BURGH, PA.

Drawn from Nature Lithographed & Published by Wm Schuchman, Pittsburgh, P.

FORGING
A MAJORITY

The Formation of the Republican Party in
Pittsburgh, 1848–1860

by Michael Fitzgibbon Holt

New Haven and London, Yale University Press, 1969

For My Mother and Father

Acknowledgments

While preparing this study I have incurred many obligations which I am happy to acknowledge. A predoctoral research grant from the Social Science Research Council allowed me to devote full time to the project during 1964–65. In that year Professors Lee Benson of the University of Pennsylvania and Samuel P. Hays of the University of Pittsburgh provided valuable methodological advice about the analysis of voting returns. During that year also Dr. Paul J. Kleppner of the University of Pittsburgh generously shared with me the results of his own research on the election of 1860 in Pittsburgh.

I am particularly indebted to Professors Alfred D. Chandler, Jr., of Johns Hopkins University, Robert F. Dalzell, Jr., and C. Vann Woodward of Yale University for reading the entire manuscript. The study has profited immensely from their trenchant critiques.

My wife Joyce typed the manuscript, and her frequent queries greatly helped me to clarify the prose. Moreover, her encouragement and sense of humor made the preparation of the book considerably more enjoyable.

My heaviest debt, however, is to Professor David Donald of Johns Hopkins University. He originally suggested this study as a dissertation topic, and he criticized thoroughly and incisively innumerable drafts of the manuscript. More important, his teaching, his remarkable enthusiasm for his students' work, and his continual inspiration contributed immeasurably to the completion of this undertaking. Perhaps only his students can appreciate the challenge of his scholarly standards and the extent and value of his aid.

Almost every page of this study is better because of the attention of these men, but I alone, of course, am responsible for any errors of fact, method, or interpretation that remain.

M.F.H.

Yale University
June 1968

Contents

Introduction

The decade before the American Civil War has received attention from many historians. Of those who have concentrated on political developments in a single state, a section, or the entire nation, many have undoubtedly been influenced by their knowledge that the Civil War occurred and have often emphasized those issues and events which led to increasing sectional conflict. For example, in tracing the collapse of the Whig party and the subsequent rise of the Republican party in the North, historians have stressed the importance of the Kansas-Nebraska Act, "Bleeding Kansas," the Lecompton constitution, and the Lincoln-Douglas debates. By focusing on political issues, these historians, with a few notable exceptions, have neglected the influence of cultural, economic, and social conditions on political behavior in the 1850s. Moreover, while excellent studies of the maneuvers and motives of national and state party leaders exist, assertions about why people voted as they did have frequently been inferred from national platforms and the rhetoric of leaders, rather than from a close examination of the voters on the grass-roots level.

Recently, however, historians have begun to point out that politics often involves the whole fabric of human interrelationships and that political alignments are frequently shaped by local social and economic factors which do not appear in formal national or state party platforms. What is needed to discover and evaluate the importance of these factors, they persuasively argue, is a more comprehensive "social analysis" of political history.[1] Moreover, the elements or interest groups that go into political coalitions are often small and local, not broad and national; therefore, investigation of these parties on the national or state level may prevent any specific identification of the kinds of men who joined them. To determine the impact of local conditions on national politics and to identify the elements which constituted political parties, more intensive studies on the local level are necessary.

This study attempts to make a social analysis of the politics of the 1850s, to integrate social and economic conditions with political developments. In order to examine more closely the nature of political coalitions than was possible in the excellent general histories of the period, I have chosen to investigate a single city. Such a detailed analysis seemed the best way to identify what elements went into the Republican party and learn how they differed from the Democrats, to compare systematically and quantitatively the leaders, appeals, and supporters of the Republican party with those of its predecessor, the Whig party, and to test in one city the influence of local factors in shaping political parties.

For several reasons I chose the city of Pittsburgh, Pennsylvania. First, it gave Lincoln a larger percentage of the vote in 1860 than any other major city in the country. The Republican party was much stronger there than in other cities, such as Cincinnati, Philadelphia, and New York, which also traded extensively with the South. The reasons for this unusual Re-

---

1. For a good exposition of this plea for a more comprehensive political history, see Samuel P. Hays, "The Social Analysis of American Political History, 1880–1920," *Political Science Quarterly, 80* (1965), 373–94.

publican dominance invited inquiry. Second, Pittsburgh was small enough (it had fewer than 50,000 people in 1860) to study with the use of certain laborious statistical methods necessary to identify party leaders and followers. Third, the population of the city grew very little between 1850 and 1860 so that the tracing of voters from one party to another was more feasible. Fourth, as a jumping-off point to the Old Northwest, it attracted a large immigrant population and was thus similar in demographic makeup to other cities with large numbers of Germans and Irishmen. Finally, newly completed railroads were rapidly transforming Pittsburgh's economic structure in the 1850s. Thus the city afforded the opportunity to investigate the impact on political behavior of the transition from a relatively simple to a complex, industrialized society—a process which undoubtedly occurred in other American cities in the nineteenth century.

While this study entails a close investigation of the city's society and economy, it is not meant to be an urban history or a comprehensive examination of all aspects of Pittsburgh in the 1850s. I have ignored many interesting questions such as the response of the municipal government to urban growth. Instead, I have concentrated on those local factors which seemed most clearly to shape political coalitions in these years.

In this study I have utilized certain methods borrowed from the social sciences which historians have only recently begun to use. To determine what differences, if any, existed between the kinds of men who led both parties, I traced the backgrounds of large numbers of leaders in city directories, manuscript census returns, and church records. To check the relative importance of issues, I often made systematic content analyses of state platforms, local resolutions, and local newspapers and thereby compared quantitatively the emphases opposing political parties gave certain appeals. Finally, to identify voting support, I have used the manuscript census returns from 1850 and 1860 to classify the city's population according to wealth, occupation, and nationality and have correlated these indices with voting returns.

It should be stated flatly at this point that these statistical methods are crude and certainly not unimpeachable. Because the federal manuscript census returns contain many palpable errors and are not precise, the indices based on them are not completely accurate. Unfortunately, there was no state census to supplement these federal returns. Hence, percentages about leaders or coefficients of correlation about voters show only general tendencies and are not exact. Another problem is that correlations only show the relations between certain characteristics of the wards and never really identify what people in those wards were voting. Thus, I am never able to prove that a definite percentage of the Germans in Pittsburgh gave their votes to the Democratic party in any election; my data permit me only to show that the more heavily a ward was inhabited by Germans, the more strongly it voted Democratic. Throughout this study, I could have qualified my findings by iterating these cumbersome formulas, but instead I have taken the figures to show certain tendencies in the voting behavior of groups. Moreover, to demonstrate that certain issues occupy more space in newspaper columns or party resolutions than others is not to prove conclusively that people thought about them more than other issues. Nor is the identification of who voted for a party necessarily the answer to why they voted that way. A statistical study cannot explain what people thought or why they acted as they did, and I have resorted to

4

more conventional methods of historical analysis in attempting to answer such questions.[2]

Stating these reservations, however, one cannot dismiss the methods as useless or discount the results of quantification. These research tools are more precise than those most historians have applied to this period, and one can certainly suggest with more assurance why some people did something if he first knows who they were and how they differed from those who did not do it. Therefore, the results of this investigation of political behavior and its relation to other aspects of life in Pittsburgh suggest the need for rethinking the traditional interpretations of the politics of the 1850s.

The standard interpretations of the rise of the Republican party do not suffice for Pittsburgh. Some historians have stressed the importance to Republicans of Northern desires for specific economic measures such as a protective tariff, internal improvements, and a homestead act. The tariff was supposedly crucial in Pennsylvania. In Pittsburgh, however, these economic issues made no discernible contribution to Republican strength. Neither workingmen nor employers there apparently cared very much about the tariff in times of prosperity, and its influence in winning Whig or Republican support at those times is questionable.

Nor do interpretations of Republicans as an antislavery party capitalizing on humanitarian outrage in the North against the South's peculiar institution adequately account for the Pittsburgh Republican party. Don E. Fehrenbacher and Harry V. Jaffa in their brilliant analyses of Lincoln's "House

2. For an able discussion of some of the pitfalls of quantification in historical analysis, see William O. Aydelotte, "Quantification in History," *American Historical Review, 71* (1966), 803–25.

Divided" speech have reemphasized the moral attack on slavery as the central core of the Republican party.[3] They argue that Lincoln and the Republicans denounced slavery as a moral wrong which should eventually be eradicated. The difference between the Democratic and Republican champions Douglas and Lincoln, they stress, was that one looked at slavery neutrally while the other deemed it an intolerable sin. The implication of their argument is that Republican voters, more than Democrats, were moved by humanitarian considerations and wanted to condemn slavery as a moral wrong, even if they did not call for immediate emancipation.

In Pennsylvania, however, the Republicans did not make slavery or even its extension their primary target. As William Dusinberre's study of Philadelphia in this period also shows,[4] Pennsylvania and Pittsburgh Republicans apparently cared more for the rights of white men than of Negroes. They complained less about slavery in Kansas than about the attempt to force it on Northern settlers against their will. Republican appeals were aimed at the unfair power of the minority South and its aggressions against the rights of the Northern majority, rather than at slavery. Republican rhetoric in Pittsburgh opposed slavery expansion primarily to hurt the South and preserve the territories for white men, not to help the Negro. Indeed, one reason Republicans played down their antislavery appeal and spoke instead of white men's rights was a respect for the anti-Negro prejudices of many of the people in the city.

3. Don E. Fehrenbacher, *Prelude to Greatness: Lincoln in the 1850s* (New York, 1964); Harry V. Jaffa, *Crisis of the House Divided: An Interpretation of the Issues in the Lincoln-Douglas Debates* (Garden City, N.Y., 1959).

4. William Dusinberre, *Civil War Issues in Philadelphia, 1856–1865* (Philadelphia, 1965).

Nor did the slavery issue alone shape voting patterns in Pittsburgh. Most people disliked slavery and the South, and the anti-Southern free-soil appeal of the Whigs and Republicans undoubtedly won them votes. But politics did not revolve exclusively around those issues just as politics today does not revolve around communism, although most people dislike it. Instead, social, ethnic, and religious considerations often determined who voted for whom between 1848 and 1861. Divisions between native-born Americans and immigrants and between Protestants and Catholics, rather than differences of opinion about the tariff or the morality of slavery, distinguished Whigs and Republicans from Democrats. Until 1853 the Whig party ordinarily triumphed in local, state, and national elections. The city's business and social elite who shared many economic and private interests also shared the leadership of its majority party. The bulk of Whig voting strength, however, came from middle- and working-class native-born Americans. The minority Democratic party, hampered by the unpopular platforms of the national party, drew its support primarily from poorer Catholic and immigrant groups. A combination of hostility to the slave power and antagonism toward immigrants apparently accounted for the Whig success, but after the passage of the Kansas-Nebraska Act in 1854 these sentiments divided the components of the coalition into competing groups. Debates about the violation of the Sabbath by Catholics, temperance laws, the allocation of public school taxes to support parochial schools, and the role of Catholics in politics sharply rent the community and even cut across ethnic lines so that Protestant Irishmen and Germans repudiated their Catholic countrymen and voted differently from them. Anti-Catholic sentiment fostered the nativist Know-Nothing party which initially overshadowed the fledgling antislavery Republican party as the opponent of the Democracy. Only in 1856 when the Republican party wooed Know-Nothing support did it combine the foes of the Democrats into a winning alliance. By carefully maintaining that partnership in 1860 the Republicans continued the Whig hegemony in the city. Apparently most Republicans in Pittsburgh voted not for Negro equality but against the hated Catholics and the impudent South, both of which the Democracy represented.

Interpreting the rise of the Republican party in the North solely in terms of hostility to slavery or economic issues is, therefore, too simplified. While Republicans inherited the free-soil position of the Whigs, they also inherited the ethnic antagonisms from which Whigs had benefited. Moreover, the smoldering anti-Catholic bias, which was fanned by events in the 1850s, brought additional voters into the Republican ranks and became a vital element of the party. Because national and state platforms focused on national events does not mean that these issues attracted the support the parties won. In Pittsburgh and probably in many other areas, local conditions and the mutual dislike by the members of one party for those of the other fixed traditional voting patterns that contributed as much to Republican strength as did national questions.

In a larger sense, moreover, confining one's examination of the 1850s to causes of the Civil War obscures rather than clarifies certain significant trends. Beneath the surface rhetoric about slavery and the South, politics in Pittsburgh developed along lines historians have generally ascribed to the Gilded Age. The social and economic dislocation caused by industrialization produced political responses that presaged those around 1900. Bloc voting by Catholic immigrant groups and

8

many native-born Protestants emerged when parties wooed their votes, as parties would later, on terms of ethnic allegiance. Such bloc voting as well as the power of political bosses in party primary conventions seemed to many people a perversion of democracy, and in response to these evils the Know-Nothings rose as a reform party similar in certain aspects to urban progressives in the early twentieth century. To stop ill-considered voting by ethnic allegiance, they would increase the naturalization period for immigrants. To curtail the power of political bosses, they demanded a direct primary system. Changes in Pittsburgh's economy in the 1850s also gave politics there a more modern tinge. Railroads were destroying the city's function as middleman between East and West, and men turned to new industrial endeavors. Resentment against railroad practices boiled over in the 1850s in an outburst that augured later antirailroad and antitrust protests, and railroad politics dominated the last years of the decade. The convergence of the increasing political power of immigrants, the emergence of a new lower- and middle-class leadership among Know-Nothings and then Republicans, and the uprising against the railroads which forced both parties to defy the courts drove from politics the wealthy merchants, manufacturers, and lawyers who had formerly dominated them through the Whig party—an abdication by the "best men" which has customarily been placed in the postwar years. These developments also helped erase the sharp class lines which had distinguished Whigs from Democrats and produced a marked class similarity between Republican and Democratic leaders —an homogenization of party leadership which historians have called characteristic of the Gilded Age.

Such facts suggest that by concentrating on events leading to the Civil War, historians may have been neglecting the essential elements of continuity in politics between the prewar and postwar years. Economic historians have already pointed out that railroads began in the 1850s institutions and developments that had normally been attributed to later periods. Perhaps political historians should recognize that political patterns shaped by the complex economic and ethnic issues of an industrial society also emerged in the decade before the war.

One

AN UNFULFILLED PROMISE:
PITTSBURGH, 1800–1850

Pittsburgh grew because of its location. In the eighteenth century the British and French had fought for control of its strategic site at the head of the Ohio River in western Pennsylvania, and Pittsburgh was the product of the British triumph in 1758. The portal to the Ohio Valley, the town first expanded because of the lucrative business of outfitting settlers who passed through on their journey west.[1] In the early nineteenth century the natural advantages of the position fostered both commerce and industry and promised increasing prosperity. To its place at the threshold of the burgeoning West and its fortunate proximity to coal and iron deposits, Pittsburgh owed its livelihood.

The city's position at the forks of the Ohio allowed it substantial trade on three rivers. Down the Monongahela from western Virginia and southwestern Pennsylvania came tons of coal, potential energy for the city's various industries. Settlers along the Allegheny River, which stretched 325 miles down from western New York, shipped lumber, produce, and pig iron to Pittsburgh in return for manufactured articles.

1. Richard C. Wade, *The Urban Frontier: The Rise of Western Cities, 1790–1830* (Cambridge, Mass., 1959), p. 11.

Important as these rivers were, however, most of the river traffic came on the Ohio, the highway to the west.

Trade with the West and South increased steadily in the first half of the nineteenth century. Tonnage received at Pittsburgh from the Ohio rose from 22,440 in 1825 to 381,539 in 1848. Until railroads tapped the northern portion of the Old Northwest in the 1850s, goods going to Pittsburgh came primarily from that section's southern portion whose rivers flowed into the Ohio. Steamboats regularly deposited flour, whiskey, hemp, pork, tobacco, and pig iron at Pittsburgh's wharves in the 1830s and 1840s. Those from Louisville, St. Louis, Memphis, and New Orleans carried increasing amounts of cotton as well.[2]

Pittsburgh's trade with the Mississippi valley expanded as the Southwest was settled and grew. Steamboats plied westward down the Ohio laden with bar iron and nails, castings, stoves, safes, steam engines, springs and axles, shovels, forks, picks, plows, coal, and household goods imported from Philadelphia.[3] New Orleans purchased so heavily from Pittsburgh that a Southern editor complained in 1860 that "Pittsburgh spreads herself in New Orleans very extensively" and that "Pittsburgh, Pittsburgh, *Pittsburgh* stared us in the face wherever we went." [4]

2. Catherine Elizabeth Reiser, *Pittsburgh's Commercial Development, 1800–1850* (Harrisburg, 1951), pp. 51, 101; A. L. Kohlmeier, *The Old Northwest as the Keystone of the Arch of American Federal Union* (Bloomington, Ind., 1938), p. 150.

3. For a discussion of Pittsburgh's commerce with the Ohio and Mississippi regions, see Freeman Hunt, ed., *The Merchants' Magazine and Commercial Review, 10* (1844), 323; J. D. B. DeBow, ed., *The Commercial Review of the South and West, 18* (1855), 505.

4. *New Orleans Bulletin* quoted in the *Pittsburgh Daily Gazette*, Jan. 21, 1860.

Trade with the Northwest and other areas sprouted even more rapidly than that with the South. Merchants advertised that western customers would find the goods they wanted in Pittsburgh at prices which matched those of eastern cities. Buying in Pittsburgh could save western shopkeepers the trip east.[5] By 1850 the city's merchants no longer looked to New Orleans as their major market and supplier. The towns along the upper Ohio, the villages of Ohio and western Pennsylvania, and especially the cities to the east by then attracted the larger portion of their business.[6]

Pittsburgh's position as middleman between East and West was even more important than river traffic in its commercial growth. Since the completion in 1834 of the Pennsylvania Canal System, a chain of canals, portages, inclined planes, and railroads, much of what the city received from the West its merchants forwarded to the East. Conversely, much of what they shipped west had come from the manufacturers and importers of the coastal cities. Furs, flour, bacon, whiskey, tobacco, cotton, and wool flowed in increasing quantities eastward to Philadelphia. From the east came salt, glassware, hardware, dry goods, chinaware, furniture, and iron products.[7] Because of their opportunity to forward goods both east and west, the city's merchants prospered in the early part of the century.

By the 1840s, however, location alone did not suffice to keep them ahead of their rivals to the west—Cincinnati, Louisville,

5. For example, see William L. Russell, Kennedy and Sawyer, and Murphy, Wilson & Company advertisements, Nov. 1, 1849, and the John D. McCord advertisement, Feb. 1, 1850, all in the *Gazette*.

6. Reiser, pp. 45, 51.

7. Ibid., p. 107. Tables which list the entire trade over the Pennsylvania Canal System from 1835 to 1850 can also be found on pp. 213–24.

and St. Louis.[8] Because these cities were closer to New Orleans and the expanding western market and could trade with the East via Ohio canals and the superior Great Lakes-New York route, they passed Pittsburgh, which was dependent on the outmoded Pennsylvania Main Line Canal, in the commercial race for the western market. Competition from both east and west underlined the inadequacies of Pittsburgh's reliance on water routes. Trade on rivers and canals came to an abrupt halt during the winter when they froze and during the summer when low water prevented navigation. As an editor complained in 1848, just when Pittsburgh's merchants should have been reaping the benefits of a brisk east-west exchange, its "rivers [were] so low that navigation [was] seriously obstructed, and both travel and goods [were] taking the Lake route." He estimated that Pittsburgh would lose nine tenths of the western trade that autumn to the Great Lakes route which connected with railroads and the Erie Canal in New York.[9] The northern route was superior to the Pennsylvania System not only because it did not suffer from low water in the summer but also because the numerous inclined planes and places where transshipment was necessary on the Pennsylvania Main Line made it much slower. Completion of the Cincinnati and Sandusky Railroad to Lake Erie in 1848 also helped divert the Ohio River trade from Pittsburgh to New York.[10]

8. A writer in Hunt's *Merchants' Magazine* noted in 1847 that "Pittsburgh's trade has been somewhat diverted to Cincinnati and other points elsewhere, upon the Ohio River." "Pittsburgh: Its Trade and Manufactures," Hunt's *Merchants' Magazine, 17* (1847), 589; Wade, p. 190.

9. *Gazette,* Sept. 14, 1848.

10. Julius Rubin, "An Imitative Public Improvement: The Pennsylvania Mainline," in Carter Goodrich, ed., *Canals and American Economic Development* (New York, 1961), p. 107. See the letter of S. V. Merrick, president

Just when new railroads in Ohio and New York were de-priving Pittsburgh of part of the western trade, a competitor to the south threatened to drain off the remainder of it. The Baltimore and Ohio Railroad had originally seemed like a godsend to Pittsburgh's merchants who were anxious to find a direct route to the Atlantic Coast so that they could contend with the Great Lakes-New York route. The trunk line across Maryland could provide a fast, all-weather alternative to the canal. Enthusiastic businessmen secured a charter for the Pitts-burgh and Connellsville Railroad Company, which would connect with the Baltimore and Ohio south of Pittsburgh, in order to induce the Maryland road to make Pittsburgh its Ohio River port. But when Philadelphia lobbyists, fearful of losing the western trade to rival Baltimore, frustrated the efforts of the Baltimore and Ohio to secure a right of way through Pennsylvania, the president of the company decided to make Wheeling, Virginia, located on the Ohio below Pitts-burgh, its western terminus.[11] The fear that Wheeling might siphon off a substantial portion of their trade stirred the citizens of Pittsburgh to active support of railroads.

At first, the course of action for the anxious citizens was not clear. Advocates of three different roads clamored for support. Some men wanted to continue the Pittsburgh and Connellsville project, build south across the Pennsylvania state line, and then connect with the Baltimore and Ohio at Cumberland, Maryland. Others who argued that Pittsburgh's

---

of the Pennsylvania Railroad, to the Pittsburgh Board of Trade in the *Gazette,* Oct. 2, 1848.

11. Joseph S. Clark, Jr., "The Railroad Struggle for Pittsburgh," *The Pennsylvania Magazine of History and Biography, 43* (1924), 1–37. See also Festus P. Summers, *The Baltimore and Ohio in the Civil War* (New York, 1939), p. 20.

destiny lay with the West wanted to build a road west from Pittsburgh into central Ohio at Crestline in order to tap the Ohio trade which was going to New York. Forming the Ohio and Pennsylvania Railroad Company, these men began to sell stock by January 1, 1848. A third group advocated support of the Pennsylvania Central Railroad, a through line to the East. Backers of all these schemes urged investment by the city and by Allegheny County, in which it was located.[12]

Because the Pennsylvania Railroad seemed the readiest response to New York's competition and to the Baltimore and Ohio, it received public support first. In April 1848 the Pittsburgh Board of Trade urged that the county commissioners subscribe to its stock. When the commissioners submitted the question of subscription and a bond issue to public referendum, the advocates of subscription won in a very close vote, and on June 1, 1848, the commissioners exchanged $1,000,000 worth of 6 percent county bonds for twenty thousand shares of Pennsylvania Railroad stock. The company guaranteed to pay a 6 percent dividend on its stock annually, and this dividend was to be applied to paying the annual interest on the county bonds. In effect, the railroad company contracted to pay the annual interest on the government bonds.[13]

Public subscription to other roads followed on terms similar to those made with the Pennsylvania Railroad. The cities of Pittsburgh and Allegheny, situated across the Allegheny River from Pittsburgh, each pledged $200,000 to the Ohio and Pennsylvania road in April 1849. In 1851 a threat that Philadelphia and the Pennsylvania Railroad would support the proposed

12. *Gazette,* Mar. 27, Aug. 31, Sept. 1, Nov. 16, Dec. 4, 7, 1847, Jan. 1, Apr. 28, May 18, 1848.

13. *Gazette,* Apr. 10, June 1, 1848; *Daily Commercial Journal* (Pittsburgh), Apr. 28, May 31, 1848.

Hempfield Railroad, a line from Greensburg, Pennsylvania, east of Pittsburgh on the Pennsylvania route, directly to Wheeling, and thus bypass Pittsburgh spurred railroad backers to frantic activity. Anxious citizens proposed numerous plans to combat the Hempfield scheme. Some backed the Allegheny Valley Railroad which would run north from the city and, hopefully, join with the Erie Railroad in New York. Such a route would be a way to escape the control of the seemingly treacherous Pennsylvania Central. Others urged that the Pittsburgh and Connellsville project, neglected for four years, be revived. Still others advocated the Pittsburgh and Steubenville Railroad, a direct line to Wheeling and then across the river into Ohio which would run south of the Ohio and Pennsylvania Railroad and draw off the trade which the Hempfield road was supposed to capture. A road from Pittsburgh to Washington, Pennsylvania, where it would intercept the proposed Hempfield line, also attracted backers. All of these projects eventually received public support, and by 1855 the bonded debt of the city for railroads was $1,800,000 and that of the county, not including the subscription to the Pennsylvania Railroad, was $2,300,000.[14] Faced with the loss of their western customers, merchants and manufacturers heartily endorsed public subscription to the railroads in order to improve their competitive position.

Manufacturing played an even larger role in Pittsburgh's economic growth than commerce. The city's industries at-

14. *Gazette*, Apr. 28, 1848, Apr. 27, 1849, July 10, 12, 1851, May 14, 1852; George Thornton Fleming, et al., *History of Pittsburgh and Environs* (4 vols. New York, 1922), 2 ,90; Frank C. Harper, *Pittsburgh: Forge of the Universe* (New York, 1957), p. 130.

tracted and employed most of its residents. Moreover, the location of mills, factories, and workshops determined the city's geographical pattern of settlement and tied it closely to surrounding towns. To a large degree the community's industries were responsible for its physical outlines, the size of its population, and its economic health.

Like the merchants, Pittsburgh's manufacturers originally flourished because of their geographical advantages. The Monongahela River allowed them to tap the vast bituminous coal fields of southwestern Pennsylvania and Virginia. These regions produced more coal than Pittsburgh's factories and homes could consume, and the surplus of coal kept its price down. This abundance of cheap fuel drew raw materials to the city's iron, glass, and cotton mills.[15] Easy access to a western market which needed manufactures also facilitated the city's rise as the Birmingham of America.

The prominence of industry distinguished Pittsburgh from her commercial rivals along the Ohio, such as Wheeling, Cincinnati, and Louisville. By 1830 manufacturing overshadowed commerce in economic importance in Pittsburgh.[16] By 1840 almost three times as many men worked in manufacturing as in commerce and the navigation of the rivers and canals combined. One out of every nine persons in the city worked as a

15. A writer in 1857 gave figures to show how the excess of coal kept the price down in Pittsburgh. In 1856 the total Pittsburgh consumption was 33,405,000 bushels; the total exported to other areas was 20,372,159 bushels. The value of the Pittsburgh sales was only $1,670,250 while that of the smaller export tonnage was $3,000,240. George H. Thurston, *Pittsburgh As It Is; or Facts and Figures, Exhibiting the Past and Present of Pittsburgh, Its Advantages, Resources, Manufactures and Commerce* (Pittsburgh, 1857), p. 63. Local citizens were well aware that manufacturers would locate where the fuel was cheapest. See *Gazette*, Nov. 20, 1847.

16. Wade, p. 47.

factory hand or artisan.[17] By 1860 almost one out of every five persons living in the city was involved in industry.[18] Nor should the influence of industry be measured only by the numbers it employed. In the manufacturing community many men such as grocers, butchers, bakers, and other shopkeepers depended on factory operatives as customers. Their fortunes were fused to those of industry.

Ironmaking was the city's major business. Rolling mills, foundries, machine shops, and boiler yards employed about half the working force in Pittsburgh and its immediate vicinity.[19] In value of goods produced, iron manufacturers consistently led glass and textile manufacturers, their closest rivals.[20] Because of the nature of their market and product before 1860, Pittsburgh's ironmasters saw no need to integrate and centralize the entire ironmaking process there. Content

17. According to the U.S. census of 1840, of Pittsburgh's total work force of 3,329, 2,345 (70%) were employed in manufacturing or trades, 589 (18%) in commerce, and 248 (7%) in the navigation of canals, lakes, and rivers. Hunt's *Merchants' Magazine*, 7 (1842), 339.

18. No figures are available for 1850. Out of 49,217 people in the city in 1860, 8,837 (18%) were employed in manufacturing. U.S., Bureau of the Census, *Eighth Census of the United States: 1860. Mortality and Miscellaneous Statistics* (Washington, D.C., 1866), p. xviii.

19. From the tables given in the census of 1860 I estimate that about 35 percent of all males employed in manufacturing in Allegheny County worked in one of the basic iron industries. U.S., Bureau of the Census, *Eighth Census of the United States: 1860. Manufacturing*, pp. 493–95. Thurston listed all the men employed in each type of business and occupation in Pittsburgh and the surrounding towns. Of the total work force of approximately 14,800, those engaged in rolling mills, foundries, machine shops, and boiler yards numbered 7,277 (approximately 49%). The textile industries, cotton mills, and other clothing houses employed 2,330, and the glass factories employed 1,982. Thurston, passim.

20. See Table 1, Appendix A. All tables cited in subsequent footnotes in this study are in Appendix A.

to machine and fashion iron into finished products, they did not smelt pig iron from ore. Rather they brought it from Ohio, Kentucky, Tennessee, and Missouri. The principal suppliers of pig iron, however, were the furnaces of the upper Allegheny region and of the central and eastern counties of Pennsylvania. Pittsburgh's location at the threshold of the western market determined the type of iron products Pittsburgh produced. Its manufacturers concentrated on merchantable bar iron, which could be sold to western blacksmiths, steam engines, nails, and tools; they did not produce railroad iron.[21]

Cheap fuel and accessibility to markets also encouraged other industries to locate in Pittsburgh. The city's flint glass, pressed glass, and lamp chimneys were famous throughout the country. The glass industry ranked second to iron, and in 1857 nineteen glass firms operated thirty-four factories in and around the city. Five cotton factories in Pittsburgh and Allegheny City, across the river from Pittsburgh, employed many women and children and contributed significantly to the growth of the community. Copper and brass foundries, which brought their copper ore from the Great Lakes region, also flourished. Steamboat construction for river traffic on the Ohio and Mississippi continued to be an important activity. Steamboat builders used the iron shaped in Pittsburgh's mills in the 1840s. Others utilized the lumber from the Allegheny region to make furniture, wagons, and carriages.[22]

Because of prosperity in the 1830s the city's manufacturers

21. Louis C. Hunter, "The Influence of the Market upon Technique in the Iron Industry in Western Pennsylvania up to 1860," *Journal of Economic and Business History, 1* (Nov. 1928–Aug. 1929), 241–81; Thurston, p. 106; *Gazette,* Dec. 3, 1859.

22. Thurston, pp. 76, 135, 142; *Gazette,* Dec. 23, 1850; *Pittsburgh Morning Post,* June 19, 1851; Leland D. Baldwin, *Pittsburgh: The Story of a City* (Pittsburgh, 1937), p. 191.

complacently expected that cheap raw materials and proximity to markets would continue to give them a competitive edge over manufacturers in other locations. By 1850 this hope was proving increasingly delusive. Because competitors in Cleveland, Cincinnati, Wheeling, and St. Louis adopted cost-saving innovations and more aggressive sales tactics such as extensive advertising, they were leaving far behind the manufacturers in Pittsburgh who continued to rely solely on the savings gained from their location. Businessmen even in Pittsburgh looked more and more to other places to obtain goods at a lower price than they could get from Pittsburgh manufacturers. By that date engine makers in Cincinnati could undersell Pittsburgh's manufacturers in their own city.[23]

Poor banking facilities combined with complacency to prohibit "a favorable competition with other manufacturing and commercial cities in the West." [24] Despite heavy investment by entrepreneurs, the cost of the machinery and buildings of Pittsburgh's factories drained off most of the city's banking capital. The funds available after industrial investments by the banks were woefully insufficient to meet the everyday needs of the business community. Between 1837 and 1850, while the volume of business increased and the population doubled in size, the amount of banking capital decreased by $1,500,000. A state banking law confined note issue to three banks within the city and forbade entirely the issue of small notes. Because of the chronic shortage of money, merchants and manufacturers who had to accept long-term notes from western cus-

23. *Pittsburgh Daily Dispatch,* Apr. 17, 1850; the *Massillon News* (Ohio) quoted in the *Gazette,* Apr. 25, 1853.

24. Charles Shaler to William Bigler, Pittsburgh, Apr. 14, 1852, William Bigler MSS (Historical Society of Pennsylvania). Hereafter the Historical Society of Pennsylvania will be cited HSP.

tomers had difficulty discounting them in Pittsburgh. One editor estimated that banks could "only discount four out of fourteen millions of choice business paper, annually created by the usual and legitimate business of [the] city." Brokers who charged higher discount rates than the banks handled the remainder of the business. Some were "compelled to go to Washington, Wheeling, Steubenville, Cleveland, and other places to obtain discounts." As a result Pittsburgh businessmen could not "carry on [their] commercial and manufacturing operations successfully." [25]

Difficulties of monetary exchange, the lack of funds, and competition stunted Pittsburgh's industrial growth. Men who needed capital to start new businesses could not get it because an established group of customers monopolized the loans of the banks.[26] The two largest industries, iron and glass, failed to grow significantly between 1837 and 1850.[27] The overall rate of manufacturing expansion declined sharply. Between 1826 and 1837 the total annual value of manufactures had jumped from $2,500,000 to $11,606,305; yet by 1850 the total annual value for all of Allegheny County had climbed to only $16,686,032. Because of the pervasive influence of manufacturing, its troubles slowed the growth of the entire economy of the city.[28]

25. Thurston, p. 38; *Gazette*, Mar. 7, 1849, Mar. 22, 1850; *Dispatch,* Apr. 25, 1849, Mar. 22, Apr. 18, 1850; George P. Hamilton to William Bigler, Pittsburgh, Apr. 19, 1852, and Lecky Harper to William Bigler, Pittsburgh, Apr. 20, 1852, Bigler MSS.

26. *Dispatch*, Apr. 18, 1850. For a discussion of how the lack of capital hindered iron manufacturers in Pittsburgh, see Louis C. Hunter, "Financial Problems of the Early Pittsburgh Iron Manufacturers," *Journal of Economic and Business History*, 2 (Nov. 1929–Aug. 1930), 520–44.

27. See Table 1.

28. While the annual value of the total amount of business in the city rose from $7,500,000 in 1826 to $31,000,000 in 1837, it only increased to

Despite these economic difficulties, more people settled in Pittsburgh in the 1840s than ever before. Still, the city failed to draw as many newcomers as western rivals such as Chicago, St. Louis, and Cincinnati, and in the 1850s, when the real effects of the slowed growth rate were felt, the city's population only increased from 46,601 to 49,217.[29] More people chose to pass through the "Gateway to the West" than to reside there.

The large number of newcomers who remained there in the 1840s forced the city to expand its boundaries. As the urban center of Allegheny County, Pittsburgh attracted many more people than did the rural areas of the county.[30] Mechanics, shopkeepers, and manufacturers crowded into the triangular plot bounded by the Allegheny and the Monongahela. Draped in a shroud of black smoke from the numerous factories, the city spread back from the Monongahela wharves to the mills along that river to the congested streets of the downtown area, a mélange of red brick and frame office buildings and hotels, public structures like the courthouse, and pseudo-Gothic churches such as the First Presbyterian. (For a picture of Pittsburgh and of Allegheny City across the river in the 1850s, see the frontispiece.) During the day the streets teemed with hucksters, draymen, and laborers; at night, many remained in this downtown area and lived close to where they worked.

$50,000,000 in 1850. For both sets of figures, see Samuel Jones, *Pittsburgh in the Year Eighteen Hundred and Twenty-Six* (Pittsburgh, 1826), pp. 85, 87; Isaac Harris, *Harris's Pittsburgh Business Directory for the Year 1837* (Pittsburgh, 1837), p. 187; J. D. B. DeBow, *Statistical View of the United States* (Washington, D.C., 1854), p. 301; and Samuel Fahnestock, *Pittsburgh Directory of 1850; Containing the Names of the Inhabitants of Pittsburgh, Allegheny, & Vicinity* (Pittsburgh, 1850), p. 118.

29. See Table 2.

30. Except in the 1850s the rate of growth of the city was faster than that of the county, especially in the 1840s. See Table 3.

Others moved to the hills to the east where the air was cleaner and houses were less crowded together. The city had been divided into four wards in 1833 with a fifth added in 1837, but the spread of the population away from the point where the rivers met necessitated the creation of four more wards in 1845 and 1846. These new wards, east of the business district, and the suburbs across the two rivers grew the fastest in the 1840s.[31]

As the population overflowed into the suburbs, Pittsburgh became the center of an industrial complex of seven contiguous towns which were economically and socially virtual parts of the city. Across the Allegheny River, Allegheny City, with a population of 21,262 in 1850, ranked next to Pittsburgh in size and importance. East Birmingham, Birmingham, and South Pittsburgh housed many glass factories and iron mills on the south bank of the Monongahela. An editor estimated that in those three boroughs "nearly one-half the entire manufacturing capital of [the] community [was] invested." Laborers living close to the factories where they worked comprised almost the entire population of those mill towns. Many manufacturers who lived in Pittsburgh built their mills across the Monongahela closer to the coal deposits where the land was cheaper than in the city.[32] Other men whose businesses were located in

31. James Howard Thompson, "A Financial History of the City of Pittsburgh, 1816–1910" (unpublished Ph.D. dissertation, University of Pittsburgh, 1948), p. 15; *Gazette*, Oct. 24, 1846. Of the older wards in the city, the third and the fifth with large working-class and immigrant populations grew the fastest. *Gazette*, July 15, 1847.

32. *Post*, May 7, 1853, June 9, 1860; *Gazette*, Feb. 27, 1847, Mar. 19, 1849. The other boroughs in the complex were Lawrenceville, Duquesne, and Manchester. In Pennsylvania the term "borough" referred to an urban area smaller than a city, while a township was a much more rural area.

Pittsburgh made their homes in Allegheny where the coal smoke belching from the iron mills was less dense.

The economic slump of the 1840s underlined class and ethnic differences in the society. The decline in Pittsburgh's rate of economic growth at the same time that its population was doubling created problems. People who came there expecting jobs and prosperity often found only slashed wages and unemployment. As a result many strikes broke out in the 1840s, and this labor strife became one of several sources of friction in Pittsburgh's diverse population.

As a jumping-off spot to the Northwest and an industrial center, Pittsburgh attracted a mixed population of free Negroes, native-born whites, and immigrants, especially Germans, Irishmen, and Welshmen who worked in the coal mines and iron mills. The number of Negroes was small, but immigrants constituted more than a third of the city's population in 1850.[33] Many of the foreigners were single men, and in the adult white male population of Pittsburgh and Allegheny City in 1850 only 5991 (36.7%) of the 16,323 total were native-born. The Germans numbered 3,295 (20%); the Irish, 5,104 (31%); and the English, Scottish, and Welsh, 1,638 (10%).[34]

33. The published U.S. census of 1850 does not list the numbers of immigrants in the city, but the foreign-born in the county numbered 43,414, or 31 percent of the population. In 1850 Negroes constituted 4.1 percent of Pittsburgh's population. U.S., Bureau of the Census, *Seventh Census of the United States: 1850* (Washington, D.C., 1853), pp. xc, 158. Hereafter this census is cited as *Census of 1850*.

34. *Journal*, Jan. 31, 1850. These figures for Pittsburgh and Allegheny City are based on the tabulation of the federal manuscript census of 1850 explained in Appendix B. I am deeply indebted to Paul J. Kleppner of the University of Pittsburgh who shared with me his findings on the distribution of ethnic groups among the city's wards.

Assimilation of the various ethnic groups into the society was incomplete before the Civil War. The Negroes who by local custom did not attend the public schools established a separate facility financed by a school fund paid only by the Negro residents of the city. The Germans' language prevented them from blending fully with their English-speaking neighbors, and they too developed institutions of their own. For example, they established a German Thespian Society, a German Library Association, and German-language newspapers, held their own charity balls, and formed separate religious congregations with services held in German. Not only did the Germans consider themselves different, but the rest of the community regarded them as a separate breed. Newspapers made a point of identifying them as Germans when they described any incident in which they were involved. The Welsh also maintained a distinct identity and established their own Congregational, Baptist, Calvinistic Methodist, and Wesleyan Methodist churches by 1850. Though speaking English, the newer Irish immigrants also tried to preserve some of their traditional characteristics and formed military companies such as the Irish Greens. Disgusted with the influx of immigrants and their attempts to cling to their traditions, some native-born Americans formed exclusive groups of their own and held social functions to commemorate the American past. The Sons of America held a ball on Washington's birthday in 1850. Antiforeign prejudices took political expression by 1847 in the form of a Native American Party.[35]

Living in close proximity to fellow countrymen reinforced

35. *Post*, Jan. 24, 26, Feb. 4, 5, 9, 16, 23, 1850, Sept. 9, 1851, Oct. 1, 1859, Feb. 5, 1860; *Journal*, Jan. 15, 17, 31, 1850; *Gazette*, May 12, 1847; Fahnestock, pp. 113–16. For further discussion of the nativist reaction to immigrants, see below, Chap. 4.

group consciousness among immigrants and natives. Most of the Negroes clustered together in an area known as Hayti which ran through the third, sixth, and seventh wards of the city. Close to them in a part of the third ward and the contiguous section of the sixth ward were heavy concentrations of Irishmen. Irish and German laborers also gathered in the fifth ward, a jungle of breweries, glassworks, and iron foundries, and in the eighth ward, which housed the rolling mills and glass factories along the Monongahela. Skilled English and Welsh ironworkers settled in the latter ward near the factories in which they worked. The native-born Americans and older residents of the community remained primarily in the original four wards of the city where the business district and older homes were located.[36] (For the location of these wards, see map, facing p. 31.)

Religious differences further fragmented the community. Although there were many different Protestant groups, the major division was between Protestants and Catholics. Conscious of their distinct character and exclusion from many upper-class Protestant organizations such as the board of managers of the Pittsburgh and Allegheny Orphans' Asylum and the Young Men's Mercantile Library Association, the Catholics developed their own institutions such as the German Catholic Orphan Asylum of Allegheny, the Young Men's Catholic Literary Association, and their own newspaper, the Pittsburgh *Catholic*.[37] Protestant sects also founded their own

36. See Table 4. About 61 percent of the Irish concentrated in the third, fifth, and sixth wards.

37. *Post*, Feb. 1, 1850, May 5, 1854; Fahnestock, p. 113. The wives of some of the city's most prominent citizens were members of the board of managers of the Orphan Asylum. In a sample of 30 of these women, I could identify the religion of 21; all were Presbyterians or Episcopalians. For lists of managers, see the *Gazette*, May 13, 1847, and May 13, 1853.

journals such as the *Presbyterian Advocate* and the Methodist *Pittsburgh Christian Advocate*. The more numerous Protestants in the city regarded with suspicion what they considered the spread of papal influence in their society.[38] These religious differences cut across ethnic lines; German Lutherans and German Catholics continued feuds started in their homeland as did Irish Catholics and Irish Protestants. The anti-Catholic Protestant Association had a large German and Irish membership and was patterned after the English organization of the same name. The formation of an anti-Catholic Protestant party in 1850 also reflected the religious tension in the society.[39]

As in most cities, vast differences of wealth also divided the community. Among the adult white male population of Pittsburgh, according to the manuscript census of 1850, only 4 percent owned or were members of families which owned real property evaluated at $10,000 or more. At the same time, 84 percent, many of whom were newly arrived immigrants, owned no real property of value.[40] Most men were workers

38. The *Gazette* carried on a running dispute with the Pittsburgh *Catholic* about the despotism of the Pope. For example, see the issues of the *Gazette* for July 1849. Exact figures on the number of Protestants and Catholics in the city are impossible to find, but it is fairly evident that the Catholics were outnumbered in 1850. In 1842, 46 of 76 congregations in the city were Presbyterian. Baldwin, pp. 250–51. In 1850 the county contained 12 Catholic churches with a combined seating capacity of 13,790, yet at the same time there were 69 Presbyterian and 54 Methodist churches. *Census of 1850*, pp. 200–05.

39. *Gazette*, Sept. 11, 1850, Sept. 12, 1854; *Dispatch*, Sept. 4, 1850, Jan. 4, 1855. The political manifestations of the hostility between Catholics and Protestants are discussed in more detail in the following chapters.

40. See Appendix B for a description of the property evaluations listed in the manuscript census of 1850. For the distribution of wealth in each ward, as measured in that census, see Table 5. To see the numbers of immigrants among the poor (propertyless), see Tables 4 and 5 and compare the wards

rather than employers. The proportions of adult white males in the city engaged in different types of occupations were: unskilled laborers, 33 percent; skilled artisans, 30 percent; small manufacturers, 8.7 percent; clerks and shopkeepers, 21 percent; lawyers, doctors, and editors, 3 percent; large manufacturers, 1 percent; merchants, 2.5 percent; bankers and retired gentlemen, .4 percent.[41] A small minority of the community owned most of its property and controlled its business ventures.

The homes, carriages, and furnishings of the rich contrasted so glaringly with the shabby cottages of the poor that they could not help but be aware of the differences of rank in the society. The poor developed a sense of class identity and their own class interests. A letter written to the *Pittsburgh Morning Post* said that many workingmen in Allegheny County opposed the county subscription to the Pennsylvania Railroad because the road would benefit only the "gentlemen of large estate" and harm the poor by increasing their tax burden.[42] Seemingly incessant strikes exacerbated the relations between employers and employees as owners cut wages to compete during the industrial slump. The puddlers and boilers of the iron mills struck for better wages in 1842, 1845, and 1850. In 1843 the brickmakers of the city walked off the job; the journeyman tailors followed suit in 1847. Girls working in the cotton mills of Allegheny struck in 1845 and rioted in 1848

---

with large concentrations of those owning no real property of value with the wards with large concentrations of immigrants—i.e. the third, fifth, sixth, eighth, and ninth.

41. To arrive at a social profile of the city, I calculated these percentages by categorizing each white male over 21 listed in the manuscript census of 1850 by occupation. For a discussion of this method and a description of the groups included in the different categories, see Appendix B.

42. *Post*, May 4, 1848.

during a dispute that lasted for years.[43] During the ironworkers' strike of 1850, certain laborers denounced the "capitalistic aristocrats" who "lolled on sofas and lounges in their princely mansions" and ground their workers into poverty.[44]

Exactly how oppressive the life of the working classes was is unclear. Workdays varied from eight to twelve hours,[45] but for these days workers in Pittsburgh generally received less than laborers in cities to the east and west.[46] Wages ranged from 75 cents a day for common laborers to over $90 a month for some glass workers. In the iron industry in 1850 puddlers received about $32.50 every two weeks, while their helpers earned only $13.75 for the same period. Boilers, refiners, scrapers, and heaters earned even more than puddlers.[47] If the wages of the unskilled were low, fuel was cheap; moreover, most men with families could still afford to rent their own cottages.[48] Many single men lived in boarding houses,

43. Norman Ware, *The Industrial Worker, 1840–1860* (Boston and New York, 1924), pp. 27–30, 141, 201, 229; *Post*, Jan. 30, 1844; *Gazette*, Aug. 1, 1848.

44. See letters signed "A Puddler" and "Vox Populi" in the *Post*, Jan. 23, 26, 1850.

45. Ironworkers complained that they had to work in intolerable heat from ten to twelve hours a day, not eight hours a day as their employers claimed. Ibid. For the arguments of iron manufacturers that skilled ironworkers only put in eight-hour days, and actually worked only four of those hours, see the *Gazette*, Jan. 21, 1850. The accepted working day in the cotton mills was twelve hours, at least until the passage of the Pennsylvania Ten Hour Law in 1848.

46. Thurston boasted (p. 50) that wages in Pittsburgh were 20 percent lower than in any city west of it. The letter signed "Vox Populi" in the *Post* in 1850 asserted that any man would rather work in the East than in Pittsburgh at the current wages. *Post*, Jan. 23, 1850.

47. Thurston, p. 191; *Gazette*, Jan. 21, 23, 1850; Ware, pp. 28–29.

48. The average number of families per dwelling in Pittsburgh in 1850 was only 1.11. I found the numbers of dwellings and families in each

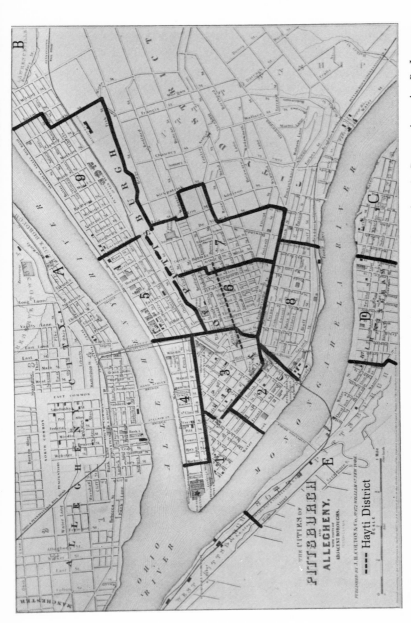

Map of the cities of Pittsburgh and Allegheny in 1855, showing ward boundaries and boroughs: A Duquesneborough, B Lawrenceville, C East Birmingham, D Birmingham, E South Pittsburgh. Courtesy of Carnegie Library of Pittsburgh.

but the stifling hell of crowded tenements and slums was as yet unknown in Pittsburgh.

In fact, if there was any crowding, it seems to have been done by the wealthier, native-born Americans in the older wards of the city. An editor observed that instead of building their homes on the hills of the newer wards above the smoke-polluted air of the lower parts of the city, "the men of wealth huddle[d] together in [the] crowded streets" of the business district "and at the same time thrust to the outskirts the miserable abodes of the thriftless." Much of the crowding probably occurred among the workers and immigrants who lived in these wards, particularly in the third ward, but the majority of business leaders also concentrated there.[49] Because of its large numbers of workers the third ward did not attract as many of the wealthy as did the first, second, and fourth wards. Of the 149 men in Pittsburgh who owned real property worth more than $25,000 according to the manuscript census of 1850, 133 (89%) lived in the original four wards, but only nine resided in the third ward. Almost half of them (71) lived in the fourth ward. Preferring the social prestige of the more established neighborhoods, and especially the stately old mansions along Penn Street in the first and fourth wards, the wealthy remained in the downtown district which was becoming more congested each year. There they were close to the churches which they attended and which exercised social leadership in the community—the First and Third Presbyterian, the First Cumberland Presbyterian, and the Trinity

---

ward listed in the manuscript census of 1850. Thurston boasted in 1857 that workers could rent cottages for from $6 to $11 a month, depending on their size. Thurston, p. 190.

49. *Post*, Mar. 11, 1854. See Table 7, which shows that most people in the upper-class occupations remained in the original four wards.

Episcopal churches.[50] Tradition and convenience still held the older inhabitants of the city in its most cramped sections by 1850.[51]

The established economic leaders of the community were primarily businessmen. In the early days of the century leading merchants had formed a tight social clique, but by 1850 manufacturers rivaled if they did not surpass their influence in the city. Middle-aged or fairly old by 1850, the wealthy were predominantly native-born Americans and Protestants. Of 83 men owning real property worth $25,000 or more and whose religion could be identified, 47 were Presbyterian, 34 were Episcopalians, and only two were Catholics. Of the foreign-born among the elite, many were Scotch-Irish Presbyterians who had resided in the community for a long time and had achieved social as well as economic success.[52] For example,

50. People had moved to Penn Street in the 1820s, and it remained the most socially prestigious in the 1850s. Wade, p. 206; Baldwin, p. 277; Adelaide M. Nevin, *The Social Mirror* (Pittsburgh, 1888), p. 122. On the churches, see John Newton Boucher, ed., *A Century and a Half of Pittsburgh and Her People* (4 vols. n.p., 1908), 2, 201.

51. See Table 6, which shows that by almost every index of wealth the richest wards were the most crowded. Note that the low per person real estate values in the new wards indicate how ramshackle the homes of the poor really were.

52. Wade, pp. 107, 201. From the manuscript census of 1850 I compiled a list of one hundred eighty-six men in Pittsburgh and Allegheny who owned real property worth $25,000 or more. The occupational, ethnic and age breakdowns of this sample are as follows:

Occupation		*Nationality*		*Age*	
Manufacturers	50 (27%)	Native	128 (69%)	20–29	16 (9%)
Merchants	46 (25%)	Irish	48 (26%)	30–39	33 (18%)
Professional	31 (16%)	German	6 (3%)	40–49	55 (30%)
Bankers	8 (4%)	British	4 (2%)	50–59	50 (27%)
Grocers	11 (6%)			60–69	18 (10%)
Innkeepers &				70–79	10 (6%)
Shopkeepers	9 (5%)			80 plus	1
Artisans	5 (3%)				
Other	26 (14%)				

Alexander Laughlin, a wealthy pork merchant, was born in Ireland in 1795 but came to this country early in the century. In 1832 he was elected elder of the very prestigious First Presbyterian Church, was one of the original managers (trustees) of the Western Pennsylvania Hospital, and served as a director of the influential Bank of Pittsburgh. Another example of the type of foreigner who gained entrance to the social elite was Frederick Lorenz, who was born in Germany in 1795 but who prospered as an iron and glass manufacturer in Pittsburgh and became an elder in the Third Presbyterian Church by 1834.[53]

These rich entrepreneurs often had mutual rather than antagonistic economic interests because of common investments and business endeavors. Merchants branched out into manufacturing and communications. For example, merchants C. G. Hussey, James M. Cooper, and Waterman Palmer were partners with others in the Pittsburgh and Boston Mining Company, which opened the Lake Superior copper fields and established copper rolling mills in Pittsburgh.[54] Similarly, James Laughlin, a pork merchant like his brother, shared the interests of iron manufacturers because he was a partner in an iron mill. The closest student of the early iron industry in Pittsburgh concludes that merchants were the most important source of capital for the industry other than the manu-

---

Of the 50 manufacturers, 34 were iron makers. Of a list of 57 bank directors in 1848 and 1850, I could identify the religion of 34: there were 21 Presbyterians, 12 Episcopalians, and 1 Catholic. The lists of these bank directors can be found in the directory of 1850 and the *Gazette,* Nov. 21, 1848. From the newspapers I compiled a list of 35 prominent Catholics. Of these only 2, G. L. B. Fetterman and Christian Ihmsen, were in my sample of bank directors and 186 wealthy men. For the sources of religious affiliation, see Appendix B.

53. In 1850 Laughlin owned real property valued at $80,000, and Lorenz owned real property worth $200,000.

54. *Gazette,* Oct. 21, 1846; *Post,* June 19, 1851; Thurston, p. 133.

facturers themselves.[55] Lewis Hutchinson, a leading forwarding and commission merchant, was a director of the Pittsburgh, Cincinnati, and Louisville Telegraph Company along with bankers and manufacturers.[56] Manufacturers, particularly ironmakers, invested in railroads along with merchants. Among the twelve original directors of the Ohio and Pennsylvania Railroad, there were a wealthy banker, a lawyer, a rich retired newspaper editor, a large glass manufacturer, and eight iron manufacturers.[57] Merchants and manufacturers also shared interests as directors of banks and insurance companies. In 1850 thirteen merchants and thirteen manufacturers were evenly distributed among the boards of directors of Pittsburgh's three major banks.

Social ties combined with common economic interests to weld the rich into a social elite with shared values. Thirty-two of the men in Pittsburgh and Allegheny who owned property valued over $25,000 were members of the First Presbyterian Church. The wealthy also mixed together in charity work. Among the twenty-four officers of the newly established Western Pennsylvania Hospital in 1850, there were ten prominent manufacturers, six merchants, three bankers, two lawyers, and one judge. The wives of the wealthy managed such organizations as the Pittsburgh and Allegheny Orphans' Asylum. Exclusive social functions also helped establish a sense of upperclass status. A newspaper announced an "Upper Ten Ball," and members of wealthy families went on sleigh rides together

55. Hunter, "Financial Problems of the Early Pittsburgh Iron Manufacturers," p. 527.

56. *Gazette*, June 12, 1849. Other directors were J. K. Moorhead, an iron and cotton manufacturer, Thomas Bakewell, a glass manufacturer, Charles Avery, who had investments in cotton mills and copper mining, and Joshua Hanna, a broker.

57. *Gazette*, Dec. 7, 1847.

in the winter, attended the same teas and parties, and courted each other.[58]

Tightly knit by social and economic ties, the upper classes, then, differed from the majority of the people in the city—the propertyless. The founders or scions of well-established families, they lived in the traditionally desirable residential sections in the old wards. Their wealth, occupation, nationality, or religion distinguished them from the more numerous but less privileged classes—free Negroes, Catholics, immigrants, and workingmen. While skilled artisans, shopkeepers, or small manufacturers could probably rise from the middle classes into this elite when they made enough money, it remained a distinct group in the 1850s.

The various tensions which emerged in the community in the 1840s were reflected in the local government. Because of diffuse responsibility, sporadic administration, and inadequate powers, the city and county governments dealt inefficiently with the problems of growth in that decade. Nevertheless, the elections for municipal officers in January and county officials in the fall gave political parties opportunity for almost constant campaigning and usually aroused much interest.

Most municipal authority was held by the city councils which combined both executive and legislative powers. The Select and Common Councils met only once a month, and their members received no pay. Each ward had two members

58. The list of hospital managers can be found in Fahnestock, p. 112. For a description of the social life of the young among Pittsburgh's elite families by a scion of one of them, see the entries for Feb. 20, 21, Mar. 2, 6, 16, Apr. 16, May 15, June 30, Sept. 28, and Oct. 2, 16, 1846, in the Diary of Robert McKnight (MS, Darlington Memorial Library, University of Pittsburgh).

in the Select Council; they had two-year terms and were elected in alternate years. The thirty members of the Common Council were elected annually and were apportioned among the nine wards according to the number of taxable residents each contained. Joint standing committees of the councils had the responsibility for the various functions of the government such as finance, planning, and provision of services to the city. The councils levied taxes, issued bonds, controlled the allocation of public funds, and supervised their expenditure. The state legislature, however, closely restricted their fiscal powers.

Although the councils elected the city officers, the major struggles within them were not partisan battles for control of patronage but rather concerned the extent and location of public improvements within the city. After 1846 editors noted a clear "line of demarkation" between the old and new wards in the councils over this issue. Demanding improvements for which the citizens of the entire city would have to pay, the sixth, seventh, eighth, and ninth wards met only "patrician antipathy" from the older wards where most of the wealthy citizens of the city lived. An editor observed that there was "no community of interest between the heart and the extremities" of the city, only "a cry of 'Old Wards' and 'New Wards', a buttoning up of all aid on the one side, and a grasping of everything that can be seized hold of on the other." Old wards refused to pay for the grading and paving of streets, the installation of gas lights, and the extension of water pipelines to the new wards where many of the poorer newcomers to the city lived. Older residents of the city resisted the efforts of the "outsiders" while recently arrived settlers denounced them as "Old Hunkers." [59]

59. *Post*, Nov. 8, 1847, Mar. 11, 1854. For examples of the demands to the councils, see the petitions in the report of the councils' meeting in the

Ward representation in the councils reflected in part the different types of people that lived in the new and old wards. Neither political party had many immigrants among its council candidates in the years 1848–51, but the representatives followed pretty closely the makeup of those wards so far as wealth was concerned. Of Whig and Democratic council candidates who owned property valued over $10,000, according to the census of 1850, 37 came from the four old wards and only 14 from the other five. Most typical of the men from the newer wards were Robert Hill, a machinist from the ninth ward, William G. McCartney, an Irish gunsmith from the fifth ward, and William Dickson, an Irish carpenter from the sixth ward, all of whom were propertyless according to the manuscript census of 1850.[60] While the resistance by members from the older wards to improving the new demonstrates a general wish to avoid taxation for the benefit of others, it was also an expression of the resentment the wealthy and established families felt toward the incursion of newcomers.

If the councils exercised the real power of municipal government, the mayor was its symbolic head. Actually he was

---

Journal, Apr. 28, 1848. A protest against improvements in the new wards by certain members of the Common Council demonstrates the opposition of the old wards. Of 16 members who signed the protest, 15 were from the first five wards. Those five wards had a combined representation of 22 members in the common council. See the *Gazette*, May 31, 1848.

60. The sample from which these councilmen and council candidates were taken is described in Appendix B. There was no marked difference in the ethnic backgrounds of men from the old and new wards who were candidates for the councils. Of the candidates of both parties from the old wards there were 53 native Americans, 16 Irishmen, 3 Germans, and 1 Englishman. Of those from the new wards, there were 40 native Americans, 15 Irishmen, 1 German, and 5 Englishmen. At this point, differences between the candidates of the Whig and Democratic parties are not important. They will be investigated at length in Chap. 2.

little more than a combination of police chief and magistrate. Charged with enforcing local ordinances, he appointed the police force, meted out fines to violators, and sentenced those guilty of misdemeanors. Because the mayor's chair was the only municipal office to be filled in a citywide election, political parties contested for it hotly every January.

The county officials were elected in October along with delegates to the state legislature, state officers, and congressmen. The sheriff and county commissioners were the most important officials, and their offices the most sought after. One of the three commissioners was elected each year. They had the privilege of issuing bonds, as they did to finance the railroads, and also the power of levying taxes. Their taxing powers, however, like those of the city councils, were strictly defined by the state legislature. Both the county and municipal corporations remained very much under the thumb of the state legislature before the Civil War.

By the middle of the nineteenth century Pittsburgh had failed to achieve the prosperity augured in the 1830s. Until 1840 the advantages of location, water transportation, and old business methods had spurred economic growth. By 1850, however, merchants had suffered increasing competition from the north and feared it to the south. The settlement of the trans-Mississippi region had helped their competitors in St. Louis, Chicago, and Cincinnati much more than themselves, and they anxiously looked to the railroads to improve their competitive position. The advantages of cheap fuel and proximity to western markets also failed to sustain rapid industrial growth. Plagued by poor monetary facilities and by increasing competition, manufacturers also looked to railroads both as a market and as a link to new markets. The decline in economic growth disappointed the expectations of a growing population and produced lower wages and labor strife in the 1840s. In such a climate the palpable differences between native Americans and immigrants, between suspicious Protestants and Catholics, could easily become embittered. Already the tension between the established families of the older wards and the new residents had flared in the city councils. Increasingly, men would look to the political arena to achieve their economic aspirations and express their social frustration, and their efforts would do much to shape the political battles of the next decade.

Two

A NATURAL MAJORITY, 1847–1850

When Pittsburgh's citizens went to the polls in the 1840s, they consistently supported the nominees of the Whig party. Whig presidential candidates won majorities in the city in 1840, 1844, and 1848, and its voters elected five Whigs and only one Democrat to Congress during that period. The anti-Democratic candidate for governor carried the city in all four elections between 1840 and 1850. The local coalition of Whigs and Antimasons exerted similar control over offices in the county and delegates to the state legislature. The Antimasonic tradition of opposition to the Democracy apparently remained strong in Pittsburgh, for the local party kept the title "Whig and Antimasonic" until 1853. Moreover, a Democratic politician complained that he had suffered continual defeats in Pittsburgh because of his opposition to Antimasonry. Indeed, the victory of this combination of Whigs and Antimasons was also a constant theme in municipal elections.[1] This ability of

1. Elections for governor were held every three years—in 1841, 1844, and 1847. The death of the governor in 1848 necessitated a special election in that year. In 1841 a separate Antimasonic candidate won, while in all the other years Whig candidates carried the city. From 1840 to 1850 Whigs placed 31 delegates in the state legislature while the Democrats elected only 11; during that period 27 Whigs and only 8 Democrats served as county officials. From 1840 to 1849 the Democrats won the mayor's office only once, and from 1840 through 1847 the Whigs elected 184 out of 216 city councilmen. Election results may be found in Pittsburgh's newspapers every

Pittsburgh's Whigs to mold a triumphant coalition contrasted sharply to that of the state Whig organization which managed to carry the state only in 1840 and 1848, and it suggests that certain special factors differentiated them from the Democrats in the city.

Historians have disagreed as to what elements distinguished the Whig party from the Democrats in the 1840s. Arthur M. Schlesinger, Jr., has identified the Whigs with the same business interests and upper classes as the Federalists, and the Democrats with the common men and other sections of the community who struggled against the business elite. In his excellent monograph, *The Whig Party in Pennsylvania,* Henry R. Mueller gives some support to this thesis and asserts without entirely convincing evidence that the Whigs because of their more attractive programs won the support of "the vast majority of those possessing vested interests." Others have denied that the division between rich and poor, businessmen and nonbusinessmen, distinguished the parties. Richard Hofstadter and Bray Hammond have asserted that the conflict between enterprising newer capitalists on the make and older entrenched capitalists who had already accumulated wealth and power shaped the political battles of the 1830s and 1840s. On the other hand, Lee Benson in a more recent work ex-

---

January for municipal elections, in October for county, state, and congressional elections, and in November for presidential elections. On the power of Antimasonry in the city, see John B. Butter to Simon Cameron, Allegheny Arsenal, June 10, 1854, Simon Cameron MSS (Library of Congress). Hereafter the Library of Congress will be cited LC. See also Henry R. Mueller, *The Whig Party in Pennsylvania,* Columbia University Studies in History, Economics, and Public Law, 101 (New York, 1922), 94–95 n.; and Charles McCarthy, *The Antimasonic Party: A Study of Political Antimasonry in the United States, 1827–1840,* Annual Report of the American Historical Association, *1,* (New York, 1902), 428, 482, 502.

pands an hypothesis from his research on the leadership, support, and ideologies of the parties in New York State and argues that ethnic and religious factors, not economic ones, divided the two parties.[2]

To determine what factors differentiated the Whigs from the Democrats in Pittsburgh, I concentrated on the parties in the late 1840s rather than in the entire decade, for my primary concern was to trace party continuity into the 1850s. Systematic investigation of the sources of leadership and voter support and of the appeals of the two parties between 1847 and 1850 revealed that economic, ethnic, and religious divisions all significantly influenced political activity in the late 1840s. Together these factors and others prevented the Democrats from constructing a coalition which could replace the dominant Whig majority.

One way to determine how the Whigs differed from the Democrats was to examine and compare the backgrounds and origins of their most active and prominent men. Two groups of leaders, those who ran for office and those who ran the party by attending local and state conventions between 1847 and 1851, constituted the present sample of chieftains. The list of candidates contained 97 Whigs and 97 Democrats while the group of secondary leaders numbered 119 Whigs and 107 Democrats. Together these lists included the most prominent

2. Mueller, p. 245; Arthur M. Schlesinger, Jr., *The Age of Jackson* (Boston, 1945), pp. 132–43, 201–09, 261–321 (esp. 279, 307), 505; Richard Hofstadter, *The American Political Tradition and the Men Who Made It* (New York, 1964), pp. 44–66; Bray Hammond, *Banks and Politics in America from the Revolution to the Civil War* (Princeton, 1957), pp. 326–68; Lee Benson, *The Concept of Jacksonian Democracy: New York as a Test Case* (New York, 1964), pp. 331–32.

42

men in each party in the late 1840s, and investigation of their backgrounds revealed whatever significant class divisions, if any, existed between the types of men who led the two parties.[3]

The Whigs drew more of their leaders from the wealthier classes of society than did the Democrats. Of 76 Whig candidates almost half owned property valued at $10,000 or more while only 28 percent of the Democratic candidates did. Similarly, among the secondary party leaders the proportion of Whigs owning real property valued over $10,000 was almost twice as large as the proportion of Democrats.[4]

If the Whigs were more likely to choose rich men as candidates and delegates in Pittsburgh, the Democratic leaders more clearly represented the poor. Only one fourth of the Whig candidates owned no real property of value according to the census, but two fifths of the Democratic candidates were propertyless. Over half of the Democratic secondary party leaders but only 35 percent of the Whigs owned no real property of value.[5]

Richer than their Democratic counterparts, Whig leaders were also much more involved in the business enterprises of

3. See Appendix B for a discussion of how the samples of leaders were chosen, what criteria were used to measure social status, and how backgrounds were determined.

4. See Tables 8 and 9. Although the total samples of Whig and Democratic leaders were larger, the numbers and percentages about those leaders given in the text refer only to the men from those larger samples about whom I found information in the manuscript census or some other source. Such is the practice throughout this study.

5. See Tables 8 and 9. For the sake of stylistic convenience, throughout this study I refer to the group listed in the manuscript census as owning no real property of value as "poor" or "propertyless." Those terms are meant to be relative rather than absolute indicators of the lack of wealth since almost everyone so listed was poorer than those who owned some real property. For an explanation of the deficiencies of the census of 1850 as an index of property ownership, see Appendix B.

the city. The Democrats turned to professional men and newspaper editors for leadership much more frequently than did the Whigs. Lawyers, doctors, and editors formed a total of 29 percent of the Democratic candidates for office, but only 13 percent of the Whig candidates came from those professional groups. Instead, the majority party relied on businessmen to run for office. Their candidate for Congress in 1850, Thomas M. Howe, was cashier of an influential bank. Robert McCutcheon, the Whig candidate for mayor in 1850, was a wealthy wholesale grocer and iron manufacturer; John J. Roggen, the candidate for mayor in 1851, also manufactured iron. Morgan Robertson, one of the Whig candidates for the state assembly in 1851, owned a large glass factory. Active businessmen were also more prominent among Whig than among Democratic party leaders.[6] Iron and glass manufacturers, commission merchants, and shopkeepers familiar with the economic needs of the community, Whig leaders were deeply concerned about the failure to expand business pursuits in Pittsburgh, and they sought measures to improve the city's competitive position.

Representing the community's dominant economic groups, Whig leadership also came from the established native-born families of the city more often than did the Democratic leaders. Both parties usually nominated native-born Americans for

6. See Tables 10 and 11. Robert McCutcheon owned $15,000 worth of real property in 1850. Roggen, who also served as a Whig councilman in 1848 and 1849, owned real property valued at $25,000 in 1850. It should be admitted that in both parties most of the candidates for the state legislature or Congress were lawyers. This predominance was natural for any party then, and probably still is today. Although many workingmen voted Whig, the Whigs very rarely nominated them for office, charged a Democratic editor. See the *Post*, June 4, 1849. Nor did the Democrats, however.

office, yet three fourths of the Whig nominees were natives while only two thirds of the Democrats were. Of the 78 Whig candidates, only one was born in Germany. He was Frederick Lorenz, the wealthy and socially prominent glass manufacturer who had long resided in Pittsburgh and had been an elder in the Presbyterian church since 1834. The Germans were little better represented among the Democrats; only four of their candidates were German. Irishmen, however, constituted a larger portion of the Democratic candidates than they did of the Whig candidates.[7] Moreover, of the fifteen Irish-born Whig candidates, six were Protestants who had lived in this country for a long time. Typical of these men was Henry Coulter, a wholesale grocer who owned $64,000 worth of real property in 1850 and who had joined the socially prominent First Presbyterian Church in 1837. Another was William Young, a wealthy leather merchant and a United Presbyterian, whose twenty-year-old son had been born in Pennsylvania. On the other hand, only three of the seventeen Democratic Irish candidates could be identified as Protestants.

Differences in national backgrounds were more pronounced between secondary party leaders than between candidates. Seventy percent of the Whigs in this group were native-born while fewer than half of the Democrats were. On the other hand, the proportion of Irish among the Democrats was twice as large as that among the Whigs. Representatives of immigrant groups seemingly had more of a voice at Democratic conventions than at Whig meetings.[8]

Similarly, Democrats chose Roman Catholics as leaders much more often than the Whigs did. Over one-third of the

7. See Table 12.
8. See Table 13.

Democratic candidates whose religion could be identified were Catholic, yet of forty Whig candidates not one was Catholic.[9] There were only three Catholics among the Whig party leaders, and one of these, G. L. B. Fetterman, belonged to an extremely wealthy family.[10] On the other hand, seven (30%) of twenty-three secondary Democratic leaders were Catholic.

Presbyterians and Episcopalians were the dominant Protestant groups from which the parties drew their leaders, but Presbyterians were far more prominent in the Whig leadership.[11] Out of all the Presbyterians found in both ranks of leaders, forty were Whigs and only eight were Democrats. As shown in Chapter 1, many of the wealthy social elite were Presbyterian and, since more of the rich were Whig leaders, the large proportion of Presbyterians among the Whig leadership is predictable. At the same time, however, abolitionism spread through the Presbyterian church in the 1830s, and the stronger antislavery stand of the Whigs may have influenced these Presbyterians in their choice of party. Finally, many Whigs were former Antimasons, and Presbyterians, especially United Presbyterians, had been the major source of Antimasonic strength in Pittsburgh.[12]

9. See Tables 14 and 15.

10. According to the manuscript census of 1850, Fetterman's mother owned real property valued at $200,000.

11. See Tables 14 and 15. Because my sources on Presbyterians and Episcopalians were much fuller than those on any other denomination, the disparity in numbers would naturally result. At the same time, however, Whig leadership came from the economic and social elites of the community, and those men were predominantly Presbyterians and Episcopalians. For my sources on denominational membership, see Appendix B.

12. Gilbert H. Barnes discusses the spread of abolitionism through the Presbyterian Church in *The Antislavery Impulse, 1830–1844* (New York, 1933), p. 94. See also McCarthy, pp. 428, 482, 502, 542. I really cannot account for the equal recruitment by both parties from the Episcopalians except to argue that their religion was probably much less influential in de-

The Whig leaders, then, came from the upper and middle classes of the city, from the established Protestant families in the community. Businessmen such as Joseph Pennock and John Bissell, wealthy Presbyterian iron manufacturers who owned real property valued at $41,000 and $150,000 respectively in 1850, and James B. Murray, a wealthy Episcopalian banker, represented the Whigs in the city councils. Even the lawyers who led the Whigs were a different type from those who were Democrats. Harmar Denny, who served as councilman and had been an Antimasonic and then a Whig congressman, was the son of General Ebeneazer Denny, a Revolutionary War hero and one of Pittsburgh's first settlers. Owning property valued at $3,000,000 in 1850, Denny was an elder in the First Presbyterian Church and a leader of the social elite. Robert McKnight, a Princeton-trained lawyer who was a Whig councilman and later congressman, came from an extremely wealthy family with heavy investments in iron manufacturing. Also a member of the First Presbyterian Church, he married Harmar Denny's daughter.[13] Social ties

termining political affiliation than that of the Presbyterians who were in the forefront of various reform movements and who probably carried a more vigorous antipathy toward Catholics than did Episcopalians. Scotch-Irish Presbyterians from northern Ireland were numerous in Pittsburgh. Then too, Charles McCarthy, p. 381, points out that many Masons joined the Democratic party around 1830 because of the violent animosity of Antimasons. Since most Democratic Episcopalians in Pittsburgh were older men who had joined the party when Andrew Jackson was President, and since the Episcopalian Church, unlike the Presbyterian, showed no proclivity for Antimasonry, Democratic Episcopalians could have been former Masons. In short, the different reactions of Presbyterians and Episcopalians to Masonry may explain why Presbyterians were more often Whigs than were Episcopalians.

13. McKnight describes the interwoven life of the social elite in Pittsburgh in a very interesting diary. He shows that such Whig families as the McKnights, Dennys, Herrons, Pennocks, and Blairs all frequented the same

thus bound the Whig leaders together and gave them common interests. If any party was the party of the upper social stratum, it was the Whigs.

The Democratic leaders lacked the social prestige of the Whigs. As James Buchanan wrote of David Lynch, his good friend and trusted political lieutenant in Pittsburgh, "He does not move in the first circle of fashionable society but exercises more influence than any other Democrat in that region." [14] The lawyers who led the Democrats were men like John J. Mitchell and John N. McClowry, both propertyless Roman Catholics.[15] Indeed, the leadership of the Democratic and Whig parties reflected the ethnic, religious, and economic divisions within the society. Although both parties nominated wealthy men as candidates, the lower classes—the poorer people, the immigrants, and especially the Catholics—found a greater representation in the Democratic than in the Whig party. Conversely, a larger proportion of the Whig leadership than the Democratic came from the wealthy, well-established families who dominated the social and economic life of the city.

The issues dividing the Whig and Democratic parties varied in importance from 1847 through 1849, but in general the approach each party took to the voters mirrored the same divisions as did the leadership of the parties. Led by the rich,

---

parties and were connected socially. See entries for Feb. 21, Mar. 6, Sept. 28, and Oct. 16, 1846, in the Diary of Robert McKnight.

14. James Buchanan to Harriet Lane, Nov. 4, 1851, James Buchanan MSS (LC).

15. Neither owned any real property of value in 1850. Democratic lawyers such as Wilson McCandless and Robert Woods were very wealthy men, but they were exceptions.

the Whigs expressed a paternalistic concern for the entire community by arguing that the welfare of everyone in the society depended on the prosperity of their own mercantile and manufacturing pursuits. While the Whigs stressed the mutual interests of employer and employee, the Democrats insisted that the interests of the upper and lower classes differed sharply, and they concentrated on winning the votes of the less privileged groups by posing as champions of the common man.

In all three years, particularly in 1847 and 1848, the Whigs basically appealed to the acquisitive desires of the voter. They especially emphasized the tariff issue because the Democratic Walker Tariff of 1846 offered much less protection to the coal mining and iron manufacturing interests of Pennsylvania from foreign competition than had the higher, specific rates of the Tariff of 1842. Pennsylvania's farmers, miners, and manufacturers needed a high tariff to shield them from the competition of "pauper labor" in Britain, protested the Whigs, who argued that "the protection of American manufacturing and independence of American labor" were inseparable. Increased competition from abroad would mean fewer jobs for American workers and lower wages for those who did work. All three state platforms in 1847, 1848, and 1849 denounced the Democratic tariff of 1846, which "jeopard[ized] the interests of a confiding and betrayed people" in Pennsylvania. Always coupled with these Whig attacks were specific references to the woes of Pennsylvania's industries and workers.[16]

16. For the Whig state platforms in these years, see the *North American* (Philadelphia), Mar. 12, 1847, the *Journal*, Sept. 16, 1848, and the *Gazette*, Aug. 22, 1849. Hereafter, these platforms will be cited without newspaper references. I have emphasized the state platforms of the Whigs so much because the national Whig platform of 1848 purposefully avoided statements of principle and merely lauded the Whig presidential candidate,

Local Whig meetings and the party newspapers, the *Pittsburgh Daily Gazette* and the *Daily Commercial Journal,* echoed these cries about the tariff. The *Gazette* trumpeted in 1848, "We fight for our own workshops, for a market for our farmers and for the general prosperity of the country when we rally around the Protective policy." No matter what the office at stake, the Whig press harped on the issue. The *Gazette* argued in 1849 that the election of a Democratic state canal commissioner or of a Democrat to any local or state office was a vote of approval for the "British Tariff" of 1846.[17]

The Whigs also promised that efficient Whig administrators would promote the "interests of [the] state and the prosperity of her public works." A Whig governor would effect the "restoration of prosperity and credit to the immediate interests of Pennsylvania." Representing "the practical men who [were] concerned in the prosperity of the Commonwealth, the development of its resources, and the protection of its industry," they would provide a better atmosphere for business expansion in the state.[18]

For those manufacturers and merchants in Pittsburgh who depended on river trade for their livelihood, the Whigs demanded "liberal appropriations by the General Government for the improvement of our Lakes, Rivers, and Harbors." [19] They denounced the usurpation of power by the executive

Zachary Taylor. Thus the national organization left it to the state and local parties to create the party's ideology in the various parts of the country.

17. *Gazette,* Feb. 1, Mar. 21, Apr. 4, 5, 1848, Sept. 14, 20, 1849. For examples of the resolutions of the local Whig organization on the tariff, see the resolutions of the Whig county convention and of the meeting in Pittsburgh's third ward, *Gazette,* Aug. 24, Sept. 4, 1848.

18. Whig state platforms of 1847 and 1848. The public works were the canals in the state and the Pennsylvania Main Line System.

19. See the resolutions of the Whig county convention in the *Gazette,* Aug. 24, 1848.

and his extensive use of the veto power to block congressional appropriations for internal improvements.[20] By using the government to protect manufacturers from foreign competition, to clear the channels of domestic commerce, and improve the credit facilities of the state, the Whigs proposed to help businessmen and thereby workingmen.

In contrast to the Whigs, the Democrats of Pennsylvania and Pittsburgh apparently considered the tariff issue a thorny problem. In times of depression the iron, glass, and coal interests of the state demanded protection; therefore, Pittsburgh's Democrats lamented the passage of the Walker Tariff even in 1846.[21] Because of the necessity of party orthodoxy, however, especially in 1848 when the national Democratic platform endorsed the Walker Tariff, Pennsylvania Democrats praised it in state platforms for producing prosperity and benefiting "all sections of the country" and boasted that "the Democracy of Pennsylvania cling to it as one of the crowning measures that has rendered the present National Administration [of the Democrat James K. Polk] illustrious on the page of history." More outspoken than the formal party resolutions, the local organ of the Democracy, the *Pittsburgh Morning Post* vehemently denied that the tariff injured the iron interests of Pittsburgh.[22]

20. State platforms of 1847 and 1848. See also the resolutions of the Whig ratification meeting and of the Whig county executive committee in the *Gazette*, June 15, Aug. 14, 1848.

21. Diary of Robert McKnight, July 25, 1846. The authority on the tariff issue in Pennsylvania notes that manufacturers raised calls for tariff protection only when prices were low rather than when the amount of imports was large. Thus the prices Pittsburgh manufacturers could get, not the volume of British imports at the Atlantic coast, would determine the degree of support they gave to tariff agitation. See Malcolm Rogers Eiselen, *The Rise of Pennsylvania Protectionism* (Philadelphia, 1932), pp. 268–69.

22. See the Democratic state platforms of 1847 and 1848 in the *Pennsyl-*

When depression crippled the iron industry in the latter part of 1848 and in 1849, the Democrats changed their tune. President Taylor on a visit to Pittsburgh in the spring of 1849 was told that four fifths of the iron mills in Allegheny County had failed during the previous eighteen months.[23] A wealthy Pittsburgh friend of James Buchanan described what he considered to be the effect of this depression when he bluntly wrote him that the protective tariff cries of the Whigs caused the Democratic defeat in 1848 and that the "Whigs as a party would go *down down if it was not* [for] *the tariff principle which keeps them up.*"[24] Chastised by the 1848 defeat and forced to face the reality of depression, the Democrats in 1849 no longer boasted of the Democratic tariff but only "adhere[d]" to "the present revenue laws [because] they were the measures of the Democratic party." Democrats in Pittsburgh were particularly embarrassed, and at an 1849 county convention the resolution endorsing the 1846 tariff met strong opposition. One delegate bitterly complained that "no candidate for office, addressing the people of Allegheny county, dare[d] adhere openly to the Tariff of 1846, for it would certainly kill him."[25]

Although party loyalty forced the Democrats to mention the tariff, they usually tried to divert attention from it by stressing

vanian (Philadelphia), Mar. 8, 1847, and the *Post*, Mar. 13, 1848; see the resolutions of the Democratic county conventions in the *Post*, Jan. 13, June 22, 1848; see also the *Gazette*, Apr. 4, 1848.

23. Eiselen, p. 220. For additional evidence of the iron depression in Pittsburgh, see the report of a meeting of ironmasters in the *Gazette*, Aug. 21, 1849.

24. Robert Orr to James Buchanan, Allegheny City, Oct. 4, 1850, James Buchanan MSS (HSP).

25. See the Democratic state resolutions for 1849 in the *Post*, July 11, 1849, and the report of the Democratic county convention in the *Gazette*, Sept. 6, 1849.

other issues. While the Whigs emphasized the interests of the people and their prosperity, the Democrats spoke of the rights of man, not his interests.[26] Indeed, the Democrats gave far less attention to the economic theme in their ideology than did the Whigs.[27]

26. An actual count in the state platforms of both parties for the years 1847–49 shows that the Whigs used the word "interests" fifteen times while the Democrats, whose platforms were much longer, used it only four times and the phrase "industrial pursuits" once. On the other hand, Democratic platforms employed the words "rights" and "liberties" six times, and the Whigs used them only twice.

27. From four sets of Democratic county resolutions in 1848 and 1849, I found forty which dealt exclusively with issues rather than merely lauding candidates. Of these only three concerned the tariff and one other, additional economic issues. Only 180 (8%) of the 2,232 words in these sets of resolutions devoted exclusively to issues dealt with the tariff. For these resolutions, see the *Post*, Jan. 13, June 22, 1848, and Mar. 22, 1849, and the *Gazette*, Sept. 6, 1849.

In the three Whig state platforms in 1847, 1848, and 1849, out of 1,482 words which did not merely praise the honesty of candidates or pledge allegiance to the party, 397 words (27%) concerned a protective tariff. In addition, 254 words (17%) urged that Whigs be elected to bring prosperity to the state and nation. Thus a total of 44 percent of the actual platforms dealt with the economic theme. Of seventeen resolutions which dealt exclusively with issues, four dealt with the tariff and two concerned the prosperity of the state. I have not included in this count the two resolutions which denounced the strong executive and the use of the veto although these referred indirectly to the problem of federal internal improvements.

In contrast to the Whigs, the Democrats devoted only 285 words (12%) of a total of 2,388 words exclusively concerning issues in their state platforms in the three years to the tariff. An additional resolution of 59 words concerned prosperity, so that only 14 percent of the actual Democratic platforms made the economic appeal. Only four of 35 resolutions dealing solely with issues concerned economic prosperity. I have not included in this count the six resolutions in the Democratic platforms which denounced privileged monopolies, paper money, and banks. The emphasis of these resolutions seems to me to have been protection from infringements of individual liberty rather than positive advancement of economic interest. The Democratic state platforms may be found in the *Pennsylvanian*, Mar. 8,

53

Just as the Whigs utilized the national stand of the Democrats on the tariff against their Pittsburgh rivals so they exploited the issue of slavery in the territories. Most people in Pittsburgh and Allegheny County seem to have opposed the extension of slavery beyond the boundaries of the Southern states. Theodore Dwight Weld, the leading prophet of abolitionism in the West, attended a Presbyterian synod meeting in Pittsburgh in 1836 and converted it to abolitionism, and the Presbyterians, the sect in the city most imbued with the abolitionist spirit, were its most numerous denomination. In fact, a visitor to the city asserted after Weld's visit that there were more abolitionists in proportion to the population in Pittsburgh than in any other city in the country. The strong Antimasonic tradition in the city, with its demand to purge society of moral impurities, probably contributed to the particular strength of free-soil sentiment among the Whigs. The Pittsburgh Democrat who complained of Antimasonry linked it with the dominant antislavery feeling: "I have suffered more (as a politician) for my opposition to abolitionism and Antimasonry than from any other cause!" [28] With the prospect of territorial cession by Mexico to the United States, the debate about extending slavery into the territories became a vital issue in 1847 and 1848.

Pennsylvania's Whigs consistently denounced the very prospect of expansion. All the state platforms from 1847 through

1847, the *Post*, Mar. 13, 1848, the *Pennsylvanian*, Sept. 8, 1848, and the *Post,* July 9, 10, 11, 12, 13, 14, 16, and 17, 1849. In 1848 the Democrats held two state conventions, and each issued a slate of resolutions.

28. Barnes, pp. 84, 94; John B. Butter to Simon Cameron, Allegheny Arsenal, June 10, 1854, Cameron MSS (LC). On the moralistic aspects of Antimasonry and the continuation of that tradition among the Whigs, see Benson, pp. 21–26, 193–97, 206–07, 213; see also Robert J. Rayback, *Millard Fillmore: Biography of a President* (Buffalo, 1959), pp. 66, 100.

1849 contained resolutions opposing the extension of slavery into any newly won territories although they made no specific reference to the right or duty of Congress to prohibit such expansion.[29] In 1848 the Whigs protested the extension of "perpetuated bondage . . . which would degrade the nation and bring reproach upon republican principles." [30]

In most cases, however, Whig complaints against slavery expansion did not merely chorus the moral rhetoric of the abolitionists. They supplemented their antislavery appeal with a protest against the political power of the South. Confident of the support of those whose conscience would cause them to vote against slavery as a moral evil, they broadened their free-soil appeal so as to attract as well the apparently numerous white men in Pennsylvania who were more concerned with their own profits than with the immorality of slavery or the welfare of the Southern Negro. The 1847 Whig state platform asserted "that the interests of North and South, the welfare of the race, and the honor of the nation, demand that territories should not be acquired for the purpose of the extension of slavery." In 1849 the Whigs viewed

> slavery as an infraction of human rights—opposed to the enlightened spirit of our free institutions—destructive of equality of power in the general government, by enlarging where it exists, the constitutional representation—possessing an influence against Northern and Western policy and interests, by producing a system of laws destructive of domestic industry and vitally affecting free labor—retarding the natural growth of the population and improve-

29. The free-soil resolutions of the three Whig state platforms contained 235 words (16%) of the total devoted only to issues.
30. Whig state platform of 1848.

ment, by appropriation of large tracts of land for the benefit of the few to the injury of the many.[31]

To oppose the political power of the South which produced the disastrous economic policies of the Democrats, one had to oppose the extension of slavery.[32]

Pittsburgh Whigs resisted slavery extension even more determinedly than did the state party. In 1848 the Whig county convention required candidates for any office from county coroner to congressman to pledge support to the Wilmot Proviso which would legally bar slavery from the territories won from Mexico.[33] One of the candidates for the Whig presidential nomination that year, General Zachary Taylor, had little following in Pittsburgh, where, for most of the Whigs in the city, "the antislavery antipathy [was] stronger than the appetite for warriors." When the Louisiana slaveholder Taylor did receive the nomination, D. N. White, the editor of the *Gazette,* asserted that "almost nine-tenths of the Whig voters of the county" were disappointed.[34] Embarrassed by this selection, local Whigs assured the voters that if Congress should pass a law barring slavery from the territories, Taylor would sign it while Lewis Cass, the Democratic presidential nominee, was pledged to veto it.[35] In order to defend

31. Whig state platforms of 1847 and 1849.

32. In the most recent study of the Wilmot Proviso, Chaplain W. Morrison argues brilliantly that the North was so strong in its support of the Proviso because people really resented the spread of the slavery faction, not just because slavery extension was a symbol of the moral iniquity of slavery. Morrison, *Democratic Politics and Sectionalism: The Wilmot Proviso Controversy* (Chapel Hill, N.C., 1967), pp. 60–62. My study of appeals and popular attitudes in Pittsburgh confirms his conclusions.

33. *Journal*, June 15, 1848; *Gazette*, June 15, Aug. 14, 1848.

34. James Dunlap to John McLean, Pittsburgh, Dec. 29, 1847, John McLean MSS (LC); *Gazette*, June 10, 1848.

35. *Gazette*, Aug. 24, 1848.

the antislavery orthodoxy of the Whig candidates from the charges of both the Democratic and Free-Soil parties, the Whig *Daily Commercial Journal* republished a pamphlet entitled: "A statement proving Millard Fillmore, the Candidate of the Whig Party for the Office of Vice President to be an Abolitionist by a Review of his course in the 25th, 26th, and 27th Congress. Also, showing General Taylor to be in favor of extending the Ordinance of 1787 over the Continent, beyond the Rio Grande; in other words to be in favor of the Wilmot Proviso." [36]

Because of the prevalence of antislavery feeling in Pittsburgh both major parties viewed with dismay the appearance of a national antislavery party in 1848. Organized in Buffalo, New York, in August 1848, the Free-Soil party condemned both the Whig and Democratic parties for nominating presidential candidates whom no true antislavery man could support and declared a fixed opposition to the extension of slavery and the admission of any more slave states into the Union.[37] Staunch foes of slavery in Pittsburgh had applauded the Free-Soil movement from its inception, and, led by Edward D. Gazzam, a local doctor who had belonged to both the Whig and Democratic organizations, and William Larimer, Jr., a rich banker and normal Whig, they organized a local Free-Soil party and nominated a slate of candidates for county offices, the state assembly, and Congress. They also requested the formation of a state organization which would nominate a separate Free-Soil candidate for governor and recommended Gazzam for the post, but in the end, the state convention nominated

36. *Journal*, Sept. 12, 1848, quoted in Mueller, p. 154.

37. A copy of the Free-Soil platform may be found in the *Gazette*, Aug. 21, 1848. The Free-Soil party was almost a one-issue party; ten of fifteen resolutions of the national platform concerned the slavery question.

no candidate.[38] Still, local Free-Soil candidates remained in the field against the Whigs and Democrats in 1848.

The threat that the Free-Soil party would draw off some of their support panicked the Whig leaders and press. The *Gazette* criticized the Free-Soil platform for its failure to demand a protective tariff; White also argued correctly that the platform promised really to do no more against the extension of slavery than did the Whigs, although it openly called for a congressional statute. He excoriated as traitors Whigs who would follow former Democrats such as Martin Van Buren, the Free-Soil candidate for President, and Gazzam, men who "brought about the annexation of Texas, the extension of slavery, the disgraceful Mexican War, the prostration of the Protective Tariff, and the numerous other evils which have affected the country." Constantly White vilified Van Buren as an unconverted Jacksonian, a deadly foe of tariff protection, and an insincere opponent of slavery.[39] The great exertions of Whig papers to discredit him suggest that they considered those who supported the party because of its free-soil stand an important segment of the coalition.

If the Free-Soil party loomed ominous to the Whigs, it appeared a calamity to the Democrats of Pittsburgh because, unlike the Whigs, they were shackled by a national platform which avoided the territorial question, and they could not offer an equivalent to the Free-Soil antislavery position. Ap-

38. See the letter of some Pittsburgh men to the meeting of Barnburner Democrats in Utica, New York, which organized the New York state Free-Soil party, *Gazette*, June 24, 29, 1848. For the activities of the state and local Free-Soil conventions, see ibid., Sept. 7, 18, 1848.

39. *Gazette*, Aug. 7, 21, 28, Sept. 4, 8, 21, 22, 26, 1848. That the Northern Whigs greatly feared the Free-Soil party in 1848 is also the conclusion of the most recent work on the Wilmot Proviso. Morrison, p. 156.

parently the majority of Democrats in western Pennsylvania opposed the extension of slavery and disagreed with any policy that tacitly tolerated it. Despite the pressure from such men, a Democratic county convention in 1848 endorsed the national Democratic platform and refused to pass a resolution approving the Wilmot Proviso.[40]

Therefore local Democratic leaders feared the Free-Soil party as a real threat to lure antislavery Democrats who would never vote Whig but might follow Van Buren. Lecky Harper, the editor of the *Post*, denounced the local leaders of the movement as political opportunists "who have absolutely been driven out of the other parties, on account of a lamentable lack of character." Sincere opponents of slavery, admitted Harper, were willing to support the Whigs, and those running as Free-Soilers were mere office seekers. Nevertheless, the Free-Soil party attracted more Democrats than Whigs in Pittsburgh, and at least two editors blamed the Democratic defeat in the state as a whole in 1848 on Democratic defections to the Free-Soil ranks.[41]

Shaken by their disastrous defeats in both the gubernatorial and presidential elections of 1848, the Democrats included in their state platform of 1849 a resolution which denied "the power of any citizen to extend the area of bondage, beyond its present dominion" and declared that it was not "a part of the compromise of the Constitution, that slavery should forever travel with the advancing column of our territorial

40. *Dispatch*, Oct. 12, 1848; *Post*, June 22, 1848. Morrison (pp. 143–44) traces how the Democrats were purposely vague on the territorial question in the national platform in order to preserve unity between the Northern and Southern wings of the party.

41. *Post*, Sept. 7, 15, Nov. 18, 1848; *Gazette*, Aug. 11, 1848; *Dispatch*, Oct. 12, 1848. See Table 16.

progress." The 1849 state platform also adopted from the 1848 Free-Soil platform the demand for popular election of all public officials.[42]

Following the lead of the state organization, Pittsburgh's Democrats also tried to win back the votes lost to the Free-Soil party. They came out against the extension of slavery, for an elective judiciary, and for other measures demanded in the Buffalo Platform of 1848 such as cheap postage, the abolition of unnecessary public offices, and grants of homesteads to actual settlers. Harper of the *Post* censured slavery as "a deep stain and curse upon [the] country" which he wished to "be abolished throughout the world." [43] Because only a state canal commissioner, members of the state assembly, and county officials were to be elected in 1849, the Democrats could make such free-soil appeals. The interest of the Pittsburgh and state parties in persuading local antislavery constituencies conflicted, however, with that of the national organization which relied on the Southern branch of the party to supply votes in presidential elections. In order not to offend sensitive Southerners about slavery or the tariff, therefore, in most elections, Democrats in Pennsylvania relied primarily on trying to ignore or avoid those issues and stress other matters.

Unable to prick the voter's antislavery conscience in 1847 and 1848, the Democrats appealed to his sense of patriotism and desire for national expansion. In answer to the Whig charges that the Mexican War was President James K. Polk's responsibility alone, they defended Polk's course as necessary to preserve national honor, praised the activities of Pennsyl-

42. *Post*, July 16, 1849.

43. See the resolutions of the Democratic county convention in the *Gazette*, Sept. 6, 1849; *Post*, July 16, 1849.

vania's troops, and bitterly condemned the Whig congressional opposition to the war as "treasonable." They vaunted that they "did not fear the extension of the Union" and lauded Polk for acquiring a large portion of Mexican territory.[44] The Whigs, in contrast, long opposed to expansionism as a Democratic policy and anxious to avoid the disruptive issue of slavery expansion, questioned the desirability of annexing any territory.[45]

In addition to emphasizing the Mexican War much more than the Whigs, the Democrats more blatantly appealed to the immigrant vote in their state platforms. Calling for contributions to the starving Irish in 1847, the Democrats in 1848 excoriated the British, "the most selfish, proudest, and haughtiest aristocracy which the world ever saw" for reducing the Irish to slavery. The Whigs said little about the revolutions of 1848 in their state platforms of 1848 and 1849.[46] Refugees from revolutions in Germany and famine in Ireland found more

44. See the resolutions of the county convention in the *Post*, Jan. 13, 1848, and the Democratic state platform in the *Pennsylvanian*, Sept. 8, 1848. See also the Democratic state platform for 1847 and the other one for 1848. Of the 25 resolutions dealing exclusively with issues in the Democratic state platforms of 1847 and 1848, 12 defended the Mexican War or denounced the Whigs for hindering its prosecution. Of 1,747 words devoted to issues, 891 (51%) were devoted to this issue. In contrast, only one resolution out of a total of seventeen in the Whig platforms of 1847 and 1848 concerned the war itself, and this praised the troops.

45. Whig state platform of 1847. Harry V. Jaffa argues that because Jefferson rather than Hamiltonian Federalists acquired Louisiana, Federalist-Whig foreign policy always opposed territorial expansion. See Jaffa, *Crisis of the House Divided,* p. 70.

46. *Pennsylvanian*, Mar. 8, 1847, and Sept. 8, 1848; *Post*, July 13, 1849. In the three years, the Democrats devoted 4 of 35 resolutions and 259 words (11%) of the state platforms to the European situation. In contrast, the Whigs devoted to this issue one resolution out of seventeen and 63 words (4%) of their total devoted to issues.

apparent sympathy in the official statements of the Democrats than in those of the Whigs.

Democrats in Pittsburgh directed even blunter appeals to the Irish and German immigrants. In 1849 they "offered all [their] sympathies to the patriots of Ireland, Germany, and Rome." In 1848 the *Post* charged that both William F. Johnston, the Whig candidate for governor, and Zachary Taylor were hostile to immigrant groups. "THE ELECTION OF JOHNSTON IS THE SURE VICTORY OF NATIVISM," declared one headline, and another editorial was addressed to "Natives of Ireland, Natives of Germany, and all other adopted citizens." Harper frequently charged that the Whigs were allied with "Abolitionists" and "Churchburners." [47] Because Harper could not make open appeals for the antislavery vote in 1848, he thus linked the militant Protestant zeal behind the antislavery conscience with the Protestant antipathy toward Catholics. By kindling anti-Catholic bigotry, he argued, Whig moralistic appeals to arouse the Protestant sense of sin menaced German and Irish Catholics. Indeed, his contention contained much truth, for Presbyterian Antimasons had criticized Catholicism since 1835 in western Pennsylvania.[48]

While Whig state platforms were silent on the European situation, Pittsburgh's Whigs courted the foreign vote almost as eagerly as the Democrats. Local Whigs expressed their sympathy "with oppressed Ireland in her present efforts to

47. *Gazette*, Sept. 6, 1849. See also the *Post*, Sept. 25, Oct. 3, 5, 6, 1848. For Harper's other editorials accusing the Whigs of nativism, see the *Post*, Sept. 29, 30, Oct. 31, Nov. 7, 1848.

48. McCarthy, pp. 470, 482, 502. Ray A. Billington discusses the burning of Catholic churches in Philadelphia in the early 1840s in *The Protestant Crusade, 1800–1860: A Study in the Origins of American Nativism* (Chicago, 1964), pp. 228–30. For another discussion of the interrelationship between the antislavery and nativist spirit, see Jaffa, p. 74.

establish her independence." Defending Taylor from the *Post*'s charges of nativism, the *Gazette* asserted that Lewis Cass was responsible for the failure in Congress of an Irish Relief Bill, which would have sent government financial aid to Ireland. To woo the German vote, the Whig candidate Johnston conspicuously appointed as an aide, Leopold Sahl, an influential German Catholic in Pittsburgh. Speaking in German at rallies throughout the city, Sahl praised Johnston and accused the Democrats of nativism.[49]

Conceding the support of most wealthy businessmen to the Whigs, the Democrats concentrated on the workingmen's vote, stressed the differences in class interests, and claimed to be the champions of the poor. When they could no longer maintain that the low tariff of 1846 produced prosperity, they changed tack and condemned protection as class legislation. Protective tariffs gave "bounties to particular interests to the detriment of the great industrial classes of the Country . . . and sought to aggrandize the few at the expense of the many," the Democrats railed. If the tariff were raised, argued the *Post*, cheap British ironworkers would come over to America because of the higher wages and compete with Americans for jobs. Rather than helping workers, a protective tariff "oppress[ed] the poor and benefit[ed] the rich, [built] up monopolies with special privileges, which were inimical to the well-being of society. Hence the Whig party, as a matter of course, became its peculiar champions, and the Democrats, its foes."[50]

49. See the resolutions of the Whig county convention in the *Gazette*, Aug. 24, 1848. See also the editorials therein, July 20 and Nov. 4, 1848, and in the *Post*, Oct. 6, 1848. Newspapers reported various German-language Whig rallies—e.g. *Journal*, Nov. 2, 1848.

50. *Post*, Jan. 13, 1850. See also the resolution of the 1849 Democratic state platform and the discussion of it, *Post*, July 11, 1849.

Democrats also constantly condemned the "encroachments of corporate power on the individual rights of the people." They invoked the Jacksonian ideal of the individual who advanced only by his own merits and attacked special privileges and monopolies. While the Whigs complained about executive vetoes, the Democrats applauded Democratic governor, Francis R. Shunk, for vetoing corporation charters "by which an exemption was thus asked and conferred from the ordinary responsibilities of individual enterprise." National and state platforms pledged unwavering opposition to the rechartering of a national bank and support of the Independent Treasury System initiated by Martin Van Buren. Democrats would tolerate no new banks without individual liability and stringent restrictions on note issue. Banks which could issue "a depreciated paper currency" in the form of bank notes were a threat to cause speculation; the only safety to the profits of labor lay in the "constitutional currency—gold and silver coin." Although Pittsburgh desperately needed expanded banking facilities, Democrats there "continue[d] to look upon the whole Banking system with disgust," and they denounced "swindling banks and monopolies."[51] Unlike Whigs who demanded positive legislation to promote business interests,

51. *Gazette*, Sept. 6, 1849; *Pennsylvanian*, Mar. 8, 1847, Sept. 8, 1848; *Post*, July 10, 1849. In the Democratic state platforms from 1847 to 1849, 6 of 35 resolutions and 17 percent of the words dealing exclusively with issues attacked special privileges, banks, and paper currency. Next to the Mexican War this issue was the most prominent in the Democratic state platforms. It received even more attention from Pittsburgh's Democrats. From four sets of county resolutions, forty resolutions dealt exclusively with issues. Of these ten denounced banks and paper money. These resolutions contained 23 percent of the words devoted to issues, more than any other topic. In sharp contrast to the Democrats, the Whigs made no specific reference to banks or currency in any local or state platform in these years.

Democrats bitterly assaulted institutions which would facilitate the organization and financing of business enterprises.

The Democratic denunciation of paper money assumed particular importance in 1849 because of an over-issue of municipal scrip in Pittsburgh. The cities of Pittsburgh and Allegheny and the county commissioners had printed the fiat currency to finance the laying of water pipelines and the construction of streets. An excess of the scrip decreased its value, and in 1849 bankers and brokers refused to exchange it at face value. When the city delayed redemption of the scrip at par, laborers who had no savings had to sell it at about a 15 percent loss. Then the city announced that it would redeem the scrip at full value, and "rich capitalists" scrambled frantically to buy it up.[52] To the angry workers who could not afford to hold it until redemption in the depression times of 1849, the paper money seemed to benefit only the rich and rob them of a fair wage.

Seizing the opportunity afforded by local discontent, the Democratic press accurately charged that the "entire shinplaster system is closely allied to Whiggery; indeed the Whigs [city councilmen and county commissioners] are the authors of the system." "Shinplasters, issued by municipal or other corporations, we denounce as false representatives of money, by which labor is defrauded of its just reward," they vowed in state and local resolutions. The *Post* warned that "the workingmen of Pennsylvania, and especially of Allegheny county . . . should have nothing to do with Whiggery, if they wish to see the shinplaster system put down."[53] While

52. *Gazette*, Apr. 18, 1849; *Dispatch*, Apr. 25, June 5, 1849.
53. *Post*, Mar. 22, 1849; *Gazette*, Sept. 6, 1849. See also the plank from the 1849 Democratic state platform and the editorial discussion of it in the *Post*, July 12, 1849.

the Whigs concentrated on national issues in 1848, the Democrats grasped a local issue in 1849 to discredit the Whigs with the workers.

Just as the scrip controversy in Pittsburgh allowed the Democrats to pose as defenders of workingmen from Whig policies, the rise of a direct conflict between manufacturers and factory operatives over a factory law gave the *Post* a chance to exploit class tensions for political purposes. Passed in March 1848, the Pennsylvania Ten Hour Law forbade female and child operatives in cotton factories to work over ten hours a day and required that children under sixteen years of age attend school at least three months out of the year. Attached to the law was a proviso which would allow special contracts between factory owners and employees. In practice, this proviso permitted an employer to continue operating his factory the normal twelve hours a day.

Application of the law in the mills of Allegheny quickly provoked trouble. When the girls reported to work on July 1, 1848, the first day the law was to go into effect, they discovered that their wages had been cut 16 percent rather than being kept at the level of a twelve-hour day. Furious at this apparent treachery, the operatives refused to work until the old wages had been restored for the shortened workday. Finally, some workers signed a contract at the old wage for a twelve-hour day under the special contract proviso of the law, and they returned to work at the Penn Mills in Allegheny on July 31, 1848. Enraged, the other strikers and a mob of bystanders rioted, pelted the owners of the mill with rocks, flattened the fence surrounding the factory, splintered its doors with axes, and attacked those operatives inside who were on their dinner break. When the county sheriff tried to intervene, the mob assaulted him and then smashed windows and machinery in the factory. On August 18 most of the strikers resumed work at the reduced wage. Seventeen rioters had been arrested, and their sensational trial which dragged on through January 1849 kept the memories of the violence alive.[54]

Whig and Democratic editors took opposite sides in the dispute. White of the *Gazette* denounced the lawlessness of and destruction of property by the rioters and criticized the Ten Hour Law as grossly unfair to manufacturers. If cotton manufacturers operated their factories only ten hours daily, argued White, they could not compete with those in New England and to the west who operated twelve or more hours, and they would go out of business. Industrial depression would throw many operatives out of work and paralyze the rest of the community dependent on supplying the operatives. When the factories did shut down in 1849, White crowed about the accuracy of his forecast.[55] The *Post*, on the other hand, vigorously defended the action of the rioters; Harper vilified the factory owners for reducing the wage and utilizing the special contract proviso which violated the spirit of the law. One editor said that Harper's advocacy of the cotton mill rioters was a major reason for the Democratic defeat in the elections of 1848.[56]

At first the official positions of the opposing parties on the issue were similar. In 1848 neither party mentioned the law in its state platform, but both Pittsburgh organizations endorsed it. The Democrats "heartily concurred" with the law after its passage and proposed that labor on public works be limited to ten hours a day and that violation of the Ten Hour Act be punishable by imprisonment. Moreover, all the Democratic

54. *Gazette*, Aug. 1, 1848; Ware, *The Industrial Worker*, p. 148. See also the report of the trial of the rioters in the *Gazette*, Jan. 22, 1849.

55. *Gazette*, Aug. 4, 1848, Apr. 6, 12, 1849.

56. *Dispatch*, Oct. 12, 1848.

candidates for the state assembly in 1848 made speeches in favor of the law. The Whigs, thrown on the defensive by their responsibility for the scrip issues and by their reputation as a party of businessmen protested as "a base slander the often repeated charge that the Whigs are not the sincere and consistent friends of the working classes." Both parties also declared that their candidates for governor favored the law.[57]

In 1849 the special contract proviso became the crucial point of debate between the parties. The Democrats vaunted their defense of the "interests and rights of labor" and demanded the repeal of the proviso which they called a Whig measure in violation of the spirit of the law. They charged that in failing to repeal the proviso the Whigs had "shamefully violated" their "distinct and emphatic pledge and promise made before the last Governor's elections . . . to perfect the Ten Hour Factory Law and the elevation of the laboring classes." [58] Although the Whig state platform endorsed the extant law as "a proper and judicious safeguard against oppression" of child labor, it did not emphasize the issue so much as the Democratic platform nor did it say anything about repealing the contract proviso. In Pittsburgh the Whigs seem to have adopted the *Gazette*'s position that the law crippled the city's cotton manufacturers, and the 1849 county convention failed to mention it. Lecky Harper pointed out this omission and asserted that the Democrats of Pennsylvania were "more deeply wedded" to the Ten Hour measure than to any other. Charging that the Whig newspapers had tried to help capital

57. See the Democratic county resolutions in the *Post*, June 22, 1848; see the resolutions of the Whig county convention in the *Gazette*, Aug. 24, 1848, and the report of the Whig meeting in the sixth ward, *Gazette*, Oct. 8, 1848. See also the *Post*, Oct. 4, 1848, and the *Gazette*, Aug. 14, 1848.

58. *Post*, Mar. 22, July 9, 1849.

"crush labor" in the recent strikes, he ridiculed "the false professions of the Federal [Whig] party" to be the friends of labor and declared, "If the Industrious Classes wish to accomplish anything for their own good, they must unite with the Democratic party." [59]

Taking their cue from Harper, the Democrats tried to appear as progressive as they could in advocating the rights of labor. To establish their image as friends of labor, they ran their candidate for mayor in January 1849 as a "Citizens' and Workingmen's Candidate." The resolutions of an 1849 county convention lauded former Governor Francis R. Shunk as a "firm and radical Democrat" and "claim[ed] the ten hour law and elective judiciary as radical and progressive Democratic measures." At that same convention, Robert Woods, a very wealthy lawyer, defended his opposition to a resolution endorsing the Tariff of 1846 by asserting that "he was as radical in feeling as any man" among the Democrats. Harper disparaged "the Federal Whigs and their natural allies the Conservatives." [60] To be a "radical" friend of labor and foe of the tariff became the criterion of one's party loyalty as the Democrats strove in 1849 to win the labor vote.

The adoption of the "radical" prolabor policy by some Pittsburgh Democrats produced an open conflict between the progressive and conservative wings of that party. During the cotton riots, Harper of the *Post* openly tempted class warfare as he venomously censured "the unholy and unjust attempts of the capitalists to crush and destroy the souls and bodies of men, women, and children." Protariff business leaders in the

59. Whig state platform of 1849; *Post*, July 9, 1849.
60. *Gazette*, Sept. 6, 1849; *Post*, July 11, 1849.

Democratic party increasingly opposed the crusading editor. A correspondent of James Buchanan had written him as early as November 1847 that the *Post*, because of Harper's policies, had "become generally unpopular with *leaders* and people." These businessmen objected to Harper's condoning the factory rioters "who have trampled on the majesty of the law and dared to stop the wheels of industry in this city." In 1849 the owners of the cotton mills, led by James K. Moorhead and Pollard McCormick, wealthy Democrats, addressed the most prominent Democrats of the county and asked if they agreed with the *Post*'s attacks on the manufacturers. Many of these leading Democrats including William Wilkins, former United States Senator, wrote back criticizing the efforts of Harper to incite the operatives against the factory proprietors as "opposed to the interests of the Democratic party, and of society in general." When Harper printed this reply, however, he published simultaneously a much longer list of men who supported his position.[61]

Determined to silence Harper, the conservative wing of the party started their own newspaper in order to demolish the reputation of the *Post* as the Democratic organ. Edited by Joseph Snowden, the *Pittsburgh Daily Morning Mercury* was more than likely financed by James K. Moorhead, the wealthy iron and cotton manufacturer, a protariff conservative, and a disappointed aspirant for the Democratic congressional nomination in 1848.[62] Claiming to voice the true Democratic

61. *Post*, Feb. 6, 28, 1849; John Coyle to James Buchanan, Pittsburgh, Nov. 30, 1847, Buchanan MSS (HSP); see also the letter signed "Harkaway" in the *Gazette*, Feb. 13, 1849.

62. *Gazette*, June 22, 1848. There is no definite evidence that Moorhead financed the *Mercury*, but in 1850 Harper said that Snowden had "allowed himself to be duped by designing and ambitious men—men who would hazard their very souls for a Congressional or Gubernatorial nomination in

principles of Jefferson and Jackson, the *Mercury* denounced the *Post* for "the most pernicious and detestable" demagoguery in its attempts to array labor against capital and dismissed such agitation as useless because the Whigs always captured a large portion of the labor vote. Recognizing the need of banks in Pittsburgh, Snowden called for more of them. Venting the frustration of the protariff wing of the Pittsburgh Democracy, he declared Pennsylvania "a Tariff State" and ridiculed Democratic acquiescence in the low tariff policies of the national party. Finally, he protested that "*all the Agrarians, Fourierists, Socialists and other lazy loafing dreamers and whiners in the community have foisted themselves upon us,* and the party has been stumbling along under their odious and fanatical doctrines." He vowed his intention "*to rescue the party from the lead of all this filth and rubbish*" and bring back the wealthy and intelligent men who had been driven away from it.[63]

In defense, the *Post*'s editor carried the fight to his subscribers. Even before the appearance of the *Mercury* he complained that certain manufacturers and their friends were plotting to bankrupt the *Post* by withdrawing all advertisements from the paper. Charging that these conservative "conspirators" had done more harm to Democratic party than all the Whigs in the state, he derided the idea "that a few monied men in this community shall put down a democratic newspaper for advocating the rights and interests of the industrious classes." The election of delegates to the Democratic county convention

---

the Democratic party." See the *Post*, Apr. 30, 1850. Because Moorhead sought both offices and because in 1849 he was ejected from the county executive committee, Harper probably referred to him.

63. *Pittsburgh Daily Morning Mercury* quoted in the *Gazette*, Apr. 9, 1849. For comments on the protariff wing of the Democrats, see the *Gazette*, Aug. 31, 1846, Mar. 26, 1849, Dec. 1, 1849.

in 1849 developed into a battle between the opponents and defenders of Harper's antibusiness policy. The prolabor faction won, and the convention passed a long resolution thanking Harper for his independent advocacy of the Ten Hour Law and the "rights of labor" and called his course "proper and perfectly Democratic." To establish its complete control of the party the prolabor faction also pushed through the convention a resolution demanding "that the name of J. K. MOOR-HEAD be stricken from the County Committee of Correspondence and that a Democrat be put on to fill his place." [64]

Although the ideological conflict over such issues as the tariff, banks, and labor was genuine, the battle also derived from the struggle for power within the state organization of the Democratic party. Conflicting factions in Pittsburgh consisted of those who favored or opposed James Buchanan's control of the Pennsylvania Democracy. Harper backed Buchanan, recommended him for the Presidency in 1848, and frequently attacked his enemies such as Simon Cameron. Moorhead opposed Buchanan, and he backed Lewis Cass in 1848 as did most of Buchanan's foes in the Pennsylvania Democracy. Buchanan condemned both Cameron and Moorhead as "men who make a trade of politicks [sic] to fill their own pockets." [65] Therefore, Moorhead's loss of the congressional nomination in 1848 to a Buchanan man and his ejection from the county

64. *Post*, Feb. 6, 17, 1849. See the report of the convention, *Post*, Mar. 22, 1849.

65. *Post*, Jan. 31, 1848, July 2, 1850; *Gazette*, Dec. 1, 1849; Coyle to Buchanan, Nov. 30, 1847, Buchanan MSS (HSP); Roy Franklin Nichols, *The Democratic Machine, 1850–1854* (New York, 1923), p. 47; James Buchanan to David Lynch, Aug. 23, 1850, Buchanan MSS (LC). Actually Simon Cameron supported Buchanan in 1848 and only turned against him in 1849 and 1850. Erwin Stanley Bradley, *Simon Cameron, Lincoln's Secretary of War: A Political Biography* (Philadelphia, 1966), p. 83.

committee of correspondence in 1849 were in some respects victories for the Buchanan faction in Pittsburgh.

Local Whigs also split in their preferences for national Whig candidates, and they, too, fought with each other for the patronage. For example, in the presidential election of 1848 the *Daily Commercial Journal* early boomed Zachary Taylor, although he was unpopular locally, while the *Gazette* backed Henry Clay. "Very acrimonious feelings" also existed between the supporters of Winfield Scott, the other Mexican War hero, and those of Clay.[66]

These battles originated in a split in the local party between ins and outs, or, as the *Post* termed them, the "Old Hunkers" and the "Young Whigs." A Whig nomination almost assured election; therefore, bitter fights repeatedly occurred among the Whigs for nomination. Because city councilmen were not paid, the state and county offices were the most hotly contested by office seekers. A small group headed by George Darsie, a lawyer from Allegheny City, always seemed to win the nominations for state legislature. For example, in 1847 seventeen candidates vied for the four Whig nominations to the assembly; six of these were Young Whigs, but none received nomination. Nor did C. B. M. Smith, the candidate of the Young Whigs, defeat Darsie for the nomination to the state senate. The Young Whigs found their opportunity after the Whig state and national victories in 1848. When both factions sought to arrange the reception for President Taylor when he visited Pittsburgh in the spring of 1849, the newly elected Whig governor William F. Johnston sided with the

66. *Journal*, Nov. 20, 1847; *Gazette*, Mar. 25, 1848; Cornelius Darragh to John McLean, Pittsburgh, Mar. 2, 1848, McLean MSS; *Post*, Feb. 25, 1848. For evidence of continued feuding between Whig factions after Taylor's election, see the *Post*, Feb. 8, July 21, 1849.

leaders of the Young Whigs, whose chief, Cornelius Darragh, he appointed State Attorney General, and the Young Whig faction managed the reception. Because Johnston controlled most federal appointments in the city, the Young Whigs received most of the national patronage too.[67] In effect, the Old Hunkers usually were able to manage the nominations for elective office while the Young Whigs won the bulk of the appointive offices after 1848.

In its internal struggles for patronage the Whig party closely resembled the Democracy, but the serious ideological clash among Democrats was not found among the Whigs. Because the Democrats in Pittsburgh very rarely won office, they accepted the unpopular national stands of their party and tried to align with the state and national leaders whose victory might result in a patronage post for themselves. While constant defeat exacerbated the Democratic split, Whig factionalism grew out of victory, and the struggles for nomination rent the party, at least temporarily, almost every year. Both Whig and Democratic newspapers attempted to back a winner because they wanted government printing.[68] Unfortunately, it is difficult to estimate how much these intraparty struggles weakened the parties at the polls, but those of one party were probably no more debilitating than those of the other.

Two facts stand out about the voting support of the two parties. First, the vote for both parties was larger in state and national elections than in local elections. Second, the size of the vote in local elections was almost constant. In almost all

67. *Post*, June 4, 1847, Aug. 17, 19, 1849.
68. *Post*, July 21, 1849; Coyle to Buchanan, Nov. 30, 1847, Buchanan MSS (HSP).

elections the minor parties, the Native American and Free-Soil, had a small but consistent following. On the other hand, in the local elections of 1847, 1848, and 1849 the Whig vote was consistently around eighteen hundred, and the Democratic vote always remained around fifteen hundred. In the gubernatorial and presidential elections of 1848, however, the size of the Whig vote increased by more than half, and the size of the majority rose sharply even though the Democratic vote also increased.[69] The overwhelming turnout for the Whigs in 1848 when the issues were slavery extension, the tariff, and Taylor's nativism suggests that national issues and a chance for the people in Pittsburgh to express antipathy toward slavery and the obstructionist South could draw out the full natural majority of the Whigs. Conversely, the small votes and majorities in local elections when many Whig voters were apparently apathetic indicate that Democrats could make the greatest inroads into Whig strength on local issues.

Despite the fluctuation in the size of the vote, the sources of support for the Whigs and Democrats were fairly constant in most elections. The Whigs were the strongest in the wards with the largest numbers of well-to-do merchants, manufacturers, and lawyers. Conversely, the wards in which they were weakest had large concentrations of propertyless people.[70] Most of the wealthy men in the community tended to

69. See Table 16.

70. See Table 17 and note the coefficients of correlation between the Whig percentage of the vote and the percentage of white males over 21 who owned real property valued at $10,000 or more in 1850. Note also the coefficients of correlation with the percentage of merchants, manufacturers, and bankers, professional men, and clerks and shopkeepers. See Appendix B for an explanation of the meaning of coefficients of correlation and of the methods used to calculate them. Unless stated otherwise, all coefficients of correlation in this study are calculated on the basis of the product-moment formula described in Appendix B. Hereafter, therefore, I shall refer to coefficients of

support the Whigs. Of a total of 187 men in Pittsburgh and Allegheny City who owned real property worth $25,000 or more according to the manuscript census of 1850, the political affiliations of 77 could be found. Of these 77, 58 (75%) were Whigs, and only 15 (20%) were Democrats. The other 4 joined the Free-Soil party in 1848, but 2 of these, William Larimer, Jr., and Hugh D. King, had been active Whigs before then and would return to the Whig fold. The editor of the *Pittsburgh Daily Dispatch* declared that the *Post*'s defense of cotton factory rioters united the opponents of the Democracy in 1848, and it is likely that calls for class war united the rich behind the Whigs.[71] A more important reason for their support was simply that the economic and social elite backed the party which their friends led and which expressed a practical concern in forwarding the business interests of the state.

Others who lived in the wards with the rich followed their lead, for the wealthy alone were far too few to provide the Whigs with their majorities. Harper of the *Post* admitted, and others asserted, that despite Democratic efforts to coalesce the working classes against their Whig employers, a large number of mechanics and workingmen belonged to the Whig ranks.[72]

correlation calculated with percentages on a ward-by-ward basis merely as correlations between two groups.

71. *Dispatch*, Oct. 12, 1848; *Post*, July 3, 1848. To check the political affiliations of wealthy men, I examined lists of party candidates, delegates, ward vigilance committees, and the signers of petitions asking men to run for the various parties.

72. *Post*, June 4, 1849; see also the *Mercury* quoted in the *Gazette*, Apr. 9, 1849. Note also in Tables 17 and 18 the correlations between the Whig and Democratic votes and the unskilled laborers and the group which owned "None" (no real property of value according to the census). The insignificant positive correlations with the Democrats and negative correlations with the Whigs indicate that either many among these groups did not vote normally or they split their vote among the parties or both.

The Whig economic appeals in times of depression and un-employment may have had more effect than the Democratic rhetoric on these men. Workers were probably more interested in maintaining decent wages than in reattaining individual freedom and responsibility, concepts which were becoming increasingly unreal for them as the industrial system spread.

Other factors, however, also account for the widespread Whig support. In all segments of the population, workers and employers, rich and poor, the native-born Americans tended to give very solid support to the Whigs.[73] Indeed, the original four wards which were strongly Whig and where most of the city's wealthy men resided also contained the largest concentrations of native Americans. There is little evidence that the workers who supported the Whigs were immigrants, so many of them must have been native-born citizens.[74] Native-born artisans and laborers disliked immigrant workers who competed for their jobs and threatened their position in the society. Norman Ware, an authority on workers in the mid-nineteenth century, asserts that the immigration in the 1840s and 1850s rendered solidarity impossible among the workers and lowered their standards.[75] In Pittsburgh disgruntled native workers expressed their antagonism to newcomers by backing the Whigs, whose leaders were almost ex-

73. See Tables 17, 19, 20, and 21 and Chap. 1.

74. See Table 17 and note the negative correlation between the Whigs and the Germans and the Irish. Wards 8 and 9 appear to contradict the analysis of native American support for the Whigs, for the proportion of native Americans in them was small while the Whig strength in both was great. The absolute vote in both, however, was very small, and there were enough native Americans in both to account for the entire Whig vote. The exceptional Whig strength in both probably resulted from apathy and the disfranchisement of large numbers of potentially Democratic immigrants by naturalization laws.

75. Ware, *The Industrial Worker*, p. 10.

77

clusively native-born Protestants and whom the Democrats labeled anti-Catholic nativists.

The preference of native-born workers for the Whigs prevented the Democrats in most cases from forming a coalition of the poorer classes which could defeat the Whigs. While the Democrats were not the party of all the working classes, however, they did draw most of their support from the lower classes, especially immigrants and Catholics. The Democrats were strongest in those areas with the fewest native Americans, and the Irish particularly tended to give them strong support. Most Germans who voted probably also tended to be Democrats although some may have voted Whig.[76]

Several factors, however, prevented the Democrats from winning the complete support of the poor immigrant population. For one thing, according to Pennsylvania law only those who paid state or local taxes on real or personal property could vote, and some of the propertyless were undoubtedly disfranchised by this requirement.[77] More important, the five-year naturalization period required by federal law for immigrants before they could become citizens and vote prevented many

76. See Tables 17 and 18. The insignificant correlations of both parties with the Germans until 1849 indicate two things. First, some Germans probably voted Whig; second, many Germans either did not or could not vote.

77. See the Pennsylvania General Assembly, *Laws of the Commonwealth of Pennsylvania Passed at the Session of 1838–39* (Harrisburg, 1839), pp. 532–34. The law meant that a man who owned no taxable property whatsoever probably could not vote. The possible impact of this law on voting is discussed in Appendix B.

The immigrants formed a large segment of the poor working classes. As a group the Germans were probably poorer than the Irish. The correlations between the percentage of Germans in the adult male population and the percentage of those owning no real property, of skilled workers, and of unskilled laborers were $+.70$, $+.52$, and $+.63$ respectively. The correlations between the Irish and those same groups were $+.06$, $+.24$, and $+.56$ respectively.

newly arrived Germans and Irishmen from voting in the late 1840s. Thus, although immigrant adult males outnumbered native-born males in the city by 1850, legal prohibitions kept them from voting in sufficient numbers to secure a majority for the Democrats.

Moreover, those immigrants who did vote may have divided because of the antagonism between Protestants and Catholics within the city. Protestant Irishmen and Germans belonged to anti-Catholic Protestant Associations, and in the 1840s fear of the anti-Catholic spirit inherent in the Whig free-soil appeals and anti-Catholic biases of Antimasons caused most Catholics in the city to vote Democratic. Of 98 prominent Catholic laymen, 23 could be identified as Democrats in the period 1848–51 while only 5 were identified as Whigs. Because the Democrats gave much more opportunity to Catholics to lead than did the Whigs, and because the Whig *Gazette* seemed to attack Catholics while the Democratic *Post* defended them, the Catholics supported the party which best represented their interests.[78] It seems reasonable to assume that hostile Protestants would vote for the Whigs whose leaders were so predominantly Protestant. This religious split combined with the more basic antagonism between native-born citizens and immigrants, legal restrictions, and apathy to prevent the Democrats from forming the working-class coalition they sought.

The only exception to this pattern in the late 1840s appeared when the Democrats elected one man to the state assembly in

78. I compiled the list of Catholic laymen from the newspapers. These lists may be found in the *Post*, Mar. 29, 1855, Sept. 22, 1857, Feb. 2, May 9, 1860, and the *Gazette*, June 16, 1851. See the issues of those two papers in July 1849 for examples of the feud over the supposed despotism of the Pope. Although these were not official campaign appeals, this identification of the party organs on opposite sides of the question probably had much influence in shaping the vote.

1849. That year they finally managed to rally a fairly solid vote among the poorer elements by harping on virulent economic grievances. The Democrats made one Whig candidate, Caleb Lee, the special target of their campaign, a symbol of everything the workingmen could detest. Lecky Harper called him a "purse-proud aristocrat," the choice of "the monopolists and old hunkers of the federal [Whig] party" who opposed the Ten Hour Law which the Democrats deemed so vital.[79] Emphasizing their radical prolabor program and trying to use to advantage the workers' anger at strikes, unemployment, and the municipal and county scrip debacle in 1849, the Democrats sought to pit one class against the other at the polls.

The appeals partially succeeded as Lee drew about 300 fewer votes than Whigs normally won in local elections while the triumphant Democrat, Jonas R. McClintock, polled about 300 more votes than Democrats usually did. The Whig drop probably occurred among the poor, especially some Germans, for Lee retained the support of the wealthy and of many natives. On the other hand, the Democrats won the most support they ever had in a local election among the poor, working-class groups; because the Germans were a large segment of the propertyless they appear to have come into the Democratic camp more solidly than ever before. Only specific local economic grievances drew out this vote, however, and in the election for state canal commissioner the same day, the Democratic vote dropped to the normal level in local elections as the working-class coalition disintegrated.[80]

79. *Gazette*, Sept. 26, 1849; *Post*, June 4, 7, 14, 1849. According to the manuscript census of 1850, Lee owned property valued at $66,000.

80. See Tables 16, 17, and 18. Note the difference between the correlations between the Germans, the group owning "None," and skilled artisans, and the Democratic vote for sheriff and Jonas R. McClintock in 1849 on

Thus the different appeals and types of leaders of the Whig and Democratic parties attracted different kinds of voters. Although the Democrats did not win all the votes of the working classes, most of their support came from immigrant and Catholic workers. On the other hand, the supposedly aristocratic Whig party did attract the votes of most of the wealthier, more socially prominent groups in the community.[81] These rich businessmen were also usually native Americans and Protestants like the Whig leaders. To ask if they voted Whig because they were rich or because they were natives is to raise a false, and probably unanswerable, question. Both these conditions as well as their Protestantism gave them a superior social status in the community, and they voted for the party of the socially dominant groups. On the other hand, ethnic considerations probably did influence much more the less wealthy native Americans who followed the wealthy leaders and gave the Whigs their majority. Possibly attracted by economic appeals, some of these native-born workers and shopkeepers also voted Whig to express their resentment against and disassociation from the immigrants and Catholics whom they considered Democrats. For these poor Protestants, to vote with the party of the "better people" was to express their social superiority over newer groups whom they deemed inferior to themselves.

Another factor undoubtedly also drew native Americans,

the one hand and the correlations between those groups and the Democratic vote for state canal commissioner in 1849 on the other.

81. These findings about the political affiliation of the urban rich—that a vast majority were Whigs—probably reflect a national trend. In a recent reexamination of party affiliation in New York City, Frank Otto Gatell arrives at the same conclusion. See Gatell, "Money and Party in Jacksonian America: A Quantitative Look at New York City's Men of Quality," *Political Science Quarterly, 82* (1967), 235–52.

whether rich, middle-class, or poor, to the Whigs. Not only direct ethnic antagonism but different viewpoints on issues inspired by religion or old political affiliations shaped voting behavior. Many Whigs may have come out of the Antimasonic tradition which remained strong in Pittsburgh. They took a different moral view on issues than did those who belonged to the Democratic party. With crusading zeal these people wanted to perfect society by purging moral wrongs, and they would be more receptive to the strong free-soil stand of the Whigs than to the expansionism of the Democrats. Thus the presidential election of 1848 in which the Whig state platform, unhampered by a national Whig platform, contrasted so sharply with the Democratic platforms brought out the latent Whig strength which lay untapped in local elections. Moreover, the aroused Protestant conscience of the Whigs could have in turn increased their antipathy towards Catholic immigrants, for anti-Catholicism indeed appears to have been the reverse side of the coin of Protestant moralism in politics. The Antimasonic tradition was especially strong among native and Scotch-Irish Presbyterians in Pittsburgh, and these groups disliked Catholics intensely.

The palpable importance of traditional political hostilities and of ethnic and religious antagonisms on voting behavior raises questions about the influence of platforms in drawing out the vote. Although the Whigs stressed the tariff issue and Democratic observers bemoaned its importance in the depression year of 1848, the voting returns do not clearly verify the efficacy of that appeal. Many manufacturers could have voted Whig because of the party's tariff program, but because Democrats were agitating class hatreds against them, they may have voted Whig simply as members of the economic and social elite which that party represented. In short, there is little evidence that the tariff was the only or even the decisive reason why businessmen voted Whig. It is, however, the split along ethnic lines among the workers who constituted the vast bulk of the electorate that especially weakens the argument about the importance of the tariff. If laborers and operatives suffered in a depression, why should the tariff have more appeal to native-born workers than to immigrants, who were probably the first to lose their jobs? It is possible, of course, that the appeal of the tariff was not economic but ethnic—that is, the Whig promise that a tariff would protect American labor from foreign competition appealed to nativist biases. In this case, however, the tariff would only be reinforcing traditional antagonisms and voting patterns which would have continued anyway. Not the tariff, but the strength of free-soil and anti-Southern sentiment in Pittsburgh and the numerical superiority of native-born citizens among eligible voters contributed most to Whig strength there. Only when Democrats could divert attention from national issues and overcome ethnic and religious antagonisms within the community could they make incursions into the Whig majority.

Three

THE END OF WHIG
HEGEMONY, 1850–1853

During the years 1850–53 politics in Pittsburgh followed the same pattern as in the late 1840s. As long as the Whig national organization remained strong, the Whigs in Pittsburgh continued to win remarkably large majorities in national and major state elections. On the other hand, in county and municipal elections over local issues which reflected social and religious antagonisms, the Whig majority diminished and the Democrats benefited. In some elections apathy greatly reduced the size of the Whig vote; in others, defections to other candidates produced Whig defeat. Examination of the changing appeals and voter support of the two parties after 1849 and the striking difference between the voting behavior in national and state elections on the one hand and local elections on the other suggest that not national issues, but local ones led to the collapse of the Whig party.[1]

The congressional election of 1850 shows well the pernicious effect of local issues on Whig majorities in local elections. Although the Whig candidate won, his vote was small compared to the normal Whig total of eighteen hundred votes. Local

1. See Table 23.

conditions engendered political apathy and the small vote for both parties.

At first it appeared that national issues would dominate the congressional canvass. The opposing parties in the spring prepared to fight the campaign over Henry Clay's compromise measures of 1850, which coupled the admission of California as a free state to bills which would organize the Utah and New Mexico territories without reference to slavery, settle a Texas boundary claim dispute, abolish the slave trade in the District of Columbia, and provide more stringent measures for the capture of fugitive slaves. In sharp contrast to 1849, when local issues and prolabor appeals were so prominent in Democratic programs, the Democrats in both the state platform and Allegheny County resolutions discarded all reference to the Ten Hour Act, scrip frauds, and paper money, and concentrated on national issues. Each of the five resolutions of the Democratic county convention in March advocated one of the major proposals of Clay's Omnibus Bill. The state platform called for "such compromise of the existing controversy as will secure the constitutional rights of every portion of the Union" and for the immediate organization of the territories of Utah and New Mexico "on the principle of *nonintervention,* thus disposing forever . . . the embarrassing subject of domestic servitude." [2]

2. See the report of the Democratic county convention and the state platform in the *Post,* Mar. 21, June 11, 1850. The state platform repeated many resolutions of the Democratic national platform of 1848, but of the new planks 635 words were devoted specifically to issues. Most of these concerned national as opposed to state issues: 355 (56%) concerned cries for Union, the necessity of compromise, and the Compromise measures themselves; 94 words (15%) denounced the Whig state administration; 106 words (17%) dealt with the corruption in Taylor's administration; and 80 words (12%) defended "the present revenue laws of the general government" (i.e. the Walker Tariff).

While the local and state Democratic organizations backed Clay's plan, Pittsburgh's Whigs initially opposed it. This para-dox of Democrats supporting and Whigs opposing the Whig compromise plan reflected the division in Congress where, as Holman Hamilton has shown, Northern Democrats gave much more support to the compromise bills than Northern Whigs.[3] Instead, Pittsburgh's Whigs, like the majority of free-soil Whigs in Congress, advocated the proposal of President Zachary Taylor which called for the immediate admission of California as a free state without connection to any other bills. Taylor would delay any action on the territories until they were ready to come into the Union as states. The *Gazette*, the Whig state platform issued in June, and the resolutions of the Whig county convention in Pittsburgh earlier in the month all demanded that California be admitted immediately without reference to other problems.[4]

Later in the summer, however, the clear-cut division between the parties on the compromise measures blurred. President Taylor died on July 9, 1850. When the new Whig President Millard Fillmore supported and then signed into law the compromise bills, the Whig newspapers in Pittsburgh, which competed for the official printing, faced a decision of whether to go along with Fillmore or to continue to back the antislavery faction headed by William H. Seward, Fillmore's archfoe in New York. The *Gazette*, which had won the patronage early in 1850, continued to oppose the Fugitive Slave Act, and the *Daily Commercial Journal*, which had lost the printing to the

3. Holman Hamilton, *Prologue to Conflict: The Crisis and Compromise of 1850* (New York, 1964), pp. 142–50.

4. *Gazette*, Apr. 21, 25, 1850. For a report of the Whig county convention and the Whig state platform, see the *Gazette*, June 6, 25, 1850.

Gazette, backed Fillmore and the national Whigs.[5] If the Whig papers and officials no longer formed a bloc against the plan, the Democrats also dropped the issue because a Whig President backed it and because the fugitive slave provisions proved a divisive issue among them. In an August county convention to nominate a ticket for the fall elections, Pittsburgh Democrats did not even mention the compromise measures in the resolutions.[6]

Passage of the Fugitive Slave Act in September completely eliminated it as an issue in the campaign. Reaction to the act was immediate, widespread, and vehement, but nonpartisan. Large meetings in Pittsburgh and Allegheny City condemned the law. Censuring slavery as "anti-republican and anti-constitutional," the Pittsburgh meeting declared: "That in view of the momentous interests of humanity and freedom which have called us together, we shall regard party names as 'mere baubles' and that we shall unite and stand shoulder to shoulder" until the law is repealed. In response to this sentiment, all of the candidates for Congress in 1850 pledged to vote for the repeal of the law should they be elected.[7]

When the Compromise ceased to be an issue, both parties endeavored to take advantage of discontent with a prolonged depression which had strangled Pittsburgh's business pursuits

---

5. See the *Post*, July 21, 1849, Mar. 2, 1850. For examples of the opposing positions of the two Whig papers on the Fugitive Slave Act, see the *Gazette*, Sept. 9, 24, and Oct. 21, 1850. On the division between the free-soil and pro-Compromise Whigs in the North, see Robert J. Rayback, *Millard Fillmore*, pp. 213–67, especially pp. 255–67.

6. *Post*, Aug. 30, 1850.

7. See reports of the protest meeting, *Post*, Sept. 30, Oct. 1, 1850. At the synod meeting of the Pittsburgh Presbytery one minister said that most of the people in the community opposed the law. See *Gazette*, Oct. 24, 1850.

since 1848. Increasing competition at home and from the British drove iron prices down through 1851, and they did not rise until the summer of 1852. A glutted market, the high price of raw cotton, and the alleged inability to compete because of the Pennsylvania Ten Hour Law forced two cotton mills in the Pittsburgh vicinity to shut down in November 1849, and the cotton industry flagged throughout 1850. An interruption of the river trade in 1849–50 because of a cholera epidemic in the lower Ohio Valley and of low water on the Ohio stunted the business of Pittsburgh's merchants. Finally, the *Pittsburgh Daily Dispatch* asserted that the redemption of municipal and county scrip with bonds and the resulting decrease of the city's circulating currency also caused "the general depression of business." [8]

Slackened business activity brought misery to the poor. The scrip frauds and the closing down of the iron mills in 1849 particularly hurt the working classes. The long-sought Ten Hour Act inflicted hardship on cotton operatives by forcing their children who worked in the factories to go to school. The law required that children under sixteen attend school at least three months a year. Toward the end of 1849 employers dismissed them in compliance with the law and hired the many already unemployed adult applicants for the jobs thus opened. Families dependent on the earnings of their children spent a cold and hungry winter in 1849–50 because they could no longer afford to buy food or fuel. The prolabor *Post* admitted

8. Malcolm Rogers Eiselen, *The Rise of Pennsylvania Protectionism*, pp. 208, 223; *Gazette*, Nov. 22, 1849, May 3, Aug. 15, and Oct. 28, 1850, Jan. 13, June 17, 1851, and Mar. 2, July 24, 1852; *Journal,* Feb. 5, Apr. 24, 1851; *Post*, Nov. 23, 1849; and the *Dispatch*, Aug. 20, Sept. 20, 1850. For a discussion of the scrip crisis, see Chap. 2.

that workers were suffering but insisted that they must sacrifice so that their children could be educated.[9]

Depression also produced hardship among ironworkers. Low prices forced the iron manufacturers to cut the wages of puddlers and boilers in January 1850, and about fifteen hundred men struck in protest. Although the public initially favored the strikers and applauded their efforts to set up a producers' cooperative and build their own mill, the iron magnates imported workers from eastern Pennsylvania to break the strike. Some infuriated wives of the puddlers then rioted on two successive days, beat up the eastern puddlers in two rolling mills, and destroyed some of the furnaces in them. Nine rioters were later arrested, and six were sent to jail. The violence destroyed public sympathy for the strikers and aroused fears of labor radicalism just as the cotton mill riots had done in 1848. By the end of March the mills were filled with imported help working at reduced rates. Many strikers left the city, and those who remained were forced to return to the mills by the summer.[10]

Despite the failure of the strike, skilled workers in Pittsburgh made an effort to organize permanently to forward their cause. In April 1850, fourteen trades, including puddlers and boilers, combined to form the United Trades and Labor Organizations of Allegheny County. This Workingmen's Congress held weekly meetings and discussed banks, cooperatives, and separate political organization for workers. Spurning the solutions offered by employers to help labor, a majority

9. *Gazette*, Jan. 24, 1850; *Post*, Jan. 19, 22, 1850. See also the letter signed "A Merchant" in the *Journal*, Jan. 21, 1850.

10. *Post*, Jan. 18, 24, Feb. 5, 16, Mar. 2, 1850; Ware, *The Industrial Worker*, p. 129.

of them at one meeting also opposed any mention of a protective tariff in their prolabor program.[11]

Ignoring the evident disenchantment of laborers with the tariff, the Whigs in 1850 stressed the same economic appeals as before to win working-class support. The Whig state platform and the Whig county convention in Pittsburgh emphasized their demand for the repeal of the Walker Tariff of 1846, and Pittsburgh Whig newspapers denounced it for ruining the iron industry there. Anticipating a plank in the Whig state platform, the *Daily Commercial Journal* charged that the 1846 tariff was "the product of a reciprocal scheme" between the Southern "cotton planting interest" and British manufacturers.[12] In contrast to the Whigs, the Democrats did not mention the tariff at their first county convention, and the state platform defended the existing revenue measures. Despite the evident apathy of workers, a Democrat lamented to James Buchanan:[13]

The Sing Song of the Whigs continually harping on the tariff and crying out against the democratic party as the

11. *Gazette*, Apr. 16, May 10, 1850; Ware, p. 235.

12. *Journal*, Mar. 9, 1850; *Gazette*, Apr. 14, 1850. All in all, of 517 words devoted strictly to issues in those Whig county resolutions, 224 (42%) concerned the tariff, 162 (30%) dealt with the question of California and praised Taylor's plan, 113 (24%) praised Whig Governor Johnston for his economic administration and reduction of the state debt, and 18 (4%) lauded Johnston for standing up to Southern states when they complained about fugitive slaves escaping through Pennsylvania. The first three resolutions concerned the tariff.

Including a resolution lauding Secretary of the Treasury William M. Meredith for a message to Congress asking for a protective tariff, the section of the state platform covering the tariff constituted 29 percent of its space devoted to issues. In contrast, the Democrats gave only 12 percent of their platform to a defense of the Tariff of 1846.

13. Robert Orr to James Buchanan, Allegheny City, Oct. 4, 1850, James Buchanan MSS (HSP).

free trade party is clipping us of a good many votes that would prefer voting with the democratic party but firmly believe they are pursuing the wrong course on the subject of the tariff.

Even the Whig position on the slavery question concerned the political and economic power of the South more than the moral wrong of slavery. Slavery, rather than being the target of a Whig crusade, was instead a frustrating issue which stymied the vital economic measures which the Whigs really desired. In a letter to the Whig county convention in Pittsburgh, Congressman Moses Hampton protested that "the interests of Pennsylvania and other manufacturing states [were] broken down and destroyed" and thousands were unemployed and demanding relief, but Congress refused to act on any economic legislation until the slavery question was settled. The Whig convention adhered to the views of this letter and declared: "That this Convention regard the postponement of the repeal of the Tariff of 1846, until the question of slavery shall be compromised, as wrong and unjust, and that the great interest of American labor ought not to be postponed for the consideration of other and sectional questions." Both state and local resolutions denounced Southerners for complaining about the value of lost fugitive slaves when Pennsylvania's interests lost so much revenue because of the Walker Tariff.[14]

14. See the Whig county and state resolutions in the *Gazette*, June 6, 25, 1850. The complaint that the slavery issue was blocking necessary tariff legislation was a common one among the Whigs. Indeed, Daniel Webster, in order to get backing for the Compromise from his Massachusetts constituents, said that nothing could be done about the tariff until Southern Whigs were satisfied that the slavery question was solved. See David D. Van Tassel, "Gentlemen of Property and Standing: Compromise Sentiment in Boston in 1850," *New England Quarterly, 23* (1950), 317–18.

While the Whigs attempted to use the tariff to win over disgruntled workers, the Democrats, after dropping the compromise measures, reverted to the prolabor, class-based appeals which had brought them some success in 1849. The county convention in August censured "all partial Legislation for the aggrandisement of Capital at the expense of Labor," denounced "the Federal [Whig] promise that the 'rich will take care of the poor' [as] alike *degrading* and *false*," and advocated "*Equal Rights* . . . in opposition to special privileges" and all measures which would forward the education of the people and wide, unqualified enfranchisement.[15] In an open appeal to the workers in the city, the Democrats nominated for Congress James Salisbury, a glass blower from the industrial borough of Birmingham across the Monongahela from Pittsburgh, and for an expected interim seat in Congress opened by Moses Hampton's predicted resignation, they named Jonas R. McClintock, the man who had won enough of the labor vote to defeat Caleb Lee for the state assembly in 1849. Lecky Harper called Salisbury the true representative of the working classes, vituperated the Whig candidate, Thomas M. Howe, the cashier of the Exchange Bank, as the "candidate of Bankers, stock-jobbers, and speculators," and boasted that the Democrats had the first workingmen's ticket ever nominated in the city.[16]

Recognizing the working-class discontent and remembering its effects in 1849, the Whigs fought back. D. N. White denied

15. *Post*, Aug. 30, 1850. The reference to suffrage was to the requirement that a man pay state or county taxes before he could vote. The emphasis on education shows the belief that the Ten Hour Law passed the state legislature only because it had the support of those people who wanted to extend public education throughout the state. See Louis Hartz, *Economic Policy and Democratic Thought: Pennsylvania, 1776–1860* (Cambridge, Mass., 1948), pp. 187–88.

16. *Post*, Oct. 2, 3, 4, 1850.

that Salisbury was the only workingmen's candidate or that he necessarily represented their views; he charged that in fact Salisbury was still an operative only because he had once failed as an owner of a glass works and was therefore too incompetent to be a congressman. Howe, he boasted, "appeal[ed] to no particular class for support by catering to social prejudices," and his business record proved him to be a friend of the workingmen. That such social tensions were factors in the campaign was further attested to by the prediction, which later proved incorrect, that many Democrats would not vote for James K. Moorhead, one of the Democratic candidates for the state assembly, just because he had once owned a cotton factory.[17]

Despite the efforts to capitalize on the workers' dissatisfaction, editor White noted early in September an unusual apathy for a congressional election, and in October no candidate received a very large vote.[18] The absence of a direct confrontation on the Fugitive Slave Act in part explains the lack of interest. The labor strife, the dilemma of local workers, and the failure of both parties to suggest a remedy also probably caused the drop in the vote. While the Whigs seem to have maintained the vote of the rich and while the party vote split again along lines of native-born citizens versus Irish and Germans, neither party was successful in interesting its customary number of working-class voters with its economic appeals.[19] Skilled artisans in 1850 sought a nonpolitical solution to their problems through the Workingmen's Congress, and the vote in that association suggests that the Whig issue of protection had little

17. *Gazette*, Sept. 26, 1850; *Dispatch*, Sept. 20, 1850. Moorhead did not receive fewer votes than other Democrats, but all Democrats received small totals.

18. *Gazette*, Sept. 4, 1850; see Table 23.

19. See Tables 24 and 25 and note the lack of solid support for the Democrats from the groups of skilled artisans and those owning "None."

appeal to that segment of the population. Moreover, native American workers were not so willing to follow the merchants and manufacturers who led the Whigs in a year when riots had poisoned relations between employers and employees. Nor were the Democrats much more successful. Some workers were probably not convinced that Salisbury represented their interests, and even if he did, it was not clear what he could do for them in Congress. The Democrats had succeeded in drawing out the labor vote against Caleb Lee in 1849 because they ran on issues which had relevance to the workers—scrip frauds and the Ten Hour Law—and because a state assembly-man could actually do something about these questions in the state legislature. In 1850 neither the issues nor the office at stake seemed vital to workers, and although the Whigs failed to stir the electorate, the Democrats could not attract enough votes from the poor and skilled laborers to repeat their triumph.

In the gubernatorial election of 1851 and the presidential election of 1852 when national rather than local issues were stressed, both parties attracted large votes. The Whigs again drew out much of their natural majority even though their position on issues changed markedly from one year to the next. In 1851 the Whigs adopted their customary anti-Southern stance and defended the record of incumbent Governor William F. Johnston. In 1852 the necessities of gaining national support for the presidential ticket forced them to modify these traditional stands; still, they won an impressive majority.

In 1851 the depression remained an important issue in Pittsburgh. Although the rest of the business community found improved conditions that year, the low prices and resulting stagnation in the iron industry continued. White complained in June that many iron manufacturers had been forced to sell out. As late as March 1852 he reported that many iron mills and manufacturing establishments were shut down and that businessmen feared to invest any more money in manufacturing. Because of the depression, a Democrat wrote James Buchanan that many men in iron and coal production who influenced "a very large number of voters" wanted an immediate change in the tariff rates.[20]

To take advantage of the depression the Whigs once again emphasized their economic programs, especially the tariff. White declared frequently in editorials that the tariff was the central issue of the campaign. The first four resolutions of the state platform echoed earlier demands for tariff revision and protection of American workingmen.[21] Local and state platforms also praised Governor Johnston's record of fiscal economy, debt reduction, and the completion of state canals, without raising taxes. In a speech in Pittsburgh Johnston stressed these economic themes. He carefully explained the relevance of the tariff to workingmen who had been so apathetic about it in 1850. He pointed out that many state improvements such as the canals to the eastern coal regions had been

20. *Gazette*, June 17, 1851, Mar. 2, 1852; see also the *Journal*, Apr. 24, 1851; James May to James Buchanan, Pittsburgh, May 5, 1851, Buchanan MSS (HSP).

21. For example, see the *Gazette*, July 10, Aug. 20, 1851. In the Whig state platform, 241 words (42%) of those dealing exclusively with issues concerned the tariff. A total of 56 percent dealt with economic matters—i.e. measures to advance the state's prosperity. This count does not include a resolution praising Johnston's financial record. The Whig state platform can be found in the *North American and United States Gazette* (Philadelphia), June 25, 1851. Hereafter, no newspaper reference will be given for this platform.

built with the expectation that the revenue from the tolls on those canals would pay for their construction. Because the low tariff crippled the industries which used coal, the demand for coal and, consequently, the freight traffic on the canals decreased. Less traffic meant less revenue from tolls, and the resulting treasury deficit could be made up only by increased taxes on all the citizens of the state. Taking yet another tack, he argued that protection assured constant employment and decent wages so that workers' children could go to school rather than having to work to help support the family. He promised, "Give protection to home industry, and education will be given to all through it." He iterated this theme when he boasted about his reduction of the state debt, which, he charged, the Democrats had accumulated. Reduction of the debt would eventually release state revenue for greatly increased support of the public school system. Because he had devised a sinking fund to retire the debt, argued Johnston, "he thought he had a right to calculate on the support of the friends of education." [22]

To the dismay of Johnston, who wanted to run on his own fiscal record and Whig economic policies, the Democrats stressed primarily national, not state, issues in the campaign. Pittsburgh's Democrats admitted that the tariff needed adjusting, although the Democratic candidate William Bigler disagreed in a speech there in December. Bigler also denied that

22. For the resolutions of the Whig county convention, see the *Gazette,* June 5, 1851. For the report of Johnston's speech which was given in Allegheny City, see the *Gazette,* Aug. 20, 1851. The newspaper report of the speech measured 61⅝ column inches. Twenty-six inches (42%) were devoted to the tariff, 15 inches (24.5%) to defending his financial record as governor, and 20½ inches (33.5%) to the supposed threat to the Union occasioned by his veto of a bill to repeal the sixth section of the state's 1847 antikidnapping law.

Johnston should receive any credit for reducing the debt since taxes levied by Democrats provided his revenue. For the most part, however, the Democrats ignored economic issues.[23] Instead, they seized the Compromise of 1850 as their primary offensive weapon and insisted on the danger to the nation involved in the gubernatorial campaign. Emphasizing their love of the Union and determination to carry out all the compromise measures, including the Fugitive Slave Act, they denounced all who opposed the acts as traitors and blamed Taylor's administration (i.e. free-soil Whigs) for "the spirit of discord and alienation which at present prevails between north and south, on the question of domestic slavery . . . threatening as it does to dissolve the Union." Although many people in the city still disliked the Fugitive Slave Act, the Democrats made obedience of congressional law the issue and charged that Johnston was opposed to carrying it out. They accused him of being an abolitionist because he delayed executive action against the rioters who shot and killed two slave-catchers at Christiana in the eastern part of the state. Therefore, they contended, the election of Johnston would hurt the pro-Compromise elements in the South and assure a take-over by secessionists.[24]

23. See the Democratic state platform for 1851 in the *Pennsylvanian,* June 7, 1851, and the resolutions of the Democratic county convention in the *Post,* Aug. 21, 1851. For a report of Bigler's speech, see the *Post,* Sept. 15, 1851. While 42 percent of the Whig state platform was devoted to the tariff, only 11 percent of the Democratic state platform was. In the speeches in Pittsburgh, Johnston's tariff remarks occupied 42 percent of his speech, but the tariff issue filled only 10 column inches (12%) of the report of Bigler's speech. The address to the voters of neither the Democratic state central committee nor the Democratic county executive committee mentioned the tariff at all. *Post,* Aug. 12, Sept. 30, 1851.

24. The basis of the Democrats' charge was that Johnston in the spring of 1851 had pocket vetoed a bill to repeal the sixth section of the Pennsyl-

In reply to these charges of treason and threatening the Union, the Whigs essayed to mollify conservatives. Johnston went to some length in his speech in Pittsburgh and also in one in Lancaster which was reprinted in the *Gazette* to scoff at charges that his election would provoke secession and to deny fostering resistance to the Fugitive Slave Act.[25] The Whig state platform contained several resolutions which pledged "an unalterable determination to maintain the supremacy of the Constitution and laws" and proclaimed a deep reverence and love for the national Union.

Despite these avowals of Unionism and moderation, the Whigs in the end did seem much less anxious to obey the Compromise measures than did the Democrats. Where the Democratic state platform promised to "observe and execute" the Compromise acts, the Whig state platform only said the laws would "be faithfully observed and respected by the Whigs." Moreover, as the address of the Democratic state central committee boasted, the Whig state convention refused to pass a resolution which explicitly called for "faithful, manly, and unequivocal support" of the Fugitive Slave Act. Like the Whig state platform, Pittsburgh's Whigs pledged to execute the constitutional provisions on slavery (as distinct from congressional laws) but the local Whigs also remained "utterly hostile to its [slavery's] further extension." [26]

---

vania antikidnapping law which forbade the retention of captured Negroes accused of being fugitive slaves in the jails of the state. See the Democratic state platform of 1851, the county resolutions, the address of the state central committee, and the address of the Democratic county executive committee. See also Bigler's speech in Pittsburgh. In the Democratic state platform, 243 of 489 words were devoted to pleas for the Union and the Compromise measures. Of the local resolutions, three with about 61 percent of the words dealt with these themes.

25. *Gazette*, July 2, Aug. 20, 1851.

26. Whig and Democratic state platforms of 1851; *Gazette*, June 5, 1851.

160725

Similarly, the Whigs seemed much more hostile to the South than the Democrats did. By the summer of 1851 the Whig party in the North had split into a pro-Compromise wing which backed President Fillmore and a free-soil wing which opposed the Fugitive Slave Act and wanted to defy the South. This latter faction supported Winfield Scott for the presidential nomination in 1852. Most of Pittsburgh's Whigs belonged to this free-soil wing, and the Whig county convention in Pittsburgh had boomed Scott for President in June 1851.[27] Whig newspapers in Pittsburgh constantly ridiculed the Pennsylvania Democracy for being allies of slavery and for their fear of standing up to Southern slaveholders.[28] In his speeches Johnston turned on the South with venom. At Lancaster he complained that Southerners were trying to interfere with the internal affairs of Pennsylvania by threatening secession if he should be elected. In Pittsburgh he said that while the Fugitive Slave Act should be obeyed as the law of the land, he would have voted against it. Protesting that he was not trying to agitate the public into disobedience as the Democrats charged, he defended the right of both Negroes and whites to trial by jury and urged the people to speak out against the law and to refuse to let Southerners abridge their freedom of speech by threats.[29] The Whig anti-Southern position on the Fugitive Slave Act and the tariff was probably attractive in Pittsburgh where, as a Democrat wrote Buchanan, "there [was] extreme

27. See the resolutions of the county convention in the *Gazette*, June 5, 1851. On the Whig split in the North, see Rayback, *Millard Fillmore*, pp. 334–46. On the split between the Woolly Head (free-soil) and Silver Grey factions in Pittsburgh, see *Post*, Apr. 9, 12, 1851; *Journal*, Apr. 28, 1851.

28. For example, see *Journal*, June 17–19, 1851, and *Gazette*, Sept. 18, 1851.

29. *Gazette*, July 2, Aug. 20, 1851.

jealousy among [the] people towards the South, and considerable sensitiveness on the subject of the tariff." [30]

Essentially, therefore, the gubernatorial contest was unmarred by local issues which cut across party lines, and it attracted the large vote for both parties which important statewide elections normally produced. The Whigs won a large majority as both parties tended to draw their vote from the same sources which had supported them in the presidential election of 1848.[31] Since most unskilled laborers tended to vote Democratic while the vote of the skilled artisans was divided, the influence of the Whig economic appeals to workingmen in their victory is unclear.[32] Rather, three other factors allowed the Whigs to draw out much of their natural majority in 1851. First, no debilitating local dissatisfaction divided the Whig ranks that year, and evidently most native American workers were once again willing to follow the lead of wealthy Whig businessmen.[33] Second, the antagonisms between native-born citizens and immigrants again played an important role. While most native Americans went Whig, the bulk of immigrants who voted tended to support the Democrats. There especially appears to have been an increase in the German support for the Democrats since 1848.[34] Nevertheless,

30. George P. Hamilton to Buchanan, Pittsburgh, May 31, 1851, Buchanan MSS (HSP).

31. See Table 23. The correlation between the Whig vote for President in 1848 and the vote for Johnston in 1851 was +.72. The correlation between the Democratic vote for President in 1848 and the vote for Bigler in 1851 was +.77.

32. See Tables 24 and 25.

33. See Table 24 and note the correlations between the native Americans and the Whigs, and between those owning over $10,000 worth of property and the Whigs.

34. See Tables 24 and 25 and note the sharp difference in voting behavior between native Americans on the one hand and Germans and Irishmen on the

not enough immigrants voted yet to overcome the Whig majority. Hostility to Catholics may have reinforced the pronounced ethnic division of the vote. The Democratic candidate for State Supreme Court Justice, James Campbell, who was specifically identified as a representative of the Catholics, drew only ninety-three fewer votes than Bigler, and perhaps Protestants who were aligned against Campbell also voted against Bigler. Third, the positions taken by the parties on the Fugitive Slave Act clearly established the Democrats as a pro-Southern party and the Whigs as an anti-Southern party, and the large Whig vote represented the desire of many in Pittsburgh where there was "extreme jealousy . . . towards the South" to defy the Southern demands.

In the presidential campaign of 1852 Pittsburgh's Whigs lost their advantageous position on issues. By the summer of 1852 the iron industry and all phases of business in Pittsburgh had escaped the depression and were thriving.[35] Because cries for a protective tariff were almost superfluous with prosperity, the local and state Whig platforms, while advocating protection, deemphasized the tariff issue and made no specific attacks on the Walker Tariff as they had done in 1851.[36] Indeed, the na-

---

other. The correlation between the Germans and Democrats in the 1848 presidential election was +.18; in 1851 it was +.51. The apparent increase in support probably resulted from an increase in the number of naturalized Germans in those three years. In any case, the increase in the number of Germans among the Democratic voters probably explains the drop in the correlation between the Democrats and the Irish, rather than any absolute drop in Irish support.

35. *Gazette*, July 24, 1852; Eiselen, *Rise of Pennsylvania Protectionism*, p. 230.

36. Only 25 percent of the 1852 Whig state platform was devoted to the tariff as compared to 42 percent of the 1851 state platform. The Whig county resolutions and state platform of 1852 can be found in the *Gazette*, Mar. 11, 30, 1852.

tional Whig platform of 1852 echoed Democratic platforms of the past by calling merely for a sound tariff policy with "a just discrimination, whereby suitable encouragement may be afforded to American industry, equally to all classes, and to all parts of the country." [37]

Because Southerners opposed a protective tariff, part of the reason for soft-pedaling the tariff in the state and national platforms may have been the effort to moderate the Whigs' anti-Southern position to appease conservatives and unite the party for the presidential campaign. While Johnston had swept Pittsburgh in 1851, he had lost the state as a whole when conservative Whigs apparently abstained because of his opposition to the Fugitive Slave Act. The Whigs had lost in every Northern state in 1851 where they made open defiance of the Fugitive Slave Act their platform; therefore, they attempted to tone down their position.[38] The major emphasis of the 1852 state platform, which appeared before the convention met, was this reassurance of friendship for Southern Whigs. It asserted that Pennsylvania's Whigs had "none but the kindest feelings for their Whig brethren of the whole country" and "earnestly appeal[ed] to them to forget past differences, forgive past grievances, and move in a solid column, and act as one man" against the common Democratic foe. Other resolutions asserted their firm attachment to the Constitution and their opposition to any efforts to break up the Union.[39]

37. The national Whig platform can be found in Kirk H. Porter, ed., *National Party Platforms* (New York, 1924), pp. 36–37.

38. Rayback, p. 345; Allan Nevins, *Ordeal of the Union* (2 vols. New York, 1947), *1*, 400.

39. The Whig state platform gave most emphasis to appeasing the Southern Whigs, for the resolutions calling for Whig unity and vowing attachment to the Union contained 185 words (69%) of the 269 words devoted exclusively to issues.

Pennsylvania's Whigs, however, failed to mention the compromise measures of 1850 in their state platform. The omission occurred because the free-soil wing controlled the Whig state organization. In 1852, pro-Compromise Whigs backed Fillmore or Daniel Webster for the presidential nomination while free-soil Whigs who hated the Fugitive Slave Act supported Winfield Scott. Pennsylvania's Whigs had been divided since 1851 on this issue, but Scott men dominated the state convention and instructed the delegates to the Whig national convention to go for Scott.[40] These men could not accept the Fugitive Slave Act as a finality, and their efforts to appease Southerners and conservatives in Pennsylvania included no pledges on it.

No qualms about that act impeded the delegates to the national Whig convention in Baltimore. There the Fillmore nationals prevailed in composing the platform. It expressed concern for the security of states' rights and the permanency of the Union, urged people to obey the laws of Congress, explicitly pledged that the Whig party would maintain "and insist upon [the] strict enforcement" of the Compromise of 1850, including the Fugitive Slave Act, and opposed any further agitation of the slavery question in Congress.[41] Even the nomination of Scott could not counteract the pro-Southern nature of the platform.

40. For actions at the Allegheny County and state Whig conventions, see *Gazette*, Mar. 11, 29, 30, 1852. On the split among Pittsburgh Whigs between Scott and Fillmore men, see the *Gazette*, Nov. 4, 1852. On the Whig division in the nation, see Rayback, pp. 335–52, and Nevins, 2, 22–38. On the state party in 1852, see Henry R. Mueller, *The Whig Party in Pennsylvania,* pp. 194–95.

41. Rayback, p. 357. Five of the eight resolutions of the Whig national platform pledged adherence to the Union, states' rights, and the Compromise of 1850.

The Whig emphasis on moderation mirrored that of the Democrats. If anything, the Democratic state platform was more conservative than the Whig platform. It pledged the Pennsylvania Democracy's adherence to states' rights, firmly denied the right of Congress or a state to interfere with the domestic institutions of another state, insisted that all Democrats in the country accept the Compromise of 1850, and promised a "faithful execution of the fugitive slave law" and a repeal of the 1847 Pennsylvania antikidnapping statute. The national Democratic platform echoed this concern for the rights of the South. As the platform of the Free Democratic party, the successor to the Free-Soil party, accused, both parties endorsed the compromise laws, and very little separated their official positions on the slavery issue.[42]

Pennsylvania Democrats gleefully pointed out the similar positions of both parties on the old issues. The addresses of the Democratic county executive committee and state central committee to the voters insisted that the Whig platforms revealed the supposed Whig concern about the extension of slavery and the industrial interests of Pennsylvania as bogus. Where they had once demanded repeal of the Walker Tariff, they now adopted the same tariff position as that on which James K. Polk had run in 1844, and they nominated for Vice-President a well-known free trader, William A. Graham of North Carolina. Deserting the free-soil position of 1848, the Whigs in their national platform of 1852 espoused as much pro-slavery doctrine as Southern slaveholders demanded. On that

42. The Democratic state platform of 1852 can be found in the *Post*, Mar. 9, 1852. The national Democratic platform can be found in the *Gazette*, June 8, 1852. The Free Democratic party, the successor to the Free-Soil party of 1848, held its national convention in Pittsburgh in 1852. Its platform can be found in Porter, pp. 32–36.

platform, declared the *Post*'s Lecky Harper, Winfield Scott must stand.[43]

The argument that Southerners controlled Whig policy especially embarrassed Whig leaders in Pittsburgh, where bitterness toward the South was increasing among their followers. Scott men had dominated the Allegheny County convention, and Pittsburgh's delegates to the state and national conventions had voted for Scott. Before the national convention both Whig newspapers had criticized the Southern opposition to protection, and both had protested against the unreasonable demand of Southerners that Northern Whigs acquiesce in the Fugitive Slave Act. In May, White of the *Gazette* had condemned slavery as a moral sin and had called for the North to separate itself from the South to rid itself of the association with the institution. Riddle of the *Daily Commercial Journal* had declared, "To secure the election of General Scott, we will not consent to go forward and renew our vows at the shrine of slavery." This determination, he asserted, "represent[ed] the feelings of the great body of Whigs" in Pittsburgh.[44]

Aware of the continued hostility toward the South in Pittsburgh, Whigs there tried to deny the validity of the national and state platforms as statements of policy. Even though the Pittsburgh delegate to the national Whig convention, like most Pennsylvania delegates, had voted for the national platform, the Whig meeting in Pittsburgh to ratify Scott's nomination refused to endorse it. White deplored the platform and

43. Copies of the addresses of the county executive committee and the state central committee can be found in the *Post*, Sept. 22, Oct. 8, 1852. For Harper's remarks, see the *Post*, July 15, 1852.

44. *Gazette*, Mar. 11, 30, Apr. 23, May 19, June 19, 22, 1852; *Journal*, Feb. 28, Apr. 16, 1852.

declared that the plank calling for Whigs not to agitate the slavery issue was a nullity because a party platform could not bind men's consciences. As a correspondent wrote Governor William Bigler about the Whigs, "They almost all curse that platform." [45]

Shackled by an unpopular national platform as the Democrats had been in 1848, the Whigs in Pittsburgh in 1852 turned to other issues. Less able to appeal to the antislavery conscience of zealous Protestants, the Whigs courted the Catholic vote. The Catholics of Pittsburgh threatened not to support the Democratic party as usual in 1852 because James Campbell, the only Catholic candidate for state office in 1851, had been the only Democrat to lose throughout the state.[46] To capture support from some of the disgruntled Catholics, the Whigs accused the Democratic presidential candidate Franklin Pierce of being anti-Catholic because New Hampshire, his native state, had a law which prohibited Catholics from holding public office. Whig papers also asserted that the Democratic candidate for the state supreme court, George W. Woodward, was a nativist who had opposed Campbell in 1851.[47]

The Democrats wooed the Catholic vote more ardently and successfully than the Whigs. The *Post* protested that Pierce had opposed the New Hampshire proscription of Catholics and that in fact the Whigs were responsible for it. Harper denied that Woodward was a nativist, and the Democrats even brought James Campbell to Pittsburgh to speak on be-

45. See the report of the Whig ratification meeting in the *Gazette*, June 24, 1852. For White's remarks, see the *Gazette*, June 23, 28, 1852. See also Lynde Eliot to William Bigler, Pittsburgh, July 13, 1852, Bigler MSS.

46. Lynde Eliot to William Bigler, Pittsburgh, Sept. 20, 1852, Bigler MSS; *Gazette*, Mar. 3, 1853.

47. *Post*, June 15, 16, 1852; *Gazette*, July 13, Sept. 8, 16, 29, 1852.

half of both Pierce and Woodward. The Catholics seemed to remain loyal, and Woodward wrote to Governor Bigler from Pittsburgh that "the Whigs are plying the native nonsense with great industry, but I think, with small effect" and that "the Catholics here profess great friendship." Most important, the Democrats gave the Catholics what they demanded after Campbell's defeat—candidates. The Democratic congressional nominee in Pittsburgh in 1852, P. C. Shannon was a Catholic, and as Lynde Eliot, an editor of the *Pittsburgh Daily Union,* an organ established by the Bigler men in Pittsburgh, reported to Bigler, "We have put upon our ticket for the Assembly and County officers, some three or four other Roman Catholics, and our County Committee, as I am told, consists of nearly one half members of that church." Eliot went on to deplore the "positively and openly fraudulent" effort to appease the Catholics because the popular vote in the Democratic ward meetings was utterly disregarded in choosing the ticket and the county committee.[48]

Similarly the Democrats neutralized the Whig appeals to the growing immigrant vote. Besides calling Woodward a nativist, the Whigs declared that all Irish-Americans who opposed British policy should vote for Scott, because the British ardently disliked him while they supported Pierce.[49] In reply, the Democrats censured Scott as a nativist, produced a letter which he had written in 1841 calling for stringent measures to deny foreigners their rights as citizens, and pointed to

48. *Post,* June 15, 16, Sept. 30, 1852; George W. Woodward to William Bigler, Pittsburgh, Sept. 10, 1852, and Lynde Eliot to Bigler, Pittsburgh, Sept. 20, 1852, Bigler MSS.

49. *Gazette,* Aug. 9, 1852; see also the Whig address to the voters, *Gazette,* Oct. 23, 1852.

his statements on aliens as evidence of his unfitness for the Presidency. Harper chided that the Whigs turned to seeking the immigrant vote only because they had lost their thunder on the tariff, and he exulted that because Scott was such a well-known nativist the Democrats would receive the entire German vote.[50]

Although the appeals of the parties, especially the formal platforms, seemed very similar, Scott drew a larger vote than Johnston had in 1851 and won a good-sized majority. His vote was, however, several hundred less than Taylor's in 1848. White blamed the decrease on residual bitterness from the struggle for the nomination between Scott, Webster, and Fillmore, on the pro-Southern Whig platform, and on a "coldness produced among zealous Protestants from the [Whig] courting of the Catholic vote."[51] White exaggerated, however, for Scott's vote was quite large and his majority was very big compared to his showing elsewhere in the North. Moreover, most native Americans apparently continued to vote Whig while immigrants, most of whom were poor laborers—the Catholics whom the Democrats wooed—again tended to vote Democratic.[52]

That Scott captured such a large vote when the national platforms of the two parties were virtually the same, is most significant. The Whigs could draw out their natural majority

50. *Post,* July 23, 24, 1852; see also the county and state Democratic addresses, *Post,* Sept. 22, Oct. 8, 1852.

51. *Gazette,* Nov. 4, 1852.

52. See Tables 23, 24, and 25. Note that the votes for congressman and sheriff in 1852 indicate that the Irish still tended to vote Democratic. See n. 34 for an explanation of the drop in the correlation between the Irish and the Democrats. Additional evidence that the Irish voted Democratic is that the *Gazette* on Sept. 4, 1854, said that the Catholic vote had been solid for Pierce in 1852.

in a national election when no local issues or grievances crippled them.[53] Many among this majority voted for the Whigs in Pittsburgh because they still seemed to be more of an anti-Southern party than the Democrats. Another factor, though, was the influence of traditional loyalties and dislikes in bringing out the vote even when the Whigs surrendered their popular position on national issues. The antipathy of native-born citizens toward immigrants and of Protestants toward Catholics caused them to continue to align against the Democratic party whose leaders, appeals, and voting support established it as the party of immigrants and Catholics. Finally, this evidence of habitual voting despite the supposed issues again raises questions about the importance of the tariff issue in drawing out the Whig vote in other elections.

In contrast to the state and national elections of 1851 and 1852, when they continued to draw out large majorities, the Whigs faltered badly in local elections on local issues in the years 1850–53. How labor strife and the lack of receptiveness of workers to Whig economic appeals reduced the Whig vote in the congressional election of 1850 has already been shown. In other county elections and especially in mayoral contests, the mishandling of social issues, local grievances, and religious biases brought about Whig defeat.

Discontent in the winter of 1849–50 produced a break in the monotonous record of Whig triumph. Dissatisfaction with excessive taxes during the depression, antagonism between em-

53. The vote for both parties in 1852 came from the same sources as in 1848. The correlation between the Whig votes for President in 1848 and 1852 was +.71. The correlation between the Democratic votes for President in 1848 and 1852 was +.79.

ployers and employees, and an open outbreak of the Protestant animosity toward Catholics contributed to the defection
of many normal Whig voters from the party of the rich in
the election for mayor in 1850 and to the victory of an independent candidate who specifically represented some of the
poorer classes.

Maladministration of municipal government which could
be attributed to the Whigs damaged them in January 1850
as it had in the fall of 1849. Even editor White of the *Gazette*
declared that if the Whigs did not nominate a man of high
caliber for mayor in 1850, Whig voters should not support
the candidate out of mere party loyalty. J. Heron Foster, the
editor of the independent *Pittsburgh Daily Dispatch*, urged
the nomination of independent candidates for mayor and
councilmen, men who would favor the replacement of the city
council form of government with three city commissioners
who could keep a tighter rein on the city's finances and prevent the extravagant expenditures which had raised the city's
debt to over $1,000,000. As though they wished to satisfy the
demand for reform candidates, the Democrats offered John
B. Guthrie, a steamboat captain, as an independent "Citizens'
Candidate" and promised not to consider his victory a Democratic triumph. An "Independent Citizens' Ticket" for city
councils entered the canvass in the second ward. The meeting
which nominated it complained of the miserable financial administration, grossly extravagant expenditures, and increasingly excessive taxation in order to pay off the debt under
Whig management.[54]

Coupled with economic discontent heightened by unemployment, wage cuts, and high taxes, religious antagonisms

54. *Gazette*, Nov. 8, 1849; *Dispatch*, Oct. 16, 25, Nov. 6, 1849, Jan. 8,
1850; *Post*, Jan. 1, 1850.

greatly influenced the mayoral election of 1850. Against Guthrie the Whigs nominated Robert McCutcheon, a wealthy Presbyterian grocer. To gain the support of Catholics for Guthrie, the Democrats called McCutcheon an Orangeman —i.e. a member of the anti-Catholic Protestant league in Ireland and England. On other occasions, in order to discourage Protestants who hated Catholics from voting for McCutcheon, they called him a pet of the Roman Catholics and of their leader in Pittsburgh, Bishop Michael O'Connor.[55] A third candidate, Joe Barker, a jobless street-corner orator renowned only for his venomous anti-Catholicism, was nominated by his friends as a "People's and Anti-Catholic Candidate" even though he had been jailed in November 1849 for inciting an anti-Catholic riot in the fifth ward, a working-class area crammed with Germans, Irishmen, and bars and notorious for its shiftless, brawling vagrants and gangs.

The election brought out an abnormally large vote for a municipal campaign, a vote almost as large as that in the gubernatorial campaign of 1848. Despite Barker's lack of training and his reputation for lawlessness, he won the mayor's office from his jail cell. The Democrats maintained their customary number of votes (about fifteen hundred) and the Whig candidate trailed a distant third. The party of the Catholics, the Democrats seem to have retained the support of the Irish, but they lost their normal degree of support from other poor laborers. The Whigs lost almost half of their normal vote, and newspaper editors agreed that some of the defectors voted for Barker either because of anti-Catholic prejudice or because they feared McCutcheon had no chance of defeating Guthrie.

55. *Journal*, Jan. 5, 1850. Lecky Harper attributed McCutcheon's nomination to his leaning toward Barkerism (anti-Catholicism). See the *Post*, Dec. 27, 1849.

Since the wealthy business and professional groups again tended to vote Whig, the drop in the Whig vote appears to have occurred among the poor native American workers. In addition to the Whig defectors who supported him, Barker drew out a new vote from the lower classes, and the *Daily Commercial Journal* asserted that the majority of his support came from the carousing and rowdy elements of the population to whom all law was tyranny.[56] Barker drew out most of his support from the first, third, fifth, and eighth wards where there were the heaviest concentrations of workingmen and Germans. Indeed, the propertyless throughout the city tended to vote for him, but one suspects that most of these were Protestants, because Catholics probably would not support him.

Whig defeat in January 1850 occurred over local grievances and anti-Catholic bias rather than over the national policies of the Whigs. The apparent support for Barker among Germans suggests that some of them were Protestants who bitterly hated Catholics or that Germans wanted as a chief of police (mayor) a man from the poorer classes who seemed less likely to prosecute tavern owners for the sale of liquor on Sundays than did the other, more respectable candidates.[57]

56. *Post*, Jan. 9, 1850; *Gazette*, Jan. 10, 1850; *Journal*, Jan. 12, 1850. See Tables 23–26. The correlation between the Whig vote and the native Americans dropped from +.81 in October 1849 to +.60 in January 1850.

57. I use the term "apparent support" from the Germans because it is difficult to believe that Catholic Germans voted for Barker. The wards with large concentrations of Germans also had large numbers of propertyless native Americans and Irishmen, and the high correlation with the German group only indicates that Barker was strong in the wards with many Germans. The vote actually could have come from poor native-born Protestants in those working-class wards who may have been much more hostile to Catholics than wealthier Protestants exactly because they lived in areas where they were surrounded by Catholic immigrants.

Many working-class Protestants who had previously voted Whig now refused to follow their wealthy Whig leaders and supported a jobless demagogue who was palpably more hostile to Catholics than the Whig nominee. The importance of religious bias in elections became even clearer in the fall elections of 1850 when a separate Protestant party entered a slate of candidates in addition to the Native American and other candidates.[58]

Joe Barker ran for reelection in 1851 and 1852, and he continued to cause enough voting across party lines and to draw off enough customary Whig votes to prevent the Whigs from electing a mayor in those years. Barker broke with his formal anti-Catholic affiliations in November 1850 and ran in those years as an independent reform candidate. According to both Whig and Democratic newspapers, however, his term of office was characterized by harassment of Catholics, reckless actions, and marked laxness in enforcing laws banning the sale of liquor on Sundays. The *Gazette* stated flatly that he was the worst mayor the city had ever had.[59] Apparently because of this record, Barker remained a favorite among the propertyless working classes. In both elections his greatest strength was in areas with heavy concentrations of poor, unskilled laborers, many of whom were German. Some of these men probably voted Whig in state and national elections, for the *Post* asserted that the Democrats in 1851 "with a few exceptions" voted for Guthrie. Much of the vote, however, came from the groups who normally voted Democratic.[60]

While Barker drew away some Whig supporters, he drove

---

58. *Dispatch*, Sept. 20, Oct. 14, 1850, for election returns.

59. *Dispatch*, Aug. 6, Nov. 11, 1850; *Gazette*, Oct. 3, 9, 1850, Oct. 6–8, 1852; *Journal*, Jan. 6, 7, 13, 1851.

60. See Tables 23–26 and *Post*, Jan. 15, 1851.

others over to the Democrats, and in both 1851 and 1852 the Democratic candidate Guthrie won. In both elections, newspapers agreed, many Whigs (up to six hundred in 1851, estimated one editor) supported Guthrie in order to defeat Barker and, they asserted, to restore responsible government to the city.[61] Indeed, the wealthy businessmen and native-born Americans who had so consistently tended to support the Whigs in other elections did not do so in the municipal elections, and some of them obviously voted for Guthrie, since those groups demonstrated a marked tendency to vote against Barker.[62] Upset by the Whig defections to both candidates, the *Gazette* in 1852 criticized the "carelessness and indifference of Whig voters" while Robert M. Riddle, editor of the *Daily Commercial Journal*, protested after Guthrie's second victory, "This abandonment of Whig nominees, by known Whigs, *must* stop here, or the party fails utterly for all good ends." [63] It only stopped in the mayoral election of 1853 when the Whigs finally won again. Because Barker did not run in that election, there was no attractive non-Democratic alternative for working-class Protestants to support.

The same issues which crippled the Whigs in municipal elections appeared in the county and congressional elections of 1852. Bankrupt on national issues that year, the Whigs attempted to utilize the growing temperance crusade for a state law which would forbid the manufacture or sale of liquor in the state. In the spring of 1852 many of the leading figures in both parties complained about drinking on Sundays and signed a petition favoring such a liquor law, but the law

61. *Post*, Jan. 15, 1851; *Journal*, Jan. 17, 1851; *Gazette*, Jan. 16, 1851.
62. See Tables 24, 25, and 26.
63. *Gazette*, Jan. 4, 1852; *Journal*, Jan. 10, 14, 1852.

failed to pass both houses of the state legislature. Viewing the apparent mass support for prohibition, the Whig county convention in 1852 adopted a resolution instructing the Whig members of the state legislature to vote for a prohibitory law.[64] Because the Democrats took no official position on the liquor law, the Whigs seemed much more the party dedicated to temperance reform.

The issue was particularly important in the October election because Joe Barker, the ex-mayor renowned for his failure to enforce liquor laws, announced that he would run for sheriff in 1852 on an independent ticket. The sheriff would have much of the responsibility for enforcing any prohibition law, and Barker seemed to represent a clear-cut opponent of liquor legislation. His candidacy was even more of a threat to the Whigs, for the reportedly fraudulent nomination of their candidate for sheriff alienated many Whig voters.[65]

Dissatisfaction with local Whig officeholders and unpopular candidates also weakened the Whigs for the upcoming elections. Whig county officials had been incompetents for some time, and even the *Gazette* complained that the Whigs must improve the quality of their candidates or the party would collapse. White acknowledged that the low pay of only $1.50 a day discouraged qualified men, who could make more in business, from serving the local government; but the necessity of perpetuating the party demanded good candidates. Harper pointed out that because of the new congressional redistricting the Whigs, most of whose leaders came from Allegheny City, would have a difficult time finding a quali-

64. See the long list of temperance advocates in the *Gazette*, Mar. 8, May 17, 1852; *Journal*, Apr. 10, 1852; *Gazette*, June 3, 1852.
65. *Post*, Sept. 18, 1852.

fied man for Congress in Pittsburgh. David Ritchie, the man they finally nominated, was distasteful to many Whigs because of his religion, Swedenborgianism.[66]

In October the Whigs drew a small vote even though it was a presidential election year. In part, this little vote is explained by the absorption of Whig voters by the Native American and Free Democratic candidates. White of the *Gazette* insisted that the temperance issue severely hurt the Whigs because the proponents of prohibition did not vote as a bloc for the Whigs while its opponents did—against them. This result caused White to assert that in the future the Whigs should not take political stands on moral issues.[67]

These same local issues helped the Democrats defeat the Whigs in the fall elections of 1853, but another factor added to Whig difficulties then. After the election of 1852 the Whig national organization appeared to be disintegrating, and this collapse dissipated loyalty to the party. Editors of both Whig papers in Pittsburgh blamed the defection of Southern Whigs for the defeat of Scott. After his loss Riddle called on Northern Whigs to discard their Southern allies and to form a new, strictly Northern party.[68]

Not only defeat but the seeming loss of distinctive principles harmed the Whigs. White attributed part of the Whig

66. *Gazette*, May 26, 27, 1852; *Post*, May 10, June 3, 1852; Lynde Eliot to William Bigler, Pittsburgh, Sept. 20, 1852, Bigler MSS. In the spring of 1852 a reapportionment of congressional districts according to the census of 1850 split Allegheny County in two so that Pittsburgh and Allegheny City were in different districts.

67. See Table 23. The vote and percentage of vote for the Whig congressional candidate in 1848 was 2,421 (52.1%). Thus the 1852 Whig Congressional vote was considerably smaller. *Gazette*, Oct. 14, 15, 1852.

68. *Gazette*, May 28, Sept. 12, 1853; Mueller, *The Whig Party in Pennsylvania*, p. 202.

difficulties in 1853 to the pro-Southern policies of Fillmore and the national platform of 1852 which resembled so closely that of the Democrats. Nor did the Whig state platform of 1853 provide any strong principles around which Whig voters could coalesce. A one-resolution statement, it merely affirmed that "the Whigs of Pennsylvania . . . adhere steadfastly to the cherished and often avowed principles of their party." [69]

The loss of distinctive principles and of the national significance of the Whig party engendered an apathy among Whig voters. White complained that no one cared about politics "in these halcyon days when parties have become so mixed up that it puzzles an outsider to tell 'which from t'other.'" Again he observed, "Party ties are measurably weakened, and partially broken. Indifference and apathy have taken possession of the public mind." Lack of enthusiasm was so great that when a Whig rally could only muster a procession of small boys carrying Whig placards, Harper jeered at the "ridiculous attempt to galvanize . . . Whiggery" and pronounced that the party had been dead since 1852. [70]

An increased business prosperity contributed to the lack of interest in party matters. Merchants, manufacturers, and railroad men all flourished in 1853 as business boomed. Business was so good that the Democratic state platform once again openly defended the Walker Tariff for benefiting the iron interests of Pennsylvania. Merchants and manufacturers who led the Whigs turned to their business pursuits, and men became so intent on building railroads and making Pittsburgh the railroad center of the West that William Wilkins wrote

69. *Gazette*, Sept. 12, 1853; for the Whig platform see the *Gazette*, Mar. 28, 1853.
70. *Gazette*, May 17, 25, 1853; *Post*, May 9, 1853.

to James Buchanan at the end of the year, "Railroads seem to swallow up everything else with us." [71]

If general apathy sapped the strength from the local Whig organization, evidence of incompetence and chicanery among local Whig officials again tarnished the party's image. A pamphlet published in 1853 by the county auditors showed that when the Whig county commissioners had issued county bonds in 1849 and 1850 to redeem the undervalued scrip so troublesome in those years, they redeemed more scrip than had ever been issued. One of the commissioners accused in the scandal was William Magill, the present sheriff who had won by such a narrow margin in 1852. He became the focal point of another scandal when the Whig county commissioners accused him of speculating on the price of food he purchased for the prisoners in the county jail and charging the county more than double what it actually cost for the sustenance of the prisoners. White admitted that this evidence of local mal-administration contributed to dissatisfaction among Whig voters, and Harper rejoiced, "The rascally Scrip business and the recent doings of Sheriff Magill are enough to arouse every honest tax-payer and cause a complete revolution of politics in Allegheny County." [72]

Equally damaging was the continuation of factionalism within the Whig party. Neither of the other Whig papers in the city, the *Gazette* and the *American*, supported Robert M. Riddle, the editor of the *Daily Commercial Journal*, when he ran for mayor in 1853. Disputes between the *Gazette* and the *Journal* over the question of Catholics and public schools

71. *Gazette*, Apr. 19, 1853; *Post*, Mar. 5, 1853; William Wilkins to James Buchanan, Homewood, Jan. 1, 1854, Buchanan MSS (HSP).

72. *Gazette*, May 18, Sept. 12, 1853; *Post*, Feb. 2, May 9, 1853. The excess amount of script redeemed was $20,451.

widened the rift between the party organs. The Whig county convention, held later in the year than usual, resulted in uncommonly long and bitter primary campaigns for nomination and in less time for patching the party together before the election. White called the feuds within the party harmful in both the elections of 1852 and 1853, and he predicted that the party could never succeed while they continued.[73]

Factionalism also wracked the Democratic party in 1853. Both Lecky Harper and James P. Barr, editors of the Democratic *Post* and *Pittsburgh Evening Chronicle* respectively, failed in their efforts to win appointments from President Pierce, and both blamed Democratic Governor William Bigler. Not only did both editors criticize his policies, particularly his vetoes of bills chartering desperately needed new banks in Pittsburgh, but they fought with his newspaper in Pittsburgh, the *Daily Union,* and together with other men made determined efforts to prevent the passage of resolutions applauding Bigler's administration in the Democratic county convention.[74] Although feuds divided the party newspapers and the county convention, however, the Democrats did retain their strong national organization.

The Whigs, on the other hand, devoid of national issues to campaign on, dying as an organization, and embarrassed by the exposure of local graft, seized the temperance crusade once again to save the party from oblivion. The Whig county convention accepted and incorporated into its minutes a communication from the Temperance Association of Allegheny

73. *Post,* Jan. 13, 1853; *Gazette,* July 7, Oct. 13, 1853.

74. See Alfred B. McCalmont to William Bigler, Pittsburgh, June 8, 1853; Charles A. Black to Bigler, Pittsburgh, June 11, 1853; John Hastings to Bigler, Pittsburgh, June 12, 1853; John C. Dunn to Bigler, Pittsburgh, Sept. 8, 1853; and David Lynch to Bigler, Pittsburgh, Sept. 8, 1853, all in the Bigler MSS. For a report of the county convention, see the *Post,* Sept. 8, 1853.

County and specifically chose as candidates men known to favor legal prohibition, although they did not adopt an explicit resolution demanding it. In contrast, the Democrats refused to endorse the same communication and, as White charged, thus expressed their disapproval of the prohibition principle. Although White had once warned against the adoption of moral issues by political parties, he now insisted that the major issue between the parties was temperance or intemperance. The Whigs favored prohibition, and the Democrats opposed it. On that issue, boasted White, the Whigs were willing to stand or fall.[75]

Fall they did in October. The Democrats elected the state senator, the district attorney, and one assemblyman in the normal Whig stronghold. White blamed the Whig defeat on apathy produced by the collapse of the Whig national organization, local Whig feuds, the failure of the protemperance men to vote while the foes of prohibition voted as a bloc for the Democrats, and the defection of the entire German Whig vote because of the temperance issue. In his letter to Buchanan William Wilkins agreed that the temperance issue caused the Whig defeat.[76]

An examination of the vote for state senator reveals how the Whig majority diminished. The Whig candidate, James Carothers, was a well-known temperance man, while the Democrat opposed the liquor law. White called Carothers one of the best men in the party and predicted flatly that "the defeat of such a man would ruin the Whig party." He urged Pittsburgh's Whigs not to destroy the local organization just

75. *Gazette*, Sept. 12, 17, 1853.
76. *Gazette*, Oct. 13, 1853; Wilkins to Buchanan, Jan. 1, 1854, Buchanan MSS (HSP).

because it was disintegrating nationally.[77] In spite of White's pleas, Carothers received less than the normal eighteen hundred votes for a Whig while the Democrat received more than the customary fifteen hundred votes of the late 1840s. While many old-line native American Whigs obviously abstained because the Whig party had changed, they did not defect to the Democrats in 1853. Rather the Democratic vote came from the immigrants and particularly the Germans who were concerned by the temperance issue.[78] As more and more immigrants became naturalized and could vote, they appeared to align with the Democrats. Because of this increasing vote and the apathy and discontent of Whig voters, the Whigs by the end of 1853 could no longer guarantee the election of their best nominees. Their control of Pittsburgh politics had been broken, and indeed, the party appeared to be disintegrating.

A variety of factors led to the Whig downfall between 1850 and 1853. In state and national elections uncomplicated by local issues, the Whigs remained remarkably strong. It was in local elections that the Whigs first met defeat. Depression, labor discontent, temperance reform, party squabbling, inferior local officeholders, and the loss of distinctive anti-Southern principles in 1852 all contributed to the collapse. Especially important, however, was the growing antipathy between Protestants and Catholics, and between native Americans and immigrants as the foreign-born vote grew. The ready willingness of working-class Protestants to desert their wealthy Whig leaders for an anti-Catholic candidate shows the influence of

77. *Gazette*, Sept. 1, 12, 1853.
78. *Gazette*, Sept. 12, 1853. See Tables 23, 24, and 25.

religious bias on certain voters. To regain these voters and reestablish the natural anti-Democratic majority, a party would have to capitalize on this issue or divert attention from it by campaigning on national issues. Judged on their performance in 1853 when their national party was already moribund, the Whigs would not be that party.

Four

"THE POWER OF POLITICAL
FRENZY," 1854–1856

Between 1853 and 1856 party alignments fluctuated rapidly throughout the Northern states. The Whig party, weakened after 1852, disappeared, and old politicians frantically tried to mold new coalitions. Because of the habit of shaping the history of the 1850s into a pattern of events leading to the Civil War, historians have traditionally stressed these years as the period in which the reaction to Stephen A. Douglas' Kansas-Nebraska Bill destroyed the Whig party, shattered the Democratic organization in the North, and prompted the formation of anti-Nebraska coalitions of Whigs, Free-Soilers, and those Democrats who opposed the further extension of slavery into Kansas. Channeling the aroused antislavery sentiment of the North, these new parties swept the Democrats out of office in the fall elections of 1854. Only transitory bodies, they then evolved into Republican parties by 1856.[1]

1. See, for example, Andrew Wallace Crandall, *The Early History of the Republican Party, 1854–1856* (Boston, 1930), p. 20; James G. Randall and David Donald, *The Civil War and Reconstruction* (2d ed. rev. Boston, 1961), pp. 96–97; Nevins, *Ordeal of the Union*, 2, 121, 316–46. Nevins in his chapter on the break up of the parties after the Kansas-Nebraska Act gives some attention to the emergence of the Know-Nothings in Pennsylvania, but his primary theme seems to be that the reaction to the Kansas-Nebraska Act caused the Democratic defeats in 1854 (p. 345). A somewhat different treat-

However accurately this pattern describes events in some Northern states, it does not completely explain developments in Pittsburgh during this period. Not the Kansas-Nebraska Act alone, but a combination of factors coincided to split the Democratic party and precipitate political realignments there. Nor did a Republican party grow up quickly, for by the beginning of 1856 no viable Republican organization yet existed in Pittsburgh. As the Whig party was disintegrating nationally and Whigs in Pittsburgh were looking for a new vehicle, they were offered two choices—an anti-Nebraska coalition and the nativist Know-Nothing party. In contrast to western states where an anti-Nebraska Republican party emerged rapidly, in Pennsylvania and many other eastern states the Know-Nothing order grew more substantially in the years 1854 and 1855.[2] Indeed, it enjoyed phenomenal, if ephemeral, success.

An analysis of the causes of the rise of the Know-Nothing order and its real nature explains much about how the Pittsburgh Whig party divided in these years. Moreover, this investigation of the social bases of political developments in these years casts light on the rivalry between Democrats and their foes during the whole period from 1848 to 1860. The ethnic and religious tensions reflected in the rise of the Know-Nothings influenced political behavior both before and after their appearance. Because of the enduring importance of these

---

ment of the period can be found in Billington, *The Protestant Crusade*, pp. 262–436. Billington concentrates on the Know-Nothing party during these years, but even he asserts that at "the latter part of 1854, when the full effects of the Kansas-Nebraska act were realized" America sublimated its hatred of Catholics and immigrants to sectional hatreds over the slavery question (p. 262). For an intelligent questioning of this trend among historians, see Joel H. Silbey, "The Civil War Synthesis in American Political History," *Civil War History, 10* (1964), 130–40.

2. Rayback, *Millard Fillmore*, pp. 384–85.

factors, any monistic interpretation of the politics of the pre-Civil War decade based on the hardening of sectionalism and antislavery sentiment seems unreliable for Pittsburgh and probably for the other areas where the Know-Nothings were strong.

Prostrate at the end of 1853, the Whig party in Pittsburgh found new hope at the beginning of 1854. In the mayoral election in January, the Whig candidate Ferdinand E. Volz decisively reversed the Democratic gains of 1853 by thrashing his opponent.[3] The Whigs also received a tremendous boost from the widespread anger about the Nebraska Bill introduced into the Senate in December 1853. Douglas' Bill in its final form organized two separate territories of Kansas and Nebraska. It also specifically repealed the Missouri Compromise provision of 1820 which prohibited slavery in those areas and others of the Louisiana Purchase north of the 36° 30′ line. In Pittsburgh mass meetings of indignant Whigs and Free-Soilers and of Germans, and a separate meeting of Protestant clergymen, castigated slavery as "a curse to mankind," denounced "the outrages designed to be inflicted on our rights and honor," and condemned the bill as "propaganda in the interest of traffickers in human flesh." [4] A worried Democrat begging Governor Bigler to come out against the bill wrote, "I feel well convinced that at least *nine tenths* of *all* the *voters* in the *State* would if left free from *all kind* of party influence cast their votes against that Douglas Bill or any other Bill to

3. *Gazette*, Jan. 7, 1854. See Table 27.
4. *Gazette*, Jan. 15, 28, 1854; *Post*, Jan. 31, 1854. Actually, the Germans held two meetings; for reports of both, see the *Gazette*, Feb. 9, 20, 1854. For a report of the meeting of the clergy, see ibid., Mar. 23, 1854.

extend the institution of slavery over the new Territory."[5]

The Whigs moved quickly to use the aroused antislavery fervor in the gubernatorial campaign of 1854. A county convention in Pittsburgh declared opposition to the bill as early as February, and the Whig state platform of March censured it as "a deliberate breach of plighted faith and public compact, a high-handed attempt to force slavery into a vast new territory now free from it by law, [and] a reckless renewing of quieted agitation." Whig newspapers constantly attacked the bill, and D. N. White also castigated the Democrats and their newspapers in Pittsburgh, the *Daily Union* and the *Post*, for trying to spread slavery. He pointed out that the Democratic state senator from Allegheny County elected in 1853 had voted against resolutions in the legislature censuring the bill.[6]

Outrage at the act encouraged Whig leaders to think they could rebuild the Whig majority in Pittsburgh. White crowed that the Whigs were stronger in the city now that they were openly in opposition to slavery extension. A prominent Pittsburgh Whig wrote to James Pollock, the Whig candidate for governor, that "the Whig party of the North is, this day, stronger than in any former period" because the Democratic policy on Kansas had fused it into a unit.[7]

If Douglas' bill enhanced the chances for a comeback by

5. James May to William Bigler, Pittsburgh, May 25, 1854, Bigler MSS. It should be pointed out that Bigler received a letter the next day from another Democrat who told him to disregard May's fears about the reaction to the Nebraska Act. See John Hastings to Bigler, Pittsburgh, May 26, 1854, Bigler MSS.

6. For the resolutions of the county convention and the Whig state platform, see the *Gazette,* Feb. 2, Mar. 20, 1854. For White's editorials, see also the *Gazette,* Feb. 10, 11, 25, Mar. 1, May 17, 1854.

7. *Gazette,* Mar. 24, 1854. See also the letter from William Larimer, Jr., to James Pollock, *Gazette,* May 3, 1854.

the Whigs, it badly crippled the Democratic party. As a worried adviser warned Simon Cameron, "Those opposed to the Nebraska Bill have the moral & religious feeling and sense of the community to fall back upon. Those who have supported it—must sooner or later fall." [8]

The Democrats in both the city and state tried to ignore the Nebraska issue entirely, just as they had done in 1848 when embarrassed by the national party's stand on slavery extension. Neither the Democratic county convention held before the passage of the act nor the one held after its adoption referred to it in resolutions, although they both endorsed the records of the state and national Democratic administrations. Nor did the Democratic state platform, written before the final passage of the act, mention it, but rather it concentrated on old issues such as prosperity, the record of the Democratic candidate Bigler as governor from 1851 to 1854, and the evils of special charters of incorporation. More important, it declared that the Pennsylvania Democracy stood by the Compromise of 1850 and the Baltimore Platform of 1852, which condemned any further agitation of the slavery issue. [9]

Unlike the Pittsburgh Democracy, the Democratic state organization could no longer afford the luxury of silence when the bill became law in May. When the state central committee finally issued an address which justified the act, however, Democrats in Pittsburgh tried to deny that it was an issue between the two parties in the gubernatorial campaign. The *Post*, which had once tried to defend the act before it became

8. John B. Butter to Simon Cameron, Allegheny Arsenal, June 10, 1854, Cameron MSS.

9. For the Democratic county resolutions, see the *Post*, Feb. 23, Sept. 7, 1854. For the Democratic state platform, see the *Pennsylvanian*, Mar. 13, 1854.

clear how unpopular it was, spoke of "the entire disconnection of our *State* administration with the Nebraska law. Governor Bigler had no more to do with the passage of the law than did the Whig candidate, or any man in this state; and is in no way responsible for the law be it good or evil." [10]

The seeming enormity of the Kansas-Nebraska Act threatened to splinter the Democratic ranks. White gleefully exulted that the Democracy of the North could not survive the defections of Germans bitterly hostile to the act. His predictions appeared partially justified when the editors of the Democratic German-language newspaper, *Der Pittsburgh Courier*, quit the Democratic ranks and merged with the Whig *Western Pennsylvania Staats Zeitung* to support the Whig ticket, in part because of the Democratic alliance with slaveholders. Another sign of discontent appeared at the Democratic county convention in February when a delegate from the sixth ward, George L. McCook, a former Free-Soil Democrat, introduced resolutions protesting Douglas' bill. After a bitter struggle within the convention, spokesmen for Bigler and Pierce quashed the resolutions. Then the Democrats of the sixth ward held a meeting and endorsed the actions of their delegates in the county convention. They also censured Douglas' bill as "deeply injurious to the people of the North" and "TREASON to the Democracy" and warned that they would not feel bound to support Democratic candidates if the state platform endorsed the Kansas-Nebraska Bill.[11] A correspondent wrote to Bigler in June, "The Democracy here are closing up their ranks with tolerable alacrity; still, Nebraska makes many

10. *Post*, Aug. 22, Sept. 15, 1854. For earlier defenses of the act, see the *Post*, May 25, 31, 1854; *Gazette*, Aug. 23, 1854.
11. *Gazette*, Feb. 9, Apr. 1, 1854; *Post*, Feb. 23, Mar. 6, and Apr. 4, 1854.

halt, who were heretofore first to sound the charge." [12] A friend of Simon Cameron probably expressed the disgust of several Democratic leaders in Pittsburgh when he complained that Southern slave policies had put his back to the wall there:

> I have suffered more (as a politician) for my opposition to abolitionism and Antimasonry than from any other cause! Some of the Southern men have neither discretion, heart, or consideration! They require and exact too much of us! In a word they (many of them) are arrogant, & presuming d—d rascals! [13]

Other factors besides the Nebraska Act, however, weakened the Democrats in 1854. For one thing, Bigler's inept handling of patronage angered many Democratic regulars. Democrats had long complained that the Western Penitentiary outside of Pittsburgh had been run by Whigs. To remedy this situation the Democratic-controlled state supreme court had appointed three Democrats as inspectors of Western Penitentiary, who had in turn replaced the Whig warden with Andrew J. Gribben, a Democratic ward politician, and appointed a leader among the German Democrats named Ryser as his assistant. Then both Gribben and Ryser were fired and replaced with Whigs. David Lynch warned Bigler that the dismissal of Ryser would "create disunion in the Dutch camp" and that if both men, but particularly the influential Gribben, were not reinstated before the fall elections, it might cost Bigler as many as two thousand votes in the county from angry party regulars. Frightened, the fumbling Bigler ap-

12. John C. Dunn to William Bigler, Pittsburgh, June 23, 1854, Bigler MSS.

13. John B. Butter to Cameron, Allegheny Arsenal, June 10, 1854, Cameron MSS.

pointed Gribben as one of his aides, but this sop did not content the bawling Democrats of Pittsburgh. Another correspondent wrote Bigler later in the year that many of the most active and prominent Democrats, angered at his handling of Gribben and Ryser, were determined to use their influence against Bigler or not vote at all.[14]

A schism between the ins and outs in the Pittsburgh organization also plagued the Democrats. Young men in the party chafed under the tyranny of the Buchanan-Bigler faction which seemed to appoint all candidates and officeholders. In 1853, before he retired as editor of the *Post*, Lecky Harper had warned that a "cabal of trading politicians" managed the party in Pittsburgh through their control of nominations.[15] At the Democratic county convention in February 1854, William Ward, the second delegate from the sixth ward, proposed a resolution that no state or federal officeholders be allowed to serve as delegates to the Democratic state convention which would nominate the candidate for governor. Defending his resolution, Ward protested that the party had been led too long "by old fogies who were now reaping their reward in fat offices; that Young America should have a chance; that there was no more certain mode of destroying the party than by allowing it to be governed by a certain clique." The Democratic meeting in the sixth ward which endorsed George McCook's anti-Nebraska resolutions also backed up Ward. It emphasized the necessity of keeping the county convention free from the influence of government patronage and charged "that the Democratic minority in this county is attributable

14. *Post*, Apr. 25, 1854; David Lynch to William Bigler, Pittsburgh, Apr. 3, 1854, and John B. Guthrie to Bigler, Pittsburgh, June 28, 1854, Bigler MSS.
15. *Post*, June 22, 1853.

in a great measure to the influence of officeholders and party leaders in our primary meetings and conventions." [16]

That a clique of officeholders actually did control the local Democratic organization became clear in the county convention itself. The men who opposed Ward's resolution and those of McCook were: David Lynch, Buchanan's faithful lieutenant; John Coyle, a longtime correspondent of Buchanan and an officeholder in the post office; John N. McClowry, a seasoned worker for Buchanan; John Hastings, owner of the *Pittsburgh Daily Union*, Bigler's newspaper in Pittsburgh, and the collector of the custom house in Pittsburgh; Alfred B. McCalmont, an editor of the *Daily Union* who was later appointed collector of the custom house when Hastings was forced to retire; and P. C. Shannon, whom Bigler had appointed judge of the district court when the Whig incumbent died in 1852. These same men forced the passage of resolutions endorsing the Bigler administration over the opposition of Ward and others at the September county convention.[17]

Another discordant note which shattered the harmony of the Democratic party was the jealousy which several Protestant Democrats felt toward the influence of the Roman Catholic Church in the party. Lynde Eliot wrote Bigler in 1852 that he was retiring as editor of the *Daily Union* because the outside pressure of Jesuitism interfered with his editorials and because he wanted to hasten his "connection with a *free* Democratic paper, not to be controlled by any *clique,* and still less

16. For a report of the county convention and then the sixth ward meeting, see the *Gazette*, Feb. 23, 1854, and the *Post*, Mar. 6, 1854.

17. See the reports of the two Democratic county conventions in the *Gazette*, Feb. 23, Sept. 7, 1854. For information on the men, see the *Post*, Dec. 1, 1852, Mar. 24, 1855; *Gazette*, May 10, 1853. See also John Hastings to William Bigler, Pittsburgh, Feb. 18, 1854, and David Lynch to Bigler, Pittsburgh, Mar. 2, 1854, Bigler MSS.

by the enemies of Republicanism." He bitterly protested against the favoritism shown Catholics in the party and dismally predicted that the "tiara of Rome or the ermine of Russia" would soon control the Democratic party. How widespread this antipathy was among other Democrats is difficult to determine, although Eliot said that others shared his view, and White noted that there were in the city and state thousands of Democrats who were indignant at the supposed influence of Roman Catholic bishops and leaders on appointments to office. It is significant, moreover, that the editors of the German Democratic *Pittsburgh Courier* attributed their defection to the Whigs to the "yielding and truckling" of the Democratic party to the papacy as well as to its allegiance with slavery.[18]

Such railings against the political power of Catholics were only manifestations of much broader anti-Catholic sentiment festering in the early 1850s. Joe Barker's electoral strength, the activities of the secret Protestant Association, and the long war of certain newspapers like the *Gazette* against the Catholic Church testify to the intensity of this bigotry. In general, Protestant Americans probably tolerated the religious beliefs of the Catholics, but they feared the secular power of the Pope. D. N. White constantly warned that the tyranny of Rome as exercised through its agents, Archbishop John Hughes of New York and Bishop Michael O'Connor of Pittsburgh, violated the concept of American liberty. In 1852 and 1853 Protestant spokesmen debated Archbishop Hughes as to whether or not

18. Lynde Eliot to William Bigler, Pittsburgh, Aug. 25, Sept. 20, 1852, Bigler MSS; *Gazette*, Apr. 1, Sept. 4, 1854. Catholics did have a large influence on the Democratic leadership as shown in Chap. 2. Of the men listed above who defended the administration clique, Coyle, McClowry, and Shannon were Catholics.

the Catholic Church was inherently incompatible with the civil and religious liberties of America. Reprinting Catholic newspaper articles and documents as evidence, White charged that Catholics were disloyal to the Constitution, threatened the freedom of thought in America, and more important, admittedly hated Protestants. Expanding Romanism, warned White, spawned drinking and lawlessness on Sundays and endangered Christianity and morality in America.[19]

In the early 1850s several specific blunders by the Catholic Church crystallized the fears of a papal conspiracy and intensified the Protestants' hatred of Catholics. Archbishop Hughes, the recognized head of the Catholic Church in America, reopened the demand for ownership of church property by the clergy rather than by laymen, a system which would increase the economic power of priests. Nativists quickly denounced the undemocratic character of such ecclesiastical ownership. A more serious mistake was the mission of a papal envoy, Gaetano Bedini, to the United States. Nativist newspapers represented Bedini, who actually came to clear up some disputes about church ownership in Buffalo and Philadelphia, as an agent of the papal plot to subvert American freedom. This symbolic extension of papal authority into the United States greatly angered American and German Protestants, and when Bedini came to Pittsburgh on a tour of the country in December 1853, a mob jostled him roughly.[20]

19. See Billington, *The Protestant Crusade*, p. 345 and passim, especially his explanation of the saturation of the country with anti-Catholic feeling in his chapter on propaganda. For White's attacks on Catholics and reprints from other papers, see the *Gazette,* Mar. 22, May 17, 1852, Mar. 7, 9, 11, Sept. 10, Dec. 21–23, 1853, Mar. 3, Oct. 4, 1854. See also the *Journal,* Apr. 12, 1852.

20. See the summary of grievances against the Catholic Church in the *Gazette,* Mar. 3, 1854. See also the excellent treatment of these matters in Billington, pp. 289–321.

By far the most catastrophic policy of the Catholic Church in Pittsburgh, however, was the ill-conceived attack on the public school system. Archbishop Hughes and Bishop O'Connor had first complained that Catholic children were being corrupted and driven from their parents' faith in public schools because of Bible reading and other practices. Bishop O'Connor then protested that it was unfair to tax Catholics to support such schools, and he demanded a separate school fund for Catholics to support an independent system of parochial schools. In early 1854, Jonas R. McClintock, the Democratic state senator from Allegheny County elected in 1853, acted for the Catholic Church and introduced a bill into the legislature calling for such a division of the public school fund. Anti-Catholic editors charged that this war on the school system originated in Rome and was part of the papal conspiracy to destroy the freedom of thought and love of liberty in America. Only by perpetuating ignorance and depriving Catholic children of a good open education, they chided, could the Catholic church survive.[21]

The strong bias against Catholics complemented the anti-Nebraska sentiment. In one of his early editorials trying to agitate protests against the Kansas-Nebraska Bill, White argued that if American Protestants cried out against Catholicism "and its ancient cruelties," they must logically denounce slavery and try to save Nebraska from it. Thus White pointed out the connection between the anti-Catholic and antislavery

21. For these and other charges against the Catholics, see the editorials and clippings from other newspapers in the *Gazette*, Feb. 23, Mar. 2, 26, 28, June 1, 4, 8, 1853, Mar. 3, 1854. See also Helen Dorothy English, "The Political Background and Republicanization of Allegheny County, 1844–1856" (unpublished M.A. thesis, University of Pittsburgh, 1936), p. 67.

aspects of Protestant zeal which Democrats had long since noted in their efforts to woo the Catholic vote. Moreover, naturalized Germans seemed to hate the Pope as much as they did slavery. The mass meeting of Germans which denounced the Kansas-Nebraska Bill also passed an even longer set of resolutions against recent Catholic aggressions. The Germans protested against the Bedini mission, against the use of the religious power of the Catholic priests in politics, against "the attempt of the Catholic Hierarchy to destroy our common schools," against the efforts of the Pope, "a wordly tyrant," to extend his power throughout the world, and against the Catholic press in the United States for trying to "uproot the love of liberty and selfgovernment." White applauded the Germans' attack on the "two greatest evils of the day"— slavery and the papal conspiracy.[22]

In the first few months of 1854 the Whigs expressed as much anti-Catholic sentiment as they did antislavery feeling. The resolutions of the Whig county convention in early February which only included a line against the Nebraska Bill also declared:

> That we are in favor of a *liberal system of education,* and to effect the promotion of civil and religious liberty, we pledge ourselves to support, with unfeigned effort, the *Common School System,* as the great bulwark of our Institutions.

In other words, they would brook no division of the public school fund. The Whig state platform declared that universal education and religious liberty should be goals of all state legislation, and the address of the Whig state central com-

22. *Gazette,* Feb, 10, 20, 1854.

mittee charged that Governor Bigler favored a division of the school fund.[23]

In the first part of 1854, the Whig press also blatantly identified the Whig party with Protestantism and the Democrats with Catholicism. White boasted, "The Whig party always was and is, the standard bearer of Protestantism and Free Soilism, whilst the Democratic party represents the opposite principles." Later he insisted "that the great mass of Catholic voters in this county are members of the Democratic party" and "that the papers and leaders of that party have always been ready to yield to the wishes and demands of Popery as far as they could venture without driving away their Protestant supporters." Earlier White had denounced Franklin Pierce's appointment of James Campbell as Postmaster General as a blatant appeal to Catholic support and warned that he would live to regret the favoritism of that denomination. During the campaign he commented that major reasons for opposition to Bigler were his connection with Campbell, whom he had appointed State Attorney General, and the widespread disgust with the political power of Catholics. Combining the issues, White insisted that the gubernatorial canvass would turn on the Nebraska Bill and opposition to popery.[24]

After the passage of the Nebraska Act in May, however, the Whigs ceased to agitate the anti-Catholic issue and concentrated solely on slavery expansion in order to form an anti-Nebraska coalition. As early as March the *Gazette* called for a fusion of all Northern opponents of slavery extension into a sectional party. Magnanimously White declared on several occasions, "We are willing to make any reasonable sacrifice of party ties to a great and undying principle"—"resistance

23. *Gazette*, Feb. 2, Mar. 20, 1854; *Post*, July 21, 1854.
24. *Gazette*, Mar. 3, 1853, Mar. 20, Apr. 1, 10, Sept. 4, 1854.

to all future encroachments of slavery." [25] The second Whig county convention in June tried to transform the Whig party into an anti-Nebraska party by luring Free-Soil Democrats while maintaining the Whig name. Dropping now all talk of issues, such as the tariff, internal improvements, and the school fund, found in the February resolutions, this later convention dealt exclusively with the Nebraska Act. Adopting virtually the Free-Soil position on slavery, the Whigs condemned the effort "to propagate, confirm, and diffuse that national sin and shame" of slavery and vowed to oppose its further extension, the admission of any more slave states, and additional compromises with the South. Defiantly the Whigs warned that "for the future the South must take care of itself—take care of its peculiar property; supply its own bloodhounds and doughfaces; the freemen of the North design to and will crush out the breeds." In a final gesture to win over the Free-Soilers, they added: "That in view of the dangers of the crisis—a crisis overriding all former party distinctions—we hereby pledge ourselves in the camp of Freedom—we inscribe Free Men to Free Labor and Free Lands upon our banner, and enlist for the whole war." In addition to adopting this familiar pledge which the Free-Soil Democrats had reaffirmed at a state convention a few days earlier, the Whigs placed on their ticket for state assembly William E. Stevenson, a Free-Soiler whom the *Post* called a "well-known abolitionist." White lauded this nomination as proof that the Whigs would make concessions to draw Free-Soil support and reiterated that political antecedents would not matter in the new anti-Nebraska party. When the address of the Whig state central committee in July dropped other issues, denounced the Nebraska Act, and called for an assertion of

25. *Gazette*, Mar. 27, May 29, June 23, 1854.

Northern rights against the South, White called it a "platform broad enough to secure the cooperation of every Anti-Slavery man in the State." By the time of the election the Free-Soil party agreed to support both the local and state Whig tickets, and in effect, an anti-Nebraska party had been formed under the Whig name.[26]

But when the Whigs dropped their anti-Catholic appeal, another movement emerged which stressed it. It is not exactly certain when the Know-Nothing order, a secret organization dedicated to the proscription of foreigners and Catholics from public office, was first formed in Pittsburgh, but newspapers first referred to its existence around the beginning of July. Although the order had political goals, it was organized initially in fraternal lodges whose membership was drawn from all the old political parties. Gradually, however, the order evolved into a political organization as its members were sworn by oath to support the candidates selected by the lodges. It must be emphasized at this point that the new Know-Nothing order was a separate and distinct entity from the Native American party which had existed since the late 1840s, had far fewer supporters than the Know-Nothings, and was open in its organization.[27] Throughout the 1850s this Native American party maintained its open existence and held open conventions, while the larger Know-Nothing order chose its candidates secretly. For a variety of reasons this new political order rivaled the Whig party for the anti-Democratic vote.

For one thing, many native-born citizens who had voted

26. *Gazette*, May 26, June 1, 2, 5, July 20, 22, Aug. 31, 1854; *Post*, June 3, 1854.

27. *Post*, July 3, 12, 1854. See reports of the American county conventions in the *Gazette*, May 3, July 19, 1855. See also the *Dispatch*, May 3, Sept. 18, 1855.

Whig were genuinely outraged at Catholics and immigrants. Not only Catholic aggressions but certain evils attributed to immigrants aroused native-born Protestants in these years. Immigrants filled the poorhouse, huckstered illegally in the city's marketplace, drank on Sundays, and increased the crime rate, cried editors in Pittsburgh.[28] To escape the seemingly pernicious impact of aliens, the wealthy native-born citizens who could afford to moved away from their old strongholds, the first, second, and fourth wards, and were replaced by Germans. Newspapers commented that because of the much improved means of transportation offered by the plank roads and passenger railroads the men of means moved to country homes to escape the crowded city.[29]

Because the actual increase in the numbers of immigrants in Pittsburgh between 1850 and 1860 was so small, the virulent nativism which appeared in 1853 and 1854 probably resulted from anger at the increasing political participation by the foreign-born and Catholics. Forbidden to vote until the five-year naturalization period expired, many Germans and

28. *Dispatch,* Sept. 11, 1854; *Gazette,* June 3, 1853, Mar. 15, 1855; *Journal,* Jan. 5, 1855. For a summary of the resentment of the immigrants, see Billington, pp. 322–44.

29. See Table 31 and note that the numbers of native-born men and Germans over 21 increased between 1850 and 1860 while the numbers of Irishmen and Englishmen dropped. Still, the increase in the percentage and numbers of Germans in each ward was small. Note also the decline in the numbers of native Americans in the four old wards and their replacement by Germans. For other evidence that wealthy native-born citizens moved out of the city into the country, see the *Dispatch,* Aug. 14, Sept. 16, 1856, Nov. 9, 1858; the *Post,* June 8, 1860; Edward McPherson to J. B. McPherson, Pittsburgh, Apr. 28, 1856, Edward McPherson MSS (LC); and Charles C. Arensberg, "Evergreen Hamlet," *Western Pennsylvania Historical Magazine,* 38 (1955), 117–33. Other reasons than the influx of immigrants also prompted men to move out of the city. Two of the main ones were probably high taxes and smoke.

Irishmen who had come over in the late 1840s were beginning to vote in the early and mid-1850s. J. Heron Foster, an admitted Know-Nothing, later declared that resentment of the political power of foreigners and Catholics, and especially of the courting of the foreign-born vote by both old parties, had been a primary motive for starting the movement. Because the Know-Nothings were dedicated to the proscription of Catholics and immigrants from political office and demanded a total repeal of naturalization laws or the extension of the period to twenty-one years, they seemed a more likely vehicle than the Whigs to redress the grievances of native-born Americans.[30]

Another reason why men joined the Know-Nothings was to clean up politics. Not only bloc voting by immigrants but the corruption of the ward primary meetings and of the county nominating conventions by party bosses angered many citizens. Foster wrote in 1855:

> One great reason the American orders swelled so rapidly in numbers was the profound disgust every right-thinking man entertained for the corrupt manner in which the machinery of the party had been perverted to suit the base purpose of party wireworkers—an evil they honestly believed the orders would remedy.

A correspondent wrote Simon Cameron that the Democrat J. K. Moorhead defected to the Know-Nothings because of disgust "with the trickery and rascality of the old parties." In brief, many complained that ward primary meetings were infiltrated by outsiders and that county conventions were

30. *Dispatch*, Sept. 5, 1855. For the Know-Nothing program, see the national American platform framed in 1855 and Foster's editorial comments in the *Gazette*, June 18, 1855; *Dispatch*, Jan. 4, 9, 1855.

dominated by professional politicians who often chose candidates distasteful to the party's voters.[31]

Through secrecy and a direct primary system the Know-Nothings hoped to correct these faults. They kept a tight discipline on party membership through oaths and then had direct primaries in the wards in which every member of the order handed in a ballot with his choices for all the nominations on the county ticket. An executive committee then named as the ticket the men who had received the most votes for the respective offices.[32]

In 1854 the movement was new, and it secretly selected its slate of candidates from the tickets of the three existing parties—Whig, Democratic, and Native American. Secrecy was so tight that the *Gazette*, which knew of the arrangement, was far wide of the mark in its predictions of the number of Democrats and Native Americans the Know-Nothings would support. In 1855 the party held secret primaries before the mayoral and county elections, but announced the tickets publicly before the elections.[33]

The very newness of the Know-Nothings combined with their expression of nativist hostilities and desire for political reform to make the party an attractive alternative for Whigs and Democrats. Many Whigs who opposed slavery may have preferred the American party to their altered organization because the Whigs were clearly dead as a national party while the Know-Nothings appeared on the rise. This growing strength became especially apparent after the Know-Nothing

31. *Dispatch*, Sept. 15, 1855; see also the *Dispatch*, Sept. 5, 1855, and the *Gazette*, July 25, Sept. 26, 1855. John B. Guthrie to Simon Cameron, Pittsburgh, Dec. 10, 1854, Cameron MSS.

32. *Gazette*, Aug. 5, 1854, Sept. 19, 26, 1855; *Dispatch*, Sept. 18, 20, 24, Oct. 17, 1855.

33. *Gazette*, Oct. 2, 1854; *Dispatch*, Jan. 4, May 3, Sept. 18, 1855.

victories in 1854 in Massachusetts, Pennsylvania, and New York. Moreover, to many Whigs, Know-Nothingism probably seemed a better way to rally antislavery sentiment against the Democrats than the Whig anti-Nebraska coalition. By joining the Know-Nothings, native-born citizens could express simultaneously their nativist antipathies, their desire for political reform, and their free-soil hostility to the South. The new Whig party was less attractive because it campaigned after June on the slavery issue alone. To Democrats who wanted to leave their party for any reason, the Know-Nothings as a new and amorphous party were more appealing than an anti-Nebraska coalition controlled by their old foes—the Whigs.[34]

White of the *Gazette* recognized the appeal of this new order to native Americans who had previously voted Whig, and he considered it a great threat to the incipient anti-Nebraska coalition he had struggled for. An old Antimason who could not tolerate secret organizations of any kind, he repeatedly denounced the stealthy methods of Know-Nothings as "unwise, dangerous, and Anti-American," so akin to the tyranny of popery that American Protestants should resist the movement. He complained that by exploiting the nativist issue, the Know-Nothings were preventing the anti-Nebraska sentiment of the North from uniting behind one party. In October, immediately before the election, he begged Whigs not to go along with Know-Nothing schemes which might send pro-Nebraska, proslavery Democrats to the state legislature. White greatly exaggerated the number of Democrats

34. In his reminiscences, Alexander K. McClure, an old Pennsylvania Whig and Republican leader, says that when the Kansas-Nebraska Act aroused antislavery sentiment among the Democrats, the Know-Nothings found a wide field for recruitment among them. McClure, *Old Time Notes of Pennsylvania* (2 vols. Philadelphia, 1905), *1*, 196.

with Know-Nothing backing, but two of the three Democrats whom the Know-Nothings did support in October had endorsed the Nebraska Act.[35]

If the rise of the Know-Nothings threatened to divide the old Whig majority, it also reshaped the Democratic canvass. Already trying to ignore or deny the relevance of the Nebraska issue, the Democrats after July concentrated on appearing as staunch opponents of the order to win the immigrant, Catholic, and Antimasonic vote. The *Post* early charged that the Whigs initiated the movement and that James Pollock, the Whig gubernatorial candidate, had joined it, and urged Democrats to avoid this Whig hoax. A Democratic state address iterated this charge and boasted that the Democratic party was the haven of foreigners. In an editorial listing Democratic principles the *Post* cited first, advocacy of religious freedom. The resolutions of the Democratic county convention in September denounced secret political organizations and vowed "that the Democracy of Allegheny County, publicly tenders the right hand of fellowship to their adopted fellow citizens without reference to creed or country."[36]

The Democrats also endeavored to capture the votes of disenchanted Whigs. They pointed out that since the Whig leaders had discarded their old principles for the single plank of abolitionism, they were a sectional party which endangered the Union and that old-line Whigs who had followed Webster and Clay now had much more in common with the Democrats who espoused many of their principles. Moreover, insisting that Pollock was a Know-Nothing they questioned

35. *Gazette*, July 15, 28, Aug. 5, Sept. 4, Oct. 4, 1854; *Post*, Oct. 12, 26, 1854.

36. *Gazette*, July 15, 20, 1854; *Post*, July 3, 12, Aug. 14, Sept. 1, 7, 8, 1854.

how former Antimasons who hated secret political organizations could join the order. Summarizing the dilemma of some Whigs, they asked, "Can the sincere and honest old Antimasons vote with the Know Nothings? Will the Whigs be sold to the Abolitionists?" [37]

The Democrats concentrated, however, on preventing the defection of foreign-born Protestants who deeply resented the connection between the Democratic party and the papacy. The *Gazette* predicted that the Irish and German Protestants who belonged to the secret Protestant Association, but who were not Know-Nothings because of their foreign birth, would not vote for Bigler "as his election this fall [would] be considered the triumph of the Campbell and Romanist party." Admitting that "even the Know Nothings themselves openly boast that Protestant Germans and Protestant Irish will vote with them for Pollock," the *Post* repeatedly warned that the Know-Nothings were just as much antiforeign as they were anti-Catholic and that any vote for Pollock would be an invitation to proscription.[38]

By the time of the election, then, several issues, not just the Nebraska Act, commanded attention. White appealed to the opponents of slavery to vote solidly for the coalition of Whigs and Free-Soilers, and proclaimed, "The great conflict *is hastening to its final and desperate issue*. Freedom and Slavery cannot exist much longer together. These differences are irreconcilable and vital." On the day of the election, however, he angrily complained that the Know-Nothings had prevented a clear-cut vote on the Nebraska Act.[39] Trying to avoid the slavery-expansion issue, the Democrats posed as the defenders

37. *Post*, Sept. 8, Oct. 3, 1854.
38. *Gazette*, Sept. 12, 1854; *Post*, Aug. 21, Sept. 21, Oct. 4, 1854.
39. *Gazette*, Sept. 8, Oct. 10, 1854.

of Catholics, foreigners, and open political action. Finally, the murky Know-Nothing organization ignored the slavery issue and recommended political action and proscription to stem the tide of immigration and remedy evils attributed to the immigrant and Catholic populations.

Nor did the results of the election in October reveal an overwhelming anti-Nebraska outrage which swept the Democrats out of office. True, both James Pollock and David Ritchie, the Whig gubernatorial and congressional candidates, won crushing victories, but the Know-Nothings backed both men. On the other hand, of the ten remaining men on the Whig state and county tickets, only two assemblymen won office, and these, as the *Gazette* later admitted, also were supported by Know-Nothings. The election for members of the state assembly should particularly have revealed the impact of anti-Nebraska sentiment, for the legislature was to choose a new United States Senator, who could presumably take a strong stand for the repeal of the Nebraska Act. For the five openings in the assembly from Allegheny County, each of the three parties had nominated five men. Two Native Americans, one Democrat, and only two Whigs were elected, and all five had Know-Nothing support. William E. Stevenson, the Free-Soiler placed on the Whig ticket explicitly to fuse and rally antislavery sentiment, had the smallest vote of all five Whig assembly candidates. Thus of a total of twelve men elected in 1854, four were Whigs, three were Democrats, and five were Native Americans. Since all had Know-Nothing backing, the election was hardly a triumph for the anti-Nebraska party.[40]

40. *Post*, Oct. 4, 9, 12, 26, 1854; *Gazette*, Oct. 16, 1854, July 25, Sept. 26, 1855. See Table 27. It should be noted that in certain instances, for example the campaigns for the clerk of courts and county register, the Whig

Because Stevenson lost so decisively and because the Democrats won almost as many offices as the Whigs, the *Post* asserted that the Kansas-Nebraska Act had nothing to do with the result. It was clearly a Know-Nothing victory. A lieutenant of Bigler's blamed his chief's defeat on "excited religious prejudice." "It is idle to talk of *causes* for the result," he wrote. "There was but one, and that was the momentary supremacy of bigotry and prejudice. It was the power of political frenzy." [41] These assertions, however, are exaggerated. At least one editor argued that the Know-Nothings received votes from many unsuspecting Whigs and Democrats who had been handed ballots at the polls by their old party friends, secret members of the order, and who had voted for what they thought was the regular party ticket.[42] Moreover, although the Know-Nothings backed two Democrats who had supported the Nebraska Bill, many Whigs in the order probably did so only because they were under oath. More than likely many of these Whigs opposed the Nebraska Act as well as the political power of Catholics.

In the vote for governor, the Whigs and Know-Nothings

---

candidate had a plurality in the city of Pittsburgh but lost in the county as a whole, in the first case to a separate Know-Nothing candidate (i.e. Native American) and in the second case to a Democrat with Know-Nothing support. In general, the Know-Nothings were much stronger in the small boroughs and rural townships than they were in Pittsburgh and Allegheny City, probably because there were more Catholics in the cities and because the ties to the Whig party were stronger there. The Know-Nothings boasted that their main strength was in the rural areas of the county. See the *Gazette,* July 19, Sept. 26, 1855.

41. *Post*, Oct. 16, 1854; Alfred B. McCalmont to William Bigler, Pittsburgh, Oct. 16, 1854, Bigler MSS.

42. See the discussion of the 1854 Know-Nothing vote in the *Gazette*, July 25, Sept. 26, 1855.

almost reestablished the coalition which carried Pittsburgh for William F. Johnston in 1851.[43] Native Americans, both rich and poor, employer and employee, tended to vote for Pollock. Pollock's support from the wealthy business leaders and shop-keepers, however, was somewhat less solid than that given Whigs in previous elections, and perhaps the desertion of old Whig principles and the adoption of the free-soil platform frightened away some of the conservative businessmen who once voted Whig. Indeed, these men may have voted for the Democrats, who had wooed their votes.

Pollock's vote as a whole did not tend to come from the poor Irish and German workers, but the Democrats for once failed to win any united support from those groups.[44] What prob-ably happened was that the immigrant vote divided along religious lines as Protestants voted against the Catholic countrymen they hated. Pollock had Know-Nothing support, and almost every newspaper analyst both before and after the election agreed that the Protestant immigrants, organized in the secret Protestant Association or another group known as the Muscovies, voted with the Know-Nothings against the Democrats. Members of these groups had taken oaths to op-pose any political party which gave Catholics nominations. These organizations of foreign Protestants cooperated with the Know-Nothings only so long as there was hope they would drop their nativism and convert the order solely into an anti-Catholic body. When it became evident that they op-

43. The correlation between the vote for Pollock in 1854 and the vote for Johnston in 1851 was + .82.

44. See Tables 28 and 29. See Appendix B for a discussion of possible difficulties in correlating 1854 and 1855 voting returns with socioeconomic indices based on the 1850 census.

posed foreigners too, the Irish and German Protestants swung back to the Democratic, or anti-Know-Nothing, party in the mayoral election of 1855.[45]

While the Whigs benefited from anti-Catholic animosities and American support in the gubernatorial election of 1854, the Know-Nothing movement, not free-soil sentiment, actually destroyed the Whig majority coalition. In the election for state supreme court judge in which the Whigs, Democrats, and Know-Nothings all ran a separate candidate, the parties split and the traditional alignment of votes disappeared. None of the three parties won the bloc support of any ethnic, economic, or occupational group. One may reasonably assume that the vote split along religious lines with native-born citizens and Protestants tending to divide between the Whigs and the Know-Nothings. Indeed, the combined vote of the Whig and Know-Nothing candidates almost duplicated that of Pollock. Most newspapers pointed to the election for judge as a model to show the respective strength of the three parties, and one can estimate roughly how many voters the old parties contributed to the Know-Nothings if he compares these returns with those for state supreme court judge in 1852. Between the two elections, the Democrats lost about 350 votes while the Whigs lost around 800. If one assumes these voters joined the secret order and then adds the 200 votes which the Native American party normally drew, he has a total of 1,350 which closely approximates the Know-Nothing vote in 1854. In short, of the original Know-Nothing vote, about 25 percent came from the Democrats and about 60 percent came from the Whigs. Unfortunately this estimate is very crude because one cannot tell how many Whigs abstained and how many

45. *Gazette*, Sept. 12, 1854, July 25, Sept. 26, 1855; *Post*, Sept. 21, Oct. 4, 1854; *Dispatch*, Jan. 4, 9, 1855.

new voters from the working classes the Know-Nothings drew out. Nor can one tell how many of the Democratic converts were foreign-born Protestants who voted with but did not belong to the order.[46]

Examination of the election for clerk of courts, another three-way race, reveals equally significant voting trends. In this election, the native-born Americans again split their vote between the Know-Nothings and the Whigs. The wealthy among them and the professional groups, however, supported the Whigs. The Whigs did not tend to draw votes from the poor, and the Democrats apparently won the support of the Germans, the propertyless, and the unskilled laborers. It is evident, however, that since most of the poor were German and Irish, the Native American workers probably voted Know-Nothing; many native-born citizens, except the wealthy, tended to vote that way. Moreover, many skilled artisans who resented economic competition from immigrants also seem to have voted for the Know-Nothings, although that group did not tend to vote as a bloc for them.[47]

Various factors contributed to the decision of old Whig voters to support the new party or remain loyal to the trans-

46. There were no significant correlations between the vote for any of the three candidates and any ethnic or economic group. See Tables 28, 29, and 30. Again, the possible unreliability of correlations with the indices based on the 1850 census must be noted. See Appendix B. Compare Tables 27 and 23 to see the 1852 and 1854 returns. See also John B. Guthrie to James Buchanan, Pittsburgh, Sept. 8, 1856, Buchanan MSS (HSP).

47. See Tables 28, 29, and 30. Note the fairly high correlation between the Know-Nothing vote and the skilled artisans. It is possible that since the Germans seem to have voted as a bloc for the Democrat, some only deserted that party in the vote for governor because Bigler was specifically associated with favoritism of Catholics and held responsible for the dismissal of Ryser from the Western Penitentiary. On the other hand, the correlation figures may be suspect.

formed Whig organization. Allan Nevins has suggested that many of the conservative Whigs went into the American party because it was the only alternative to the more radical anti-Nebraska coalitions which became the Republican party, and because they were disgusted with the apparent results of immigration. In Pittsburgh, however, what distinguished those Whigs who refused to join the Know-Nothings from those who did join was that, as most newspapers pointed out, many of the former were old Antimasons, while the latter were not. Until 1853 the Whig county convention always assembled under the name "Antimasonic and Whig," and Antimasons were a powerful element in the party. Traditionally antislavery men, they voted for the stiff free-soil, anti-Southern platform of the Whigs in 1854. They could not join the Know-Nothings because they "abhor[red] secret, oath-bound political societies." [48]

On the other hand, there was also some economic basis to the split between the Whigs and Know-Nothings. Some of the wealthy native-born citizens, who could afford to, moved out of the city in the face of the immigrant invasion. Those

48. Nevins, *Ordeal of the Union*, 2, 330; *Gazette*, July 25, 1855. See especially the *Post*, Oct. 5, 1854. Lee Benson correctly emphasizes the lingering influence of Antimasonry in shaping voting in New York state in the 1840s in *The Concept of Jacksonian Democracy*, pp. 155–56, 312–13. Moreover, one should recall Butter's letter to Cameron in which he emphasized that opposition to abolitionism and Antimasonry were both political suicide in Pittsburgh. The standard work on the Antimasonic party stresses its continuing influence in Pittsburgh, but the author's assertion that because Antimasons hated Catholics they became a primary source for Know-Nothings seems incorrect. McCarthy, *The Antimasonic Party*, pp. 470, 482, 502. McCarthy does point out, however, that United Presbyterians, who were a major part of the Antimasonic strength, were forbidden by their church to belong to secret organizations. These men, who hated Catholics, may have constituted the bulk of those Whigs who adamantly refused to join the Know-Nothings and later started the Republican party.

who did not, but whose wealth protected them from direct social and job competition with Catholic foreigners, voted for their old party, the Whigs. In contrast, the poorer and middle-class native-born citizens, more exposed to competition from newcomers and possibly more susceptible to the sensational anti-Catholic propaganda which had pervaded the country for years, went into the Know-Nothing movement immediately. Alexander K. McClure, a Whig, asserted that the Baptists and Methodists, many of whom were poor, joined the Know-Nothings more readily than other Protestant sects because they were more aggressively anti-Catholic. Too poor to move away from the immigrants, these native-born Protestants found a political channel for their hostility to foreigners. Along with them voted the Protestant Irish and Germans. In this first appearance then, the Know-Nothing vote seems essentially to have been an anti-Catholic rather than a nativist one.[49]

Desire to stamp out the Know-Nothing flare-up caused both Whigs and Democrats to abandon their separate organizations in the mayoral election of 1855. Warning that the Whigs should hold no more formal conventions because the Know-Nothings controlled their primaries, White urged them to fuse with all the other opponents of the secret order to rid the party and the city of the menace. The Democratic city executive committee announced that the Democrats would not nominate a separate candidate and told the Democrats to support an independent. Both Democrats and Whigs signed a long petition and persuaded incumbent Whig Mayor Volz to run as an Independent Fusion candidate against B. T. C.

49. McClure, *Old Time Notes*, *1*, 240; *Dispatch*, Jan. 4, 1855.

Morgan, who all knew was the Know-Nothing candidate. White emphasized that there was only one issue in the municipal election—whether the secret society would gain control of the city government.[50]

Both parties waged a bitter campaign. White warned that the Know-Nothings would try to stir up the anti-Catholic prejudices of the German and Irish Protestants, but he confidently predicted that "the foreign Protestants of this city know that Mr. Morgan has sworn to proscribe *all* foreigners whether Protestant or Catholic, and simply *because* they are foreigners." He cautioned that Know-Nothings intended to vote early and then challenge all voters, particularly foreigners. Also they would try to insult immigrants and provoke fights to keep them from the polls. The other Whig paper, the *Daily Commercial Journal*, whose editor had joined the Know-Nothings, came out for Morgan. Foster campaigned openly for him and appealed to the temperance sentiments of native Protestants by criticizing Volz for his lack of vigor in enforcing liquor laws and preventing huckstering. He complained that the Fusion tickets were "selected by a few wireworking politicians" while the ostensibly secret Know-Nothing tickets were nominated by the mass of American Protestants in the respective wards.[51]

Though the Fusion party elected the mayor and the bulk of the city councilmen, the Know-Nothing vote showed an increase of almost 55 percent since the previous October as more native-born Whigs joined the party. Dedicated free-soil men, these new converts could not stomach an alliance with pro-Nebraska Democrats. Other Whigs, many of whom were

50. *Gazette*, Dec. 12, 18, 22, 25, 28, 1854; *Post*, Dec. 21, 1854.
51. *Dispatch*, Jan. 4, 6, 9, 1855; *Gazette*, Jan. 9, 1855; *Journal*, Jan. 5, 1855.

former Antimasons, joined the fifteen hundred Democrats in supporting the Fusion ticket. Foster moaned that the Democrats, Roman Catholics, foreign Protestants who had once supported Pollock in order to proscribe Catholics, and former Antimasons who wanted "to oppose the secresy [sic] of Know Nothingism" backed Volz.[52] Most native-born Americans tended to move into the Know-Nothing camp while most immigrants—Protestants and Catholics—combined to oppose the order.[53]

Estimating the makeup of the parties is difficult. It would seem that about nine hundred of the Whig and Antimasonic remnant joined the Fusion coalition while five hundred now went into the Know-Nothing party. But foreign Protestants who had backed Know-Nothing, not Whig, candidates in October 1854 also switched, so that it is probably more correct to estimate that about six hundred Antimasonic Whigs and three hundred foreign Protestants went into the Fusion party while about eight hundred more Whigs joined the Know-Nothings.

52. *Post*, Aug. 4, 1855; *Gazette*, Sept. 26, 1855; *Dispatch*, Jan. 9, 1855.

53. See Tables 27, 29, and 30. The apparent insignificant correlation between the Germans and the Fusion vote may have resulted from the fact that many Germans could not or did not vote, rather than the fact that they split their vote between the two parties. In other words, most of the Germans who voted supported the Fusion ticket, but not enough voted for the Germans to appear as a bloc vote. Contrary to Foster's commentary, the Catholic vote may not have been solidly Democratic, for the correlation between the percentage of Catholics in 1860 and the Fusion vote was only +.36. Since this index of Catholics was based on the 1860 census and other calculations, it may not have accurately described the proportional strength of Catholics in 1855 and therefore may not be valid for correlation with the 1855 vote. It is also possible that many of the Catholics listed in 1860 were unnaturalized immigrants in 1855. For the proportions of Protestants and Catholics in Pittsburgh's wards, I relied on Table 3 in Paul J. Kleppner, "Lincoln and the Immigrant Vote: A Case of Religious Polarization," *Mid-America, 48* (1966), 176–95. Kleppner explains in detail how he ingeniously constructed this index reproduced in my Table 35.

Although the *Post* later asserted that the Democrats lost many more voters to the Know-Nothings than they gained from the Whigs, the vast bulk of Know-Nothing voters by 1855 were probably former Whigs, since most native-born Protestants had voted for that party. A former Democrat in the order complained to Simon Cameron, who joined the Know-Nothings in 1854,

> It requires the most indomitable energy to overcome the deeprooted Whig *prejudices* that still exist in this county *notwithstanding* the change which has occurred through the influence of the new organization. There are nearly 8000 order men in this *county,* but the bloated visage of Whiggery still peers from under the cloak of Americanism.[54]

An examination of the Know-Nothing leadership confirms this Whig predominance and casts light on the type of men who joined the movement. Identifying Know-Nothings is difficult since membership was secret, but from published lists of candidates in 1855 and 1856 and of delegates to the open conventions of the American party, most of whom belonged to the secret order as well, and from letters to Cameron, a list of 143 Know-Nothing leaders could be constructed. The former political affiliation of 64 of these was determined; 39 (61%) were former Whigs, while 20 (31%) had been Democrats, four were members of the old Native American party, and one had been a Free-Soiler.[55] In order not to appear a mere

54. *Post*, Jan. 30, 1860; James A. Dean to Simon Cameron, Allegheny City, June 1, 1855, Cameron MSS; Erwin Stanley Bradley, *Simon Cameron*, p. 93.

55. These lists of Know-Nothings can be found in the *Gazette*, Jan. 10, Feb. 24, Sept. 19, 1855, Jan. 9, Mar. 20, 1856; *Dispatch*, May 3, Dec. 31, 1855; *Post*, Jan. 7, 1856

continuation of the Whig party and frighten off Democrats, however, the Know-Nothings chose their slates of candidates equally from the old parties. The Know-Nothing county ticket in 1855, for example, was evenly divided between seven Whigs and six Democrats, with one Free-Soiler holding the balance.[56] Of the men whose ages were determined, over half were younger than thirty-five in 1855. Sixty percent owned property valued at less than $5,000.[57] Thus Know-Nothing leaders were young men who generally came from the middle or lower classes. Like the Whig voters who joined the order, Know-Nothing chieftains who had been Whigs were not as wealthy as the old patrician Whig elite. To be sure, there were eight Know-Nothing leaders who owned property worth more than $25,000, but five of these had been Democrats; the former Whigs were unusually poor for political leaders.

Nor had the leaders often been in positions of control in their former parties. Opposition newspapers characterized the American leaders as "broken-down politicians and persistent office-hunters." This name-calling is perhaps too hostile, but the

56. *Dispatch*, Sept. 19, 1855.
57. The figures on age, occupation, and property holdings of these men were taken from the manuscript censuses of both 1850 and 1860. The distribution among categories of age, occupation, and property holdings were:

Age in 1855		Wealth		Occupation	
21–25	2 (3.5%)	$25,000+	8 (15%)	Iron & Glass Manufacturers	5 (7%)
26–30	9 (16 %)	$10,000–24,999	5 (10%)	Other Manufacturers	8 (11%)
31–35	19 (33 %)				
36–40	7 (12 %)	$5,000–9,999	8 (15%)	Merchants	6 (9%)
41–45	2 (3.5%)	$1,000–4,999	16 (30%)	Brokers & Gentlemen	3 (4%)
46–50	10 (18 %)	$100–999	7 (13%)	Professional	15 (21%)
51–55	6 (10.5%)	$1–99	1	Clerks & Shopkeepers	17 (24%)
56–60	1	None	8 (15%)	Artisans	16 (23%)
60 plus	1			Unskilled Laborers	1

outs of both the Whigs and the Democrats who desired to improve their lot did turn to the Know-Nothings, not to the anti-Nebraska coalition. C.O. Loomis, once called the leader of the Young Whig faction, joined the movement. Both of the Native Americans elected to the state assembly by the Know-Nothings in 1854 and nominated to the American ticket again in 1855, C. S. Eyster and D. L. Smith, were former Whigs who had tried unsuccessfully for nominations in their party in 1853 and 1854. The nominee for state senator on the 1855 American ticket, Francis C. Flanegin, had been an office-seeker and former officeholder in the Whig party, and Ephraim Jones, the Know-Nothing candidate for sheriff, had sought that nomination in the Whig party for nine years.[58]

The Democrats who bolted also had grievances against their party. Simon Cameron, the unsuccessful foe of James Buchanan for control of the Democratic state organization, sprang into the Know-Nothing ranks when he realized that his chances for high office were negligible in the Pennsylvania Democracy, and when his correspondents told him that everyone connected with Douglas' act would fall. James K. Moorhead and William M. Edgar, prominent anti-Buchanan Democrats in Pittsburgh, joined the new movement shortly after the fall elections of 1854.[59] Other Pittsburgh Democrats among Know-Nothing candidates for the state assembly or the city councils such as John M. Kirkpatrick, Samuel Morrow, William Ward, and George L. McCook had also clashed unsuc-

58. See the report of the Know-Nothing meeting and White's analysis of the Know-Nothing ticket in the *Gazette*, Feb. 24, Sept. 19, 1855.

59. Edgar had once been chairman of a meeting booming George M. Dallas for President in 1848. Anti-Buchanan Democrats in Pennsylvania often supported Dallas to stop Buchanan. *Post*, Jan. 4, 1848; Nichols, *The Democratic Machine*, p. 47.

cessfully with the dominant Buchanan-Bigler wing of the party.[60]

Whether they fled the Democratic party because of anti-Nebraska fervor, disgust with the influence of Catholics within the party, dissatisfaction with Bigler's patronage policies, or impatience with the power and exclusiveness of the "in" Bigler-Buchanan clique, these dissenters went into the Know-Nothing party. New and leaderless, it was more attractive to old Democrats than an antislavery party already headed by the established Whig leadership. Once in it, they could adopt the Whig principles of the majority of Know-Nothings. Early in 1855, the new Assemblyman Kirkpatrick addressed ten questions to Simon Cameron, the leading candidate for the United States Senator to be chosen that year, in order to learn his position on various issues. The first six dealt with opposition to slavery extension and the Fugitive Slave Act. Three others concerned a protective tariff and rivers and harbors improvements; only the last took up a repeal or extension of the naturalization laws.[61] That the former Demo-

60. Kirkpatrick had run for the state assembly as a protemperance Democrat in 1853 and had been defeated because of opposition by antiprohibition elements in the party. Morrow had been slapped down by the Bigler-*Daily Union* clique when he opposed pro-Bigler resolutions in the Democratic county convention in September 1854. Ward and McCook were the rebellious delegates from the sixth ward who had bucked party leaders in the county convention of February 1854. See the *Gazette*, Oct. 14, 1853, Sept. 7, 1854. For the Know-Nothing city council and assembly tickets see ibid., Jan. 10, Sept. 19, 1855.

61. John M. Kirkpatrick to Simon Cameron, Harrisburg, Feb. 9, 1855, Cameron MSS. The questions were phrased so that it was obvious what answers Kirkpatrick wanted: firm opposition to any proslavery act, advocacy of tariff protection and rivers and harbors improvements, and endorsement of a change in the naturalization laws.

crat Kirkpatrick tried to get Cameron's endorsement of these essentially Whig positions on slavery and economic issues is very significant. One of the major functions of the Know-Nothing party in Pittsburgh was to allow Democratic politicians, long saddled with the unpopular stands of their party on national issues, to swing over to the more popular Whig positions once they had bolted the Democratic ranks. Because it also offered a chance for Democratic politicians to lead, the Know-Nothing party, not the anti-Nebraska coalition, was the halfway house through which Democrats passed on their journey into the Republican party.

While the antislavery Whigs in Pittsburgh and Pennsylvania had followed divided counsels in 1854 and 1855, antislavery men in other states had been more effective in uniting anti-Nebraska opinion. In Massachusetts Henry Wilson had led the bulk of free-soil Whigs into the Know-Nothing party, and its triumph in 1854 was in part a victory of anti-Nebraska men. In western states, such as Iowa, Michigan, and Wisconsin, anti-Nebraska parties had been formed and crushed the Democrats at the polls in 1854. These parties were rapidly adopting the common name "Republican," and by the middle of 1855 the Republicans looked to many like the best party to combine anti-Democratic sentiment.

This successful rise of a unified anti-Nebraska party made the position of some Antimasonic Whig leaders in Pittsburgh all the more intolerable after the mayoral election of 1855, in which they had combined with Democrats against Know-Nothings. In the first part of the year the Democrats endeavored to preserve that Fusion coalition by authorizing the chairman of the county convention to "appoint a county committee of correspondence with the authority to form such a ticket as will unite in its behalf all who are favorable to open, independent, political action in opposition to secret, irresponsible, and unlawful combinations." [62] The Antimasonic Whigs, however, balked at a permanent alliance because as a minority they could not persuade the majority Democrats to adopt their antislavery views. Editor White, who had led old Antimasons into the Fusion party, wrote in June that there could "be no fusion, strictly speaking, between the Anti-Nebraska men of the Free States, and the Pierce pro-Nebraska Democracy. Elements so diverse cannot fuse." They could only manage local unity on specific questions. An exultant Know-Nothing told Cameron, "The much talked of fusion party in this county is an abortion, void of form, strength, or energy, the antislavery feeling having completely overpowered, and scattered their boasted legions to the winds." [63]

What White and other anti-Nebraska men wanted to do, when it became clear that no fusion was possible with Democrats, was to form an antislavery Republican party with the Know-Nothings. He pointed to the growth of Republican parties in western states and to the need to organize a united free-soil party for the presidential campaign of 1856. The American party could not be such a vehicle, he maintained, because its national platform issued in 1855 "abjectly accepted" the present laws on slavery and demonstrated that Southerners had taken it over. Even though Northerners had walked out

62. See the report of the Democratic county convention in the *Gazette*, Apr. 19, 1855.

63. James A. Dean to Simon Cameron, Allegheny City, June 22, 1855, Cameron MSS; *Gazette*, June 13, 16, 18, 1855.

of the American national convention in Philadelphia because of that platform, the weak Know-Nothing state platform insisted "that the question of Slavery should not be introduced into the Platform of the American Party." But what the North needed, insisted White, was exactly a party which would treat "the question of slavery as one that *should* be introduced into its platform." The slavery aggression in Kansas was the major question of the day, not nativist proscription of Catholics and foreigners, and a Republican party, "a Northern backbone party," should be formed to coalesce the free-soil sentiment of the North. Such a party, he boasted, would win the solid support of the Antimasonic Whig remnant who could not join the Know-Nothing party and of many within the Know-Nothing ranks who hated slavery more than Catholicism.[64]

The first attempts to organize the new party went smoothly. The *Gazette* printed a call for a Republican county convention signed by many prominent Whigs and Free Soil Democrats which urged the opponents of the Nebraska Act and any other extension of slavery to unite "for the protection of the rights and interests of Freedom and Free Labor." That paper also issued a call for an organizing convention to initiate a state Republican party in Pittsburgh on September 5, 1855. People seemed receptive. Even Foster, a Know-Nothing but also a bitter opponent of the Democratic Kansas policy, praised the party at first and advised all opponents of slavery extension to

64. *Gazette*, June 13, 18, 27, July 9, 19, 25, Aug. 4, Sept. 26, 1855. The editors of the *Post* confirmed White's confidence that many antislavery Know-Nothings would join a Republican party. "But there are thousands in the new party throughout the state with whom the antislavery sentiment is stronger than all other political purposes, and they will leave the ranks of the K.N.'s for the more congenial fellowship of the antislavery party, which is to be rendered more attractive under the ill-fitting name of *Republican*." *Post*, Aug. 4, 1855.

join it. "For one," he declared, "we go into the organization heart and soul." [65]

Both the Whig remnant and Free-Soil parties were fertile ground for recruitment. The county convention of Free Democrats had insisted that "moral suasion and voting must go hand in hand" and that antislavery men should make "liberty and free territories the 'ONE IDEA'" for political action. The convention had nominated no ticket and had advised Free-Soilers to vote for men who seemed most likely to stand up to slavery aggression. The Whig county executive committee urged all Whig voters to go into the new Republican party. To protests about this sacrifice of the name "Antimasonic and Whig," the leaders of the committee, most of whom had signed the call for the Republican convention, argued that the adoption of the name "Republican" was vital, so that the new party would have a basis for uniting with the Republican parties already flourishing in other Northern states.[66]

Attended mainly by former Whigs, the Republican county convention called "the slavery question as now presented the predominant all absorbing issue of the day," urged the formation of a party based on the single principle of opposition to slavery expansion, and nominated a county ticket headed by ex-Free-Soiler E. D. Gazzam for state senator. Later the state Republican convention passed similar resolutions concerned solely with slavery extension and nominated for state canal commissioner Passmore Williamson, an antislavery martyr famous because he had been arrested for violating the Fugitive Slave Act. The state platform invited all who agreed with the

---

65. *Gazette*, July 19, Aug. 8, 15, 1855; *Dispatch*, July 21, 1855.

66. For the Free-Soil convention, see the *Gazette*, Aug. 2, 1855; for a report of the meeting of the Whig executive committee, see ibid., Aug. 15, 1855.

single principle to join the party without regard to former political affiliation.[67]

Despite their intention to concentrate solely on the slavery issue and to form a new party which former Antimasons could support, Republicans immediately ran into problems with the Know-Nothings. To attract Whigs from the Antimasonic tradition, Republicans hoped to create an organization unsullied by Know-Nothing influence, but the Know-Nothings attended and dominated the initial Republican state convention in September 1855. After the convention Know-Nothings secured nineteen of twenty-five positions on the first Republican state central committee. White's coeditor was so discouraged by this infiltration that he later confessed to Salmon P. Chase that the Republicans would probably have to start from scratch to organize a party which all antislavery men could support in good conscience.[68]

If the Know-Nothings undermined the attempt to form a state Republican party by taking over its machinery, their particular principles and the influence of the anti-Catholic spirit spoiled the efforts of the party in Pittsburgh to mold a viable free-soil coalition. Put briefly, the Republicans faced the problem of wooing a sufficient number of men from the Know-Nothing ranks without at the same time antagonizing Germans on the one hand, and, much more important, the Antimasonic Whig remnant to whom all vestiges of secret societies were anathema, on the other. Both the Whig and Free-Soil parties in 1855 had shattered on exactly the same

67. See the reports of the Republican county and state conventions ibid., Aug. 30, Sept. 6, 1855.
68. *Gazette*, Oct. 1, 1855; *Dispatch*, Oct. 3, 1855; John M. Kirkpatrick to Simon Cameron, Pittsburgh, Oct. 3, 1855, Cameron MSS; Russell Errett to Salmon P. Chase, Pittsburgh, Nov. 2, 1855, Salmon P. Chase MSS (LC).

problem. People complained that resolutions introduced into those parties' last meetings welcoming men of all nationalities and religions seemed to prohibit Know-Nothings from joining in the single-idea crusade against slavery extension.[69]

To court both Antimasons and antislavery nativists the first Republican county convention in Pittsburgh passed unanimously a carefully worded resolution: "That we are in favor of open political action and discarding all objections to men on account of birthplace, will esteem character, capacity, and principles as the only true test by which to judge those who aspire to public favor." Thus the Republicans welcomed the foreign-born antislavery voters, and at the same time, by saying nothing about religious discrimination, they covertly bid for those foreign and native Protestants who had voted for Pollock and Ritchie in 1854 as much to express their opposition to Catholics as to voice a protest against slavery expansion. Significantly, White printed an editorial about this time in which he admitted that while he opposed the methods of the Know-Nothings he still hated the spread of papal power. Like White most Antimasons had always disliked Catholics. The *Post* quickly recognized and censured the effort by Republicans to attract the anti-Catholic vote by leaving the door open for religious prejudice.[70] Still, the Republicans could not accept the Know-Nothing program entirely, and by calling for open political action they implied a criticism of secret political organization. Although the provision alienated many Know-Nothings, it was absolutely necessary to attract the old Anti-

69. See J. Heron Foster's protest on the issue in the report of the Free Soil convention in the *Gazette*, Aug. 2, 1855. See also the protests of D. N. White and Henry Woods at the meeting of the Whig executive committee ibid., Aug. 15, 1855.

70. *Gazette*, July 18, Aug. 30, 1855; *Post*, Aug. 31, 1855.

masonic Whigs who were reluctant to sacrifice their party name and principles.

Essentially, though, the Republicans made their main case on the slavery-extension issue. White repeatedly pointed out that good Whigs could not vote for the Democrats because of their proslavery policy. Nor could they vote for the Know-Nothings, not only because of their proscriptive policies, but because they shied away from the real issue of the day and did not provide a firm enough bulwark against slavery aggression. The Know-Nothings had prevented the formation of an anti-Nebraska party in 1854, charged White, and they must not be allowed to continue this obstruction. When the American executive committee printed the Know-Nothing ticket which had been chosen in the secret direct primaries, White announced that six of the fourteen candidates were Democrats who had gone along with their party in 1854. Only the Republicans could triumphantly express the old Whig free-soil attitude, he insisted.[71]

Despite the success of the Know-Nothings in infiltrating the Republican state organization, Know-Nothings in Pittsburgh viewed the new party correctly as a threat to drain off some of their support. Although there was no official platform locally, Foster of the *Pittsburgh Daily Dispatch* tried desperately to show that the Know-Nothings were a more effective anti-Nebraska coalition than the Republicans because they combined temperance and nativist reforms with antislavery demands. "The foreign Catholic vote is almost unanimously cast for slavery," he argued, and "the mass of the rum party, composed in a great degree of foreigners," was found in the Democratic ranks. To oppose Catholics and immigrants was

71. *Gazette*, June 13, July 25, Sept. 8, 19, 24, 28, 1855.

the best way to achieve multifold reforms. Calling the Republicans essentially an anti-Know-Nothing party, he denounced the Republican resolution which called for open political action and welcomed immigrants as a proscription of Know-Nothings from the new alliance. He scorned the groveling efforts of Republicans to woo the foreign-born vote.[72]

> Does not everyone in voting the Republican ticket, vote foreignism as well as antislavery—while the supporters of the American nominations in this county are placed on record as voting just as strongly antislavery, yet expressing themselves at the same time favorable to salutary changes in the naturalization laws?

Other problems than a competing anti-Democratic party vexed the Know-Nothings in 1855. Many had joined the party to escape old political bosses, yet the Allegheny County Know-Nothing delegates to the state legislature in 1855 had supported Simon Cameron for United States Senator. This action had brought a storm of protest from Pittsburgh Know-Nothings who wanted a western man, "a new man, fresh from the ranks of the people—clad in American raiment," and not a former Whig or Democratic politician.[73] Moreover, long-time leaders of the Native American party who had campaigned for changes in the naturalization laws before the formation of the Know-Nothing order demanded open political action and denounced the secrecy that former Whig and Democratic politicians such as ex-Governor Johnston and Moorhead demanded. Many in the order also found secrecy increasingly

72. *Dispatch*, Jan. 5, Apr. 23, May 25, June 1, July 2, Aug. 6, 30, Sept. 5, 1855.

73. See report of the protest meeting in the *Gazette*, Feb. 24, 1855. See the editorial, ibid., Sept. 26, 1855.

distasteful in 1855, and one warned Cameron that "the people are restive under the yoke of the secret order and ripe for open political action." By the summer of 1855 the Know-Nothing movement was split in three—the old Native American party which was open in its organization and two secret orders.[74] Finally, the Know-Nothings' endorsement of a new temperance law in 1855 which outlawed all drinking houses and prohibited any sales of liquor in quantities less than quarts won them the hostility of the Liquor League, a secret organization of about five hundred tavern owners and men in the county who demanded repeal of the law.[75]

While both Know-Nothings and Republicans strove to appear advocates of reform, the Democrats ran a defensive campaign against the barrages of the other two. They endeavored to prevent all the antislavery men in the community from combining behind the Republicans. First, they tried to reassure voters they too were against slavery expansion. The *Post* announced that it opposed the establishment of slavery in Kansas because most settlers there disliked it. The Democratic state platform tried to counter anti-Nebraska appeals by playing upon the racist fears among whites in the state and opposed any amendment of the state constitution which would give suffrage to Negroes because "we are not willing that that class of Americans shall rule this part of America." Moreover, the *Post* justly charged that Williamson had no qualifications for office

74. For reports of the two American conventions, see the *Gazette*, May 3, July 19, 1855; for the weaknesses of the Know-Nothings, see the *Dispatch*, June 25, 1855, and James A. Dean to Simon Cameron, Allegheny City, June 22, 1855, Cameron MSS. For evidence of the rupture of the Know-Nothings into three divisions, see the *Gazette*, June 27, Sept. 26, 1855, and the *Dispatch*, Oct. 3, 1855.

75. *Gazette*, July 27, 1855; *Dispatch*, Sept. 27, 1855; C. S. Eyster to Simon Cameron, Pittsburgh, Sept. 22, 1855, Cameron MSS.

and won notoriety only because he was in jail for helping a fugitive slave. Fearful that Catholic opponents of slavery might join the new coalition, the *Post* warned that the Republicans and especially White were just as anti-Catholic as the Know-Nothings.[76]

The Democrats tried desperately to hold together the anti-Know-Nothing coalition of January, and, as they had done in 1854, they concentrated on winning the votes of those groups most alienated by the order. After the formal attempt to prolong the Fusion party failed, the Democratic county executive committee adopted a resolution pledging that its members were not and never had been members of secret political societies, although some on that committee complained that it would proscribe foreigners who had been Muscovies or had belonged to the Protestant Association. The Democratic state platform denounced the Know-Nothing party by name and insisted that citizens should not be discriminated against because of place of birth or religion. Obviously these planks were aimed at immigrants and Catholics. Less clearly, but equally important, by establishing their anti-Know-Nothing pedigree, the Democrats, like the Republicans, courted the Antimasonic Whigs. Because of the secrecy and ineffectiveness of the Know-Nothings in the legislature, boasted the *Post*, staunch old-line Whigs as well as Democrats, old and young, were out campaigning to rid the city of the Know-Nothing plague.[77]

The election results bore out the editor's confidence. The Democrats carried their entire ticket over the Know-Nothings, and the hapless Republicans, despite White's calls to Armaged-

76. *Post*, July 30, 31, Aug. 4, 31, Sept. 1, 7, 1855; see the Democratic state platform in the *Gazette*, July 9, 1855.

77. *Gazette*, July 9, Aug. 16, 1855; *Post*, Oct. 6, 1855.

don to do battle against the advance of slavery in Kansas, received only a small fraction of the vote. If one assumes that the separate Native American vote came from men who voted Know-Nothing in January, then about 330 Know-Nothings joined the Republicans, and about 300 antislavery Whigs left the Fusion ranks for the new party.[78] Many who voted Republican were evidently Antimasonic Whigs who could not accept coalition with either Democrats or Know-Nothings. In any case, the failure of the Republicans to draw enough votes away from the Know-Nothings brought their defeat.

Explanations for the Know-Nothing loss varied, but all agreed that the result revealed a disgust with the Americans rather than any particular preference for Democratic principles. Both the *Gazette* and the *Post* maintained that many Whigs joined the Democrats to overthrow the Know-Nothings.[79] If one assumes that three hundred former Whigs left the Fusion party between January and October, about six hundred former Whigs and foreign-born Protestants remained with the Democrats. An anti-Know-Nothing coalition had been continued in fact, if not in name. Contrary to predictions, the antislavery sentiment could not keep Whigs and Democrats from acting together when a local issue, the presence of the Know-Nothings, seemed more vital and relevant to them than the crisis in Kansas.

Indeed, the voting followed the same patterns as in January

78. See Table 27 and the *Gazette*, Oct. 11, 1855. White, however, asserted that none of the Republican votes came from Know-Nothings. If so, the 330 votes probably came from Antimasonic Whigs who abstained in January.

79. See *Post*, Oct. 10, 1855; *Gazette*, Oct. 11, 1855; Edward McPherson to J. B. McPherson, Pittsburgh, Oct. 12, 1855, McPherson MSS; John M. Kirkpatrick to Simon Cameron, Pittsburgh, Oct. 31, 1855, Cameron MSS; *Dispatch*, Oct. 17, 1855.

when there had been an open effort to demolish the order.[80]
Native-born Protestants again tended to vote for the Know-
Nothings while Germans and Irishmen, indeed, most immigrants, apparently voted against them.[81] Even though the
Know-Nothings adopted Whig economic positions, they
failed to win the unified support of the wealthy businessmen
who formerly voted for the Whigs.[82] On the other hand, the
other native Americans in the community who lacked the
wealth to give them social status superior to the immigrant
Catholics continued to vote Know-Nothing.[83] The *Post* pointed

80. The correlation between the Know-Nothing vote for canal commissioner in October and the Know-Nothing vote for mayor in January was
+.87. The correlation between the Democratic vote for canal commissioner
in October and the Fusion vote for mayor in January was +.92.

81. See Tables 29 and 30. Because of the year 1855, I also correlated the
election results with socioeconomic indices based on the manuscript census
of 1860. See Appendix B for the method of constructing these indices. The
correlation between the Know-Nothing vote for canal commissioner and the
percentage of Native Americans in 1860 was +.82; between that vote and
the percentage of Irish in 1860, it was —.40; and between that vote and
the percentage of Germans in 1860, it was —.71. The correlation between
that Know-Nothing vote and the percentage of Protestants in 1860, according to Kleppner's scale, was +.66. Conversely, the correlation between that
vote and the Catholics was —.66. The Know-Nothings obviously drove immigrants into the Democratic ranks, and the correlations with the 1860
indices are probably more accurate than those in Table 29. The correlations
between the Democratic vote for canal commissioner in 1855 and the proportions of total immigrants, Irish, and Germans in 1860 were +.84, +.44,
and +.50 respectively.

82. See Tables 29 and 30. The correlations of the Know-Nothing vote with
the indices based on the 1860 census are: with those owning $10,000 or
more worth of property, +.14; with those owning property valued between
$5,000 and $10,000, +.11; with merchants, manufacturers, and bankers,
+.49; with professional men, +.09; with clerks and shopkeepers, +.30.

83. See Tables 29 and 30. The vote of the poor probably split on an
ethnic basis. The indices of property holdings from the 1860 census pro-

out that while many Know-Nothings were more antislavery than nativist, many others, while opposing slavery extension, had "joined the new party for other purposes" and would not join an "abolitionist Republican party" which did not aim at those purposes—i.e. proscription of Catholics and immigrants.[84] In short, the Americans continued to win a nativist, anti-Catholic vote which the single-purpose Republican party could not capture.

Thus the voting in 1855 turned on one's opinion of the Know-Nothings. Commenting on the election a year later, a Democrat testified that German and Irish Protestants voted with their Catholic countrymen against the nativist order. Right after the election, another Democrat wrote Bigler that "the result here is mainly owing to the strong foreign vote, to the Catholic vote, to the liquor movement, and to the fact that a Republican ticket was in the field. It needed all these ele-

---

duced two groups of poorer men—those who owned property valued between $100 and $999 and those who owned property worth less than $100. The correlations with these two groups of poorer voters contrasted sharply. For example, the correlation between the Know-Nothing vote and the group owning less than $100 was +.70, indicating that the poorest people voted Know-Nothing, but the correlation between that vote and the group owning $100–$999 was —.66. Moreover, the latter group seems to have voted Democratic, for the correlation between it and the Democratic vote was +.51. These figures are of course imprecise, particularly when one remembers that the composition of the population may have been different in 1855 than in 1860, but it seems reasonable to conclude that the poorer a native American was, the more likely he was to vote Know-Nothing to express his resentment against the economic and social competition of Catholic immigrants. On the other hand, it is difficult to believe that Irish and German Catholics among the poorest group voted for the Know-Nothings. This paradox is explained in part by the fact that the group owning $100–$999 tended to be immigrant while the poorest group tended to be native American. See Appendix B for a further discussion of the construction of these indices and of the ethnic makeup of the two poor groups.

84. *Post*, Aug. 4, 1855.

ments to break down the power of the opposition in this county."[85] Devoted to opposing slavery alone and hostile to the secrecy of the Know-Nothings, the Republican party was swamped in an election for canal commissioner and local offices where slavery was an irrelevant issue. To note this fact is not to say that many in the ranks of all parties were not opposed to the extension of slavery, but to argue that because other issues were important to people at this time in this election, a party based on that issue alone could not succeed. Once again, local issues and differences prevented the reestablishment of the old nativist and anti-Southern Whig majority of 1848 and 1852.

The Americans, however, were not destroyed, and they captured the mayor's office in the election of 1856. The anti-Know-Nothing coalition split when many Democrats refused to support Volz again and supported a separate Democrat. The anti-Know-Nothings, though, had majorities in both councils.[86] Significantly, the Republican party, aborted after the defeat of 1855, did not even enter a candidate. Russell Errett, the other editor of the *Gazette*, dismally reported to Salmon P. Chase after that defeat about Republican chances: "The short and long of the matter is that, as things are now, I have no hope of Pennsylvania. I cannot see how all parties can cooperate here without a sacrifice of principle or loss of votes sufficient to insure defeat."[87] At the beginning of 1856, the Pennsylvania Republicans had not found a formula for

85. A. B. McCalmont to William Bigler, Pittsburgh, Oct. 10, 1855, Bigler MSS. See Tables 29 and 30. The correlations between the Democratic vote and the percentages of immigrants, Irish, Germans, and Catholics in 1860 were +.84, +.44, +.50, and +.46, respectively.

86. *Gazette*, Dec. 27, 1855, Jan. 9, 1856; *Post*, Jan. 4, 5, 15, 1856.

87. Russell Errett to Salmon P. Chase, Pittsburgh, Nov. 16, 1855, Chase MSS.

successful organization. The Know-Nothings had undermined the initial attempts to form an anti-Nebraska Republican party just as they had ruined the last efforts to rally the Whig party on that issue in 1854.

Before 1853 the Whigs in Pittsburgh had flourished on a combination of nativism and an antislavery, anti-Southern sentiment which was strengthened by the Antimasonic tradition. When the local Whig party began to collapse at the time of the passage of the Kansas-Nebraska Act, new parties appeared which drove apart the elements that had joined in the Whig party. At first it appeared that the Whigs would be rejuvenated as an anti-Nebraska party. Then the secret Know-Nothing order arose in response to a very real hostility to Catholics and immigrants. To many Whigs who were convinced their old party was dead, this nativist order seemed the best way to oppose the Democracy and to achieve political reform. It also attracted those native-born and, at first, foreign-born Protestants whose hatred of Catholics determined how they voted. For many former Antimasons among the Whigs, however, the methods of the Know-Nothings were obnoxious. At first, they remained in the transformed Whig party; then they joined a Fusion party with the Democrats solely in order to defeat the Americans. In the fall of 1855 they followed divided counsels. Many sincere antislavery men joined the new Republican party which tried to preserve Antimasonic principles by condemning secret political action. Others, however, remained with the Democrats in an anti-Know-Nothing coalition, for to them the menace of secret proscriptive orders seemed more real than the threat of slavery expansion in

Kansas. If any one factor destroyed the Whig party in Pittsburgh, it was not the Kansas-Nebraska Act, which actually strengthened Whigs there. It was the strength and form of organized anti-Catholic sentiment.

While the Whig party was shattering, a combination of grievances coincided with the Kansas-Nebraska Act to destroy party loyalty among Democrats. Party regulars disliked Bigler's patronage policies or the influence of Catholics within the party. Moreover, out politicians had reached the limit of their patience with the control of the in Buchanan-Bigler faction. Just at the moment when public wrath boiled over at the Nebraska Act, these disgruntled elements bolted from the party. Particularly important in their decision to switch allegiance was the availability of the American party, into which most of them went. It provided a much greater opportunity for advancement than did the anti-Nebraska coalition, led by old Whig chiefs.

By the beginning of 1856 political alignments remained confused. The Democrats had gained strength from Whigs and foreign Protestants who detested Know-Nothings. The Know-Nothings had won a large part of the Whig coalition, but their methods alienated a vital portion of it, and they could not muster a majority. The incipient Republican party had failed to rally all the anti-Nebraska voters, for it defied rather than wooed Know-Nothings and did not attract the poorer and middle-class Protestant native-born Americans who wanted to express their hostility to immigrant Catholics emphatically when they voted. As a Pittsburgh Know-Nothing wrote to Simon Cameron, the way to succeed in Pennsylvania was to drop secrecy and "step on two planks of a new platform and carry the state with a rush—viz. Americanism and antislavery." [88] In January 1856 no party had yet followed this advice.

88. James A. Dean to Simon Cameron, Allegheny City, June 22, 1855, Cameron MSS. I disagree with Ray Billington's contention. (*The Protestant Crusade*, p. 262) that Americans sublimated their hatred of Catholics and foreigners in the latter part of 1854 to sectional stands on the slavery issue. Not only did the Know-Nothing party continue through 1855 and into 1856 in Pittsburgh, but the religious and ethnic tensions reflected in its rise continued to influence voting behavior long after the party merged with the Republicans. The Republican party in 1856 was just as much a vehicle for anti-Catholic sentiment as it was for antislavery sentiment.

Five

THE OPPOSITION MERGES, 1856

The initial efforts to fuse the opponents of the Democracy under the Republican banner had failed disastrously. Know-Nothings and Republicans would not sacrifice enough principle to facilitate even an uneasy merger, and the Know-Nothings considered the Republicans a hostile party. In 1856 the opposition tried again to combine in order to support a Republican presidential campaign. These attempts to form a viable Republican party achieved partial success. John C. Frémont, the Republican presidential candidate, carried Pittsburgh, but the local and state organizations remained imperfect, makeshift combinations rather than completely fused Republican parties.

Although the new opposition coalition seemed to inherit the Whig majority in the city, it differed in several respects from its predecessor, and its changes altered the stance and composition of the Democratic party itself. An examination of the difficult process by which Republican organizations evolved on the national, state, and local levels helps identify what elements went into the two parties and suggests why. Moreover, a close investigation of the leadership, appeals, and sources of voter support of the two parties in 1856 reveals how they differed from the earlier parties.[1]

1. In this chapter I deal only with the Republican and Democratic parties

Forming a national organization to back a Republican presidential candidate proved a relatively easy task for the opponents of the Democracy. Republicans had triumphed in Ohio in 1855, and unlike Pennsylvania, most New England and northwestern states had successfully formed state organizations by 1856. Republicans in Congress in late 1855 issued a call for a national convention to be held in Pittsburgh on February 22, 1856, to form a national party. Republican leaders probably chose Pittsburgh because of its central location to the strongly antislavery, free-soil areas of western Pennsylvania, western New York, and Ohio. Moreover, the editors of the *Pittsburgh Daily Gazette*, D. N. White and Russell Errett, who were influential in the selection of Pittsburgh for the convention, favored Salmon P. Chase for the Presidency and hoped to enhance his chances for the Republican nomination by holding the meeting in Pittsburgh, a city close to his native Ohio, where he had been elected governor in 1855.[2]

The meeting attracted delegates from all over the country; they included such men as Edwin D. Morgan and Horace Greeley of New York and Francis P. Blair of Maryland. Pittsburgh Republicans had appointed a reception committee of prominent local leaders, and Errett was a secretary. The major problem debated by the delegates was what to do about the Americans (Know-Nothings) and still keep German backing. E. D. Gazzam, a delegate from Pittsburgh, told the meeting that a Republican party in Pennsylvania had to seek the

---

because the American party led by Millard Fillmore received a very small portion of the vote in 1856 and did not seem to play a major role in the campaign.

2. Crandall, *The Early History of the Republican Party*, p. 49; *Gazette*, Mar. 27, Apr. 22, 1856.

foreign antislavery vote but would welcome the support of antislavery Know-Nothings if they could tolerate an alliance with foreign-born citizens. Eventually, the convention avoided any formal statement about foreigners or Know-Nothings, proclaimed opposition to slavery extension and to the policy of the Pierce administration, the basis for uniting in the party, and called for a national convention to be held in Philadelphia in June to nominate a candidate for President.[3]

On the same day that the Republicans organized in Pittsburgh, the American party opened its national convention in Philadelphia. To coax back the Northern members who had stormed out of the Philadelphia convention in June 1855, the Americans replaced the controversial Article XII of their 1855 platform which accepted the Kansas-Nebraska Act with a resolution which denounced the repeal of the Missouri Compromise but also demanded that Congress not interfere with the "domestic and social affairs" of the territories.[4] Even this hybrid resolution failed to impress the free-soil members of the party, and they withdrew from the convention which then nominated Millard Fillmore as the American candidate for President. This choice further antagonized the Northern dissidents because of Fillmore's association with the detested Fugitive Slave Act of 1850.

3. See reports of the convention in the *Gazette*, Feb. 23, 25, 1856, and the *Post*, Feb. 25, 1856. It is not the purpose of this chapter to trace in great detail the proceedings of this national convention, the strategy behind it, or the formation of the national Republican organization. For very able discussions of these topics, see Crandall, passim; Leonard H. Bernstein, "Convention in Pittsburgh," *Western Pennsylvania Historical Magazine, 49* (1966), 289–300.

4. *Gazette*, Feb. 26, 1856; see also Billington, *The Protestant Crusade*, p. 428.

The Northern branch of the Know-Nothings assembled in early June in New York City and nominated Nathaniel P. Banks of Massachusetts for President with the understanding that he would withdraw in favor of John C. Frémont, who was expected to win the Republican nomination. For Vice-President the North Americans nominated William F. Johnston, former governor of Pennsylvania and at that time a prominent resident of Pittsburgh. When Frémont captured the Republican nomination as expected, Banks withdrew. The North Americans, however, rejected the Republican Vice-Presidential nominee William L. Dayton and kept Johnston. For a while Johnston's candidacy divided the opposition because some ratification meetings throughout the country raised Frémont-Johnston, rather than Frémont-Dayton, banners, and Know-Nothing state committees in Massachusetts and Connecticut endorsed the Frémont-Johnston ticket. Nevertheless, with the nomination of Frémont by both organizations, the Republicans were well on their way toward molding a Northern coalition of the opposition.[5]

Forming a Republican party in the state and county was more difficult. White had noted after the 1855 defeat that prospects for a union between the Know-Nothings and Republicans were dim because neither group would yield vital principles. Seeking to reform the triumphant coalition which had elected James Pollock in 1854, the American and anti-Nebraska representatives in the state legislature early in the year sent

5. See Roy Franklin Nichols, "Some Problems of the First Republican Presidential Campaign," *American Historical Review*, 28 (1923), 492–96; Fred H. Harrington, "Frémont and the North Americans," *American Historical Review*, 49 (1939), 842–48. See also Harrington, *Fighting Politician: Major General N. P. Banks* (Philadelphia, 1948), pp. 36–37.

out a call for a state Anti-Administration convention to choose
a state fusion ticket. On March 19, 1856, a county Anti-Administration, or Union, convention consisting primarily of Know-
Nothings selected two Republicans and five Know-Nothings
to the state convention. Calling for the union of all who opposed the national administration for any reason, the delegates
specifically avoided disruptive resolutions endorsing the proscriptive principles of the Know-Nothings. The state Anti-
Administration convention selected a state "Union Ticket"
and passed resolutions calling for support from all who opposed the Democratic administration because of its Kansas
policy or because of its favoritism of foreigners in the distribution of patronage.[6] Like the county convention then, the state
Union convention sought to unite the foes of the Democrats
on the single basis of opposition to a common enemy.

The incipient Republican party, especially those in its ranks
who opposed the Know-Nothings, were not willing to go
along with this effort initiated by Americans. White and
Errett, important Republican leaders in Pittsburgh as well
as editors of the *Gazette*, objected to the Know-Nothing dominance in the Republican state executive committee established
in 1855 and disliked the nativist parts of the Union platform.[7]
Moreover, the Republicans made an attempt to organize on
their own. On the same day that the county Anti-Administra-

6. *Gazette*, Nov. 2, 1855, Mar. 20, 24, 1856; *Post*, Feb. 14, Mar. 22, 1856;
Mueller, *The Whig Party in Pennsylvania*, p. 224. The Union state platform
(*Gazette*, Mar. 29, 1856) will be examined in more detail below.

7. *Gazette*, Mar. 29, 1856. White and Errett were both delegates to the
Republican state convention in 1856, and Errett was also on the Republican
state executive committee. See also the report of the meeting of the Pennsylvania delegates to the Republican organizing convention in Pittsburgh,
Gazette, Feb. 23, 1856.

tion convention met, David Wilmot, chairman of the Republican state committee, issued a call for a Republican state convention to meet in Philadelphia on June 16, 1856, the day before the national Republican convention assembled there. A Republican county convention met in Pittsburgh in early June, and only about five of approximately ninety delegates to it had also attended the Anti-Administration convention in March. Of the delegates the Republicans elected to the state and national conventions, only one, John M. Kirkpatrick, was a Know-Nothing.[8] Thus by the time of the Republican national convention, the local foes of the Democracy remained organized in two separate groups which vied to lead the opposition.

Complete combination was first achieved on the state level. The state Republican convention accepted the Union state ticket nominated in March as had a separate American convention. This ticket consisted of an old Whig for canal commissioner, a Know-Nothing for auditor general, and a Republican with Democratic antecedents for surveyor general. Apparently no separate state platform was adopted, and Pennsylvania Republicans were willing to stand on the platform of the national convention which was meeting simultaneously.[9]

Although the major elements of the opposition combined without much friction behind the state ticket, they faced problems forming a united local organization which could place a county and congressional ticket in the field agreeable to Know-Nothings, old-line Antimasonic Whigs, Republicans, and for-

8. See the lists of delegates to the two conventions in the *Gazette*, Mar. 20, June 5, 1856. For another description of the meeting, see the *Post*, June 5, 1856.

9. *Gazette*, June 18, 1856.

eigners and which could direct the campaign for Frémont in Pittsburgh and Allegheny County. The thorniest problem locally arose out of the refusal of the North American vice-presidential nominee Johnston to withdraw in favor of the Republican Dayton. J. Heron Foster, the Know-Nothing editor, immediately called for Johnston to step down so the foes of the Democracy could unite in the county, but Johnston, who was a resident of the city, president of the Allegheny Valley Railroad Company, and a leader of local Know-Nothings, held out. When a mass Frémont-Dayton rally was held in Pittsburgh in July, an equally large Frémont-Johnston ratification meeting assembled the same night in Allegheny City. Speakers from out of town traveled back and forth across the river to address both gatherings on the virtues of Frémont and the justice of the anti-Nebraska cause.[10]

To counteract Johnston's disruptive candidacy, Republicans and Know-Nothings in Pittsburgh united informally in July to campaign for Frémont by forming the Allegheny County Frémont Club. Soft-pedaling the vice-presidential question, speakers from both factions vowed that all differences between them would be sunk and that "the primary object of the organization would be to overthrow the Democratic party." Officers of the club represented both elements; of nine members of the committee of organization from Pittsburgh, four were Americans and five, Republicans.[11] The Frémont Club directed the Republican campaign in Pittsburgh in 1856, rather than a formal party organization.

10. *Dispatch*, June 21, 1856; *Gazette*, July 16, 1856.

11. See the report of the meeting in the *Gazette*, July 18, 1856, and compare the list of the committee of organization with the lists of delegates to the Anti-Administration and Republican county conventions, *Gazette*, Mar. 20, June 5, 1856.

The union between the two factions became much firmer in August. On August 20 Johnston withdrew from the race, and the way was open for further amalgamation of the pro-Frémont forces in Pittsburgh. More important, a second Union county convention that month nominated a county ticket which all the opponents of the Democracy could support. The candidate for Congress, David Ritchie, was the Whig incumbent who had had Know-Nothing support in 1854. Heading the county ticket as candidate for state senator was Gazzam, former Democrat and Free-Soiler who had occupied the same position on the Republican ticket in 1855. Among the candidates for the state legislature were William E. Stevenson, the Free-Soiler who had been placed on the Whig ticket in 1854 to help form an anti-Nebraska coalition, Nicholas Voeghtley, Jr., a former Whig born in Switzerland who had joined the Republicans in 1855, and C. S. Eyster, who had been on the American assembly ticket in 1854 and 1855. The Union candidate for county auditor had also been on the Know-Nothing ticket in 1855. Thus there were two 1855 Republicans, two old Free-Soilers, and three Know-Nothings. Of this group, three had been Whigs. The resolutions of the county Union convention endorsed the Union state ticket although they did not mention the Union state platform, denounced the effort of the Pierce administration to force slavery into Kansas, and called on all the opponents of the Democrats to unite behind Frémont. Noticeably absent were both calls for proscription of foreigners and Catholics and demands for acceptance of these groups.[12] In short, this convention avoided the mistake of the

12. See Johnston's letter to the North American national convention dated Aug. 20, 1856, *Gazette*, Sept. 17, 1856. For a report of the Union county convention held on August 20 and the Union county ticket, see ibid., Aug.

1855 Republican county convention by ignoring the divisive issues connected with Know-Nothingism.

By the time of the October elections the opponents of the Democrats had fashioned a formal alliance, but no state or local Republican party had yet been formed because of the seeming irreconcilability of the Americans with the other elements. Indeed, because of its anti-Know-Nothing connotations from the campaign of 1855, the name "Republican" could not even be used by the state and county coalitions. Supporters of Frémont sought to strengthen the merger after the October elections when they formed a Frémont Fusion electoral ticket headed by Frémont and including thirteen Republican and thirteen Know-Nothing electors.[13] Forced to combine in order to organize support in the presidential campaign, the factions of the opposition as yet tolerated only a marriage of convenience.

Such a union was vital, for the Democrats waged a strong campaign. They chose as their presidential candidate James Buchanan, the native Pennsylvanian who would have great drawing power in Pittsburgh and throughout the state. Minister to England under Pierce, Buchanan escaped the taint of the Nebraska Act, and even the pro-Republican *Pittsburgh Daily Dispatch* applauded his nomination. A Buchanan-Breckinridge Club began to direct the campaign for local Democrats as early as June. Buchanan evoked displays of enthusiasm and mass support long absent among the chronically defeated

---

21, 1856. To check the backgrounds of the Republican candidates, see the 1855 Know-Nothing ticket, ibid., Sept. 19, 1855. For identification of Voeghtley as an early Republican, see the list of nominees for county treasurer at the Republican county convention, ibid., Aug. 30, 1855.

13. *Post*, Oct. 27, 1856.

Pittsburgh Democracy. Indeed, the minority party, bolstered by its triumph in 1855, conducted one of its most vigorous campaigns in decades in Pittsburgh.[14]

One way to gauge the impact of the emerging issues of the 1850s on the nature of parties and to measure in what ways the new coalitions of 1856 had changed from the Whig and Democratic parties of the 1840s was to compare the prominent men of the Republican (Union) and Democratic parties between 1855 and 1857—both candidates and secondary leaders. The list of candidates from those years totaled 49 Republicans and 43 Democrats; that of secondary leaders included 137 Republicans and 88 Democrats. Examination of these samples revealed that the opposing parties still drew their leaders from different elements of the population. At the same time, while there was much continuity between the party leadership of the late 1840s and that of 1856, the intervening events and party realignments had brought new chieftains to the surface and thereby reduced the disparities between the leadership of the Democrats and that of their foes.[15]

Like the Whigs, the Republicans drew more of their leaders from the wealthier classes of society than did the Democrats. Even though the Democrats do not appear to have chosen so many of their leaders from among the propertyless classes as in 1848, as a group Republican leaders were richer. Almost half of the Republican candidates, but less than a third of the Democratic candidates owned property valued at $25,000 or more. Similarly, the party leaders and convention delegates of the Republicans came from the wealthier classes more often

14. *Dispatch*, June 7, Oct. 25, 1856.
15. See Appendix B for the sources of the leadership sample.

than did those of the Democrats.[16] Moreover, although the parties recruited equally from most occupational groups, Republican leaders were generally richer and more successful men than the Democrats, and more of them were influential iron and glass manufacturers who dominated the city's economy.

The differences between Republican and Democratic leadership were not, however, precisely the same as those that had existed between Whigs and Democrats. Earlier, a significantly larger proportion of the Democratic than of the Whig candidates had come from the professional groups (lawyers, doctors, and editors). Of the Republican and Democratic candidates around 1856, however, ten from each party were professional men. Moreover, while in earlier years a much larger proportion of the Whig than the Democratic leadership had come from the active business leaders of the community, the same distinction did not persist between the Republicans and Democrats. In 1856, while there were substantially more iron and glass manufacturers among Republican candidates, other types of manufacturers and store owners were stronger proportionately among Democratic candidates than among Republicans. Similarly, among secondary party leaders, while manufacturers were more numerous among the Republicans, other business leaders such as railroad officials, merchants, and store owners were equally prominent in both parties. If

16. See Tables 37 and 38, and 8 and 9. Proportions and figures in the text are based on the leaders about whom information was found, not on the total sample. Both Republican and Democratic leaders in 1856 seem wealthier as a group than their counterparts in 1848. For example, only 48 percent of the Whig candidates examined in Chap. 2 owned property valued at $10,000 or more, while 67 percent of the Republicans did. This disparity is probably explained by the differences in the censuses of 1850 and 1860. See Appendix B for an explanation of this difference.

William Robinson, Jr., the first president of the Ohio and Pennsylvania Railroad, was a Republican, his successor George W. Cass was a Democrat. If James McAuley, the wealthy president of the Iron City Bank, ran for city councilman as a Republican in 1857, Samuel Jones, another wealthy banker, was a Democratic candidate for the state assembly in 1856. Moreover, skilled artisans and unskilled laborers had an equally small representation among the leadership of both parties.[17]

If the occupational distinctions between the leaders of the Republicans and Democrats were less clear-cut than those between the Whigs and Democrats, so too were distinctions of nationality. Whig leaders between 1847 and 1851 had come from the established native-born families of the community more often than had those of the Democrats. Conversely, a much larger proportion of the Democratic leaders than of the Whig, particularly in the second rank, had been Irish. In 1856 the proportions of native-born Americans among the candidates of the two parties were about the same as they had been among the earlier Whig and Democratic candidates. The proportion of Irish-born candidates in both parties, however, had decreased since 1850.[18] This change in the ethnic groups from which the parties drew their leaders was even clearer among the second echelon of party leaders. While the proportions of natives and Irish among the Republicans were about the same as they had been in Whig leadership, the Democrats no longer chose so many Irishmen as leaders; instead, they selected many more native Americans. Some of the new leaders of both parties may have been sons of

17. See Tables 10, 11, 39, and 40.
18. See Tables 12, 13, 41, and 42.

Irishmen who had been born in this country. But in all probability, the drop in the numbers of Irishmen among leaders also reflected the evident exodus of Irish from the city, since both the absolute numbers and proportion of Irish in the adult white male population decreased between 1850 and 1860.[19]

If the number of Irishmen in the city was falling, the German population was growing, and Germans were more significant among Republican candidates than they had been in the Whig leadership. Republicans chose four German candidates and one who was Swiss. In contrast, between 1847 and 1851 only one of 78 Whig candidates had been German, and he was Frederick Lorenz, an extremely wealthy glass and iron manufacturer, an elder of the socially prestigious Third Presbyterian Church since 1834, and a resident of the very fashionable Penn Avenue area of the fourth ward—hardly a representative of the more recent German immigrants crowding into the city in the late 1840s and early 1850s. In contrast, the four Germans on the Republican council tickets in 1857 were far different types. They came from the wards with the heaviest concentrations of German workingmen, not the stronghold of wealthy native Americans, were less wealthy than Lorenz, and in no way belonged to the social elite. On the third ward ticket, J. G. Backofen was the former editor of the Democratic German-language newspaper, *Der Pittsburgh Courier*, who had merged with the editors of the Whig and subsequently Republican *Western Pennsylvania Staats Zeitung* in 1854. Nathan Gallinger from the working-class fifth ward was a dry goods merchant from Bavaria who owned property valued at only $4,000 in 1860. A. B. Berger was a successful

19. See Tables 13, 31, 41, and 42.

187

grocer from the sixth ward, and Lewis Kim from the eighth ward, which was primarily populated by operatives for the rolling mills along the Monongahela River, was a master tinner who owned property worth $4,800 in 1860.[20] Fairly successful, these men were in positions where they could be influential leaders in the German community. With these Germans, Republican leadership more than that of the patrician Whig party reflected the makeup of the population and probably was more attractive to the growing number of German voters.

If roughly the same proportions of Republican and Democratic leaders in 1856 came from the various ethnic groups, the Republicans, like the Whigs before them, chose Protestants as their leaders far more often than the Democrats did. None of the Whig candidates had been Catholic, and of fifty Republican leaders all were Protestants. In contrast, almost half of the Democratic leaders in 1856 belonged to the Church of Rome.[21]

Presbyterians and Episcopalians remained the two major Protestant denominations from which both parties drew their leaders; but, like the Whigs, the Republicans were more likely to be Presbyterians than were the Democrats. In con-

20. According to the manuscript census of 1850 Lorenz owned real property valued at $200,000. He died before 1855. On the other hand, Backofen owned no real property of value, but $6,000 worth of personal property, according to the manuscript census of 1860. A. B. Berger, the wealthiest of the four German candidates, owned property valued at $45,000 in 1860. By a count in the manuscript census of 1860, of the nine wards in the city as ranked by the number of German males over 21 living in them, the fifth ward was first, the third ward was second, the eighth ward was third, and the sixth ward was fourth. Thus the Republican German candidates came from the four wards with the largest concentrations of Germans.

21. See Tables 14, 15, 43, and 44.

trast, eleven members of each group were Episcopalians. Many of both denominations were wealthy; therefore the large number of wealthy men among the Presbyterians does not account for the difference. On the other hand, Presbyterians, much more than the Episcopalians, were leaders in the temperance and abolitionist movements which found greater expression in the Republican party. Moreover, Presbyterians more than Episcopalians believed in imposing their ethical standards on the community through political action. Perhaps because Episcopalians did not share the sense of moral stewardship and the aggressive benevolence which motivated some Presbyterians, their religion may not have influenced their choice of party, as it did that of the Presbyterians and the Catholics.[22]

In some respects then, Republican and Democratic leadership in 1856 sprang from the same sources and differed in almost the same ways as did Whig and Democratic leadership between 1847 and 1851. If the Democrats now seemed to draw almost equal proportions of their leaders from the various ethnic and occupational groups, as did their opponents, it was the increase among the Democrats of wealthier, native-born merchants and businessmen which narrowed the gap between the parties. Even so, Republican leaders were richer,

22. See Tables 43 and 44. Part of the heavy Presbyterian and Episcopalian cast in leadership derives from the fact that I found more information on these two denominations than on others. For the influence of Presbyterians in the local temperance movement, see Lloyd L. Sponholtz, "Pittsburgh and Temperance, 1830–1854," *Western Pennsylvania Historical Magazine, 46* (1963), 351, 378; George F. Swetnam, "The Growing Edge of Conscience," *The Presbyterian Valley,* ed. William Wilson McKinney (Pittsburgh, 1958), pp. 271, 277. For an excellent analysis of the manifestations of moral trusteeship which affected upper-class Presbyterians and Congregationalists especially, see Clifford S. Griffin, *Their Brothers' Keepers: Moral Stewardship in the United States, 1800–1865* (New Brunswick, N.J., 1960), passim.

more likely to manufacture iron or glass, and to be Presbyterian or at least Protestant than their Democratic counterparts.

That the origins of the early Republican leadership were closely akin to those of Whig leadership seems natural, for indeed, the majority of these men had been Whigs. The previous political affiliation of 25 of the 49 Republican candidates was identified, and 16 (64%) of these were former Whigs. Four others had been Free-Soilers, and four had been Democrats, two of whom, William Ward and Max K. Moorhead (the son of James K. Moorhead), had entered the Republican party by way of the Know-Nothings.[23] Of 69 secondary Republican leaders 60 (87%) were former Whigs. Four others had been Free-Soilers, and five had been Democrats. Of these last five, three had first defected into the Know-Nothing party. The difference in proportions of Whigs among the candidates and secondary leaders of the Republicans is significant. While the Republicans made a surface effort to put Free-Soilers or Know-Nothings on their tickets to draw the votes of different groups and change the image of the new party from that of the old Whig party, the great bulk of Republican leaders, as shown among delegates and committee members, came from the old Whigs.

Similarly, most of the Democratic leaders had belonged to the Democratic party before 1853, and many had been leaders in it. Of 23 Democratic candidates 21 had been Democrats,

23. The two other former Democrats were J. G. Backofen, the editor, and Samuel McKelvey, an extremely wealthy Presbyterian iron manufacturer from the fifth ward. The other leader of the twenty-five was C. S. Eyster, the Know-Nothing who had once been a Whig. To examine political affiliation, I checked the lists of party candidates, delegates, vigilance committees, and petitioners from 1847 to 1853.

and of 55 secondary Democratic party leaders, 54 had been Democrats. The others had been Whigs. Moreover, 55 from the total sample had been listed among the leaders from 1847 to 1851. The old Democratic leadership whose control had driven some Democrats into the Know-Nothings continued to prevail.

The contending parties also differed in their appeals to the voters in 1856. An examination of national, state, and local platforms in 1855 and 1856 as well as newspapers in Pittsburgh reveals how their strategies shaped their platforms. Basically, the Republican and Union parties strove to unite all the opponents of the Democratic administration by agitating immediate issues while the Democrats attempted to keep them apart. The efforts of both antagonists resulted in platforms which differed in certain ways from those of the earlier Whig and Democratic organizations.

The incipient Republicans concentrated primarily on establishing themselves as the sectional party of the North through which disgruntled citizens could express hostility to slavery, to the South, and to the pro-Southern Democracy. True, they adopted the Free-Soil attack on the institution of slavery as a moral wrong. The state and national platforms of 1855 and 1856 condemned slavery as "the withering curse of human bondage" and a relic of barbarism. Moreover, they complained that the civil rights of Negroes to life, liberty, and property as guaranteed in the Declaration of Independence and the Constitution would be violated if slavery were allowed to spread.[24]

24. See the Republican state platform of 1855 and national platform for 1856 in the *Gazette*, Sept. 6, 1855, June 19, 1856. See the editorials in that

But Republican appeals spoke of the moral iniquity of the institution and the unhappy plight of the Negro propagated by the extension of slavery much less than of its threat to Northern whites. Congress must prohibit slavery's expansion into free territories to protect white settlers there from being degraded to the status of poor whites in the South, warned Pittsburgh Republicans in 1856. "The question is thus one of immediate personal interest to the free white inhabitants of the Northern states," cried the *Gazette*. Earlier, editor D. N. White had summarized perfectly the basic Republican appeal:

The real question at issue between the North and the South in the present contest, is not a sentimental difference growing out of the oppression of the negro, but whether free settlers shall be allowed to occupy the free lands of the nation, in the enjoyment of free institutions, or be excluded from them.

Not only does this editorial belie the humanitarian concern for the slave and reveal that some voters obviously did not respond to slavery as a moral issue; it also shows that slavery expansion, rather than being a mere symbol of a deeper moral conflict between the sections, was itself the fundamental issue to many voters regardless of ethical considerations.[25]

---

paper for June 13, July 15, and Oct. 14, 1856. For purposes of convenience in this section, I refer to the opponents of the Democracy on all levels as Republicans although the name connotes a formal unity of principle and party which did not yet exist in the Union coalitions.

25. See the Republican national platform. See also the Republican county resolutions and state platform, *Gazette*, Aug. 30, Sept. 6, 1855, and the address and principles of the national organizing convention in Pittsburgh, the Union state platform, and the resolutions of the Union county convention, ibid., Feb. 25, Mar. 29, Aug. 21, 1856. For example of the newspaper use of

Because to Republicans the struggle in the territories was a sectional clash, they attempted to rally the entire North as a section against the power of the South in the nation. In Republican ideology slavery stood for a wide variety of evils many Northerners connected with the economic and political power of Southern slaveholders.[26] The state platforms of 1855 and 1856 called for the people of the North to unite to defend their rights against the "continual aggression of slavery upon the interests of freedom" and "to check the evils inflicted upon the country by the unjust and sectional measures adopted by the present National Administration." Republicans in Pittsburgh at their county convention in 1856 warned that Northerners were becoming increasingly impatient with the "insufferable arrogance" of planters and with the undemocratic and un-American idea that the minority South should rule the richer and more populous North through its control of the national government. Republicans would brook no more compromises with slaveholders and would oppose the admission of more slave states to block the extension of the slaveholding oligarchy.[27]

the appeal, see ibid., Sept. 8, 1855, June 5, 13, 1856, and the *Dispatch*, Aug. 8, 1856.

26. Roy F. Nichols points out that much of the Northern attack upon slavery derived actually from bitterness about the political power of slaveholders who seemed to frustrate the passage of measures which Northerners wanted. Nichols, *The Disruption of American Democracy* (New York, 1962), p. 43. Chaplain W. Morrison (*The Wilmot Proviso Controversy*, pp. 52–74) argues convincingly that the argument over the spread of slavery in the late 1840s was a basic issue, not just a symbol of a deeper moral conflict, because northerners wanted to prevent the spread of Negroes and the subjugation of their section to the slave power, not to attack slavery in the South. The Republican appeals in 1856 seem to confirm this analysis.

27. *Gazette*, Sept. 6, 1855, Feb. 25, Mar. 29, June 5, 1856.

To increase sectional antipathy toward the South, Republicans stressed the outrageous aspects of two current events— the caning of Charles Sumner, the Republican Senator from Massachusetts, by South Carolina Congressman Preston S. Brooks and the supposed civil war in Kansas.

The assault on Sumner in the Senate chamber on May 22, 1856, quickly became a partisan issue as Republicans tried to make him a martyr and Democrats tried to foil that effort by denying the seriousness of the incident. White asserted that the "cowardly attack . . . stirred up [an] indignation . . . that pervaded all classes and conditions of men," and he bitterly demanded that Northern men return blow for blow with "these cut-throat Southrons." In early June some Republicans called for an indignation meeting to protest this assault, and the *Post* scorned it as a "tardy exhibition of bottled wrath." Vigorously proclaiming the assault a crucial issue, "involving the manhood of Northern men," the Republicans at their county convention declared it a "summons louder than the first gun at Lexington to every free man of the North without distinction of party to gird on his armor at once and fall into line with his brethren with the same unanimity, which is sure to prevail in the South." [28]

Similarly, the situation in Kansas angered many Northerners. Despite the efforts of governors appointed by President Pierce to insure impartial and fair elections, some Missourians had crossed the border into Kansas to carry the territorial elections fraudulently for the slave-state forces. Many free-state men did not vote, and the majority of settlers apparently disliked the proslavery territorial legislature. Governor Andrew Reeder opposed that legislature, and free-state men resisted it. When fighting broke out between free-state settlers

28. *Gazette*, May 24, June 5, 1856; *Post*, May 24, June 6, 1856.

and proslavery border ruffians, some concerned citizens in Pittsburgh formed a Kansas Aid Society which solicited funds to send arms and supplies to Kansas.[29] Newspaper accounts fed the flames of outrage with exaggerated and purple descriptions of violence and murder.

Indignation boiled over in Republican resolutions. They censured "the organized conspiracy of the slaveholders of Missouri backed by the public opinion of the whole South" and abetted by the national Democratic administration "to force slavery into Kansas." Kansas must be made a free state, they cried. Because free-state settlers suffered sacking and burning of their towns and murder at the hands of border ruffians, the belligerent Republicans of Pittsburgh pledged, "[Their] battle is ours, and . . . if we would continue free, we must look at once to our weapons and see that our powder is dry." Moreover, not just the expansion of slavery, but the basic constitutional rights of Northern settlers were at stake. The major section of the Republican national platform decried the tyrannical attempt by Southerners and the national government to impose unconstitutional officers on the settlers of Kansas and to infringe their rights to vote, to hold office, to bear arms, and to receive an impartial jury trial. Republican victory was necessary not only to stop the spread of slavery, but also, as the Union county convention summarized, to preserve "the freedom of the public domain, the freedom of speech, freedom of press, and the Constitutional rights of a free people." [30]

29. For the efforts of the governors appointed by Pierce, see Nevins, *Ordeal of the Union*, 2, 380–93; *Post*, Feb. 19, 1856.

30. See the Union state platform, the national platform, and the Republican county resolutions in the *Gazette*, Mar. 19, June 5, 19, Aug. 21, 1856. In the Republican national platform, 388 words (46%) of 841 dealt with the deprivation of rights in Kansas.

By shifting their appeals on Kansas away from the slavery extension question to a purported defense of the rights of Northern settlers, the Republicans added to their potential vote those who were concerned with the protection of civil liberties as well as those who opposed the spread of slavery for humanitarian reasons, racist dislike of any Negroes in the territories, or a desire to curb the growth of Southern political power. They labeled the South the foe of all these Northerners, and the Democratic party the champion of the South. This emphasis on the abstract rights and freedoms of the individual differed from the Whig appeal to his economic interest, and the Republicans probably adopted it from the earlier Free-Soil platforms.[31]

In response to Republican assaults, the Democrats who sought national, i.e. Southern, backing rather than purely Northern support, essayed briefly to justify the Democratic policies on Kansas and slavery expansion. The state and national platforms of 1856 defended the Nebraska Act and the

31. Whereas the three Whig state platforms between 1847 and 1849 used the words "liberties" and "rights" only twice by actual count, they were used thirty times in the Republican and Union state platforms of 1855 and 1856 and the national Republican platform of 1856. On the other hand, the Whig platforms used the words "interest" and "prosperity" fifteen times while the Republican platforms used them only twice. William Dusinberre in a study of Philadelphia politics in the mid-1850s notes that the major stress of the Republican campaign there in 1856 was not opposition to slavery expansion, but a defense of Northern rights and the rights of settlers in Kansas against Southern aggressions. Dusinberre, *Civil War Issues in Philadelphia*, pp. 35–36. In the most recent history of the Republican party, George H. Mayer astutely suggests that the Republicans in 1856 could use the Sumner and Kansas issues to arouse Northern antagonism "without embracing the cause of the Negro" and thereby bring reluctant anti-Nebraska Whigs and Democrats into the party. Mayer, *The Republican Party, 1854–1966* (2d ed. New York, 1967), p. 38.

formula of popular sovereignty as the just and proper solution to the problem of slavery in the public domain. The national platform reaffirmed the right of the actual majority of settlers in Kansas to establish or reject slavery when creating a constitution, and the state platform endorsed the record of the Pierce regime.[32]

In Pittsburgh the editors of the *Post* denied flatly that the Democratic party was proslavery, that it favored the extension of the institution, and that there existed an actual threat that slavery would expand into Kansas or any other territory. Moreover, insisted the *Post*, the rumors of civil war and violence in Kansas were exaggerations of "the fanatics on both sides" such as the Southern hotspur Senator David R. Atchison of Missouri, "a border ruffian" and an "agitator of disunion." The absence of war in Kansas meant that Kansas was no issue and that the Republicans, whose single issue was Kansas, were bankrupt of principles.[33]

Despite the attempt to justify their actions and deny the validity of Republican charges, the Democrats preferred to avoid the questions of slavery extension and the turbulence in Kansas. They gave considerably less attention to these questions in their platforms and editorials than did the Republicans. Indeed, they boasted that while the Republicans were only concerned with Kansas and the Negro, they thought about a wide variety of issues and the whole country.[34]

32. See the state and national Democratic platforms in the *Post*, Mar. 7, June 10, 1856.

33. *Post*, Jan. 21, Mar. 22, May 28, June 14, July 14, Aug. 23, 1856.

34. *Post*, Aug. 11, 1856. In the Republican national platform, 592 words (70%) of 841 had dealt with slavery extension or Kansas. Of the Democratic platform, only 246 words (24%) out of 1,021 defended the Democratic policy on Kansas, and another 30 words (3%) demanded protection of

The Democrats stressed foreign policy in their national platform. Explicitly stating that foreign affairs were just as important as domestic matters, they gave more attention to them than to any other single question. The platform called for adherence to the Monroe Doctrine, expressed sympathy for the efforts of the filibusterer William Walker in Nicaragua by emphasizing the necessity of United States influence in a passage connecting the oceans across the Isthmus, and called for a more aggressive policy in the Caribbean and the Gulf of Mexico. When the *Post* endorsed the national platform, it cited the resolutions calling for a bolder foreign policy as the most important feature of the platform.[35] It is true that many people may have viewed the Democratic plans for ex-

---

the rights of Southern states on slavery. In the Union state platform of 1856, 255 words (44%) of 575 dealt with the spread of slavery and Kansas while in the Democratic state platform of that year 299 words (25%) of 1,212 concerned those issues. Even in the newspapers, the same difference in emphasis was evident. To measure the relative importance of issues in the partisan newspapers I counted the column inches devoted to various types of appeals and issues on the editorial pages of the *Gazette* and the *Post* for each issue during the months of August, September, and October 1856. I included both editorials and clippings from other newspapers used politically in the campaign, but I did not count other news items such as railroad stories which had no clear political significance. In the sample of editorials and articles from the *Gazette*, of a total of 1,297 column inches, 395 inches (30.5%) concerned Kansas, the spread of slavery, or the insult of slavery to workers. In contrast, of a total of 1,181 column inches from the *Post*, only 96 inches (8%) were devoted to a defense of the Democratic position on Kansas and a denial that the Democrats favored the extension of slavery. Another 15 inches (1%) denied that slavery was aggressive. The difference in the proportions devoted to slavery and Kansas between the formal platforms of both parties and the editorial columns of local newspapers indicates that both parties carried on a much broader and more varied campaign, involving other issues, on the local level.

35. *Post*, June 10, 1856. Thirty-two percent of the Democratic national platform was devoted to foreign affairs.

pansion as part of a scheme to get more territory for slavery, but by masking this goal, the Democrats, who had traditionally been expansionists, tried to appeal to the American confidence in Manifest Destiny.[36]

If the national Democratic platform emphasized foreign policy as a major issue, the basic maneuver of the Pennsylvania Democrats to counteract Republican charges was to insist that the Republican hostility to the South would provoke secession and civil war. In reply to the Republican call to arms against the South, the Democrats denounced "all sectional parties and platforms concerning domestic slavery" whose "partial and exaggerated sympathy [for the Negroes] . . . is at the peril of our dearest interests as a nation." While the Republicans emphasized the constitutional rights of individuals, the Democratic platforms argued that "the equality of the states is the vital element of the Constitution itself" and stressed that the rights of all the states must be protected. While Republicans asserted that freedom versus slavery was the issue of the campaign, the Democrats insisted "that all other evils are insignificant in comparison with the danger to the Union." [37]

The Democratic editors in Pittsburgh savagely vilified the Republicans as fanatical warmongers who would provoke civil

36. The Democrats traditionally had been expansionists, and they particularly asked for territorial or agricultural expansion. See Jaffa, *Crisis of the House Divided*, pp. 70 f.

37. All quotations were taken from the state and national platforms, found in the *Post*, Mar. 7, June 10, 1856. The Democrats gave more attention to calls for a defense of the Union, the Constitution, and states' rights and to denunciation of Republican agitators than to any other issue in their state platform of 1856. Of 1,212 words devoted to issues, 703 (54%) were devoted to the appeal. The national platform used other appeals, but 20 percent of its words were devoted to defending states' rights and, thereby, the Union.

war between North and South. The *Post* charged that "the Black Republican abolitionists" harped on the Kansas issue because their "aim is a dissolution of the Union. While the Union lasts the abolition agitators can never hold the high places of the government. In disunion rests the only hope of their diseased ambition." [38]

The frequent Democratic attacks forced the Republicans to reply. Fearful of losing the vote of conservative businessmen, the Republicans denied that they wanted disunion and that a Republican victory meant civil war. Republican papers asserted that agitators and disunionists in both the North and the South desired Buchanan's election because Frémont's triumph would settle the slavery question permanently against extension. The *Dispatch* labeled as a myth the idea of Southern secession, and White declared flatly, "We shall elect Colonel Fremont, and the South will submit very quietly." [39]

Because the Whigs had been in such a preponderant majority both parties in 1856 made appeals to their conservatism and old party loyalty to capture their vote. Where the Democrats charged that the abolitionist and sectional stand of the Republicans would provoke a civil war, the Republicans, like the Whigs, denounced the aggressive foreign policy advocated by the Democrats in the Ostend Manifesto and their platform as seeking war with England, France, Spain, Mexico, and Central America: "*This* is the entertainment to which

38. *Post*, Feb. 25, July 14, 1856. The *Post* also charged, Mar. 18, 1856, that "these fanatical agitators the Republicans well know that while the Union lasts they can never climb to power; but divide it into fragments, and they think that they may secure the control and plunder of at least one fragment."

39. *Gazette*, July 25, Aug. 4, Sept. 5, 6, 1856; *Dispatch*, Aug. 6, Sept. 6, 1856.

the old line Whigs—the peace-loving conservative men of the country—are invited." The conservatives should unite to prevent wars brought on by the "open-mouthed filibusterism" of the Democrats. Republicans also asserted that Henry Clay, the Whig hero, had hated Buchanan and that they alone continued the Whig tradition. The *Post* replied that Clay and Buchanan had been personal friends. Moreover, it said that E. D. Gazzam, the Republican candidate for state senator and an old Jacksonian, had been a bitter foe of Clay, and that hundreds of old-line Whigs were therefore working for his defeat.[40]

The efforts of Democrats to attract Whigs and establish a conservative coalition of those loyal to the Union and of the Republicans to build an anti-Democratic coalition from the old parties resulted in the clearest difference between the 1856 appeals and those of the Whigs and Democrats earlier—the absence of an economic debate. Anxious to attract anti-Nebraska Democrats and Free-Soilers, the Republicans dropped all talk of protective tariffs and paternalistic probusiness programs which would advance the prosperity of everyone because such Whig measures might alienate old Democrats. No state, national, or local set of Republican resolutions even mentioned the tariff. The Republican national platform did devote a little space to advocating a Pacific Railroad and the old Whig measures of rivers and harbors improvements, but state and local platforms did not include such calls.[41] Finally,

40. *Gazette*, Sept. 6, 1855, Mar. 29, June 11, 19, 26, 1856; *Post*, June 26, Oct. 9, 1856. The reference to war with England may have been a special appeal to former Whigs who traditionally had been pro-British while Democrats were anti-British. See Jaffa, p. 71.

41. Economic appeals formed an insignificant portion of the Republican platform when compared to the importance of economic appeals in the Whig

economic appeals occupied a minuscule portion of the editorials of the major Republican newspaper in the city.[42] At the same time, the Democrats who actively wooed conservative Whig businessmen no longer stressed their opposition to big business and measures to help business. Gone from their platforms were condemnations of banks, paper money, and monopolies. Aware of the conservative fear of class strife, they also discarded the special interest appeals to the poor and their class-conscious agitation of workers against employers which had characterized Democratic platforms in the late 1840s.[43]

Rather than playing on the economic grievances of workers, the Democrats charged that Republicans were abolitionists in order to scare into their camp white workingmen who feared emancipation and competition from the Negro.[44] The Re-

---

program. In the Whig state platforms of 1847, 1848, and 1849 an average of 27 percent of their space had been devoted to tariff appeals, and 44 percent to all kinds of economic appeals. See Chap. 2, n. 27. On the other hand, the Republicans gave no space to the tariff. The combined space allotted to economic appeals in the Republican national platform was 104 words (13%) out of 841 words.

42. Of a total of 1,297 column inches in the sample from the Republican *Gazette*, only 3½ inches concerned the tariff or any other economic appeal resembling the earlier Whig ideology.

43. The Democratic national platform of 1856 reiterated the principles of the Baltimore Platform of 1852, but the new section only mentioned monopolies and exclusive legislation once. Of 1,021 words in the new part of the platform, only 30 (approximately 3%) concerned this protest against privilege. In contrast, 17 percent of the Democratic state platforms from 1847 to 1849 had attacked privilege, banks, and paper money. Of the 1,181 column inches in the sample for the editorial page of the *Post*, only half an inch was devoted to the matter.

44. For discussions of the hostility of white laborers in the North to Negroes and of their coolness toward any scheme of emancipating the slaves, see Williston H. Lofton, "Abolitionism and Labor," *Journal of Negro History*, 33 (1948), 249–83; Albon P. Man, Jr., "Labor Competition and the New

publicans cared only for the Negro, insisted the *Post*, while the Democrats were concerned with the white race. "They [the Republicans] would abolish slavery, and bring the Negroes into the Northern States to take the places of white laborers." "To elevate the African race in this country to a complete equality of political and economic condition with the white man, is the one aim of the party that supports Fremont." On the other hand, the Democracy of the North opposed the amalgamation of the races and believed "that the white laboring masses should never be subjected to ruinous competition with the almost countless hordes of cheap and needy negro laborers." After the defeat of the Democrats in the October elections the *Post* warned, "The issue now for the balance of the contest is, the white race or the Negro race." [45]

Recognizing the extent of racist sentiment among workers in the North, the Republicans denied the Democratic allegations. Terming the charges ridiculous, White insisted that the issue was not white men versus Negroes; rather it was the contest between the slave oligarchy of the South who wanted to introduce slavery into Kansas and the free laborers of the North who wanted to save it for white workingmen. Thomas

York Draft Riots," *Journal of Negro History, 36* (1951), 375–405; and Joseph G. Rayback, "The American Workingman and the Antislavery Crusade," *Journal of Economic History, 3* (1943), 152–63. Dusinberre in his study of Philadelphia asserts that racism was an important political fact of life there and in a belt across Pennsylvania, Ohio, Indiana, and Illinois that includes Pittsburgh. He insists that the play on racist fears was a traditional Democratic appeal and a major reason for their strength in Pennsylvania. Dusinberre, *Civil War Issues*, pp. 13, 16, 28. For an opposing view which stresses the hostility of workingmen toward slavery but still recognizes the racism of many workers, see Bernard Mandel, *Labor: Free and Slave, Workingmen and the Anti-Slavery Movement in the United States* (New York, 1955).

45. *Post*, Mar. 18, July 27, Aug. 7, 11, 18, Oct. 16, 1856.

Williams, a speaker at a Republican meeting, declared that he "cared nothing for the 'nigger'; it was not the mission of the Republican party to preach rebellion—he had a higher mission to preach—deliverance to the white man." Resolutions of a Republican meeting in Birmingham, an industrial borough heavily populated by workingmen, declared that the only issue in the election was "whether the West should become the homes of white Freemen or colored slaves." In sum, both Republicans and Democrats posed as defenders of white labor against Negro competition, but the Republicans stressed the competition from slaves in the western territories while the Democrats warned of the horrors of an influx of free Negroes into the Northern states.[46]

Republicans amplified their appeal to workingmen by arguing that the very existence of the institution of slavery degraded labor and that its spread endangered them in eastern cities. "To make work the lot of slaves is to badge workingmen with the disgrace of bondage," insisted White. Moreover, Southern Democrats wanted to make all laboring men, both white and black, slaves. Because Democrats favored an aristocratic society which condoned the "lashing, clubbing, branding, and hounding of Working Men," they were "un-

46. For the resolutions of the meeting in Birmingham and the report of the Frémont Club meeting, see the *Gazette*, July 12, 26, 1856. See also the *Gazette*, Sept. 17, 1856. Two recent books reveal that the strong hostility toward the Negro in the Midwest forced both parties there to play on racism as they did in Pittsburgh. Indeed, the promise by Republicans that they would keep Negroes out of the territories was a major element of their antislavery and free-soil rhetoric there. See Eugene H. Berwanger, *The Frontier Against Slavery: Western Anti-Negro Prejudice and the Slavery Extension Controversy* (Urbana, Ill., 1967); and V. Jacque Voegeli, *Free but Not Equal: The Midwest and the Negro during the Civil War* (Chicago, 1967), pp. 1–9 and passim.

worthy of the freeman's vote." A Republican rally in the fifth ward resolved that "the working men of this—the working ward of the city—will never consent to spread over the west, a system which degrades labor, enriching a few aristocrats at the expense of labor." [47] J. Heron Foster of the *Dispatch* pointed out that the extension of slavery directly harmed eastern workers by preventing the labor surplus from moving west. If all the western states had been allowed to become slave states or if the territories were open to slavery, workingmen "would have remained here to compete with you for work and by their presence reduced the wages in your branch of trade." [48] Whether the West actually operated as a safety valve for eastern workers has been seriously questioned by historians, but the point here is that the Republicans made a special effort to warn workingmen as a group of the dangers of slavery and its spread.[49]

If the Republicans tried to arouse workingmen's hostility to slavery to overcome their racist antipathies, they also labeled Buchanan a foe of Northern labor. The *Gazette* constantly iterated the "Ten Cent Jimmy" charge: "Working men, Remember that James Buchanan, while in the United States Senate, advocated the reduction of wages of labor to

47. *Gazette*, July 15, Sept. 23, 1856; for a report of the fifth ward meeting, see the *Gazette*, July 30, 1856.

48. *Dispatch*, Oct. 29, 1856. This argument that western lands should be used to absorb the labor surplus of the East in order to keep up the wage level of eastern workers echoed appeals land reformers had been making to workers for thirty years. Evidently the response of laborers to such calls was mixed. Some were enthusiastic; some were apathetic. See Helene Sara Zahler, *Eastern Workingmen and National Land Policy, 1829–1862* (New York, 1941), pp. 27–29, 35, 67, 181–82.

49. For example, see Fred A. Shannon, "The Homestead Act and Labor Surplus," *American Historical Review*, 41 (1936), 637–51.

the European standard—Ten Cents a day." [50] In their appeal
to the class interests of workers and attempt to arouse their
class antagonism toward aristocratic planters the Republicans
differed sharply from the Whigs, who had deplored Democratic efforts to agitate workers as a separate class against
employers and who had emphasized the common interests of
rich and poor with a paternalistic theory that business prosperity meant steady employment and high wages for the
operative. [51]

Just as both parties appealed to laborers and racial fears,
both played on ethnic and religious antagonisms. Democrats
tried again to frighten the immigrants and Catholics away
from the nativist alliance between Know-Nothings and Republicans, and to preserve the anti-Know-Nothing Democratic coalition of party regulars, Whigs from the Antimasonic
tradition, foreign Protestants, and Catholics which had defeated both Know-Nothings and Republicans in 1855. The
national Democratic platform denounced groups which based
their membership on religious considerations and place of
birth, and the state platform censured the Know-Nothings by
name and announced the Democracy's opposition to secret
political orders and to "the overthrow of . . . the civil and
religious rights of the citizen." Speakers and editors warned

50. *Gazette*, Aug. 15, 1856. During the month of August, the *Gazette*
headed its editorial column almost every day with the same editorial which
elaborated this charge.

51. *Post*, June 20, July 28, 1856. The Republicans made more direct appeals to labor than the Democrats did. The Democratic appeal to labor, exclusive of the racist, occupied 38 inches (3 percent) of the editorial sample from
the *Post*, while the racist occupied 8 percent. The Republican specific appeals
to laborers in the *Gazette* covered 12 percent of the sample. In contrast to the
small Democratic effort in 1856, 17 percent of the local Democratic resolutions in 1848 and 1849 involved direct appeals to workers as a distinct class.

206

Germans and Irishmen not to support a party led primarily by Know-Nothings who wished to proscribe them. In a final editorial before the October election, the *Post* listed among the enemies of the Democrats: Frémont abolitionists who hated the white workingman, Americans who proscribed foreigners to elevate Republicans to office, and Orangemen, foreigners who had taken a secret oath to oppose any government which gave Catholics equal rights.[52]

At the same time that they denounced the alliance between Republicans and Know-Nothings, the Democrats attempted to prevent the completion of that merger. Early in the year before the partnership was sealed, the *Post* warned Know-Nothings that the Republicans could not be trusted because they had combined with the Democrats to oppose the secret order in 1855. After the organization of the Union conventions the Democrats, confident of Catholic support, charged that Frémont was a Catholic and questioned how Know-Nothings could support such a man.[53]

Meanwhile, the Republicans and Union party endeavored to attract the Know-Nothing vote to give substance to the alliance which local leaders had formed. Perhaps the crucial item in this attempt, in addition to the inclusion of Know-Nothings on Union tickets, was the Union state platform of March. Almost equal portions of this statement denounced the spread of slavery and the alleged political evils of Catholicism and the immigrants. It censured the interference "of foreign influence of every kind" in American government and thus by implication that of the papacy. It also castigated "the pandering of any party to foreign influence as fraught with manifold

52. *Post*, Feb. 25, Mar. 7, 22, June 10, 12, 24, Aug. 23, Oct. 9, 27, 1856; *Gazette,* Dec. 20, 1855.

53. *Post*, Feb. 14, June 20, Sept. 29, 1856.

evils to the country" and pledged to defend the system of universal education from any attempts "from whatever quarter" to convert it to sectarian purposes. By protesting the Catholic assault on the public school system, the chief grievance against Catholics at the time, the Union platform bid for the support of both native- and foreign-born Protestants whose hatred of Catholicism influenced their vote.[54] On the local level, the Republican press tried to retain the anti-Catholic vote by insisting that Frémont was an Episcopalian, not a Catholic. To keep anti-Catholic Protestants from supporting Buchanan, the Republicans also continued to identify the Democrats with the Catholics. White wildly charged that Archbishop John Hughes of New York anxiously awaited Buchanan's victory, and that if he did win, another Inquisition was impending.[55]

To cement the coalition Republicans tried to prevent Know-Nothings from supporting Millard Fillmore, the American presidential candidate. White charged that the rumors that Frémont was a Catholic emanated from a bargain between Fillmore Americans and the Democrats and Catholics. "It is a curious spectacle to see the Archbishops, Bishops, Priests, and editors of that Church shaking hands with the Fillmore Know-Nothings and uniting with them to foment prejudice against their own faith." White pointed out that Fillmore was

54. For the Union state platform, see *Gazette*, Mar. 29, 1856. Of 575 words in this platform, 255 (44%) were devoted to Kansas and the expansion of slavery while 172 (30%) denounced the influence of foreigners in government and politics and 76 (13%) concerned the public school question. In sum, 43 percent involved the Know-Nothing appeals of 1855, while 44 percent was devoted to the Republican appeals of 1855. The balance of the platform called for a combination of all who opposed the Democracy for any reason.

55. *Gazette*, July 22, Oct. 4, 7, 1856.

a friend of Catholics and had had his daughter educated in a Catholic convent, and he asked, "If the Know Nothings cannot vote for Mr. Fremont because he was married by a Catholic priest, how in the name of common sense can they vote for Fillmore?" The Democrats boomed Fillmore, a popular man among slaveholders, only to draw Know-Nothing votes away from Frémont.[56]

While the Republicans hoped to turn Protestants away from Fillmore by asserting he worked with Catholics, they also attempted to drive the foreign vote away from the Democrats by revealing the Democratic alliance with the Americans. Charging that Democratic Senator William Bigler was circulating and signing Fillmore literature, White demanded, "Let the people of foreign birth, especially, to whom the Buchanan men are constantly appealing, remember this fact." Another editorial asserted that three men on the Democratic county ticket were Know-Nothings. Since the Republicans identified Catholics with Democrats, it is clear that they hoped to capture only the foreign Protestant vote with such propaganda. Indeed, after the election Russell Errett, the new editor of the *Gazette*, wrote that the Republicans should give up on the Catholic vote but should make special efforts to woo the votes of foreign-born Protestants, for in time they could win as much as nine tenths of that vote.[57]

Like the leadership and ideologies of the Republican and Democratic parties, the voter support of the opposing parties in 1856 differed in some degree from that of the Whig and

56. Ibid., July 21, 22, Aug. 2, 14, 23, Sept. 6, Oct. 4, 1856.
57. Ibid., July 30, Sept. 2, 8, Nov. 11, 1856.

Democratic parties in the late 1840s and early 1850s. The primary reason for the difference was that a portion of the Whigs joined the Democrats, while some groups who had often supported the Democrats now bolted to the Republicans. The biases, issues, and party loyalties which emerged in 1854 and 1855 had much to do with this realignment of voter support in 1856.

The most noteworthy fact of the election of 1856 was the great increase in the total vote in Pittsburgh, particularly that for the Democrats, since 1854 and 1852. While the vote for Fillmore was small and that for Frémont was a third larger than the vote for James Pollock in 1854, Buchanan's vote was almost twice the size of that for William Bigler in 1854. Presidential elections normally draw out larger votes than state and local campaigns, but Buchanan's increase over Pierce's total in 1852 was much larger than the difference between Pierce's vote and that for Lewis Cass in 1848.[58] At the same time, the Republicans in this national election, free from divisive local issues, drew out a larger vote than the Whig vote in the presidential elections of 1848 or 1852 and won a majority equal to Scott's in 1852.

Some of the Democratic increase over 1854 came from party regulars who had supported Pierce in 1852 but who had refused to vote for Bigler for one reason or another. A correspondent advised Buchanan before the election that "a good many Democrats who left us two years ago [(in 1854) are] remaining with the Know Nothings and Black Republicans," and Buchanan appears to have drawn back old party regulars who merely abstained in 1854 and 1855, rather than the three

58. See Table 45. The *Post* noted this large Democratic vote, Nov. 22, 1856.

hundred or so voters who defected to new parties in those years.[59]

Still, Buchanan also drew out new supporters who had not voted Democratic before, and part of this new vote, as in other areas of the country, apparently came from former Whigs who jumped into the Democratic ranks. During the summer of 1856 various correspondents wrote Buchanan that "many of the most respectable of the Old Line Whigs of old Allegheny County" were leaning toward him, and in September John B. Guthrie assured, "We shall have a good many old line Whigs with us this fall who did not vote before and some of them will vote our state ticket." After the October elections, another man forecast that many former Whigs who would not vote for the rest of the Democratic ticket would vote for Buchanan himself.[60] These predictions were accurate, for Whigs, particularly those who did not join the Know-Nothing party, did not tend to unite very solidly behind the Republicans in 1856.[61] Moreover, the Democrats appear to

59. John B. Guthrie to James Buchanan, Pittsburgh, Sept. 8, 1856, Buchanan MSS (HSP). The Democrats gained the most votes between 1854 and 1856 where they had lost the most votes between 1852 and 1854. The correlation between the percentage decrease of the Democratic vote for Pierce in 1852 to the vote for Bigler in 1854, and the percentage increase from that vote for Bigler to the vote for Buchanan in 1856 was +.64. For a definition of "percentage increase" see Appendix B.

60. See John Anderson to James Buchanan, Pittsburgh, June 2, 1856, John C. Devlin to Buchanan, Pittsburgh, Aug. 15, 1856, Guthrie to Buchanan, Pittsburgh, Sept. 8, 1856, and Ellis Lewis to Buchanan, Pittsburgh, Oct. 9, 1856, all in the Buchanan MSS.

61. The correlation between the 1852 Whig vote for President and the 1856 Republican vote for President was only +.36. On the other hand, the correlation between the Whig vote for President in 1848 and that Republican vote was +.68. This discrepancy is possibly explained by a Whig discontent and apathy over Scott in 1852 which caused his vote to be slightly smaller

have gained the most votes between 1854 and 1856 exactly in those areas where the Whigs had been strongest in 1854.[62]

Some of the former Whigs who joined the Democrats in 1856 seem to have been wealthy business and commercial leaders. The vote of those groups, which had once been so solidly Whig, appears to have split fairly evenly between the two parties in 1856. As in other Northern cities, some professional men and particularly merchants and shopkeepers who traded with the South and feared the loss of their customers swung over to the Democrats.[63] Indeed, fear of disunion was prob-

than that for Taylor in 1848. The correlation between the Whig vote for governor in 1854 and the 1856 Republican vote for President was only +.57. But that vote for governor was a coalition with the Know-Nothings. The correlation between the Whig vote for clerk of courts in 1854, which represented the Whig remnant which did not join the Know-Nothings immediately, and the Republican vote for President in 1856 was only +.40. It should be noted, however, that these low correlations may have resulted from the fact that some of the Republican vote could have come from new sources in addition to, rather than replacing, the Whig vote.

62. The correlation between the percentage increase of the Democratic vote in Pittsburgh from the gubernatorial election in 1854 to the Presidential election in 1856 and the Whig vote for governor in 1854 was +.59.

63. See Nevins, *Ordeal of the Union, 2*, 511, for a discussion of the national trend of conservative Whigs to vote for Buchanan. See Tables 45, 46, and 47, especially the correlations with the groups owning $10,000 or more of property and the occupational categories of merchants, large manufacturers, and bankers, professional men (lawyers, doctors, editors, ministers, and civil engineers), and clerks and shopkeepers. In the presidential election of 1848 the correlation between the group owning $10,000 plus and the Whig vote was +.63 and with the Democratic vote —.45; in the 1852 presidential election, the correlation between that group and the Whig vote was +.74 and with the Democrats —.67; in the 1856 presidential election, the correlation between that group and the Republican vote was —.08, and with the Democratic vote, +.09. Since the correlations in the first two elections were calculated from the scale based on the 1850 census and the 1856 correlations were calculated with scales based on the 1860 census, I also correlated the 1856 returns with the indices based on the 1850 census. Then, the correlation be-

ably most important in influencing these conservative men to back Buchanan.

Actually the evidence on the political affiliation of the wealthy is contradictory. In 1857 the owner of the Democratic *Pittsburgh Daily Union* asserted, "The great mass of the mercantile community here" belonged in the opposition ranks.[64] To check the politics of the rich between 1855 and 1857 an effort was made to determine the political affiliation of the 235 men in Pittsburgh and Allegheny City who, according to the manuscript census of 1860, owned property valued over $25,000. Of 67 identified, 49 (70%) were Republicans. It is difficult to reconcile this heavy Republican cast with the results of election analysis, but the very inability to find the political affiliations of the other men on the list may indicate that the wealthy were not so actively involved with either party as they had been with the Whigs.[65] In any case, if more wealthy men were associated with the Republicans than with the Democrats between 1855 and 1857, they do not appear

---

tween the group owning $10,000 plus and the Republican vote for President was only +.11. In sum, there seems to have been a drop in the support the rich gave the opponents of the Democracy and an increase in the support they gave the Democrats.

64. Thomas J. Keenan to Jeremiah S. Black, Pittsburgh, Mar. 28, 1857, Jeremiah S. Black MSS (LC).

65. The 67 were only 28 percent of the 235 men. In contrast, in the sample of those who owned $25,000 or more worth of property from the 1850 census, I found the affiliations of 77 (41 percent) of 187. Possibly the low correlation figure between the wealthy and the Republican vote results from the presence of many more relatively poor voters among the Republican voters than had been in the Whig coalition. Nevertheless, the Whigs had been a majority party and necessarily had to have wide support among relatively poor workers, and at the same time, the correlations between the wealthy and business leader groups and the Whig votes were always high. Therefore, it seems reasonable to assume that the lower correlations actually do reflect a lesser degree of support.

to have voted as a group for the Republicans in the presidential election of 1856, and more of them seem to have voted for the Democratic party than earlier. Neither in its leadership nor in its ideology was the Republican party so clearly that of the businessmen as the Whigs had been, and it failed to win the kind of support from them that the Whigs had.

Not only economic considerations, but the refusal to align with Know-Nothings helped determine which Whigs joined the Democrats. In the election of 1855 for canal commissioner, the vote of the Antimasonic Whig remnant had split between the Democrats and the incipient Republican party, and with the exception of foreign Protestants, those Whigs who had supported the anti-Know-Nothing Fusion and Democratic tickets in 1855 remained almost solidly behind the Democrats in 1856.[66] Apparently the former Antimasons who had joined the party because of antipathy to Know-Nothings and other secret organizations such as the Protestant Association re-

66. *Gazette*, Oct. 11, 1855. The correlation between the Democratic vote for congressman in 1856 and the Fusion vote for mayor in 1855 was +.64; the correlation between that vote for congressman and the Democratic vote for canal commissioner in 1855 was +.82. The correlations between the 1856 Democratic vote for President and the Fusion vote for mayor and Democratic vote for canal commissioner in 1855 were +.69 and +.81 respectively. If one considers that many foreign Protestants left the party after 1855, as will be shown below, and that many other voters joined the party in 1856, these correlations are extremely high and indicate that the rest of the anti-Know-Nothing coalition, the old-line Antimasonic Whigs included, tended to vote Democratic in 1856 almost to a man.

The Democratic vote did change from 1852 because the correlation between the vote for Pierce and the vote for Buchanan was only +.52. On the other hand, the correlation between the Democratic votes for President in 1848 and 1856 was remarkably high— +.83 —as was the correlation between the Whig vote in 1848 and the 1856 Republican vote. One must point out again that the makeup of the wards, according to the censuses of 1850 and 1860, did change in these years, so the high correlation may not mean the vote came from the same people.

mained in it when the Republicans openly combined with the Know-Nothings and did not disavow their principles as they had done in 1855. Moreover, some of the Whigs who voted Democratic for the first time in 1856 could have been Antimasons who voted Republican in 1855 when that party called for open political action but who could not do so in 1856.

The final reason for the large Democratic vote in 1856 was an increased degree of support from Catholics. In 1856 the Catholic vote seems to have gone almost solidly to the Democrats. After the election Russell Errett noted that Catholics had been and always would be a unit in the Democratic camp. Much of the new Democratic vote therefore could have come from newly naturalized Catholic immigrants who had never voted before.[67]

If most Catholics voted Democratic, most Protestants tended to vote Republican, and the religious division cut across both economic and ethnic lines. Just as earlier, the poor and propertyless laborers and skilled artisans did not unite as a class bloc behind either party.[68] Moreover, many Protestant Irishmen and Germans who had voted with the Know-Nothings

67. *Gazette*, Nov. 11, 18, 1856. See Table 47. Admittedly, the scale of the proportionate strength of Catholics is imprecise, but it is significant that the correlation between the Catholics and the smaller Democratic vote in 1855 was only +.46. True, the lower correlation could have meant that more foreign Protestants voted with the Democrats in 1855 than in 1856, and this indication is correct. Still, the great increase in the correlation when the size of the vote increased is important.

68. See Tables 46 and 47. The same difference between the behavior of the group owning $100–$999 and the group owning property valued at less than $100 was evident in 1856 as in 1855. That is, the first group tended to vote for the Democrats while the latter and poorer group tended to vote against them and for their opponents. For an explanation of that difference, see Appendix B.

in 1854 apparently voted with the Republicans. Before the election Guthrie had warned Buchanan, "We shall not have that portion of the Irish and German Protestant vote, that came over to us last fall [1855]," and after the election the *Gazette* noted that while the bulk of Irish and German Catholics had supported the Democrats, the majority of Protestant Irish, Germans, Welsh, and English supported Frémont and the Union tickets. Most Germans and Irishmen seem to have voted Democratic but their support was less solid than in previous elections because of the religious division.[69]

If the immigrant support of the Democrats was less solid than in previous years, the native Americans did not seem to support the Republicans so staunchly as they had supported the Whigs.[70] Several reasons account for this apparent decrease in support. Some native-born Catholics who had been Whigs became Democrats as, evidently, did a portion of the wealthy and Antimasonic Whigs, many of whom were native

69. John B. Guthrie to James Buchanan, Pittsburgh, Sept. 8, 1856, Buchanan MSS (HSP); *Gazette*, Nov. 11, 1856. Another correspondent had predicted that the Democrats would lose as much as one-third of the German vote, and after the election the *Post* admitted that the Democrats had lost a "large portion" of that vote. See Charles A. Burgthal to Buchanan, Aug. 23, 1856, Buchanan MSS (HSP); *Post*, Nov. 22, 1856. See also Tables 46 and 47. Note the sharp decrease in the total immigrant support for the Democrats from 1855 when the Know-Nothings had driven most foreigners into the Democratic party. In 1848 the correlation between the Democratic vote for President and the Irish was $+.58$; in 1852, it was $+.46$; in 1856, it was $+.56$. In 1848 the correlation between the Germans and the Democratic vote for President was $+.18$; in 1852, it was $+.65$; and in 1856 it was $+.53$.

70. See Table 46. The correlation between the native Americans and the Whig vote for President in 1848 was $+.64$; in 1852 it was $+.83$; and in 1856 with the Republican vote it was $+.59$. On the other hand, the correlation between the natives and the Republican congressional vote in 1856 was $+.65$.

born.[71] Moreover, the seeming decrease in native support could merely have reflected the increase in immigrant backing which the Republicans won and which the Whigs had not had. In any case, most native-born Protestants who had supported the Know-Nothings in 1855 voted for the Republicans.[72]

The alliance of the opposition behind the Union tickets and Frémont achieved its desired goal. Because certain events intensified sectional animosities in the North and thus benefited the Republicans, because the party was no longer openly hostile to Know-Nothings while it maintained open political action, and because the state and local parties still appealed to anti-Catholic biases as well as free-soil sentiment, the Republicans in 1856 could combine the Whigs and Free-Soilers who had voted Republican in 1855 with those native-born Protestants who had supported the Know-Nothings then. The additional Republican strength probably came from the foreign-born Protestants who had voted with the anti-Know-Nothing coalition in 1855.

The major dividing line between the parties, then, appears to have been denominational, although Protestants and Catholics probably took different views on nonreligious issues such as slavery extension. Distinctions of wealth and occupation did not set the Republican voters apart from the Democratic voters as they had the Whigs. The Democrats' charges that Orangemen and other Protestant organizations opposed them were probably correct; many foreign-born Protestants voted Republican to express hostility to Catholics as well as to slavery.

71. The correlation between the native Americans and the Democratic vote was not so markedly negative in 1856 as it had been earlier. In 1848 it was —.51; in 1852 it was —.76; and in 1856 it was —.45.

72. The correlations between the Republican vote for congressman and President in 1856 and the Know-Nothing vote for canal commissioner in 1855 were +.82 and +.81.

Similarly, many of the poorer native Americans who had voted for Joe Barker in 1850 and 1851, had joined the anti-Catholic Know-Nothings in 1854 rather than stay in the anti-Nebraska Whig party, and had remained in that organization in 1855 rather than enter the antislavery Republican party voted Republican in 1856 just as they had voted for other parties—simply because most Catholics were Democrats.[73]

The aggressively Protestant nature of the Republicans explains why many people voted Democratic. Republican newspapers, particularly the *Gazette*, had long been hostile to Catholics. More important, those foreign and nativist groups whose professed goals included exclusion of Catholics from the government were evidently going to vote Republican. Both the nature and the membership of the local Union coalitions were anti-Catholic even if the national platform was not hostile. In sum, just as many Protestants voted Republican because the Democrats were identified with the Catholics, the Catholics voted Democratic because that party gave them a voice in leadership and because their foes were in the opposition.

The Republican party in 1856 made its basic appeal to the voters one of hostility to the South, yet the vote for that party

73. Clifford S. Griffin has noted the marked Protestant tinge of the Republican party, but he has linked it with the Protestant zeal for temperance, antislavery, and Sabbatarian reform which grew out of a tradition of moral stewardship in the nineteenth century. See Griffin, *Their Brothers' Keeper*, pp. 219–41 and passim. Many Republicans in Pittsburgh, especially the leaders, undoubtedly shared these desires for positive reforms, but the argument here is that a large number of Protestants voted Republican out of a negative reflex response to the Catholics in the Democratic party. Simply because Catholics were Democrats, and not necessarily for any positive reasons, many Protestants voted Republican.

cannot be interpreted solely as a protest against the South. The Republicans could never have succeeded without the open bargain with Know-Nothings through which they could combine antislavery and anti-Catholic elements. Moreover, the efforts of parties to choose Whigs, Know-Nothings, or Catholics as leaders and to pin on their opponents the label of Catholics or Know-Nothings show that the practical politicians of the day knew that the makeup of the opposing party influenced voting just as much as its stand on issues. Clearly, local tensions and old party loyalties had as much to do with shaping the vote as the national debate over slavery extension.

Six

THE ANTIRAILROAD
IMPULSE, 1857–1859

The Republican party matured in the free states in the years between the defeat of John C. Frémont and the election of Abraham Lincoln. The disappearance of a separate American party and the leavening of the antislavery platform with other issues facilitated a broadening of the party's base in the North. Equally important were the misfortunes and blunders during the Presidency of the Pennsylvanian James Buchanan. The Panic of 1857 broke during his first year in office, and the subsequent depression produced clamors for tariff protection which embarrassed the free-trade Democracy in the North. Troubles with the Mormons in Utah, heavy federal expenditures resulting in a large increase in the national debt, and charges of corruption discredited Buchanan and Democrats everywhere. But it was the result of popular sovereignty and pro-Southern policy which particularly weakened the Democracy in the North during these years. The Dred Scott decision forbidding statutory prohibition of slavery from the territories along with the adoption in Kansas of the Lecompton constitution which would bring Kansas into the Union as a slave state created difficult problems. Although the majority of settlers in Kansas apparently opposed this constitution, many had not voted for the delegates who drew it up or for the final product. The document was therefore technically valid, and the legalist Buchanan attempted to force it through Congress. His effort almost rent the Democracy and helped produce Republican victories in the congressional elections of 1858.[1]

Politics in Pittsburgh, however, did not revolve exclusively around these national issues which supposedly shaped events in these years; instead, complex local problems also determined the actions of both parties. The opposition had to cement the loose alliance of Know-Nothings and Republicans which had supported Union tickets in 1856. To effect complete fusion Republican strategists hoped to stress the crisis in Kansas and other national issues, but between 1856 and 1860 a local issue greatly concerned the voters of Allegheny County and threatened to shatter the fledgling Union coalition. When a popular outrage at railroads erupted, the Democrats attempted to build a new coalition based on this hostility, and the Republicans had to meet the Democratic challenge on the local question. Only by doing so and by wooing the Know-Nothing wing did they manage to remain the majority party.

The campaign of 1856 had failed to fuse the opponents of the Democracy in Pittsburgh and especially in eastern Pennsylvania. Know-Nothings who had allied with the Republicans in 1856 continued to consider themselves a distinctive entity, and Republicans and Democrats alike constantly identified Americans and Republicans as separate elements of the Union

1. For a review of these developments and their impact on the Democratic party, see Nichols, *The Disruption of American Democracy*, pp. 65–268. For the fairest account of the adoption of the Lecompton constitution and of Buchanan's reasons for supporting it, see Philip Shriver Klein, *President James Buchanan: A Biography* (University Park, Pa., 1962), pp. 292–308.

coalition. The two wings of the local party can be identified with the purely Republican *Pittsburgh Daily Gazette,* edited by Russell Errett, and the *Pittsburgh Daily Dispatch*, an old American sheet edited by J. Heron Foster.[2]

To strengthen their ties with the Know-Knothings in 1857 Republicans were willing to make some concessions. Because Americans hated the very name "Republican" and begrudged the Republican influence in the coalition, Republicans again sacrificed their name and ran on a Union ticket in Pennsylvania. Moreover, they adopted some blatantly nativist and anti-Catholic principles. The 1857 Union state platform accepted by the Republicans called for laws to end fraudulent voting practices and warned of the danger of admitting to "fair participation" in the benefits of American institutions "any man who acknowledges a foreign supremacy which he cannot conscientiously and without mental reservations abjure and forever renounce, whether the supremacy be civil or spiritual." [3]

These concessions were relatively minor, however, and the Union leaders initially hoped to preserve the victorious coalition by stressing the slavery extension issue and agitating hostility to the South as the party had done in 1856. While they granted two planks of the state platform to Know-Nothing wishes, seven other resolutions concerned slavery and more particularly the violation of Northern rights by Southern aggression. Echoing the national Republican platform of 1856,

2. See for example the *Post*, Dec. 25, 1856, Mar. 19, 1857, June 3, 9, 1858; the letter of E. D. Gazzam on forming an opposition party in the *Gazette*, Mar. 14, 1857; Russell Errett to Salmon P. Chase, Pittsburgh, Mar. 14, 1857, Chase MSS (LC); and David Wilmot to Samuel Calvin, Apr. 30, 1857, Samuel Calvin MSS (HSP).

3. For the Union state platform, see the *North American and United States Gazette*, Mar. 27, 1857.

they adhered to the principles of the Declaration of Independence and insisted on the "duty of Congress to prohibit from the territories the twin relics of barbarism—polygamy and slavery." Other planks denounced the Dred Scott decision as a step in "the conspiracy against our free institutions" and the violation of "the constitutional rights of the settlers in Kansas." Indeed, the protection of the political rights of the North, not the slavery issue, seemed the Republicans' chief concern.[4]

To implement their vigorously antislavery platform, the Republicans disregarded possible Know-Nothings and former Whigs and gave the Union gubernatorial nomination to David Wilmot, a former Democrat who had joined the Republicans in 1855 and who was renowned primarily for his free-soil proviso of 1846. Wilmot had always belonged to organizations which opposed the Know-Nothings. Although he recognized the difficulties of pleasing both the Republican and American wings of the party in different parts of the state, he seems to have hoped to run solely on the slavery issue, and in a letter to the Union state committee in May he dealt exclusively with the Kansas crisis and his opposition to slavery extension.[5]

This reliance on the slavery extension issue alone soon proved inadequate to unite the opponents of the Democracy. Know-Nothings throughout the state were apparently unenthusiastic about Wilmot, and despite the inclusion of nativist planks in the Union state platform, a separate state American

4. Union state platform of 1857. See also William Dusinberre, *Civil War Issues in Philadelphia*, pp. 12, 36. Hereafter, unless the terms "Union leaders" and "Republican leaders" are clearly distinguished from one another, they are considered synonymous.

5. Wilmot recognized that the Republican and Know-Nothing wings were mutually jealous. Wilmot to Samuel Calvin, Apr. 30, 1857, Calvin MSS; for a copy of Wilmot's letter to the Union state committee, see the *Gazette*, May 5, 1857.

party entered Isaac Hazelhurst into the gubernatorial campaign against Wilmot and his Democratic opponent, William F. Packer. Recognizing that Hazlehurst might divert Know-Nothing votes, Wilmot dropped his single-issue stance and wrote a letter to the American state central committee in which he endorsed the American state platform and criticized the Catholic church. Wilmot's protestations of nativism did not convince the American state committee, and Hazlehurst remained in the race. Nor were some Know-Nothings in Pittsburgh appeased by the maneuver, and James P. Barr, the new editor of the Democratic *Pittsburgh Morning Post*, predicted that the Republicans would get only a small share of the Know-Nothing vote in the city and in Pennsylvania as a whole.[6]

Although Pittsburgh's Republican leaders had to please two factions of the opposition coalition, they were more confident than Barr of their chances of retaining nativist support in the city. Many Know-Nothings there were antislavery men, and Republican leaders evidently thought that gestures alone could soothe the pride of Americans and that they could concentrate on pure Republican tactics. Errett of the *Gazette* explained to Salmon P. Chase, Ohio Republican chief, that while the Republicans "must honor them [Know-Nothings] for a time until they are able to conquer their prejudices," the Union movement could bring "every right-thinking 'American' to our side." Success that autumn "upon the 'Union' basis, of which Freedom will be the leading purpose," would allow Republican leaders "to build up a strong consolidated party, identified with the Republican party, and eventually [it] will be called by that name. A little experience in having that name

6. *Post,* July 27, 30, Aug. 1, 1857.

used will habituate them to it."[7] Accordingly, the two Union county conventions in the spring declared adherence to the national Republican platform of 1856 and the state Union platform of 1857, but as in 1856 they did not pass any blatantly American resolutions of their own. Just as important, where they had purposely run a Know-Nothing for mayor in January 1857, they included only two Know-Nothings on the county ticket of thirteen for the October election.[8]

As the campaign progressed, Union leaders in Pittsburgh, unlike those in the state organization, continued to rely almost solely on the slavery aggression issue and the denial of Northern settlers' rights in Kansas, rather than anti-Catholic appeals, to mold the coalition. Barr asserted that Wilmot's letter adopting the American platform angered the Republican portion of the party in Pittsburgh, and no Republican paper in the city printed it because "the German and Irish Protestants, whom they have, by false pretenses, deceived would leave the party as one man" if they learned of the letter.[9] Apparently Wilmot considered Pittsburgh an area where "a large majority of the Republicans [were] jealous of any full recognition of the distinctive doctrines of the American party," for he confined a speech there in August exclusively to the slavery extension issue. Unlike Republicans in 1856 who had

7. Russell Errett to Salmon P. Chase, Pittsburgh, Mar. 14, 1857, Chase MSS.

8. For reports of the two Union conventions and the Union ticket, see the *Gazette,* Mar. 19, June 25, 1857. I could identify only J. Heron Foster and T. A. Rowley as Know-Nothings on the Union county ticket. Others on that ticket may have been Know-Nothings, but because they were from rural districts, I could not establish their party backgrounds. See the *Post,* Dec. 25, 1856. Both parties usually held two county conventions—one in February or March to elect delegates to the state nominating conventions and one later in the year to choose county tickets.

9. *Post,* July 27, 30, Aug. 1, 1857.

fastidiously denied any sympathy for Negroes, he even ignored the prevalent anti-Negro sentiment, criticized the racism of the Democrats, and said that Negroes were God's children and "have been endowed with sacred rights we cannot disregard with impunity." [10]

The Republicans, however, overestimated the appeal of the Kansas issue and cries of battle between Freedom and Slavery. As late as August Republicans in Pittsburgh complained of a "feeling of universal apathy and indifference. . . . The campaign last fall seems to have absorbed all the energy and vitality that we ever possessed." Reliance on anti-Southern sentiment could not draw out a big vote.[11]

Just when the Republicans were worrying about their failure to stir up the electorate, the entire nature of the campaign changed. In late August, in order to remedy problems of their own, the Pittsburgh Democrats championed a local grievance at their county convention. After 1856 the Democracy in Pittsburgh seemed destined to constant defeat. Unable to win elective office, local Democrats bitterly fought for the patronage plums in the hands of the newly elected Buchanan, and this scramble exacerbated factionalism in the party. Factions seemed to crystallize around the two major Democratic papers, the *Post* and the *Daily Union*, which vied for printing

10. *Gazette*, Aug. 29, 1857; Wilmot to Calvin, Apr. 30, 1857, Calvin MSS. For a discussion of anti-Negro sentiment in the North, particularly Philadelphia, and of the necessity of all parties in Pennsylvania not to antagonize that feeling, see Dusinberre, p. 13 and passim. See also Voegeli, *Free but Not Equal*, passim.

11. John M. Kirkpatrick to Simon Cameron, Pittsburgh, Aug. 24, 1857, Cameron MSS; R. P. McDowell to Lemuel Todd, Pittsburgh, Aug. 14, 1857, Edward McPherson MSS. Todd was the chairman of the Union state committee in 1857.

contracts. Correspondents of the national party leaders constantly spoke of arranging appointments to appease both factions, and in early 1858 the editor of the *Post* wrote Senator William Bigler, "I believe you can settle the matter by giving to one side the Custom House and to us for the first time the Post Office—and satisfy both wings." [12]

More damaging to the Pittsburgh Democracy than factionalism was the yoke of the pro-Southern policies followed by the national Democratic administration. What one Democrat called "the pervading and rampant spirit of abolitionism which overrides everything else in this county" seemed to doom the Democrats.[13] In 1857, therefore, both the state and local organizations had tried to shy away from the Kansas and slavery issue as much as possible. While the two state platforms had approved the policy of the national administration and pledged faith to old Democratic principles, neither specifically mentioned the Kansas crisis nor completely endorsed the Dred Scott decision. The second platform, however, did appeal to the anti-Negro sentiment in the state by approving that part of the decision "in regard to the political rights of the negro race"—i.e. the assertion that a Negro could not be a citizen of the United States. The platforms also concentrated on state issues and attacked the record of the previous Republican legislature for increasing the number of banks in

12. James P. Barr to William Bigler, Pittsburgh, Jan. 13, 1858, Bigler MSS. See also Edward Campbell to Jeremiah S. Black, Pittsburgh, Mar. 9, 1857, and Thomas J. Keenan to Black, Pittsburgh, Mar. 12, 28, 1857, Black MSS; John Hastings to William Bigler, Pittsburgh, Jan. 3, 1858, Bigler MSS.

13. William H. Smith to J. S. Black, Pittsburgh, Dec. 24, 1857, Black MSS; for other complaints about the strength of abolitionist sentiment, see R. P. Fleniken to James Buchanan, Pittsburgh, Nov. 12, 1856, Buchanan MSS (HSP).

the state and authorizing the sale of the Main Line Canal to the Pennsylvania Railroad.[14]

In Pittsburgh the Democracy tried to avoid the slavery issue by diverting attention to local grievances. While two resolutions of the August Democratic convention lauded the state ticket and "approve[d] most emphatically" the course of Buchanan's administration, the remainder of that platform mentioned no national issues and did not even confirm the traditional Democratic hostility to secret proscriptive groups. Indeed, the Democrats placed three Know-Nothings on their county ticket, one more than the Republicans had. The inclusion of Know-Nothings was part of an effort to form a new Democratic coalition on a local question, and the remaining ten resolutions of the convention concerned exclusively the issue of taxation for railroads and echoed a virulent anger against railroads widespread among the local populace.[15]

Railroads had greatly disappointed the expectations of the citizens of Pittsburgh, particularly the merchants and manufacturers who had eagerly backed public subscription to the lines in order to improve the city's competitive position.[16] Many blamed the railroads for allowing farmers to raise food prices in the city.[17] Editors asserted that agents of the Penn-

14. There were two sets of Democratic resolutions in the state—one at the convention to nominate a gubernatorial candidate and the other at the convention to nominate candidates for the state supreme court. The first which did little other than laud Democratic candidates and denounce the American Union party can be found in the *North American and United States Gazette*, Mar. 4, 1857. The second platform which dealt with important state issues can be found in the *Post*, June 11, 1857.

15. *Post*, Aug. 27, 1857; *Gazette*, Aug. 28, 1857.

16. For a discussion of the expectations and initial investment in railroads, see Chap. 1.

17. William Wilkins to James Buchanan, Pittsburgh, Jan. 1, 1854, Buchanan MSS (HSP). The *Post* on June 30, 1857, estimated that food prices had

sylvania Railroad, since its completion to Pittsburgh in 1852, had competed with the city's forwarding and commission merchants by making forwarding arrangements from western cities to Pittsburgh or from Pittsburgh to Philadelphia without charge in order to win freight for the railroad away from the other trunk-line railroads or from the Pennsylvania Canal. The linking of the Ohio and Pennsylvania Railroad from the west with the Pennsylvania in Pittsburgh in 1857 destroyed the city's function as a transshipment center and thus displaced the many merchants there.[18] The trunk lines took goods directly through the city to points beyond and thus ruined the business of those merchants and draymen who transferred goods between riverboats and the railroads or between one railroad in Allegheny City and the other in Pittsburgh.

Editors charged that the completed railroads also helped the competitors of Pittsburgh businessmen in both the East and the burgeoning West rather than improving the city's competitive position. The Ohio and Pennsylvania, which monopolized shipments west, and the Pennsylvania, the only through line to the east, charged different rates for long hauls and short hauls and thus discriminated against Pittsburgh. For example, goods could be shipped more cheaply between Chicago or Cincinnati and New York than between Pittsburgh and Philadelphia over the Pennsylvania. Even J. Edgar

---

doubled since the arrival of railroads into the city. For the impact of railroads on the prices received by midwestern farmers, see U.S., Bureau of the Census, "Influence of Railroads on Agriculture," *Eighth Census of the United States: 1860. Agriculture*, quoted in Alfred D. Chandler, Jr., ed., *The Railroads: The Nation's First Big Business* (New York, 1965), pp. 25–30. It is also possible that the increased demand for American grain in Europe drove food prices up. See Nevins, *Ordeal of the Union*, 2, 192.

18. *Gazette*, Feb. 25, Mar. 1, 26, 1853, Mar. 31, 1858; Louis C. Hunter, "Financial Problems of the Early Pittsburgh Iron Manufacturers," *Journal of Economic and Business History*, 2 (Nov. 1929–Aug. 1930), 526–27.

Thomson, president of the Pennsylvania, admitted the rates were discriminatory.[19] Because of the lower transportation costs, western merchants bought manufactured products in New York and Philadelphia which they had formerly purchased in Pittsburgh. Competition from the East even increased in Pittsburgh itself.[20] As one editor summarized in 1858, the railroads had already ruined the commission business in Pittsburgh, were destroying the produce and jobbing business, and were crippling manufacturers and robbing them of their western markets.[21]

Particularly the policies of the Pennsylvania Railroad aroused bitter resentment in Pittsburgh. The Board of Trade lodged protests against the discriminatory rates, and in 1860 it urged the passage of a bill introduced into the state senate by E. H. Irish of Pittsburgh which would require equal rates. Moreover, the immense power of the corporation and its influence in the legislature caused the people to vilify it in rhetoric borrowed from the Jacksonian Democrats. With a capitalization of $20,000,000, the Pennsylvania Railroad was one of the largest corporations ever to exist in the United

19. For evidence on rate discrimination, see the *Gazette*, Mar. 9, June 27, 1857, Mar. 31, Apr. 7, 1858, and Feb. 21, Apr. 8, 1859; *Post*, Mar. 31, Apr. 3, 1858; *Dispatch*, Apr. 12, 1858, May 5, 1859.

20. One indication of additional competition from the East within Pittsburgh was a great increase in the advertising by New York and Philadelphia firms in Pittsburgh newspapers after the completion of the Pennsylvania to that city. The number of New York advertisements leaped from three or four a day in 1850 to eighteen in 1852. For example, compare the New York advertising columns in the *Gazette* for June 28, July 1, Aug. 1, and Sept. 2, 1850, with those in the same paper for July 1, Sept. 2, and Oct. 22, 1852. By 1855 an average of fourteen firms advertised in Pittsburgh newspapers. In January 1850, the *Journal* carried only 31½ column inches of New York advertising. By January 1855 that figure increased to 214 inches.

21. *Gazette*, Mar. 5, 1858.

States. In a cry that clearly presaged the response to trusts at the end of the century, the *Gazette* complained that such a large corporation, competing with individuals, could crush out the business of Pittsburgh and that "no company should be allowed to possess or exercise such powers. Unlike an individual, it should not be allowed to do as it pleases, because when it pleases to do an injury its power to do so is unlimited." The sale of the Main Line Canal System to the Pennsylvania in 1857 provoked further outcries, for while most people in the city favored its sale into private hands, they wanted the canal kept open and feared its purchase by a railroad company whose interest would be to close it down. When the arrangement with the Pennsylvania was announced, the Allegheny County commissioners at first tried to get an injunction forbidding the sale. Errett complained that by the sale the state fostered an "overshadowing power," a "mammoth corporation, by the side of which the United States Bank was a pigmy," because the railroad then monopolized all routes of transportation east from Pittsburgh.[22]

If the roads which were in operation by 1857 harmed and enraged businessmen, the virtual collapse that year of certain unfinished roads unleashed a widespread popular anger. Four of the roads to which the municipality and the county had subscribed bonds—the Allegheny Valley, Chartiers Valley, Pittsburgh and Steubenville, and Pittsburgh and Connellsville—were not operating successfully by 1857 for one reason or

22. *Gazette*, June 27, 1857, Mar. 4, 5, 31, 1858, Feb. 21, 22, 1860; *Post*, Mar. 31, 1858; *Dispatch*, June 20, 1857. For estimates of popular opinion on the sale of the Main Line, see the reports of the public meetings protesting its proposed sale to the Sunbury and Erie Railroad in the *Gazette*, Apr. 27, May 4, 1857. For a discussion of the sectional background of the opposition to the sale of the Main Line, see Hartz, *Economic Policy and Democratic Thought*, pp. 53, 176.

another. For example, the Pittsburgh and Steubenville, which was to run to Wheeling, Virginia and then across the Ohio River to Steubenville, began construction before it secured a right-of-way from Virginia; when it failed to secure this right-of-way, the road could not be completed and languished in debt. The companies had failed to pay any dividends after 1855, and by 1857 the interest due on the county and city bonds subscribed to them was mounting. To pay this interest, in May 1857 the county commissioners, two of whom were Republicans, raised the county tax on real and personal property from four to eight mills per dollar of assessed value.[23]

This tax increase was the last straw. Apparently very few citizens in the county owned any of the bonds, for the railroad companies either kept them, paid them to construction companies, or sold them through New York banking firms to large businesses or foreign investors.[24] With nothing to gain from the payment of interest on the bonds, many people opposed a tax which would benefit only large corporations at the expense of individual taxpayers. Soon after the commissioners raised the tax, both Democrats and Republicans assembled in a mass public protest meeting. While it avoided an expression of outright repudiation, many there supposedly fa-

23. Thompson, "A Financial History of Pittsburgh," p. 96; *Gazette*, May 23, 1857, Aug. 24, 1858. For the amount of the subscriptions to the roads by the city and county, see Harper, *Pittsburgh: Forge of the Universe*, p. 130. For conciseness, in the rest of this chapter I shall use the contemporary terms "railroad bonds" to mean the county and municipal bonds given to railroads, not the company bonds issued by those roads, and "railroad tax" to indicate the tax to pay the interest on those county and municipal bonds subscribed to railroads, not a tax on the property of the railroads.

24. In 1857 a correspondent wrote Jeremiah S. Black, "I am not a bondholder, and do not know a man who holds one." William H. Smith to Black, Pittsburgh, Oct. 26, 1857, Black MSS. See also Thompson, p. 99; and the reports of the antirailroad meetings in the *Gazette*, June 11, 24, 1857.

vored such a move. The convention resolved not to pay the interest on the bonds to those who held them as a result of fraud—i.e. who had received them without paying the full price. Moreover, it appointed a bipartisan committee to investigate the records of the railroad companies and look for fraud in their disposal of the bonds. The committee was to determine to whom and at what price the bonds had been sold and was especially to look for sales at a price too far below face value or for an exchange of bonds for iron rails from construction companies. Reflecting the prevalent hostility to railroads in general, another resolution demanded that the county commissioners fire all attorneys employed by the county who had ever worked for the railroads.[25]

The report of the investigating committee appointed by the antitax convention assailed the negligence of both the railroads and the county commissioners, demanded that the city and county sever all relations with the railroads by forbidding any commissioner or councilman to act as a railroad director, and recommended that the city and county exchange the railroad stock they held for the municipal and county bonds held by the railroads and by others. The committee also urged that voters who opposed paying off the interest support no man for county commissioner or city councils who favored paying the bonds and suggested that county commissioners be held accountable for tax receipts and expenditures.[26]

It was this hostility to railroads, both finished and unfinished, on which the Democrats in Pittsburgh concentrated to elect local candidates in the fall campaign of 1857. Although many among both parties complained about the tax and several Republicans led the protest, the Democrats tried to make the

25. *Gazette*, May 23, June 11, 1857; *Dispatch*, June 11, 1857.
26. *Gazette* and *Post*, June 24, 1857.

tax a party issue. The *Post* noted that two of the three county commissioners who raised the tax in May were Republicans and charged that Republicans were responsible for the original subscriptions because the Whigs had controlled the county commissioners and city councils which made them.[27] Before the Democratic county convention in August a Democrat complained to Jeremiah S. Black, Buchanan's Attorney-General and an influential leader of the Pennsylvania Democracy,[28]

> Thomas Williams and the Repudiating leaders of the Republicans seem to have the Democrats of this county in their hands and are moulding them like clay in the hands of a potter. . . . That a Repudiation ticket will be taken up by our convention, and that it will be elected, I have no doubt.

The writer's fears were confirmed when antitax delegates pushed a repudiation platform through the Democratic convention despite the protests of one-third of the delegates, many of whom were old, conservative Democratic leaders. The Democrats vowed their "hostility to the imposition of taxes for railroad purposes, and [their] unqualified determination to resist, by all constitutional and legal means, the payment of any tax imposed upon us illegally, either by State or county." Another resolution called on the county commissioners "not to assess any tax for railroad purposes until compelled to pay by legal process." Denouncing free railroad passes to "Judges, Legislators, Preachers, [and] Editors," the Democrats ar-

27. *Post*, June 22, 1857. Barr neglected to recollect, however, that municipal and county subscriptions were made only after popular pressure on officials.

28. William H. Smith to Jeremiah S. Black, Pittsburgh, Aug. 24, 1857, Black MSS.

ranged for a committee to interrogate their candidates and require them to pledge to carry out the resolutions of the convention.[29]

The Democrats seemed much more opposed to paying the bonds than did the Republicans. The address of the Democratic county committee asked for support because the party would resist taxation, and a Democrat confided after the election, "The democratic ticket in Allegheny county were out square for Repudiation [while] the Republicans took the opposite course." When the investigating committee of the county antitax convention asked the candidates if they would oppose any tax to pay off the interest on bonds subscribed to the railroads, the Republicans said they would support taxes to pay the legal liabilities of the county; but the Democrats supported repudiation, that is, resistance to taxation even if the debts were ruled legal. In this stress on repudiation, the Allegheny County Democracy differed greatly from the party in the rest of the state, which disavowed any such designs.[30]

The Democratic emphasis on the railroad issue greatly distressed the Pittsburgh Republicans, who had hoped to maintain their victorious coalition on the basis of the anti-Southern stance alone. D. L. Eaton, a member of the Union state committee and another editor of the *Gazette*, wrote three weeks before the election to another committee member, "In Allegheny County we have an ugly battle on our hands; this taxation business is bad. We will be able, however, I think, to draw the party lines on 'em and will succeed without doubt."

29. *Post*, Aug. 27, 1857.
30. *Gazette*, Sept. 8, 1857; *Post*, Aug. 27, Sept. 2, 1857; *Dispatch*, Aug. 27, Sept. 24, 25, 1857; William H. Smith to Jeremiah S. Black, Pittsburgh, Oct. 26, 1857, Black MSS; D. L. Eaton to Edward McPherson, Pittsburgh, Sept. 21, 1857, McPherson MSS.

Party loyalty, however, did not suffice, and the Union leaders had to answer the Democratic challenge. Charging the Democrats with repudiation and dishonor, Republican papers asserted that the Democrats "forced these railroad subscriptions upon us" because they had controlled the state legislature which authorized them. Moreover, Foster of the *Dispatch* insisted that although Democrats asked for votes because of their antitax position, if elected they could and would do no more to protect the people from taxation than the Republicans. Because Democrats were only utilizing the tax issue to secure office, the people should remember that national issues, particularly the clash between Freedom and Slavery, were the major ones at stake in the election.[31]

The Republicans, however, notably failed to draw out the normal opposition vote on these national issues in the October poll. Packer swamped Wilmot in the state, and in Pittsburgh the antislavery leader received fewer votes than even the Republican mayoral candidate the previous January. Wilmot amassed the smallest total vote for an anti-Democratic gubernatorial candidate since 1847.[32] Although the entire vote was small, probably because the campaign for governor did not directly concern the railroad issue, the local grievance prevented the Republicans from reforming the natural opposition majority, just as economic grievances had hurt the Whigs in the early 1850s.

Several contemporaries and later historians have attributed the small vote to the panic which broke out in September before the election. Russell Errett explained that many business-

31. D. L. Eaton to Edward McPherson, Sept. 21, 1857, McPherson MSS; *Gazette*, Sept. 8, 9, 17, 23, 24, 1857; *Dispatch*, Sept. 17, 1857.

32. See Table 48. It was extremely unusual to have a larger vote in a municipal election than in a gubernatorial election.

men neglected to vote because of their concrn with monetary difficulties. Historians have pointed to Wilmot's free-trade record and suggested that after the outbreak of the panic this record alienated protectionist Whigs among the Republicans and caused his defeat.[33] The Whig support for the Union ticket in Pittsburgh did drop in 1857 from that of 1856, but these Whigs who did not support Wilmot merely abstained, rather than joining the Democrats as some Whigs had done in 1856.[34] Moreover, these former Whigs were not necessarily businessmen or protectionists. For one thing, the panic hit Pittsburgh very slowly; and at the end of October, after the election, while the panic was "bad," there had as yet been no business failures because of the monetary crisis. Neither party mentioned the tariff in its state platform, and it was probably not a major issue in the campaign. Further, Democratic newspapers did not attack Wilmot as a free-trader until the beginning of October, two weeks before the election. Finally, while businessmen may not have voted in 1857, they probably had not voted solidly Republican in 1856 either; and they constituted such a small proportion of the voters that their abstention, even if new, would explain only a fraction of the decrease in the vote.[35]

33. *Gazette*, Oct. 14, 1857; Eiselen, *The Rise of Pennsylvania Protectionism*, pp. 239, 241.

34. The correlation between the Whig vote for governor in 1854 and the Republican vote for President in 1856 was +.57. The correlation between that Whig vote and the Republican vote for Wilmot in 1857 was +.35. Although the vote for governor in 1854 represented a coalition of Whigs and Know-Nothings, there is a clear relationship between it and the Whig vote, for the correlation between it and the Whig vote for governor in 1851 was +.82.

35. William H. Smith to Jeremiah S. Black, Pittsburgh, Oct. 26, 1857, Black MSS; *Gazette*, Oct. 1, 1857; *Post*, Oct. 2, 1857; see Table 49 and compare the correlations with businessmen and wealthy groups in 1856 and 1857.

Not the monetary crisis, but the Republican failure to combine effectively the Know-Nothing with the other elements of the coalition and to meet the Democratic challenge on the railroad issue caused the small vote. The coalition with Americans on the state level had failed, Wilmot's political background was unpopular, and Know-Nothing representation on the Union county ticket was sparse especially when compared to that on the Democratic ticket. Many who refused to support Wilmot in 1857 were Know-Nothings who had voted for Frémont in 1856 and for Henry Weaver, the Republican candidate for mayor in 1857 and a Know-Nothing. Particularly the poorer elements seemed disenchanted with a Union campaign which failed to stress American principles and ran a former Democrat.[36] It is also possible that Wilmot's open sympathy for Negroes alienated these working-class voters, who hated that race.

The Democratic identification with repudiation also helped cut the Republican majority. Not only was Wilmot's vote smaller than the normal opposition total, but two Democrats on the local ticket won—a candidate for the state assembly and, more important, Major John McIlhenny, the candidate for county commissioner and an avowed opponent of railroad taxation. The people of the county expressed their disillusion-

36. The correlation between the Know-Nothing vote for canal commissioner in 1855 and the Republican vote for President in 1856 had been +.81 and between that vote and the Republican vote for mayor in January 1857, +.77. In contrast the correlation between that Know-Nothing vote and the vote for Wilmot in 1857 was only +.52, and between that vote and the Republican vote for county commissioner in 1857, +.54. It should be noted that there was no large defection of Know-Nothings to the separate American party in 1857, for the vote for Hazlehurst in Pittsburgh was small. See also Tables 48 and 49 and note the drop in support given by the group owning less than $100, native Americans, and Protestants between 1856 and 1857.

ment with railroads at the election by voting overwhelmingly for a constitutional amendment which forbade governmental subscription to railroad corporations. After the election the *Dispatch* explained that "large numbers" voted Democratic to escape railroad taxation and "in effect, to repudiate the debt contracted for railroad purposes. This question has more or less affected the vote, not only for county, but for state officers." [37] The popular concern with a local economic grievance as well as the Republican nonchalance about keeping the nativist vote broke the solidarity of the native Protestant support for the opposition which had been a political fact of life in Pittsburgh since the 1840's. In 1858 the Republicans would try to correct these errors.

With the installation of the Democrat McIlhenny as a county commissioner immediately after the election, the Democrats held two of the three commission offices. Following their campaign promises, they immediately rescinded the additional four-mill tax to pay interest on railroad bonds and pledged to pay nothing in the future. Foster lamented that "the election of McIlhenny was indeed a popular mandate for the County Commissioners to refuse to pay the interest on 'railroad bonds.' " [38]

Although the Democrats elected two candidates in 1857, they faced particularly severe problems in 1858. The worsening depression after the financial panic in 1857 provoked cries

37. Hartz, p. 125. The vote was 5,560 to 431 for the amendment. See also the *Dispatch*, Oct. 14, 1857.

38. William H. Smith to Jeremiah S. Black, Pittsburgh, Oct. 26, 1857, Black MSS; *Dispatch*, Oct. 28, 1857.

for tariff protection; and the adoption of the proslavery Lecompton constitution in Kansas and Buchanan's attempt to force Congress to accept it almost wrecked the Democracy. Some dissident Democrats in Pennsylvania, such as the Philadelphia editor John W. Forney, followed the lead of Senator Stephen A. Douglas in opposing the Buchanan administration on this issue. Moreover, the ratification of that constitution gave a great advantage to the traditionally free-soil opposition party.

The Lecompton constitution particularly threatened to splinter and destroy the Democratic party in Pittsburgh where people were extremely sensitive about the spread of slavery. David Lynch, Buchanan's lieutenant, estimated that "forty-nine of every fifty Democrats in this region are in favor of Kansas joining the Union as a free state," and the vast majority of Democrats apparently disliked Buchanan's Lecompton policy and leaned toward the Douglas position.[39] Party leaders struggled to suppress this hostility to administration policy. Officeholders and friends of Buchanan and Bigler stifled any anti-Lecompton resolutions in a special Democratic convention in January, and they passed resolutions supporting the administration although not specifically endorsing the constitution. In early March, administration workers pushed pro-Lecompton resolutions through the Democratic county convention by packing the resolutions committee with their friends.[40] While the *Daily Union* immediately supported Bu-

39. David Lynch to James Buchanan, Pitt Township, Jan. 9, 1858, copy, David Lynch MSS (LC); William H. Smith to William Bigler, Pittsburgh, Dec. 21, 1857, and T. J. Keenan to Bigler, Pittsburgh, Jan. 6, 1858, Bigler MSS; William H. Smith to Jeremiah S. Black, Pittsburgh, Dec. 24, 1857, and Feb. 26, 1858, Black MSS.

40. David Lynch to William Bigler, Pittsburgh, Dec. 26, 1857, and John Hastings to Bigler, Pittsburgh, Jan. 3, 1858, Bigler MSS; Lynch to James

chanan's policy, the *Post* opposed it at first and only supported it later in an attempt to secure government printing.[41] Despite the conversion of the *Post*, most of the other papers in the city denounced the constitution, and one Democrat summarized:[42]

> Many who vote with the Democrats from habit, from education, and even from strong convictions, are not uninfluenced by the great preponderance of free-soil feeling —and while they are not going to leave the party, the incessant clamor of the anti-Lecomptonites, increased and fomented as it is by the neutral press . . . would influence them in a forced issue, to take sides against Lecompton.

When the state Democratic convention "unhesitatingly approve[d]" Buchanan's Kansas policy and said that even if the majority of free-state settlers in Kansas opposed the constitution, "their own obstinate conduct produced the result, they have no cause to complain, and their mouths should be forever closed," anti-Lecompton Democrats in Pittsburgh openly rebelled. Soon after the state convention an "immense gathering" of anti-Lecompton Democrats there denounced both the state platform and the Lecompton constitution. One delegate summed up the feelings of the meeting when he

Buchanan, Jan. 9, 1858, Lynch MSS; see also the reports of the conventions in the *Post*, Jan. 7, 1858; the *Gazette*, Jan. 8, 1858; and the *Dispatch*, Mar. 8, 1858.

41. On the *Daily Union*, see the *Dispatch*, Dec. 2, 1857. On the change in the *Post*, see it for Dec. 1, 1857, and Feb. 5, 1858. For Barr's attempts to get patronage, see James P. Barr to William Bigler, Pittsburgh, Jan. 13, 1858, and William H. Smith to Bigler, Pittsburgh, March 8, 1858, Bigler MSS; *Post*, June 12, 1858.

42. William H. Smith to Jeremiah S. Black, Pittsburgh, Feb. 26, 1858, Black MSS.

asserted that the state platform was "not a platform, but a scaffold that will hang any man who dares go on it."[43]

Not only did the Lecompton measure threaten to splinter the Democracy, but by reviving concern over the Kansas crisis, it improved Republican chances for bringing out the natural opposition majority. Republicans sought to enhance these chances by carefully wooing the various groups which disliked the Buchanan administration and by combining them in a supposedly new party under a new name—the People's Party.

To attract antislavery Republicans, the leaders stressed the Lecompton issue. Even in the mayoral campaign of 1858, the *Gazette* insisted that voters must express their opposition to Buchanan's policy. After the Democratic state platform endorsed the Lecompton constitution, that paper proclaimed that the "naked question" of slavery extension was the only clear issue between the parties in Pennsylvania for the first time. To bring the issue home to Pittsburgh workingmen Errett argued that opposition to slavery expansion reflected not only commiseration for the oppressed Negro, but also concern for the laboring men of the North "whose greatest enemies now are Southern statesmen who sneer at them as mudsills and 'white slaves.' "[44]

To court anti-Lecompton Democrats, the People's Party on both the state and local levels moderated the antislavery position of their official pronouncements. Confident of the antislavery vote, the People's Party emphasized the rights of Northerners and the perversion of popular sovereignty rather than the sin of slavery. They discarded the Union and Republican charges that slavery was a relic of barbarism and

43. *Post*, Mar. 8, 25, 1858.
44. *Gazette*, Jan. 4, 7, Mar. 10, June 25, 1858.

merely assailed the attempt to force the constitution on the settlers of Kansas against their will as a violation of "the rights of the people." To make the party more palatable to dissident Democrats, the People's state convention chose Andrew Reeder, former governor of Kansas and a Democrat, as chairman and nominated for the state supreme court John M. Read, also an anti-Lecompton Democrat.[45]

Part of the reason for watering down the antislavery position was probably to attract conservative former Whigs. To bring into the party the protectionists among these men and to woo all those suffering from the depression which followed the panic of 1857, the People's Party also attributed the depression to Democratic policies and took up the cry for a protective tariff so noticeably absent from the Republican campaigns in 1856 and 1857.[46]

Another reason for the tariff plank, however, was to help cement the alliance between Know-Nothings and Republicans and avoid the disastrous division of forces which occurred in 1857. By dropping the 1857 calls for exclusion of foreigners and Catholics from political rights, the People's Party hoped to pacify the anti-Know-Nothing elements in the party, but at the same time, the leaders took steps to secure the Know-Nothing vote by demanding protection for American labor, pure ballot boxes, and prohibition of the admission of foreign criminals into the country.[47] In Pittsburgh the Republican campaign for mayor in 1858 was openly anti-Catholic, and

45. *Gazette*, June 3, July 17, 1858; Dusinberre, *Civil War Issues in Philadelphia*, pp. 78–79; *Post*, July 16, 1858.

46. *Gazette*, June 3, July 17, 1858.

47. Ibid., July 17, 1858. William Dusinberre, p. 78, argues brilliantly that the wording of the tariff plank with its call for protection of American labor was a device to channel nativist hostility to foreigners into more politically acceptable forms.

the incumbent candidate Weaver was a former Know-Nothing.[48] For the fall campaign of 1858 the Pittsburgh People's organization gave the Know-Nothings what they wanted even more than planks in the platform—offices. The local ticket was headed by James K. Moorhead, a former Know-Nothing and Democrat, for Congress; and the party nominated Know-Nothings for the other offices which paid the most. So many former Know-Nothings and Democrats were on the People's ticket and onetime Know-Nothings so completely dominated the Republican county convention that the *Post* labeled it a Know-Nothing convention and questioned how old Whigs and Antimasons could tolerate such an unfair distribution of offices.[49]

Faced with the resurrection of the Republican and Know-Nothing coalition of 1856 and with the hostility within their own ranks to the Democratic state platform, local Democratic leaders tried again to capitalize on the palpably strong hostility to railroads and taxation, and to neutralize the equally strong antipathy to the Lecompton policy. James A. Gibson, chairman of the antitax Democratic county convention in 1857 and of the Democratic county committee of correspondence in 1858, directed maneuvers to elect part of the local ticket and perhaps even a congressman.[50]

48. The Republicans actively sought the anti-Catholic vote in January 1858. The *Gazette* printed lists of all Democratic ward candidates for aldermen, city councils, school directors, etc., and put the names of Catholics in italics, specifically to show the Catholic influence in the Democratic party. In six wards, 25 of 60 Democratic candidates were Catholic. *Gazette*, Jan. 1, 1858.

49. *Post*, June 3, July 9, 15, 1858; *Gazette*, June 4, 5, 1858. Probably to appease the nativists the *Gazette* (June 8, 1858) made a point of defending the old family backgrounds of the nominees and emphasized that the German on the Republican county ticket had lived most of his life in Pittsburgh.

50. *Post*, Aug. 28, 1858; see also the analysis of the election ibid., Oct. 18, 1858. For other evidence that the Democrats expected to elect part of the

Beginning in May, Gibson moved to combine all the elements in the county hostile to railroads. He particularly sought the aid of Republicans such as Thomas Williams, a lawyer and the foremost leader of the antitax protesters in the county, and William Robinson, Jr., the former president of the Ohio and Pennsylvania Railroad and a vehement foe of railroad taxation. When both of these men failed in their attempts to win congressional nominations in the Republican county convention in June, they set up their own newspaper, the *True Press*, in conjunction with antitax Democrats Rody Patterson, the county sheriff, and his deputy Edward Campbell, a onetime Whig. The *True Press* immediately launched a smear campaign against the Republicans as a prorailroad party. Williams also attempted to start his own independent antitax People's Party, and he flirted with old Know-Nothings to get them to join his party rather than the Republicans.[51] Gibson hoped to win the support of the *True Press* group and others by imposing an antitax ticket and platform on the Democratic party.

Editors charged that by following Gibson's orders, the antitax faction completely dominated the Democratic county convention in August. Delegates to the meeting who were described as "crazy on the subject of repudiation"[52] were new men and ward politicians under the thumb of Gibson rather than the old leaders of the party who traditionally attended

---

local ticket, see R. Biddle Roberts to James Buchanan, Pittsburgh, Aug. 21, 1858, Buchanan MSS (HSP); William H. Smith to William Bigler, Pittsburgh, Sept. 9, 1858, Bigler MSS.

51. *Post*, Oct. 18, 1858; *Gazette*, June 3, 1858; *Dispatch*, Aug. 9, 26, 1858. On Edward Campbell's background, see the *Gazette*, June 30, 1859.

52. R. Biddle Roberts to James Buchanan, Pittsburgh, Aug. 21, 1858, Buchanan MSS (HSP).

conventions. Some were recent converts and disappointed office seekers from the Republican ranks. Gibson opened the
meeting and had it appoint as chairman David D. Bruce,
onetime Whig, a Republican in 1855, and his crony on the
Democratic county committee. Bruce urged all the opponents
of taxation, regardless of former party affiliation, to join the
Democratic antitax crusade. He chose as one of the secretaries
of the convention R. C. G. Sproul, Thomas Williams' law
partner. To help cement the coalition with the *True Press*
clique, these leaders rammed through the convention the
nomination of Barnes Ford for county sheriff. Ford's only
qualification for that office was that he was the brother-in-law
of the Democratic incumbent Patterson, who along with
Campbell hoped to continue their influence through Ford.

Gibson headed the committee on resolutions which wrote
a platform that solely concerned railroads. Not only did the
convention fail to mention Lecompton or even endorse the
state and national Democratic platforms, but it also stated
that taxation was "the only question which should at the
present engage our attention" and "in order to free discussion
from other issues which might embarrass it, we are willing,
for the present, to forego the consideration of National and
State policy." The other resolutions contained the most savage
attack on railroads and elected officials thus far passed at any
convention, and the Democrats vowed not to support any man
who would consent to levy taxes for railroad purposes or who
even considered them legal or constitutional. When William
Wilkins, an old and renowned Democratic leader who had
once been Secretary of War and a United States Senator and
had been a state senator in the previous session of the legislature, attempted to introduce resolutions endorsing the Bu-

chanan administration, chairman Bruce, the former Whig, continually ruled him out of order and then pushed through a motion, introduced by Gibson, to adjourn.[53]

Successfully controlling the Democratic county organization, the antitax Democrats next moved to place Williams or another well-known leader on their ticket. Both Republicans and Democrats commented that Gibson expected Andrew Burke, the Democratic congressional candidate in the Pittsburgh district, to decline, and that congressional nomination would then be given to the *True Press* clique in return for their support of the rest of the Democratic ticket.[54] When Burke did not withdraw, the Democratic managers decided to give Williams the nomination in the other congressional district, the twenty-second, which included Allegheny City, the northern portion of the county, and Butler County. This plan was complicated by the Democratic practice of alternating the candidates between counties, for it was Butler County's turn. A week after the Allegheny County Democratic convention, Deputy Sheriff Campbell and John B. Kennedy, editor of the *True Press*, dominated a supposedly nonpartisan antitax convention in Pittsburgh which was to choose a separate antitax ticket. Most of the delegates to this third-party convention were actually Democrats carefully chosen by Campbell. R. C. G. Sproul, Sheriff Patterson, and his subordinate J. H. Phillips, the county jailer, helped organize the delegates. After hearing an address by Williams, they nomi-

53. See reports of the convention and editorial comment in the *Gazette*, Aug. 19, 20, 1858; *Post*, Aug. 19, 1858.

54. *Gazette*, Aug. 19, 1858; *Post*, Aug. 28, 1858; R. Biddle Roberts to James Buchanan, Aug. 21, 1858, Buchanan MSS (HSP).

nated him as the Anti-Tax candidate for Congress in the twenty-second district and endorsed the complete Democratic ticket for county offices and Congress in the twenty-first district. To complete the bargain, Gibson, with the aid of his adviser William Robinson, the Republican antitaxer, then foisted Williams on the Butler County Democrats at the mixed session with them. Thus, although Williams did not run for Congress in the Pittsburgh district, he was on the Democratic ticket, and his name was associated with Democrats as well as Anti-Taxers. Then the Allegheny County Democratic Committee with Bruce and Gibson at its helm channeled Democratic campaign funds to the *True Press,* and it, rather than the hostile *Post* and *Daily Union,* became the Democratic campaign paper.[55] Fusion was complete.

The Democrats then concentrated on identifying the Republicans as the prorailroad party. Williams and the *True Press* constantly ranted against railroads and Republicans and blamed the public subscriptions to the roads on that party. Two resolutions of the Democratic county convention had specifically named James K. Moorhead and Robert McKnight, the Republican congressional candidates, as undeserving of popular support because they were railroad men. Indeed, Moorhead was president of the Pittsburgh and Steubenville, while McKnight was a director of that road and a lawyer for others.[56]

These tactics outraged Democrats loyal to old party princi-

55. See reports of the *True Press* convention in the *Gazette, Post,* and *Dispatch,* Aug. 26, 1858; *Post,* Sept. 25, Oct. 18, 1858.

56. See Williams' speech at the *True Press* convention, *Gazette,* Aug. 26, 1858; for a report of the Democratic resolutions, see the *Post,* Aug. 19, 1858; for evidence on McKnight, see the *Gazette,* Aug. 24, 1858.

ples and to the national organization. The prominent leaders of the party such as Wilkins and Charles Shaler, who had been spurned by the antitax men who took it over, formally protested "the slanderous and abusive tirade contained in the resolutions" of the county convention, the failure even to recognize the national and state administrations and to adopt Democratic principles, and the tyranny of the antitax clique which dominated the convention. Many of these former leaders were businessmen who did not want to be associated with the dishonor of repudiation. They called a "National Democratic" convention which accepted most of the ticket of the former convention but nominated another Democrat to replace Williams. It also denounced the earlier meeting's desertion of "sound Democratic principles" in order to win office, called for a protective tariff, endorsed President Buchanan and Governor Packer, although it too assiduously avoided mention of the Kansas policy, and insisted "that men who fear to express their belief in the principles of the Democratic party should not hold office from those they seek to defame." This last resolution referred to the role of patronage recipients like Port Collector Gibson and Postmaster John Dunn in the coup by the antitax faction. Finally, the chairman of the convention made reference to honest Democrats who never combined with Whigs, Antimasons, or Black Republicans, and thus implied criticism of Gibson's well-known courtship of Williams and alliance with Campbell, Bruce, and Robinson. The convention also lauded the *Post* as the true voice of the Democracy, which right up to election day called railroad taxation a false issue and continually lashed at Williams, the *True Press*, and the antitax wing of the party. Even this protest convention, however, considered it necessary to pledge not to levy taxes to pay off the interest on railroad bonds until forced to by the courts.[57]

The threat that the Democrats would utilize the popularity of Williams and hysteria against railroads to draw off anti-tax Republicans frightened the opposition leaders. After Moorhead won the Republican congressional nomination, but before the Anti-Tax and Democratic parties combined, he wrote Simon Cameron, "The only fear I have at all is the Repudiation or Anti-tax party under the head of Tom Williams. They don't look formidable now, but he appeals to the pockets of the taxpayers and there is no certainty about the result." [58] As in 1857, the Republicans tried originally to campaign on national issues, and Errett continued to point out that the Democrats opposed tariff protection and to stress that although the Democrats adopted local issues, the major issue of the campaign was still slavery because "the true purpose" of the Democracy was to extend it.[59] Despite such cries, during the last months of the campaign the Republican press concentrated on meeting and negating the Democratic anti-tax offensive.[60]

57. For the protest and the meeting, see the *Post*, Sept. 7, 16, 1858; *Gazette*, Sept. 10, 1858. For examples of the *Post*'s opposition to the *True Press*, see it for July 21, Aug. 20, and Sept. 4, 1858.

58. J. K. Moorhead to Simon Cameron, Aug. 2, 1858, Cameron MSS.

59. *Gazette*, Sept. 5, 7, 9, Oct. 2, 1858.

60. To measure the emphasis given different issues by the Republicans in the last months of the campaign, I made a content analysis of the editorials in the major Republican paper, the *Gazette*, for the months of August, September, and October, up to the election. I measured column inches devoted to issues on only the editorial page although I included clippings from other papers which appeared on that page. This analysis showed conclusively that the *Gazette* was preoccupied with the railroad issue, not the tariff or Lecompton, during the last months of the campaign. It harped on three themes: it attacked the *True Press* and the attempt to form a third party on the tax issue; it denounced the Democratic bargain with Williams; and it exposed

The popular excitement over the railroad issue forced the Republicans to demonstrate that they too opposed the tax. To prevent antitaxers in the party from following Williams out of it, they declared opposition to the payment of interest until the state supreme court ruled on the question of the county's liability. The Republican county committee asserted in an address that the Republican party was in no way responsible for the railroad subscriptions because they were made before the party came into existence. Williams was a sorehead who only wanted revenge on the Republicans; his charges against Republicans such as Robert McKnight about responsibility for the city's expenditure on railroads were false.[61] Taking a different tack, the *Dispatch* argued that both parties fundamentally agreed that the courts should settle the question and that the Democratic clamor was senseless because elected officials, other than the county commissioners, would have nothing to do with the tax question. Moreover,

the railroad connections of Democratic leaders. The space devoted to various issues was:

Issue	*Column Inches*
Railroads and railroad tax	708
Lecompton and Kansas	111
Other slavery	62
Pro-Southern sympathies of Democrats	33
Tariff and the depression	58.5
Democratic corruption	112
Other anti-Democratic	108.5
Direct appeal to labor	49
Anti-Catholic and ethnic	10
Others (not necessarily political)	392

61. For reports of the county conventions, see the *Gazette*, Jan. 7, June 3, 1858; see the analysis of the Republican address in the *Post*, July 9, 1858, and the crucial parts of it reprinted in the *Gazette*, Sept. 25, 1858; *Gazette*, Aug. 10, 24, 1858.

the Republican candidate for county commissioner had vowed not to levy any tax until legally compelled to do so.[62]

To supplement this approach the Republicans attempted to play on the antipathy for taxation in another way. The county convention in June had called for retrenchment in county expenditures and blamed a heavy burden of county taxation on the Democratic county commissioners. The *Gazette* charged these Democratic commissioners with mismanagement of county funds and protested that they had levied a three-mill tax when the state law allowed only a two-and-a-half-mill tax.[63]

If the Republicans attempted to defend their own record on railroad subscriptions and taxation and to blame higher taxes on the Democrats, they also sensationally exposed the intimate connections of Democrats with railroads. Democrats had self-righteously claimed purity on this matter and insisted that any candidate tainted by relations with railroads was unfit for office. The *Gazette* dragged up old records and revealed that all the prominent Democratic leaders and candidates such as Williams, Gibson, Bruce, and John M. Irwin had either supported subscriptions to railroads, worked for them as attorneys, or taken free passes from them. A typical report maligned Thomas Farley, the Democratic candidate for county commissioner, by revealing that not only had he once supported subscriptions to railroads, but he also had two sons and a son-in-law employed by the Ohio and Pennsylvania Railroad.[64] Thus, during the last months of the campaign when Lecompton, corruption, and the tariff supposedly con-

62. *Dispatch*, Aug. 25, 1858; *Post*, July 7, 1858.
63. *Gazette*, June 3, Oct. 6, 7, 1858.
64. Ibid., Sept. 25, 1858; see also ibid., Aug. 10, Sept. 3, 4, 8, 1858; *Dispatch*, Sept. 5, 1858.

cerned the rest of the state and the North, the congressional campaigns in Allegheny County degenerated into a farce of taunts, denials, and mudslinging about former affairs with railroads.

Republican tactics proved more successful than those in 1857, and the Democrats took a drubbing in the October election. Though the vote was fairly light, Moorhead won as large a portion of it as Frémont had in 1856. Errett was jubilant at the victory of the entire Republican ticket and the estranged Democratic editor Barr confided to William Bigler, "The Repudiators here have been thrashed to death." Explanations of the triumph varied. A Democrat in Harrisburg reported that the key issue in the state as a whole was the tariff and depression, and that the People's Party won the foreign vote, both German and Irish, in a body. Errett also said that the Germans, "in a solid phalanx," supported the principles of protection to American industry and "freedom in our territories." [65] These assertions have little validity, for in Pittsburgh neither immigrant group appears to have voted solidly for the Republicans. In fact, they seem to have voted more solidly for the Democrats, especially the Irish, than they had in 1857. If any Germans and Irish supported the People's Party in Pittsburgh, they were probably Protestants, for there appears to have been a sharp split in the vote along religious lines.[66]

Assessing the impact of the tariff is difficult. Wealthy Whig manufacturers and merchants seem to have supported Moor-

65. See Table 48; *Gazette*, Oct. 13, 1858; James P. Barr to William Bigler, Pittsburgh, Oct. 18, 1858, Bigler MSS; David R. Porter to James Buchanan, Harrisburg, Oct. 14, 1858, Buchanan MSS; *Gazette*, Oct. 19, 1858.

66. See Tables 49 and 50, and note especially the difference between the correlations of the German, Irish, Protestant, and Catholic groups in 1857 and 1858.

head, an iron manufacturer and railroad executive, more solidly than they had any previous Republican candidate.[67] In part, the desire for tariff protection may explain this new support, but it also seems likely that the moderation of the slavery plank and the concern of these businessmen about the dishonor and resulting loss of credit and value of county bonds involved in the repudiation stand of the Democrats prompted their change. The attraction of the tariff for poorer voters is equally difficult to measure. Had the tariff drawn the vote of unemployed operatives, however, there would have been an increase in the support for Republicans among skilled artisans and unskilled laborers, but there does not seem to have been one.[68]

What apparently won the larger vote for the Republicans was their more adroit stand on the tax issue and their greater effectiveness in winning back the Know-Nothing vote which Wilmot had alienated in 1857. It is difficult to determine exactly how the tax issue worked, but the new Republican position on it prevented the large-scale defections which occurred in 1857. Moreover, while the vote split along ethnic and religious lines, the tax issue appears to have been important enough to prevent the customary solid support among native Americans for the anti-Democratic candidate. Because Protestant support for the Republicans seems to have increased since 1857, however, it is possible that the apparent drop in native American support really reflects an increase in support from foreign-born Protestants for the People's Party and

67. See Table 49. The correlation between the Whig vote for governor in 1854 and that for Moorhead in 1858 was +.68; it had only been +.35 between that coalition vote and the vote for Wilmot.

68. See Tables 49 and 50.

the loss of the homogeneous nature of the opposition party. It is clearer that the People's Party won the vote of many Know-Nothings who had supported Frémont in 1856 and Pollock in 1854. Indeed, before the election a Democrat had predicted the certainty of Moorhead's victory because he had "both the Republican and the Know Nothing nominations, and the majority in this district in 1856 was 2,300." [69]

Taxation for railroad bonds became more of a problem after the election of 1858. In November the state supreme court ordered the Allegheny County commissioners to levy an additional tax to pay the interest on the bonds issued to the Pittsburgh and Steubenville Railroad Company. Forced to new expedients, the commissioners in early 1859 voted the county's stock to elect all three of themselves directors of the Pittsburgh and Steubenville, and to make their agents a majority of the directors of the Allegheny Valley Railroad.[70] Whether the commissioners hoped to hasten the roads into efficient operation or to vote to exchange the county bonds still held by them for stock held by the county is not clear, but this direct intervention with the management of the roads evoked a chorus of disapproval from an antitax protest meet-

69. William H. Smith to William Bigler, Pittsburgh, Sept. 9, 1858, Bigler MSS. The correlation between the Know-Nothing vote for canal commissioner in 1855 and the Republican vote increased from +.52 for Wilmot in 1857 to +.64 for Moorhead in 1858. The higher correlation along with the larger absolute vote indicates increased support from the Know-Nothings as well as all Protestants. See Tables 48, 49, and 50. The mention of the separate Know-Nothing convention in Smith's letter was the only such notice I discovered.

70. *Gazette, Post,* Nov. 12, 1858; *Dispatch,* Nov. 15, 1858; *Post,* Jan. 11, Feb. 2, 1859.

ing in February. The meeting denounced any connection between public officials and railroads, and called for the resignation of two of the commissioners. All newspaper observers agreed that the meeting reflected a public determination to resist the court mandamus whatever the consequences.[71]

Indeed, the people of Pittsburgh and Allegheny County withstood taxation throughout 1859, 1860, and 1861 despite numerous federal and state court decisions against both the county and the municipality. When the state supreme court ruled in 1860 that the city councils had to levy new taxes, public meetings in the wards urged the councilmen to refuse such action, and a mass protest meeting flayed the court for its decision and charged that the justices, either as individuals or stockholders in insurance companies, held the bonds issued to the railroads. Both city councilmen and county commissioners were repeatedly fined, and the commissioners were jailed for contempt of court, but public officials still heeded the electorate and refused to pay. By 1862, with some sixty-five court decisions against the city and county, a compromise solution was finally reached. The city councils replaced the old 6 percent–30-year bonds issued originally to the railroads with 5 percent–50-year bonds at the ratio of 86 of the new for 100 of the old. The county achieved a similar compromise; both represented partial repudiation.[72]

The railroad crisis apparently remained a primary popular concern throughout 1859 and well into 1860. Measuring public opinion is always hazardous, but in the spring of 1860 a Republican wrote to Salmon P. Chase about the difficulties of

71. *Dispatch, Post,* Feb. 17, 1859.

72. *Dispatch,* Feb. 24, 27, Mar. 2, 22, Nov. 23, 1860; Thompson, "A Financial History of Pittsburgh," pp. 99–100; Hartz, *Economic Policy and Democratic Thought,* p. 83.

organizing the party in Pittsburgh for the presidential campaign that year:[73]

> I feel mortified and discouraged at our position; a few demagogues have complete control of this county and great influence in several neighboring counties through the antirailroad tax question, and [there is] so much excitement that men will listen to nothing else on any question.

The great importance of the local issue which rivaled concern about national issues forced both parties to pay it heed again in 1859. The canvass that year followed the pattern established in the previous two years. The Republicans tried to associate the state and local Democrats with the Buchanan administration, and the Democracy avoided the slavery and Southern question by stressing foreign policy in their state platform and the railroad crisis in the Allegheny County resolutions. In the end, both parties in Pittsburgh pledged firm resistance to taxes and denied the power of the courts to order people to pay without proper legal process and trial by jury. In response to the reigning antitax sentiment, the Republicans nominated for county judge Thomas Mellon, founder of the banking family, a political independent, and the lawyer who had led the investigation of railroad companies for antitax conventions since 1857. The Democrats were so controlled by antitaxers, asserted Barr of the *Post*, that they nominated a weak candidate for judge to insure the election of Mellon. The Democrats did nominate for county commissioner, however, Edward Campbell of the *True Press*, a Democratic antitax leader. The *Post* criticized the Democratic ticket and plat-

73. Joshua Hanna to Salmon P. Chase, Pittsburgh, Apr. 9, 1860, Chase MSS.

257

form as evidence that a man had to believe in repudiation and defiance of the courts "or he cannot be nominated by a Democratic convention in Allegheny County." [74]

If both parties openly courted the antirailroad vote, other portions of their programs were also remarkably similar. Both advocated the passage of a new tariff to protect Pennsylvania coal and iron interests, although the *Gazette* asserted that the Democrats could promise specific duties but they would never produce them.[75]

The major change in the campaign of 1859 from that of 1858 resulted from the renewed efforts of the Republicans to combine Know-Nothings with other elements of their coalition. The Republicans again attempted to camouflage nativist principles with strategic wording in the state platform. Reiterating the calls for a pure ballot box and prohibition of foreign criminals, the platform also appealed to men of all parties who wanted "to restore the Government to its original purity, and to preserve the proud heritage of American institutions." Moreover, another plank advocated a homestead bill which would give 160 acres to every citizen. By specifying citizens rather than persons, the Republicans thus excluded aliens and appealed to the nativist vote.[76]

Having granted the Know-Nothings certain sops, the Republicans then had to woo the German vote. This task proved particularly difficult in 1859 because the Massachusetts legislature, which was controlled by Republicans and Know-Noth-

74. For the Republican and Democratic state platforms of 1859, see the *Gazette*, June 10, 1859, and the *Post*, Mar. 19, 1859. See also the *Gazette*, June 2, 1859, and the *Post*, Apr. 1, June 30, and July 1, 1859.

75. *Gazette*, Jan. 17, June 10, 1859; *Post*, Feb. 1, 2, Mar. 19, 1859. Nothing appeared on the tariff in the resolutions of the Democratic county convention, and the Republicans did not pass any resolutions.

76. *Gazette*, June 10, 1859.

ings, passed a law that year which denied the vote to immigrants until two years after their naturalization. The *Post* labeled the action clear evidence of Know-Nothing domination of the Republican party and warned Germans in Pittsburgh not to support a party which considered them inferior to Negroes. Errett advised Pittsburgh Republicans to place a German on the county assembly ticket to hold the German vote, denied Barr's accusations of Know-Nothing dominance, and assured Germans that nothing in the entire Republican platform could evoke disapproval from even "the most sensitive foreign born citizens." [77]

As the campaign advanced and it became clear that Democrats and Republicans agreed on many issues, the Democrats in desperation raised the Sabbatarianism issue against the predominantly Protestant Republican party. According to Pennsylvania state law, passenger railroads could not operate on Sunday, and most Protestants who wanted strict observance of the Sabbath apparently favored the law. The *Post* charged that "a large portion of our German, Irish, and American workingmen" lived along the railroad lines and wanted to use them on Sunday, either to come into the city to go to church or to escape the city on their one day off and get out into the country. The Sunday law discriminated against the poorer classes, insisted the *Post,* because wealthier men could ride out of the city in carriages. Although the Germans demanded a repeal of the law, the *Gazette* and the Republicans with their "rank Know Nothing proclivities" opposed any change; in contrast, Democratic candidates favored it. How could Germans and Irishmen vote for such a party as the Republicans? Even though Errett declared that Germans as a whole did not ask for repeal, at election time the Democrats confidently

77. *Post*, May 18, 1859; *Gazette*, June 29, 1859.

"expect[ed] to have a large portion of the Republican German vote." [78]

As the *Gazette* noted, the Democrats who had won elections in Pittsburgh only by seizing local issues such as temperance and the railroad tax took up the Sunday railroad question when the tax issue apparently lost its usefulness in order once again to avoid national issues.[79] One must add that the Republicans as a new party with diverse support had tried to rally voters on national issues, precisely to avoid the important but divisive local issues which Democrats stressed. In response to the Democratic charges on this question, Errett criticized those Democrats who would destroy the distinction between Sunday and other days by allowing beer drinking and other activities on the Sabbath. Already outraged citizens had held meetings to denounce the drunkenness of foreigners on Sundays. At such meetings Protestant immigrants had complained about their being identified with their more rowdy countrymen, and the *Gazette* insisted that German and Irish Protestants should not be blamed for the activities of Catholic immigrants. The Presbyterian synod of Pittsburgh also denounced the frequent violations of the Sabbath. Because the question of a separate school fund for Catholics was raised again in 1859, with the *Gazette* opposing the Catholics and the *Post* supporting them, open political hostility between Catholics and Protestants, dormant in 1857 and 1858 when the economic issue of the railroad tax occupied both parties and the people, had emerged again by the October election.[80]

78. *Post*, Oct. 1, 5, 6, 1859; *Gazette*, Sept. 29, Oct. 3, 1859; James A. Gibson to Jeremiah S. Black, Pittsburgh, Oct. 7, 1859, Black MSS.
79. See the editorial, "Democratic Hobbies," in the *Gazette*, Oct. 3, 1859.
80. *Gazette*, Aug. 3, Oct. 3, 26, 1859; *Post*, Feb. 1, Oct. 1, 1859.

Although the Democrats may have in fact raised issues which troubled people as much as Southern aggressions, the Republicans swept all offices in the October election. The vote was small and the people apathetic about a canvass in which parties aped each other on the railroad tax issue and which did not involve important state or national offices. With the old antagonism clearly in the open, the Republicans won back the native Protestant support which the tax issue had apparently split the previous two years. The foreign vote, Irish as well as German, tended to divide along religious lines as well, for most Protestants tended to vote Republican. Anxious to avoid identification with their Catholic countrymen, German and Irish Protestants voted for the Protestant party. Once again, the poorest voters, many of whom were native-born Protestants, tended to give strong support to the Republicans, and the ethnic and religious divisions which had characterized voting patterns in 1856 had reappeared.[81]

Up to the time of John Brown's raid on Harpers Ferry, then, the Republicans in Pittsburgh had managed to maintain the coalition of Know-Nothings, foreign-born Protestants, and anti-Know-Nothing Whigs of the Antimasonic tradition which had triumphed in 1856. They had accomplished this feat, however, only after they appeased a public response to railroads which foreshadowed the Granger and other anti-monopoly protests after the Civil War, for the protest against the railroad tax was only a partial manifestation of a larger

81. See Tables 48, 49, and 50. The Know-Nothings continued to give strong support to the Republicans in 1859 when they voted. The correlation between the Know-Nothing vote for canal commissioner in 1855 and the Republican vote for state supreme court judge in 1859 was +.77. I used the vote for the state office because it was the largest in the election.

antipathy to all railroads.[82] Pittsburgh Democrats had been first to seize upon the local social and economic issues during these years, and their tactics forced the Republicans to supplement their platforms based on national issues alone. Rather than being upset only by events in Kansas, slavery, or the South as Republicans desired, the citizens of Pittsburgh were too angry about their own problems with railroads between 1856 and 1860 to coalesce into a sectional phalanx against the South.

82. For a good summary of the protests against railroads after the Civil War, see Edward A. Purcell, Jr., "Ideas and Interests: Businessmen and the Interstate Commerce Act," *Journal of American History*, *54* (1967), 561–78.

Seven

COALITION COMPLETED:
THE ELECTION OF 1860

Pittsburgh and Allegheny City polled larger majorities for Abraham Lincoln in 1860 than any other major cities in the country.[1] That presidential campaign culminated certain developments which had been occurring in Pittsburgh since 1855. After four years of effort, the Republicans had effected a more complete organization; like the national party, they continued to widen and moderate their appeals in order to combine diverse elements into a single unit. The resulting coalition was more heterogeneous and more representative of all elements in the city than its Whig predecessor had ever been. On the other hand, the Democrats suffered even more than previously from factionalism as the national party split into northern and southern wings with separate tickets headed by Stephen A. Douglas and John C. Breckinridge. Moreover, anxious conservatives formed a fourth party, the Constitutional Union Party, which nominated John Bell of Tennessee on a platform of preserving the Union. Although these last three tried to combine against Lincoln, the new Republican

1. See Table II in Ollinger Crenshaw, "Urban and Rural Voting in the Election of 1860," in *Historiography and Urbanization: Essays in American History in Honor of W. Stull Holt*, ed. Eric F. Goldman (Baltimore, 1941), p. 65.

maturity and unity coupled with the mortal rupture within the Democracy, produced sweeping Republican victories in the city and the state.

Pennsylvania Republicans, like those elsewhere in the North, strengthened their organizations considerably between 1856 and 1860. After the 1856 campaign, Republican chieftains in Pittsburgh took steps to improve their embryonic party structure. In 1859 Russell Errett, editor of the *Gazette* and chairman of the city executive committee, suggested a plan to prevent participation by Democrats at Republican primary meetings. He would restrict voting to confirmed Republicans and have them nominate directly all candidates to be selected at the county convention. In effect, Errett's plan would accomplish within the Republican party the reforms of the county convention system that the Know-Nothings had attempted to effect through secrecy. Thus it was also an indirect bid to those Know-Nothings whose chief complaint in 1854 and 1855 had been the corruption of democratic processes by party wireworkers.[2]

Using this plan for a tighter party control of membership and spurred on by the presidential election, Pittsburgh Republicans organized more quickly and more thoroughly in 1860 than they had in 1856. In early January they formed the Republican Club of Allegheny County to direct the campaign,

2. On the strengthening of the Republican organization throughout the North, see Allan Nevins, *The Emergence of Lincoln* (2 vols. New York, 1950), 2, 299. On the lack of organization in 1856, see Russell Errett to Salmon P. Chase, Pittsburgh, Aug. 2, 1856, Chase MSS. For Errett's plan, see the *Gazette*, Mar. 8, 1859.

and by early spring every ward in the city had formed its own Republican club. Significantly, the local groups all adopted the name Republican while the state organization clung to the less radical title, People's Party. Following the advice of Errett, a member of the People's state committee, the Republicans quickly made arrangements to draw out the vote. The local clubs canvassed every block in the city wards and every school district in the rural townships in the county to learn the name, residence, postoffice address, and political affiliation of every voter and used this information to bring out the vote of doubtful and lukewarm Republicans. To disseminate campaign literature from national and state committees, the Republicans also organized a Republican Club reading room where pamphlets, newspapers from other cities, and German- and Welsh-language papers were circulated.[3]

These local organizations had intimate connections with the state committee and could supply information to state leaders. Although the People's state committee did not organize until April, it began actively directing the campaign by the beginning of May. Having urged a canvass of the voters similar to that in Pittsburgh, Alexander K. McClure, chairman of the state committee, wrote Lincoln in the summer that every election district in the state had been "actually counted to a man, or carefully estimated by reliable men residing in the precincts." Moreover, the state committee was in direct contact with the organizations in the election districts in over half the counties of the state. Because this superior organization would produce a huge Republican vote, McClure confidently

3. See the editorial in the *Gazette*, May 28, 1860, comparing the 1856 and 1860 campaigns. See also the *Gazette*, Jan. 6, 10, Feb. 23, Mar. 6, 19, 21, 31, Apr. 13, 21, 24, 27, 1860; *Post*, Jan. 5, 1860.

predicted as early as June, Lincoln and Andrew Curtin, the People's Party gubernatorial candidate, would carry the state.[4]

In Pittsburgh the Republicans wielded the local patronage they held to improve their vote-getting machine. According to Pennsylvania law, only people who could prove they paid local or state taxes could vote. Such proof normally took the form of tax receipts from the local tax collector; therefore, the sixty-eight collectors for the county could be the nucleus of either party's machine. Both Republican and Democratic papers in 1859 had warned that whichever party elected a county commissioner that year would control two of the three commissioners and, in turn, the appointment of collectors. Hence, the Republican victory in 1859 allowed the party to appoint its workers as tax collectors in 1860. Moreover, the Republicans carried eight of Pittsburgh's nine wards in the municipal elections in January, so that city tax assessors and other officials in the wards were Republicans who could electioneer when they spoke to people in the course of their official duties.[5]

To bolster the systematic registration of voters on each block, the Republicans employed all the devices of ballyhoo to stir up voter interest and sweep normally apathetic citizens into their fold. Throughout the summer and fall of 1860 pole raisings, rallies, torchlight processions, and songfests saturated

4. People's state central committee to Edward McPherson, Philadelphia, Nov. 4, 1859, McPherson MSS; Alexander K. McClure to Simon Cameron, Apr. 12, 1860, Cameron MSS; McClure to Abraham Lincoln, June 16, July 2, Aug. 21, Sept. 27, 1860, Nos. 3109, 3248, 3569, 3812, Robert Todd Lincoln MSS (LC; microfilm in the Yale University Library; all citations from the Lincoln papers hereafter come from this microfilm collection, and only their index numbers will be given).

5. *Post*, Sept. 20, 1859, July 6, 1860; *Gazette*, Sept. 19, 1859, Oct. 8, 1860. For evidence that the county and municipal appointees were Republican, see the *Gazette*, Jan. 4, 1860.

the city. Glee clubs, marching societies such as the famous Wide Awakes, and others known as Rail Splitters, Lincoln Lookouts, Lincoln Rangers, Minute Men, and the Third Ward Invincibles held a special attraction for young men who were allured by the uniforms and quasi-military aspects of those groups. Indeed, many who belonged to these organizations which were so prominent in Republican demonstrations were probably too young to vote.[6]

A mass demonstration arranged by the Republicans for September 27, 1860, exemplifies the thoroughness of their preparations. Speakers from many states addressed a huge throng which the Republicans had carefully recruited. For every rolling mill, foundry, and glass factory in the county the Republicans appointed a committee of two, including owners as well as operatives, to organize the workers for the parade. Draymen, butchers, and the employees of at least three railroad companies were also enlisted to participate along with the marching clubs. Each company generally supplied wagons which carried workers and banners displaying the products of the company and affirming allegiance to the Republican cause. For example, one from the Juniata Iron Works read: "Free land for free labor; with Lincoln nails and Old Abe's rails we'll fence out the nigger democracy." [7] Thus, the Republicans solicited the worker at his job as well as at reading rooms, at his home, and through social and marching clubs. This complete organization at the local and state level seemed to assure Republicans in Pittsburgh of victory.

Only factionalism threatened this triumph. On both the state and local levels the Republican party split as rival wings maneuvered for the spoils of the expected victory. In Pitts-

6. *Gazette*, Sept. 3, 25, Oct. 24, 1860; *Post*, Aug. 8, 1860.
7. *Gazette*, Sept. 13, 24, 25, 27, 28, 1860.

burgh, jealousy between John Heron Foster of the *Dispatch* and Errett of the *Gazette* temporarily menaced the successful organization of the party, particularly since Foster represented the Know-Nothing branch of the coalition. Errett had obtained by election and through his influence with Simon Cameron both the office of city comptroller and the position of clerk of the state senate in Harrisburg. For several months Foster bitterly opposed his holding both positions simultaneously because it gave his faction a monopoly of offices.[8]

This local friction grew out of a larger division which weakened the party in the state—the split between the followers of Cameron and those who opposed him and rallied around Andrew Curtin. Curtin and Cameron had been foes since 1855, when they competed for the nomination for United States Senator in the Know-Nothing caucus of the state legislature, and in part their split represented the division between old Whigs and old Democrats in the new Republican party. Errett backed Cameron, continually informed him of his prospects in Pittsburgh, and boomed him for the Presidency in the influential *Gazette* as early as 1859. From his position as chairman of the Republican city committee and member of the People's state committee he worked to secure Cameron delegates to the state nominating convention in 1860 and have that body choose him as a favorite-son candidate for President. The other Republican papers in the city, the *Dispatch* and the *Daily Commercial Journal*, opposed Cameron and tried to prevent efforts to have the state convention, which Cameron men would control, rather than local congressional districts, choose the state's delegates to the Republican national convention. Eventually congressional districts did select the dele-

8. Russell Errett to Simon Cameron, Pittsburgh, Oct. 8, 1858, Cameron MSS; *Dispatch*, Dec. 1, 1859, Jan. 6, 12, 13, 1860.

gates, and those from Allegheny County were hostile to the Winnebago Chief.[9]

Undaunted by this evidence of popular disaffection, Errett continued to support the state boss. Before the Republican national convention in May he explained to delegates from all over the country by letter that "the People's Party [was] not the Republican party" but a hybrid of Republicans, old-line Whigs, Americans, and anti-Lecompton Democrats. Only a man such as Cameron who could satisfy all these groups could carry Pennsylvania. Although not an official delegate, Errett attended the Chicago convention and tried feverishly the night before the final vote to dissuade the Pennsylvania delegation from swinging to Lincoln. Even after Lincoln's nomination, Errett suggested to Cameron ways to undermine the Curtin faction in Lincoln's eyes, and he informed Lincoln that state chairman McClure, a Curtin lieutenant, was ruining the Republican chances by alienating wealthy businessmen and Know-Nothings in Philadelphia.[10]

9. McClure, *Old Time Notes of Pennsylvania, 1*, 353, 396–97; Russell Errett to Simon Cameron, Pittsburgh, Nov. 15, 1859, and Harrisburg, Jan. 8, Feb. 8, 1860, Cameron MSS; *Gazette*, Nov. 8, 15, 1859, Feb. 10, 24, 1860; see reports of the Republican county convention in the *Post* and the *Gazette*, Jan. 5, 1860; *Post*, Feb. 25, 1860; *Dispatch*, Nov. 28, 1859, May 3, 1860.

10. Russell Errett to Simon Cameron, Pittsburgh, Apr. 17, May 29, 1860, and Harrisburg, June 23, 1860, Cameron MSS; Errett to Joseph Medill, Pittsburgh, July 24, 1860, and to David Davis, Pittsburgh, Aug. 27, 1860, Nos. 3392 and 3608, Lincoln MSS. The details of the attempt to undermine McClure are complex. Briefly, Errett and Cameron tried to set up a Republican finance committee outside of the People's state committee which could get credit from Lincoln for leading the Republican campaign in Pennsylvania. On this plot, see Alexander K. McClure to Cameron, July 31, 1860; Cameron to McClure, Aug. 1, 1860, copy; and McClure to Cameron, Aug. 2, 1860, Cameron MSS. See also McClure, *Old Time Notes, 1*, 410–14; and William E. Baringer, *A House Dividing: Lincoln as President Elect* (Springfield, Ill., 1945), pp. 132–35, 152–89.

Such factionalism and potential difficulties in the Republican campaign were, however, for the most part confined to the state level. Even Errett admitted that the western counties were safe for the Republicans. Local differences of opinion disappeared in late May when Pittsburgh's Republicans enthusiastically endorsed the nominations of Lincoln and Hannibal Hamlin.[11] McClure remained confident that Curtin and Lincoln could not lose. Two sources of this optimism were the strength of the Republican organization and the widespread popular dissatisfaction with the record of the Buchanan administration.

Another cause for confidence was the open fissure in the Democratic party. If 1860 saw the perfection of the Republican organization, it also witnessed the final splintering of the Democratic party into Buchanan and Douglas wings. As in most other areas in Pennsylvania, officeholders and patronage-appointees in Pittsburgh supported the President while the rank and file of the local Democracy who disliked the idea of slavery expansion apparently favored Douglas. As early as January 1860 the Democratic county convention in Pittsburgh divided over an endorsement of President Buchanan. The antitax faction of the party along with the postmaster and customs collector dominated the convention and quashed resolutions endorsing Douglas for President and forbidding federal appointees to attend the state convention. After a bitter struggle between Buchanan and Douglas men, delegates favorable to John C. Breckinridge, Buchanan's probable choice as a successor, were sent to the state convention, but the Allegheny County Democrats refused to recommend any man for the presidential nomination. The split widened when Barr

11. Russell Errett to David Davis, Pittsburgh, Aug. 27, 1860, No. 3608, Lincoln MSS; *Gazette*, May 22, 1860.

of the *Post* supported Douglas. When the Allegheny County delegation to the Democratic national convention in Charleston, South Carolina, failed to support the Little Giant, Barr demanded that they be chastised, for, he asserted, nine tenths of the Democrats in Allegheny County favored Douglas. Thus Barr once again opposed the Democratic officeholders in the county as he had done the previous three years on the tax issue. The eventual nomination of both Douglas and Breckinridge and the support which Buchanan's Pennsylvania machine gave Breckinridge spread the chasm between the two wings.[12]

State and local Republican leaders felt confident that the Democratic split would assure Lincoln's victory. McClure wrote Lincoln that despite attempts to fuse the Democrats in a single electoral ticket, the factions hated each other so much that they could never combine. McClure asserted that the managers of Douglas' campaign, especially John W. Forney, would resist fusion to the last because in reality they hated Douglas and would oppose any move such as fusion which might allow him to win Pennsylvania.[13] Insisting on a separate electoral ticket for Douglas, both Forney and the *Post* in Pittsburgh opposed the so-called Cresson compromise electoral ticket which would have given the state's Democratic votes to the candidate with the best chance of defeating Lincoln

12. Nichols, *The Disruption of American Democracy*, pp. 334–35; *Dispatch*, Aug. 14, 1860. See reports of the county convention and editorial comment in the *Post* and the *Gazette*, Jan. 26, 1860. See especially P. C. Shannon to William Bigler, Pittsburgh, Feb. 1, 1860, Bigler MSS; *Post*, Sept. 6, 1859, Feb. 28, May 18, 1860. See also James A. Gibson to Jeremiah S. Black, Pittsburgh, Oct. 7, 1859, Black MSS. For continuing evidence of the split in Pittsburgh, see the *Gazette*, Sept. 6, 1860; and Mrs. David Lynch to James Buchanan, Pittsburgh, July 16, 1860, Buchanan MSS.

13. Alexander K. McClure to Lincoln, July 2, 1860, No. 3248, Lincoln MSS.

in the electoral college. Even when the *Post* accepted the compromise in August, the Douglas state committee rejected it, and the *Dispatch* noted that many Democrats in Pittsburgh could not stomach the efforts of Buchanan men on behalf of it. Only after the October elections did the separate Douglas ticket drop from the race.[14]

Although they were so badly split in the presidential canvass, most Democrats in the state apparently united behind Henry D. Foster for the gubernatorial contest in October. A faithful Democrat from Westmoreland County, which neighbored on Allegheny County, Foster was chosen, according to former Democrat David Wilmot, because he had no convictions and would readily submit to administration pressure. At the same time, he seemed to be an anti-Lecompton man because he was from a western county.[15] Although Forney and some other dissident Democrats hoped for the Republican Curtin's victory and attempted to embarrass Foster, Barr rejoiced that the split in the Democracy had been patched up.[16]

Most Republican leaders recognized that because the Democrats were united behind Foster, the gubernatorial election in October, not the presidential election, was the crucial poll in

14. *Post*, July 16, Aug. 11, 1860; *Gazette*, Aug. 20, Sept. 6, Oct. 20, 1860; *Dispatch*, Aug. 14, 1860; Alexander K. McClure to Lincoln, Oct. 19, 1860, No. 4056, Lincoln MSS. For a general description of the efforts to fuse the Democratic wings in Pennsylvania, see Nichols, pp. 339–40.

15. David Wilmot to James Casey, Towanda, Mar. 10, 1860, Cameron MSS. On the other hand, McClure described Foster as the strongest candidate the Democrats could put up against Curtin in *Old Time Notes, 1*, 425.

16. Alexander K. McClure to Lincoln, July 7, 18, 1860, Nos. 3283, 3335, and Russell Errett to David Davis, Aug. 27, 1860, No. 3608, Lincoln MSS. McClure quoted Forney as being "painfully solicitous" about the nomination of Curtin and said he had "corresponded and cooperated with [McClure] and others to secure" Curtin's nomination. Errett told David Davis, "Forney and his crowd do not want Curtin defeated; but they have led off for Foster and got the masses committed to him." *Post*, Mar. 6, 1860.

Pennsylvania. Moreover, victory in the early election would have a bandwagon effect which would almost assure triumph in November. Errett warned his readers, "One vote in October is worth five in November," and McClure correctly predicted to Lincoln, "When we carry Curtin in October, *your* battle will have been fought." [17] In 1860, therefore, both parties concentrated their fire on the contest for governor.

Even with the surface unity behind Foster, however, the split within the Democracy hampered local leaders and delayed their efforts to organize the state campaign. In Pittsburgh these difficulties were compounded by the Democratic tradition of late county conventions. Thus, while the Republicans formed a county club to direct the presidential campaign in early January, the Democrats did not form one until the beginning of September. While the Republican local ticket had been campaigning since June, the Democrats did not choose a local ticket until September. While Republican clubs had been enrolling and propagandizing voters in precincts, wards, and school districts since March and April, there was no mention of any local Democratic activity in the newspapers until late August and September. Moreover, an examination of the *Post* and the *Gazette* gives the strong impression that Republican rallies, marching clubs, and songfests were far more numerous than those of the Democrats. McClure warned Lincoln that the Democrats could rally more voters in ten days than the Republicans could in a month, but the Republicans had indeed been working many months longer than the Democrats in Pittsburgh.[18]

17. *Gazette*, Sept. 22, 1860; Alexander K. McClure to Lincoln, Aug. 21, 1860, No. 3569, Lincoln MSS.

18. *Post*, Sept. 1, 6, 1860; Alexander K. McClure to Lincoln, Sept. 27, 1860, No. 3812, Lincoln MSS.

The issues of the 1860 campaign are generally familiar. Numerous historians have related how the Republicans moderated the antislavery stance of the national platform, stressed their essential conservatism, and attacked the Buchanan administration for its corruption, its obstruction of laws to raise a protective tariff, make rivers and harbors improvements, and provide free homesteads, and its pronounced pro-Southern proclivities. In reply to Republican accusations, the Democrats denied the charges against them and emphasized the threat of secession by Southern states should Lincoln win.[19] In Pennsylvania both major parties followed essentially the same tack as the national parties, but the situation varied somewhat locally.

In Pittsburgh in 1860 the strategy employed by both parties to attract support from various elements of the population shaped appeals more than did principles. Republicans attempted to enlarge their coalition from that of 1856 and appealed to specific groups—Whigs, Know-Nothings, immigrants, workers, and opponents of railroad taxation. The Democrats wooed these same groups to frustrate Republican efforts. As a result, each party frequently echoed the rhetoric of the other. While similar to each other, the appeals of the Democrats and Republicans differed markedly from those of the Democrats and the Whigs in the late 1840s and early 1850s.

19. For general discussions of the issues, see Emerson D. Fite, *The Presidential Campaign of 1860* (New York, 1911), pp. 132–204; Reinhard H. Luthin, *The First Lincoln Campaign* (Cambridge, Mass., 1944); and Nevins, *The Emergence of Lincoln,* 2, 261–317. Don E. Fehrenbacher has challenged some of these traditional interpretations about how much the Republicans moderated their antislavery platform in 1860 in *Prelude to Greatness*, pp. 156–57.

Both parties wooed the antitax vote in 1860. The issue remained a major one that year, and at an antitax convention in March Thomas Williams, the chief prophet of repudiation, insisted that the tax question was more vital to the specific interests of the citizens of the county than the supposed major political question of the day—slavery expansion. The protest meeting called on the state legislature to strip the state supreme court of its power in railroad tax cases and to adopt the railroad debt of Pittsburgh and Allegheny County. To see that the assembly accomplished these goals, the meeting recommended that both parties place Williams on their assembly tickets.[20] In June the Republicans, after reaffirming their hostility to any railroad tax, heeded this advice even though Williams had bolted the party in 1858 and run for Congress as a Democrat. Once content to scorn Democrats as repudiationists and forced only by popular pressure in 1858 and 1859 to adopt a position against increased taxation, the Republicans became the major antitax party in the county in 1860. Not to be outdone, the Democratic county convention vilified the supreme court for jailing the Allegheny County commissioners when they refused to levy increased taxes and vowed adamant resistance to new taxes. Unwilling to accept Williams, the Democrats nominated John McIlhenny, one of the imprisoned commissioners and thus a martyr to the antirailroad crusade, for county clerk of courts.[21]

Both parties also used the tariff issue to attract votes. They gave almost equal attention to a call for a protective tariff,

20. Joshua Hanna to Salmon P. Chase, Pittsburgh, Apr. 9, 1860, Chase MSS. For a report of the antitax meeting, see the *Gazette* or *Post*, Mar. 22, 1860.

21. *Gazette*, June 5, 8, 1860; *Post*, Sept. 6, 1860.

one with specific rather than ad valorem rates, in their state and local platforms.[22] Each party accused the other of being a false advocate of protection. The Republicans attacked Douglas and Foster, the Democratic gubernatorial candidate, as free-traders and argued that Democratic pleas for protection were a trick to hoodwink voters. Politicians who professed they wanted protection but continued to associate with free-trade Southern Democrats could not be trusted. Democrats in Congress blocked the Morrill tariff bill in 1860, and only by helping Republicans overthrow Southern control of the government could unemployed workingmen protect their rights. At the same time that they impeached Democratic integrity on the tariff, Republicans attempted to defend the records of Lincoln and particularly Hamlin, once a Democrat, from Democratic assaults.[23]

Indeed, in sharp contrast to 1848 when Pennsylvania Democrats tried to avoid the tariff issue or denied the need for protection, Pittsburgh Democrats in 1860 waged a vigorous campaign on that issue. Defending Douglas as a tariff man and Foster as "The Poor Man's Friend," the *Post* correctly pointed out the ambiguity of the tariff plank in the Republican national platform and noted that while Republicans in manu-

22. See Republican and Democratic state platforms in the *Public Ledger* (Philadelphia), Feb. 24, Mar. 2, 1860; see resolutions of the Republican and Democratic county conventions in the *Gazette*, Jan. 5, 1860, and the *Post*, Jan. 26, 1860. In the state platforms, the Republicans devoted 104 words (10 percent) of the platform to the tariff issue; the Democrats gave it 92 words (16 percent) of their platform.

23. For the charges against the Democrats, see *Gazette*, Jan. 30, Feb. 22, 24, Mar. 7, 15, Apr. 17, May 7, June 18, Sept. 20, Nov. 5, 1860; see especially the resolutions of the first ward Republican Club, *Gazette*, Mar. 19, 1860. For the Democratic assaults on Lincoln and Hamlin, see the *Post*, June 23, Sept. 7, 1860; for Republican denials of them, see *Gazette*, June 9, Sept. 7, 14, 1860.

facturing areas boasted of it as offering protection, the New York *Evening Post*, a Republican free-trade journal, argued that the resolution actually called for reciprocal trade. Republicans in Allegheny County were so unconcerned about protection, he chided, that they failed to pass a tariff resolution at their second county convention in June while the Democrats passed a strong one. Curtin did nothing in the tariff fight of 1860 while Foster actively lobbied in Washington to have the Morrill bill passed in Congress.[24] In one long editorial Barr argued,

> When the tariff question has been in Congress this winter and heretofore, our iron manufacturers, who in Allegheny county, are mostly Republicans, have manifested the utmost indifference in regard to it. They have neither sent petitions to Congress nor delegates, to forward the tariff. Apparently they have been satisfied with the measure of their own prosperity, and manifested no earnest desire for any better protection to Pennsylvania interests than the present tariff afforded.

In contrast to Republican ironmasters in Pittsburgh, the iron-makers along the Allegheny, Connemaugh, and Juniata rivers and in districts east of the Allegheny mountains, "a large proportion of whom [were] Democrats," did the most lobbying in Congress for the tariff. "It has been the Democrats of Pennsylvania who have labored most assiduously for the manufacturing interests of the State for years past." [25]

Barr's assertions raise serious questions about the traditional interpretations of the decisive importance of the tariff issue in contributing to the Republican victory in Pennsylvania in

24. *Post*, May 28, June 6, 7, 23, Sept. 7, 10, 19, Oct. 4, 1860.
25. *Post*, Apr. 17, 1860.

1860.[26] Although the *Gazette* described banked furnaces and unemployment in the iron mills in 1860, other papers had noted recovery from the panic of 1857 by the summer of 1859 in Pittsburgh. Workingmen were happy because of "plenty of work and prompt pay." [27] With such prosperity, the tariff issue may not have had much appeal. Furthermore, iron manufacturers in Pittsburgh and Allegheny County did petition Congress about the tariff much less frequently than others in the eastern, Democratic portions of the state. A check of the House and Senate Journals from 1849 through 1860 revealed 13 petitions from Pittsburgh and Allegheny County on the tariff and 159 from other counties, most of which were in central and eastern Pennsylvania; 75 were just designated as being from Pennsylvania.[28] Explaining such apathy in Pittsburgh is difficult, for the tariff rates on Pittsburgh iron products were the same as those on products from other parts of the state—that is, Pittsburgh gained no advantage from the provisions of the law itself.[29] One can hypothesize, however, that since Pittsburgh ironmakers concentrated before 1860 on the production of merchantable bar iron and finished iron

26. Several historians have stressed that the tariff issue was crucial in the Republican victory in Pennsylvania in 1860. For example, see Luthin, p. 208; Nevins, *Emergence of Lincoln,* 2, 301, 304; Eiselen, *Rise of Pennsylvania Protectionism,* p. 260.

27. *Post,* Aug. 4, 1859; *Gazette,* Feb. 24, 1860.

28. I arrived at these totals by checking the indexes for the House and Senate Journals for the years 1849–60, from the first session of the 31st Congress through the first session of the 36th Congress. I checked under such headings as Tariff, Petitions, Pennsylvania, Pittsburgh, and Allegheny County. Most were listed in a section on petitions from Pennsylvania.

29. Rates on all iron products, whether pig, bars, or rails, were the same in the tariff of 1846. See U.S. Senate, 62nd Congress, 1st Session, "Customs Tariff of 1846 with Senate Debates Thereon, Accompanied by Messages of the President, Treasury Reports, and Bills," *Senate Documents No. 71* (Washington, D.C., 1911), p. 267.

products which they sold to western customers, they may not have suffered from the competition of British iron as much as others in different parts of the state who made different products, especially those who made iron rails. Pittsburgh manufacturers did not make railroad iron until after 1860. Moreover, since ironmakers in Pittsburgh only fashioned products from pig iron rather than producing pig themselves, they may have benefited from the low tariffs on British pig iron which would lower the price of the pig iron they bought.[30] In contrast, those furnace operators on the upper Allegheny and in the central portions of the state who smelted pig iron from ore would suffer much more from British imports and would be more apt to move for a change. In short, the nature of the iron industry in Pittsburgh until 1860 and its advantages of location may have made a protective tariff less vital to ironmakers there than to those in other parts of the state. On the other hand, it is possible that more petitions came from Democratic areas than from Republican because the ironmakers there thought it necessary to put pressure on their congressmen to support revisions, while those in Whig and Republican areas could be confident of such a vote from their congressmen.

Whatever the reason, the tariff issue was probably much less influential in Pittsburgh in 1860 than it is supposed to have been in other parts of the state. Both parties made the same appeals on the tariff, and one wonders if the Republicans were more convincing than the Democrats, particularly in the gubernatorial canvass in October, the critical election in the state. After all, Pennsylvania Democrats in Congress had fought for

---

30. On the nature of the iron industry in Pittsburgh, see Louis C. Hunter, "The Influence of the Market upon Technique in the Iron Industry in Western Pensylvania up to 1860," pp. 241–81.

an upward revision of the tariff since 1858. Moreover, the tariff was much less important in the Republican platforms than it had been in the earlier Whig platforms. For an issue that was supposedly so important, it received little attention in official programs. State chairman McClure wrote Lincoln in June that while the tariff was the "overshadowing question" in the eastern, southern, and central counties of the state, "in the West the Tariff [was] regarded of no greater importance than the slave aggressions." [31] Finally, the Republican vote in October 1860 was not much bigger than the Republican vote in 1856 when the tariff was not an issue.

If the parties adopted similar positions on certain issues, however, their main appeals were different. As in 1856 Pennsylvania Democrats stressed the threat to the nation inherent in a Republican victory. Only a Democratic triumph could prevent secession, they insisted. To establish their superiority to the sectional Republican party, they emphasized their devotion to the Constitution and the Union, "deprecate[d] the attempt of sectional parties . . . to obtain control of the Government," and deplored "any attempt to alienate one portion of the Union from the rest." Pledging their determination to protect the rights of Southerners and Southern states, Democrats in Pittsburgh castigated John Brown's misguided attempt to initiate a slave insurrection by seizing the arsenal at Harpers

31. Nichols, *Disruption of American Democracy*, pp. 237–40; Alexander K. McClure to Lincoln, June 16, 1860, No. 3109, Lincoln MSS. After the October election a correspondent wrote to Buchanan that Pennsylvania was "free-soiled and abolitionized. The tariff did something toward the result, but not all, as the terrible frontier majorities show." William S. Hurst to James Buchanan, Philadelphia, Oct. 12, 1860, Buchanan MSS (HSP). Whig tariff resolutions had always been first in the state platforms and were always the most prominent in those platforms. In contrast, in the 1860 People's state platform, the tariff plank was only the twelfth one listed.

Ferry, Virginia, as "but the legitimate consequence of the open hostility expressed by the leaders of the Republican party against Southern institutions." [32]

Barr of the *Post* openly identified the Democratic party as the inheritor of the Whig tradition of moderation. Once businessmen and others had properly looked to the Whig party as the bastion of conservatism, he admitted, but now they must look to the Democracy. The Republican program menaced not only the peace and harmony of the nation, but also the personal economic interests of the old Whig business elite in Pittsburgh. Barr and the Democratic county convention in Pittsburgh warned that abolitionist Republicans alienated Southerners and therefore threatened to terminate trade with the South, "a trade which has been a vast source of profit for Pennsylvania." To save their Southern markets merchants and manufacturers should repudiate the Republicans and sustain the Democracy. Barr harped on this economic menace of Republicanism, and the *Gazette* charged that he even threatened to publish a list of businessmen who actively supported the Republicans so that Southern merchants could blacklist them. Summing up after the Republican victories in October, Barr stated flatly that it was the duty of every conservative man in the country to vote against Lincoln.[33]

The Democrats also raised the specter of racial amalgamation augured by Republican programs. Doubtless they were

32. For the Democratic state platform, see the *Public Ledger*, Mar. 2, 1860; for the resolutions of the Allegheny County Democratic convention, see the *Post*, Jan. 26, 1860; see also the *Post*, Oct. 21, 25, 1859. The Democrats devoted 339 words (58%) of their state platform in 1860 to the themes of preserving the Union and reassuring the South.

33. See the resolutions of the county convention in the *Post*, Jan. 26, 1860; see also the editorials, ibid., Jan. 10, Mar. 6, Sept. 13, Oct. 11, 15, 31, 1860; *Gazette*, Dec. 12, 1859, Sept. 29, 1860.

appealing to the fears of the racist working masses and farmers. The *Post* argued that Republicans considered Negroes more deserving of citizenship than immigrants. In an editorial entitled "White Men, to the Rescue," Barr charged that Republicans in Massachusetts encouraged mixed marriages and that all who shared his prejudice against Negroes and wanted to preserve the free states for white men should vote Democratic.[34]

As in 1856 the Democrats also played on ethnic and religious fears. To retain the immigrant vote they condemned Curtin as a bigoted Know-Nothing and correctly stigmatized the Wide Awake Clubs as Know-Nothing in ritual. At the same time, however, the Democrats sought to keep the anti-Catholic vote out of the Republican coalition by spreading the rumor that Curtin was Catholic. They also appealed to the antiradical stream of nativism by calling Carl Schurz, who spoke before Pittsburgh Republicans, a "notorious German Red Republican infidel" and taunting Know-Nothings for being willing to listen to him.[35]

The Republicans first tried to answer Democratic charges against them. In response to Democratic threats of impending doom and Southern secession, Republicans assured conservatives that no such crises would result. In both the Republican national platform and the Pennsylvania People's state platform, the leaders emphasized how conservative the Republicans really were. They excised the antislavery rhetoric of 1856 and 1857 from their 1860 state platform, which was virtually a blueprint of the national platform. Only the heinous African slave trade rather than the institution of slavery itself

34. *Post*, Oct. 9, 11, 31, 1860.

35. *Gazette*, Oct. 3, 1860; *Post*, Apr. 23, Aug. 8, Sept. 13, 26, Oct. 2, 1860.

drew the epithet "relic of barbarism." While the state platform opposed slavery extension and denounced the Dred Scott decision in the exact words of the national platform, it concentrated on the theme of maintenance of the Union and conciliation of the South.[36] Like the national platform, the state platform, conventions in Pittsburgh, and Republican newspapers all vehemently defended states' rights, pledged that the Republicans would not interfere with slavery in the Southern states, denounced threats to the Union from either North or South, denied any Republican responsibility for John Brown's raid, and deplored "the lawless invasion by armed force of the soil of any State or Territory . . . as among the gravest crimes." Pennsylvania's Republicans "hail[ed] the people of the South as brethren in whose prosperity [they] rejoice[d]." Pittsburgh Republicans announced their desire to perpetuate commercial relations with the South. The *Gazette* asserted that not the Republicans who "desire[d] calm and quiet for the country [and] earnestly [sought] to cultivate the closest fraternal relations with their brethren of the South," but Southern fire-eaters were provoking discord.[37] Thus Errett

36. The Republican national platform of 1860 can be found in Fite, *The Presidential Campaign of 1860*, pp. 237–40. The People's Party state platform can be found in the *Public Ledger*, Feb. 24, 1860. On the efforts to moderate the national platform by watering down the slavery sections and adding economic planks, see David Potter, *Lincoln and His Party in the Secession Crisis* (New Haven, 1962), pp. 30–31; Jeter A. Isely, *Horace Greeley and the Republican Party, 1853–1861: A Study of the New York Tribune* (Princeton, 1947), pp. 288–93. The theme of conciliation of the South formed the principal part of the People's state platform. Of the words in that platform, 402 (39%) were devoted to a defense of Southern and states' rights or to pledges of loyalty to the Union and the Constitution. The Democrats devoted 339 words (58%) of their state platform to those themes.

37. See the resolutions of the Allegheny County Republican convention and of the Pittsburgh first ward Republican Club in the *Gazette*, Jan. 5, Mar.

tried to remove the onus of disunionism from the Republicans and place it on the Democracy. The implied conclusion was that true conservatives should vote Republican to oppose the party which housed disturbers of the peace.

If Republicans in Pittsburgh followed the national and state party line in mollifying conservatives, they maintained more defiant attitudes toward the South than those found in official platforms. Newspapers continually scoffed at threats of Southern secession as empty bluffs to intimidate nervous conservatives, a device the Democrats had often used before. Errett charged that talk of secession was a cheap trick to maintain political power by Southern Democrats who feared that Lincoln would use patronage appointments to create the nucleus of a Republican organization in the South. When the Democrats threatened businessmen with the loss of Southern markets, Errett called on them to place principles before markets. To one such threat in the *Richmond Whig* he replied: "This is the merest rant. It is an insulting demand from the minority to the majority to disband and give up their cherished views and purposes. The demand will not be complied with." The South had succeeded in dominating the national government through the Democratic party too long. The North should "assert its independence of Southern influence in defiance of South Carolina cockades and the idle threats of secession which are sent up to us from the cotton plantations." The *Dispatch* flatly stated that determined opposition to slavery aggressions was the key to the Republican party in Allegheny County. As Errett's statements above show, "slavery aggressions" referred to all the overweening economic and political power of the South, not just the advance of the in-

---

19, 1860. See also the editorials in the *Gazette*, Oct. 21, 25, Nov. 19, Dec. 6, 9, 1859; *Dispatch*, Oct. 19, 28, 1859.

stitution.[38] Hostility to the South, not just to slavery as a moral wrong, thus remained an important Republican theme.

To the Democratic accusations that they favored integrating the races, Republicans, who recognized in the ironworkers' demand "to fence out the nigger democracy" the racism of many workingmen, denied they were abolitionists. As in 1856 they stressed that they wanted to keep the territories free from slavery so that white workingmen and farmers could avoid degrading contact with Negro slaves. The state platform sought to mitigate racist fears by recommending the gubernatorial candidate Curtin for "his earnest fidelity to the interests of white men." [39]

Another line of defense was to accuse the Democracy of holding the white workingmen of the North in contempt. Republican papers claimed that Southerners, such as Senator Louis T. Wigfall of Texas and Herschel V. Johnson, Douglas' running mate, who spoke in Pittsburgh during the campaign, called northern workers slaves, mudsills, and criminals. The "poor men of the country [should] vindicate their honor by routing a party that dare[d] to utter so foul a libel" about them. Often Republican papers pointed to Southern opposition to a homestead law as a manifestation of this contempt for free labor. Errett noted that the Democracy had once defended

38. *Gazette*, Nov. 17, 18, Dec. 6, 9, 12, 1859, Jan. 21, Feb. 3, Aug. 6, 24, Oct. 17, 24, 1860; *Dispatch*, May 3, Sept. 3, Oct. 30, 1860. On this theme of majority resistance to the demands of the minority, see Nichols, *Disruption of American Democracy*, p. 7, and Dusinberre, *Civil War Issues in Philadelphia*, p. 12 and passim.

39. *Gazette*, Mar. 5, Oct. 9, 1860; state platform, *Public Ledger*, Feb. 24, 1860. Eugene Berwanger, *The Frontier Against Slavery*, pp. 128–40 and passim, shows that much of the Republican resistance to slavery expansion resulted from racist hostility to Negroes in the territories. Republicans insisted they were the white man's party.

the dignity of free labor, but because of Southern influence Democrats now hated poor men.[40]

Republicans also made special efforts to secure the American and foreign Protestant vote. Although the Republicans had merged successfully with the Know-Nothings in 1858 as the People's Party, they were apprehensive about maintaining the alliance. At first the major problem had been the threat that William H. Seward of New York, who openly opposed Know-Nothings but was the leading contender for the nomination, would be the Republican presidential candidate in 1860. As early as May 1859 a Pittsburgh correspondent had informed Salmon P. Chase that Know-Nothings in eastern and western Pennsylvania adamantly refused to support Seward, and McClure reminisced long after the campaign that in March 1860 "the apparently assured nomination of Seward by the Republicans would have made Curtin's election impossible by alienating the entire Know-Nothing or American element from the People's organization."[41] When historians suggest that Lincoln was more available in Pennsylvania than Seward because he was more conservative on the slavery issue, they dismiss too cavalierly the vital importance for the People's Party to have a candidate like Lincoln whom Know-Nothings could support.[42]

40. *Gazette*, Apr. 10, June 11, Sept. 25, Oct. 9, 1860. The Republicans in Pittsburgh asked that congressmen send them the speeches of these Southerners so that they could use them to stir up the workingmen. See John M. Kirkpatrick to John Covode, Pittsburgh, June 11, 1860, John Covode MSS (Western Pennsylvania Historical Society).

41. Joshua Hanna to Salmon P. Chase, Pittsburgh, May 24, 1859, Chase MSS; McClure, *Old Time Notes, 1*, 399.

42. For an example of the traditional interpretation stressing Lincoln's being more conservative, see Luthin, *The First Lincoln Campaign*, p. 73. By far the best explanation of the importance of nativism in Seward's failure

To retain nativist support in Pittsburgh Republicans included Americans on their tickets and gave them prominent positions in the local organization. Andrew Curtin had been a Know-Nothing. James K. Moorhead, the former Democrat and Know-Nothing who had led the successful People's ticket in Allegheny County in 1858, was again the Republican congressional candidate in Pittsburgh in 1860. John M. Kirkpatrick, a Democrat who had been on the American tickets of 1854 and 1855, headed the Republican county executive committee in 1859–60. Indeed, among a sample of 37 Republican candidates for office from Pittsburgh in the years 1858–60 whose former political affiliation was identified there were 13 Know-Nothings.[43]

Republicans also made blatant appeals to Know-Nothing and anti-Catholic biases. Know-Nothings had demanded clean government, and Republican papers harped on the corruption of the Buchanan administration.[44] The *Gazette* noted that Archbishop John Hughes of New York supported Douglas and that the *Boston Pilot*, the foremost Catholic newspaper in the country, and Catholic priests in eastern Pennsylvania vilified Curtin and called on Catholics to oppose him. Remembering the Know-Nothing hatred of the political machinations of the Catholic Church, Errett argued that since the friends of Foster were enlisting the whole power of the Catholic Church on his behalf, it was just as legitimate for Republicans to appeal to Protestants to support Curtin. Clearly, the political leaders of the day perceived the split between parties along denomina-

---

to win the nomination can be found in Glyndon G. Van Deusen, *William Henry Seward* (New York, 1967), p. 225.

43. *Gazette*, Jan. 4, Sept. 6, 1860; *Post*, Apr. 24, 1860. A description of the sources of this leadership sample is given in Appendix B.

44. *Gazette*, June 3, 4, 5, Sept. 22, Nov. 6, 1860.

tional lines. When Republicans became worried that the supporters of John Bell (the Constitutional Union candidate), most of whom were former Know-Nothings, would combine with Democrats to back Foster in October, they ridiculed the nativists for their willingness to join with papist Democrats. To retain the anti-Catholic vote they also denied Democratic charges that Curtin was Catholic and pointed out that he was a good Presbyterian.[45]

If the Republicans courted Know-Nothings with representation on tickets, they publicly kept quiet about their alliance and avoided open expressions of hostility to foreigners. The first ward Republican Club went so far as to "eschew all sectarian or national prejudices" and to welcome all who agreed with their principles whether native- or foreign-born. Not only did Republicans welcome immigrants and set up naturalization committees for aliens, but they also argued that Democrats, the supposed friends of foreigners, actually hated them.[46]

Courting the foreign and nativist vote simultaneously was only one of several ways in which the Republican appeals were similar to those of the Democrats. Both parties also deplored sectional agitation and held the Union and states' rights sacrosanct; both called for a protective tariff with specific rates; and both wooed the opponents of higher taxes for railroad bonds. The major differences between appeals were the ability of the Republicans to form a coalition of those who opposed the Buchanan administration for any reason and the firm opposition of Republican newspapers to the demands of the minority South on the majority North. Indeed, in Pitts-

45. *Gazette*, Apr. 25, May 28, Aug. 28, Sept. 6, Oct. 3, 4, 1860; Alexander K. McClure to Lincoln, Philadelphia, Aug. 21, 1860, No. 3569, Lincoln MSS.
46. *Gazette*, Mar. 19, May 9, Sept. 19, 21, 27, Oct. 1, 1860.

288

burgh the Republicans still identified all ills—whether low tariffs, the failure of homestead legislation, the advance of Negro slavery, or sectional agitation—with the South and hence the Democracy. They hoped to draw all resentful Northerners into the Republican ranks.

The appeals of both parties had changed considerably from those of the Whigs and Democrats in the late 1840s. Led by the business elite, the Whigs had relied primarily on a paternalistic economic appeal which stressed the harmony of interests of all elements in society and the mutual benefits for all when businessmen prospered. In their rhetoric they seemed to abhor the very idea of class consciousness and certainly deplored class conflict. In contrast, the Democrats denounced the Whig program as class legislation, stressed the different interest of workers and employers, and tried to utilize working-class unrest to build a lower-class coalition. In 1860 the Republicans used positive, probusiness economic appeals much less than the Whigs had.[47] Rather than playing down class differences, the Republicans openly appealed to workers and insisted that the Democrats hated them. Indeed, they urged the poor to take action to defend their rights from aristocratic Southern planters. Gone was the note of economic paternalism; in its place was a concern for the individual rights of Northern white men and a defense of the rights of the North as a section. When Errett called on Pittsburgh businessmen not to

47. The following table compares the space devoted to economic themes in the Whig state platforms of 1847, 1848, and 1851, all gubernatorial election years, and in the People's state platform of 1860.

Issue	1847	1848	1851	1860
Tariff	102	102	241	104
Others	134	44	87	10
Combined percentage of total	48.5%	37%	56%	11%

sacrifice principle for economic interest, he even showed a disdain for the materialistic appeal so characteristic of Whigs. At the same time, the Democrats adopted the conservative probusiness stance of the old Whigs. They, not the Republicans, appealed directly to the economic interests of merchants and manufacturers. They no longer agitated workers against employers but relied on racial and ethnic appeals to attract their vote. This new rhetoric of both parties reflected the new elements which had entered their leadership and ranks since 1854 and the new issues which had arisen since 1850. It must be noted, however, that in spite of this change in the use of economic appeals, the Republicans were similar to the Whigs in their freesoil stand and identification with Northern interests while the Democratic appeals in Pittsburgh remained much more tolerant of the South than those of their foes.

The appearance of new issues and the attempts to broaden coalitions altered the nature of Republican and Democratic leadership after 1857.[48] By 1860 the leadership of the opposing parties had also changed considerably from that of the Whigs and Democrats in the late 1840s. Those parties had recruited some of their leaders from the same elements of society, but the Whigs had differed from their Democratic counterparts in many significant ways. A markedly larger proportion of the Whig leaders came from the wealthy, native-born families of the social and business elite than did the Democratic leaders who were much more frequently Irish and Catholic. Presby-

48. My leadership sample for analysis in this chapter covers the years 1858–60 and includes 91 Republican and 83 Democratic candidates and 80 Republican and 82 Democratic secondary leaders. See Appendix B for the sources of this sample.

terian elders and Episcopalian vestrymen gave the Whig leadership a patrician tone which distinguished it from that of the Democrats. In contrast, the Republican and Democratic leaders by 1860 came from much more similar backgrounds.

True, there were some differences. Republican candidates in the years 1858–60 were slightly wealthier and more likely to be iron or glass manufacturers than the Democratic candidates, and Republican primary and secondary leaders tended to come from the same socioeconomic groups while there was a considerable difference between Democratic candidates and secondary party leaders as to wealth and ethnic background. Moreover, the Republicans continued to be almost exclusively Protestants while a large proportion of Democrats were Catholics. Of 23 Republican candidates and 13 convention delegates none was a Catholic, but 25 (44%) of 57 Democratic leaders adhered to the Church of Rome.[49]

Aside from this notable difference in religious background, however, the leaders of the two parties were remarkably alike. Democrats and Republicans drew their leaders from rich and less wealthy groups in equal proportions. The same proportions of candidates in each party owned property valued at over $50,000, and among convention delegates almost identical percentages owned property valued at $10,000 or more. Similarly, the parties drew almost equal portions of their chiefs

49. See Tables 51, 53, 55, 57, and 58. Another student of the 1860 election in Pittsburgh has also examined the religious background of party leaders. He culled a list of 474 Catholics from the official paper of the Catholic diocese for two years. From other papers he identified 218 Democratic and 167 Republican leaders. Sixty-seven (31%) of the Democrats were Catholics, but not a single Republican leader was on the list of Catholics. Although it is not clear how this student defined "leader," his results certainly confirm my own. See Paul J. Kleppner, "Immigrant Voting Behavior: Pittsburgh, 1860" (unpublished seminar paper, University of Pittsburgh, 1963), p. 7.

from among merchants, shopkeepers, doctors, lawyers, and skilled artisans. Moreover, while a larger number of Republican candidates were native-born, the convention delegates of both parties came in almost the same proportions from the native-born Americans, Germans, Irish, and British.[50] Indeed, the Republicans probably included as many Germans among their candidates as did the Democrats. Although only three Republican candidates could be identified as German-born, other men with names such as Jacob Diehl, J. J. Siebnick, William Siebert, and C. H. Bennerman, who were probably of German extraction, won the Republican nominations for city councils in the wards with large concentrations of Germans.

One reason for the new similarity between Democratic and Republican leaders was the transfer of many men from one party to another. While most of the Republican leaders whose former affiliation could be determined had been Whigs, a substantial portion were former Democrats who leavened the new coalition and helped give it a different character from the former Whig leadership. Of 37 Republican candidates 9 (24%) had been Democrats. Similarly, 21 percent of the Republican convention delegates had been Democrats. It should be noted, however, that while only 62 percent of the Republican candidates were former Whigs, 23 (79%) of the convention delegates were. Thus, again there was more representation of non-Whig elements among the candidates in order to draw new elements into the coalition. Some of the onetime Democrats among Republican leaders had come into the party by way of the Know-Nothings. Others, such as Thomas Williams, G. W. Coffin, and James Dain, had been Democrats as late as 1858

50. See Tables 51–58.

and 1859 and joined the Republicans in the middle of the 1860 campaign. While some of these converts like Samuel McKelvey and James K. Moorhead were wealthy iron manufacturers, they did not seem to belong to the social elite which had spawned Whig leaders. For example, Moorhead wrote Simon Cameron that Whigs among Republicans disliked his Democratic antecedents and that "the idea of a fellow getting up who has not come through college is very offensive to certain persons." [51]

Similarly, converts helped make the Democratic leadership seem more prosperous and somewhat different from the Democratic leadership of 1848. How the antitax faction displaced many of the former Democratic chieftains has already been described. Among the new men were former Whigs such as Edward Campbell, D. D. Bruce, perennial chairman of Democratic county conventions, and Thomas Williams. Altogether 7 (22%) of 31 Democratic candidates had been Whigs. Indeed, the *Post* complained about the inordinate number of nominations the Whigs captured in the party. Two of the Democratic delegates to the state convention in 1860 were Know-Nothings, and men such as Campbell and Bruce came to the party through the American organization. The Know-Nothings were a transitional party for people going both ways in 1854–56. [52] Like the Republicans, however, the Democrats selected more men from other parties as candidates to woo new voters than they did delegates to conventions. While 22 percent of

51. *Gazette*, Sept. 6, 1860; J. K. Moorhead to Simon Cameron, Pittsburgh, Nov. 21, 1860, Cameron MSS.

52. *Post*, Jan. 30, 1860. Barr said in the same editorial that many Democrats left the party after 1854, joined the Know-Nothings, and then went into the Republican party before 1860. For additional evidence of Know-Nothings and antitaxers in the Democratic party, see P. C. Shannon to William Bigler, Pittsburgh, Feb. 1, 1860, Bigler MSS.

the Democratic candidates had been Whigs, only 4 (13%) of 31 Democratic secondary leaders were former Whigs.

The emergence of new men with different backgrounds as Republican and Democratic leaders after 1857 also produced the new similarity between the parties. Fewer wealthy businessmen led the Republicans in 1860 than had participated in the incipient party in 1856. For example, 47 percent of the Republican candidates in the 1855–57 sample owned property valued at $25,000 or more, while in the 1858–60 sample, only 27 percent did. Among the Republican secondary leaders, the proportion owning property valued at over $10,000 was almost three times as large in 1856 as in 1860.[53] Likewise, fewer Republican leaders were large merchants and manufacturers. Among the leaders of both parties the number of lawyers and doctors also dropped, and there was an increase in the proportions of leaders who apparently were skilled artisans rising through the ranks. Even the numbers of Republicans who could be identified as Presbyterians had dropped since 1856.[54]

53. In the 1856 sample of Republican delegates 43 percent owned property valued over $10,000, but in the 1858–60 sample only 16 percent did. Similarly only 11 percent owned property valued over $25,000 in 1860, but 25 percent had in 1856–57.

54. See Tables 39, 40, 53, and 54. The number of professional men (lawyers and doctors) among the convention delegates of the Republicans dropped from 24 in 1856 to 5 in 1860. For the Democratic delegates, it dropped from 17 in 1856 to 5 in 1860. The proportion of skilled artisans among the secondary leaders rose from 17 percent to 27 percent for the Republicans and from 16 percent to 27 percent for the Democrats. The number of Republican leaders identifiable as Presbyterians dropped from 29 in 1856–57 to 15 in 1858–60. As will be argued below, this decrease suggests much about the change in the type of Republican leaders. After 1857 the old social elite abandoned politics to different men.

Of course one must allow for a possible decrease since 1856 in the proportions that occupational or religious groups such as the Presbyterians formed

These changes in Republican leadership after 1857 made it far different from that of the Whigs around 1848. While the large majority of those Republicans whose former political affiliation could be determined were Whigs, it is very significant that only 23 (25%) of a total of 91 candidates and 23 (29%) of 80 Republican delegates could be identified as former Whigs.[55] A few of the others came from other parties, but the bulk were men who either had not participated actively in either party earlier or could not do so because of age or nationality. With more Germans and Irishmen among these emerging Republican leaders, they were much less clearly representative of established native-born families than the Whigs had been. Similarly, a smaller proportion of the Republican leaders than of the Whigs came from the wealthy elite.[56] Finally, that a significantly smaller proportion of Republicans than of Whigs were leaders or members of the prominent Presbyterian and Episcopalian churches suggests

of the population in 1860 to make these comparisons exact. Since, however, the population did not grow that much in this short period, the comparisons do seem valid. On the other hand, it is true, as I have shown in Chap. 4, that many of the wealthy native-born Protestants who had lived in the city in 1850 had moved outside it by 1860.

55. In order to track down former political affiliations, I used not only lists of candidates and convention delegates, but executive committees, clubs, ward vigilance committees, and the signers of petitions to various candidates of both parties.

56. Compare Tables 51–58 with Tables 8–15. Among the secondary leaders 27 percent of the Whigs in my sample for 1847–51 owned property valued over $10,000 while only 16 percent of the Republicans in 1860 did. Since I measured Whig wealth in the 1850 returns and Republican wealth in the 1860 census returns, it is remarkable that in this one category a larger proportion of Whigs than Republicans owned property valued over $10,000. See Appendix B for a discussion of the differences in the 1850 and 1860 censuses. It should be noted, however, that I have not attempted to account for changes in the cost of living between 1850 and 1860 or in the value of money.

that fewer of the social elite participated in the Republican than in Whig leadership.[57]

Still other evidence exists that the old patrician elite which had dominated the Whigs abdicated the leadership of both parties in 1860 to other groups. After the fall election of 1859 Barr of the *Post* complained about the "neglect manifested by those who are esteemed the best men in the community to interest themselves in the political affairs of the county." He elaborated:

Those who, in fact, have the greatest stake in the government attend the least to the proper administration of that government. A large proportion of the intelligent and wealthy classes are accustomed to turn up their noses at politics and politicians, and make it their boast that they never read political articles, never attend a primary meeting and never take the trouble to vote except when it perfectly suits their convenience. . . . In this county, politics has become a trade, and men unqualified for office and regardless of public welfare, make use of the worst material in the community for the purpose of serving their own ends.

He then asked why incompetent men held local offices. "Sim-

57. My very inability to identify more Republican leaders as Presbyterians and Episcopalians is vastly significant. Among my sample of 216 Whig leaders I identified 41 (19%) Presbyterians and 25 (11%) Episcopalians, but of 171 Republicans in my 1860 sample I could find only 15 (9%) Presbyterians and 15 Episcopalians. My sources for the identification of denominational affiliation, the same used in Chaps. 1, 2, and 5, included only important laymen from many churches and the membership rolls of the most socially prominent churches. (For those sources see Appendix B.) Elders and vestrymen, I think, can well be considered members of the social elite, and the drop in absolute numbers between 1848 and 1860 indicates a defection of that elite from political leadership.

ply because good men for public position, disgusted with politics, will not serve the public. Our merchants, our manufacturers, our best lawyers, and other professional men, refuse to accept nominations for public positions." While Barr may have exaggerated, the editors of the *Gazette* and the *Dispatch* echoed his complaint about local officeholders, and the change in Republican leadership seems to confirm it.[58]

Several factors account for this abnegation by the social and economic elite. First, as always, the low salaries of local officials deterred able men who could make more money in business from seeking political office. Second, some of the former Whig leaders had died or were too old to participate actively any longer. Third, some manufacturers and merchants who had led the Whigs were probably intimidated by the threat of sectional conflict and lost markets in the South, and therefore they refused to work actively for the Republicans. Indeed, early in January 1860 a New Orleans editor called for merchants in that city to stop purchasing Pittsburgh products because the Republicans had won the mayoral election of 1860, and other Southerners continually threatened to cut off trade with Republicans.[59] Fourth, the open defiance of the law and the courts by both parties on the railroad tax issue drove some of the law-abiding commercial and social elite away from political activities. The marked decrease in the number of wealthy men among Republicans and the lawyers in both parties after 1857 especially shows this effect. New, less prominent men seized power in these crucial years. The importance of the railroad tax issue in changing the nature of leadership between 1856 and 1860 probably cannot be exag-

58. *Post,* Oct. 15, 1859; *Gazette,* Aug. 15, 1860; *Dispatch,* June 2, 1858.
59. *New Orleans Bulletin* quoted in the *Gazette,* Jan. 21, 1860; see also *Gazette,* Dec. 6, 1859, and Sept. 29, 1860.

gerated. Finally, the palpable growth of the political power of the working-class and immigrant groups allowed them to choose as leaders men of their own kind who would express their desires. Unwilling to follow the lead of the conservative elite who might want to moderate anti-Southern positions in Republican platforms or especially to honor the municipal and county debt, these groups simultaneously disgusted "the best men in the community" and displaced them as political chieftains. By the late 1850s, as in some other cities of the country, the most responsible citizens of Pittsburgh had already abandoned the governing of their city to less able men. They had also failed to retain control of the leadership of the party which supposedly represented them.[60]

The defection from politics of the city's most prominent men gave party leadership a different tone than it had had earlier. It especially made the Republicans different from the Whigs. The heads or scions of established and distinguished families in the city, Whig leaders such as Harmar Denny, Joseph Pennock, Robert McKnight, Thomas Bakewell, and Frederick Lorenz, had belonged to the same churches, attended the same

60. It should be noted, however, that newspapers continued to comment that most of the wealthy businessmen of the community were Republican in inclination (*Post*, Apr. 12, 1858). Some obviously were. Among the officers of the mass Republican rally in September 1860 were some very wealthy men who did not attend party conventions or run for office. A few of these were: James McAuley, a former Whig and banker worth $120,000; William Robinson, Jr., a Whig and former president of the Ohio and Pennsylvania Railroad, who was worth $500,000; Thomas Bakewell, onetime Whig and glass manufacturer worth $40,000; and George W. Jackson, former Free-Soiler and merchant worth $200,000. Significantly, three of these men were members of the First or Third Presbyterian Church, and Jackson was an Episcopalian vestryman. These were the types who had led the Whigs, who were affiliated with the Republicans, but who did not participate actively in the leadership of the Republican party. As officers of the rally, they were probably more symbols than influential leaders.

parties, and been imbued with common values because of so much business and social contact. Their participation in and domination of the leadership of the Whig party had been an extension of their tightly knit social connections. By 1860, however, Republican leadership was no longer an exclusive gentlemen's club; rather it was much more representative of the entire population of the city. Granted, some of the old Whigs like Denny and Lorenz had died since 1850, but others still lived and abstained from politics. If many Republicans had once been Whigs, they were often a different type than the old Whig patricians. The emergence of new parties in the 1850s gave new men a chance to run them.

Despite the change in Republican leadership, the efforts to broaden the Republican appeal, and the greatly more efficient Republican organization, the Republicans failed to win a much more impressive victory in Pittsburgh in 1860 than they had in 1856. The total vote that year was almost the same as in 1856. Although both Curtin and Lincoln polled large majorities in the city, Curtin's vote in the crucial October election was no greater than that polled by Frémont and Fillmore combined in 1856. Despite the Democratic divisions, Foster's vote almost equaled Buchanan's, although it did drop in four wards.

The split may have kept some Democrats from the polls in November, but the October defeat was more influential. Lincoln's majority was larger than Curtin's, but this increase resulted primarily from the predicted drop in the Democratic vote after the October elections rather than from additional Republican votes. The Democratic total in Pittsburgh fell from 2,847 in October to 2,079 a month later. Barr wailed, "It appears to us that the Democracy have made some mistake and neglected to vote. . . . The Democracy since the result of the state elections have been disheartened and discouraged. They have not worked with their accustomed energy." [61]

In the more representative October election, not only did both Democrats and Republicans capture almost the same number of votes as in 1856, but the votes tended to come from the same sources.[62] As in 1856, Protestants, whether rich or poor, tended to vote Republican more solidly than any ethnic, occupational, or other group. In both the gubernatorial and presidential elections, moreover, the Republicans' effort to retain the Know-Nothing vote proved successful, for they amassed the largest majorities in those wards where the Know-Nothings had been the strongest. On the other hand, the Democrats apparently continued to draw their most solid support from Catholics, particularly German and Irish Catholics in wards with relatively poor people.[63]

What slight increase there was in the Republican vote probably came from diverse sources. The natural increase in the electorate was one, and newspapers asserted that the Republicans won the votes of young men voting for the first time. The Republicans also absorbed some of the vote Fillmore had won in 1856. Finally, their more thorough canvass among the workers produced an increase in support among the very poor. Ac-

61. See Table 59; *Post*, Nov. 7, 1860.
62. See Tables 59, 60, and 61. Note the very high correlations between the vote for Frémont in 1856 and the votes for Curtin and Lincoln in 1860 and between the vote for Buchanan in 1856 and the vote for Foster and the combined Democratic vote for President in 1860 (i.e. both the Douglas straight and the Douglas fusion tickets).
63. See Tables 60 and 61. For the analysis of the ethnic and religious makeup of the group owning property valued between $100 and $1,000, and of the group owning property valued at less than $100, see Appendix B.

cording to newspapers, some of these were Democrats, and many may have been German and Irish Protestants since there is little evidence of additional support from native Americans.[64] No matter what the sources of new voters, however, the essential fact is that the major split in voting was again along ethnic and denominational lines, for neither party tended to win bloc support from workers or employers.

The division along denominational lines was predictable. Protestants and Catholics had been divided on many issues since the middle of the decade. Protestants may have disliked slavery more than Catholics did; they took a more active role in the fight against it. In 1860 some Protestants in Pittsburgh formed the Church Antislavery Society which denounced slavery as a moral sin, called on Christian ministers to treat it as such, and demanded "its total extinction" at once.[65] But the difference in attitudes toward slavery alone did not account for the different voting behavior. The Sabbatarian issue had alienated some Protestants from Catholics in 1859. The desire of foreign-born Protestants not to be associated with the Sunday

64. *Gazette*, Sept. 6, Oct. 24, 1860. Former Know-Nothings among Republicans had worked very hard with the Americans who had voted for Fillmore in 1856 to keep them behind Curtin rather than joining the Foster ranks. See L. O. Cameron to Simon Cameron, Pittsburgh, Oct. 10, 1860, Cameron MSS. For evidence that some Fillmore men supported Curtin see Table 59. For evidence that some of the additional support came from the very poor, see Table 60, and note the increase in the correlations between the Republican votes in 1856 and 1860 and the group owning property valued at less than $100. The *Gazette* in the first issue cited in this note said that many Germans had come over, and in the fifth ward where it noted as many as sixty converts to Republicanism, there was a large concentration of Germans. Moreover, it is doubtful that the increased vote came from native Americans since the correlation between that group and the Republicans decreased between 1856 and 1860. On the other hand, the size of the negative correlation with the Germans decreased. See Tables 60 and 61.

65. *Gazette*, Feb. 2, 1860.

activities of their Catholic countrymen particularly shows how divisive this issue could be and how it could split ethnic blocs. Although it was not an open political issue in 1860, the Pittsburgh synod of the Presbyterian Church had denounced the frequent violations of the Sabbath by non-Protestants since the 1859 elections.[66] This disagreement over the Sunday issue reinforced traditional voting patterns. In 1856 both native- and foreign-born Protestants had joined the Republican party because they disliked Catholics as well as because they wanted to oppose the slave power, and they remained with it in 1860. On the other hand, Catholics had remained loyal to the party most amenable to their interests. Fearful of the militant Protestantism evidenced by the ministers and laymen who espoused the antislavery stands of the Republicans, they clung to the Democratic party.

In many ways, then, the votes for and against Lincoln in 1860 did not result from a single campaign but represented the continuation of a division which had occurred earlier. The habitual dislike of the type of person who belonged to the other party and loyalty to one's own party, as much as the national issues, produced the Republican victory in Pittsburgh. V. O. Key has noted in a study of modern political behavior that political cleavages often do not come from "conflicting attachments to issues" but from "loyalties to competing groups." [67] The pattern in Pittsburgh suggests that much of the Republican vote for Lincoln throughout the North, especially in areas where Know-Nothings once flourished, may have come from habitual antagonism to the Democrats and

66. *Gazette*, Oct. 26, 1859. See Chap. 6.
67. V. O. Key, *Public Opinion and American Democracy* (New York, 1961), p. 60.

Catholics rather than from any strong feelings about the morality of slavery.

As the result of a long-term trend, the voting support of the Republicans and Democrats in Pittsburgh differed somewhat from that of the earlier Whigs and Democrats. Where the Whigs had received substantial support from wealthy businessmen, the Republicans did not, and that group no longer tended to vote solidly for either party. Instead, the Republicans received their most solid support from poor Protestants, and with a direct appeal to workingmen they won much more support from among propertyless groups than the Whigs ever had. Conversely, the Democrats who dropped their class appeals to workers by 1860 had lost much of the support from laborers and the propertyless they had once had. Similarly, the Whigs had won very solid support from native-born Americans, rich and poor, but the Republicans were not nearly so homogeneously native American in makeup.[68] Nor did the immigrant groups support the Democrats so solidly in 1860 as they had in the late 1840s. The ethnic and economic distinctions between the earlier parties had been erased and only the sharp denominational lines remained by 1860. Both parties were broader and more heterogeneous coalitions than the earlier organizations.

68. There are two ways to explain the lower correlation between the native-born Americans and Republicans than between that group and the Whigs. The first is to argue that fewer native Americans supported the Republicans than had supported the Whigs. That is, after 1854 some joined the Democrats or else abstained. The second is to argue that there were more immigrants in the Republican coalition than in the Whig coalition, and this increase of immigrants rather than any decrease of native Americans meant that the Republicans had less homogeneous voting support than the Whigs. Both are valid, but the second factor seems more important in accounting for the lower correlations. The Republicans in 1860 were much stronger in the newer wards than the Whigs had been.

Eight

CONCLUSION

Politics in Pittsburgh in the dozen years before the Civil War did not revolve exclusively around national questions. To Pittsburgh's citizens in the 1850s immediate local matters loomed much larger than they have to historians a century later. These local issues and conditions as much as national issues determined the character and makeup of opposing political parties. Any explanations, therefore, of the shift from a Whig to a Republican majority in Pittsburgh based only on national platforms or assertions about increasing sectional conflict and the slavery issue are inadequate and distorted.

To insist on the importance of local matters, however, is not to excise the slavery issue from the 1850s. Indeed, most people in Pittsburgh, Democrats as well as Whigs or Republicans, disliked slavery and especially resented the national influence of the South, and these animosities contributed to the rise of the Republican party there. The unanimity of its citizens against compromise with the South during the secession crisis is ample proof of such sentiment. In January 1861 Russell Errett wrote Simon Cameron, "Those who are familiar only with the public sentiment at Harrisburg, Philadelphia, New York, and Washington can have no idea of the fierceness of sentiment, here, in opposition to anything that looks like compromise. It amounts almost to a fury." [1] Since most men of all parties shared these free-soil and anti-Southern, and one might add, anti-Negro, sentiments, they do not seem to have been the crucial factors that distinguished the men in one party from those in the other, although they probably helped bring a greater number of men into the coalitions which opposed the Democrats. Men chose their parties often for other reasons, and local issues frequently determined the choice.

Although Democrats appealed to very real local discontent around 1850, several disadvantages prevented them from attaining a majority in Pittsburgh. Almost everyone disliked the pro-Southern policies of the national party, and men probably voted Democratic in spite of, rather than because of, the national platform. Trying to ignore national issues, the Democrats, in contrast to their opponents, stressed important local matters. In the late 1840s they seized on working-class discontent and tried to construct a coalition of relatively poor and propertyless workers. While most of their voters indeed came from these groups, not all of the poor voted Democratic. Most immigrants and Catholics who could vote were Democrats, but many native American workers who resented these newcomers apparently clung to the Whig party.

1. Russell Errett to Simon Cameron, Pittsburgh, Jan. 23, 1861, Cameron MSS. Further proof of this bipartisan anti-Southern sentiment is that Pittsburgh's outraged citizens protested almost to a man when Secretary of War John B. Floyd ordered guns shipped from the arsenal in Pittsburgh to the South in December 1860. Correspondents warned President Buchanan they would riot to prevent such a move. See *Gazette*, Dec. 25, 27, 1860; *Dispatch*, Dec. 28, 1860; James R. Speer to James Buchanan, Pittsburgh, Dec. 24, 1860, Citizens Committee of Pittsburgh to Buchanan, Dec. 25, 1860, and James May to Buchanan, Dec. 26, 1860, Buchanan MSS (HSP).

The Whigs responded to the Democratic agitation of class differences and local tensions by concentrating on national questions. Denying that different classes even existed, the Whigs stressed a paternalistic, probusiness program of positive economic legislation which would bring prosperity to both employers and workers. They also opposed the spread of slavery in order to reduce the political power of the South. Although Whig positions on these national issues were popular, it is not clear that they alone drew out the Whig vote. The bulk of the wealthy men in the community voted Whig, and they may have been attracted by the probusiness platform. Just as likely, however, they voted for the Whigs because their friends and acquaintances—the wealthy, native-born merchants and manufacturers who constituted the city's business and social elite—dominated Whig leadership and lent the party a patrician tone. Moreover, while most rich men were Whigs, the majority of Whig voters were native-born Protestants from among the middle and working classes. It is difficult to believe that Whig economic appeals had a special attraction for them and not for the foreign-born citizens who voted Democratic. The effectiveness of Whig economic appeals is particularly questionable because in 1850 a Workingman's Congress spurned the idea that the protective tariff was a prolabor measure. True, some could have voted for the Whigs because they were more anti-Southern than the Democrats, but their hostility toward the immigrants also explains why they followed the lead of wealthy, native-born businessmen. Thus, although Whigs stressed national issues, local social tensions helped them maintain the upper hand in Pittsburgh.

As long as ethnic and religious differences split economic classes, and elections did not directly involve the immediate interests or dislikes of the working classes who formed the great bulk of the potential electorate, the Whigs maintained their majority in state and national elections. In certain local elections, however, the Whigs lost some of their working-class support. A depression from 1848 to 1851 led to wage cuts, strikes, and labor riots, all of which alienated native-born workers from the businessmen who led the Whigs in the elections of 1849 and 1850. If economic grievances caused workers to overlook temporarily their ethnic differences and desert the Whigs, a more effective exploitation of religious animosities by a third candidate also injured them. When Joe Barker, an anti-Catholic demagogue, ran for mayor in 1850, 1851, and 1852, he drew the votes of poor Protestants away from the Whigs, who as the anti-Democratic party normally benefited from the anti-Catholic prejudices of those Protestants. Other local matters, such as corruption by local Whig administrators, factionalism, and an ill-advised endorsement of temperance legislation, weakened the Whigs in the early 1850s and helped the Democrats rally a unified immigrant support.

Local conditions also vitally affected the transition from a Whig to a Republican majority between 1854 and 1856, and explanations of these years only in terms of reaction to the Kansas-Nebraska Act are unsatisfactory. No straight-line evolution from a Whig to a Republican party occurred after the passage of that act. Nor did the act alone shatter existing parties. The Whigs had been weakened previously. The Democratic coalition was collapsing at that time for other reasons—dissatisfaction with patronage policies, jealousy of the influence of Catholics in the party, and the impatience of outs with the perpetual control of party ins. Finally, the proximate causes of the rise of the Know-Nothing party in

1854 appeared before the passage of that bill. Indeed, grievances against immigrants and Catholics had long existed, but they became particularly virulent around 1853 and 1854 when the five-year naturalization period expired and immigrants who had come to the city in the late 1840s began to vote.

Between 1854 and 1856 anti-Catholic and free-soil elements looked for a new party, but it was not clear in what form the new anti-Democratic Protestant coalition would crystallize. Most Whigs, many of whom were poor workers who had readily deserted the Whigs earlier to vote for an anti-Catholic candidate, eventually joined the Know-Nothings. Because the Americans combined temperance, free-soil, and political reform with nativism, they were more attractive to these Whigs than anti-Nebraska coalitions and the incipient Republican party which ran on the slavery issue alone. Almost a third of the Know-Nothings' leaders, and originally a fourth of their voters, were Democrats, but the bulk of both were former Whigs. Fairly young men, generally from the middle and lower classes, Know-Nothing leaders had been in the second ranks of the older parties; particularly some of the Democrats had been outs. For several reasons, most dissident Democrats who left their party after 1854 joined the Know-Nothings before they went into the Republican party in 1856. Unlike native-born Protestants, however, foreign Protestants, who also hated Catholics and who broke with the Democrats, could not abide the Americans. After changing sides rapidly in 1854 and 1855, they along with the Know-Nothings would join the Republicans by the presidential election of 1856.

If most Whigs eventually entered the American party, others did not join the secret order. The strength of the Antimasonic tradition which had kept many voters in the Whig ranks prevented them from becoming Know-Nothings. These men remained with the Whig anti-Nebraska coalition in the fall of 1854, and in January 1855 they combined with Democrats in an anti-Know-Nothing movement. In October of that year some went into the new Republican party, which denounced secret societies, while others remained with the Democrats as the best anti-Know-Nothing party. Indeed, the Democrats won the elections of 1855 because they gained so much additional support as a foe of the nativists. The latter group of Antimasonic Whigs stayed with the Democrats in 1856 after Republicans combined with Know-Nothings. In short, the strong Antimasonic tradition in Pittsburgh determined to a large degree which Whigs joined the Democratic party by 1856.

The Republican party lost in 1855 because it campaigned on only one issue—slavery extension—and because it openly opposed the Know-Nothings. In 1856 it corrected these errors. Dropping the name "Republican," local leaders made formal alliances with the Americans and ran as Union parties, included Know-Nothings on tickets, and adopted anti-Catholic planks in the state platform. Only by so doing and by soft-pedaling the antiforeign appeals of Know-Nothings did they win the support of native-born Know-Nothings as well as Protestant immigrants. To attract former Democrats and Free-Soilers, Republicans dropped the Whig economic appeals and campaigned primarily against Southern aggressions, but the party's leaders and supporters were still mainly former Whigs. Despite the emphasis of Republican appeals, the party was as much an anti-Catholic as an antislavery coalition in 1856, for native- and foreign-born Protestants voted against the Catholics, who solidly went Democratic.

In the years between 1856 and 1860 resistance to slavery extension alone could not sustain the Republican party in Pittsburgh. What most interested the city's voters in these years was not Catholic aggressions, slavery, the South, or Kansas, but their own difficulties with railroads and tax increases. Popular wrath at supposed railroad transgressions foreshadowed the later Granger uprisings. The Democrats first capitalized on this hostility in 1857, but soon Republicans matched their invective against new taxes to pay the interest on bonds issued to railroad companies. Indeed, the congressional campaign of 1858 revolved around railroads, not the Lecompton constitution, as it supposedly did in other Northern areas. Only by actively demonstrating their hostility to railroads and taxes and by wooing Know-Nothing support did the Republicans remain a majority.

According to traditional interpretations, the Republicans broadened their coalition considerably between 1856 and 1860 by moderating their antislavery stand and adding economic planks such as the protective tariff to attract conservative Whigs. In Pittsburgh, however, the 1860 vote was not much larger than in 1856, and it came from remarkably similar sources. This lack of change, like the lack of labor enthusiasm for the tariff, raises even more doubts about the importance of that issue in attracting Republican or Whig support. Indeed, rather than becoming more conservative in those years, the leadership of the Pittsburgh Republicans became less conservative, for many wealthy businessmen and lawyers who had participated actively in the incipient, more radical Republican party of 1856 no longer did. What drove these men away from the Republicans and the Democrats was the antitax uprising which forced both parties to defy the courts and the law.

By 1860 the parties differed somewhat from the Whigs and Democrats in the late 1840s. Although the Republicans appeared to inherit the Whig majority and although most Whigs apparently became Republicans, the new party was less patrician in leadership and in tone. The wealthy social elite did not work so actively for them as they had for the Whigs nor did they have so much influence. The Republicans had lost one segment of the old Whig coalition, part of the Antimasonic Whigs, to the Democrats, and they had apparently gained many immigrant Protestant voters. As a result, they were not nearly so homogeneously native American as the Whigs had been, in leadership or in support. On the other hand, while the Democrats maintained the support of immigrant Catholics, they gained the allegiance of Antimasonic Whigs, and their resulting coalition no longer came so uniformly from poorer groups. Indeed, as foreign-born Protestants shifted to the Republicans to vote against their Catholic countrymen, the Democrats no longer received the degree of support from the working classes they had won earlier. What clear economic differences there had been between the leadership, appeals, and voting support of the two parties in the early 1850s were now blurred.

Why did the Republican party become so strong in Pittsburgh by 1860? As an anti-Southern party it, like the earlier Whig party, undoubtedly benefited greatly from the jealousy in Pittsburgh toward the South. Moreover, the nature of its membership and that of the Democratic party indicates that the virulent animosities between Protestants and Catholics which emerged in the 1850s greatly added to the party's strength once it became the only anti-Democratic party. Disagreements over division of the public school fund, Sabbatarianism, and the political role of Catholics cut across ethnic and economic lines. Thus the strength and influence of the Protestant denominations in the city helped foster the rise of such a powerful Republican party.

The appeals and voting behavior in Pittsburgh create doubts about how much the moral issue of slavery shaped political patterns in the North in the 1850s. First, it is unclear that sectional and partisan differences grew out of a fundamental cleavage over the morality of slavery. Not the oppression of the slave, but slavery extension which threatened to bring the hated Negro into the territories and which apparently involved Southern aggression on Northern rights seems to have been the major popular grievance against the South in the North. Second, it is not certain that even sectional issues, let alone moral indignation, motivated Northern voters. Some local factors in Pittsburgh like the railroad tax crisis may have been unique, but in almost every city of the North local conditions may also have importantly shaped the nature of the Republican and Democratic parties. Anti-Catholic and nativist elements were probably fundamental blocs of Republican coalitions in other areas where the Know-Nothings had flourished.[2] One can accept Richard P. McCormick's conclusion that the second American party system "could survive only by avoiding regionally divisive issues"[3] and agree that sectional animosity intensified by the issue of slavery extension destroyed the old national party system and brought about the replacement of the Whig party in the North by the Republican party without agreeing that sectional antagonism alone explains either the defection of Northern Whigs from their party or the voting support of the new party. Why the Republican party emerged and why people voted for it are two different

2. This view finds support in an excellent essay in Joel H. Silbey, *The Transformation of American Politics, 1840–1860* (Englewood Cliffs, N.J., 1967), pp. 1–34.

3. Richard P. McCormick, *The Second American Party System: Party Formation in the Jacksonian Era* (Chapel Hill, N.C., 1966), p. 15.

questions which do not necessarily have the same answer. Southerners were correct to interpret the vote for Lincoln as an assault on their section, but it represented as well the continuation of voting patterns which had formed in the 1850s because of traditional party loyalties and bitter religious hatreds.

Appendix A

Tables

TABLE 1

ANNUAL VALUE OF MANUFACTURES IN PITTSBURGH[a]

Type	1826	1836	1850	1860[b]
Iron	$1,155,094	$ 6,290,000	$ 6,300,000	$ 7,315,461[c]
Glass	199,804	1,260,000	1,000,000	2,075,173
Cotton	288,032	500,000	1,500,000	1,076,333
Total	2,553,549	11,606,350	16,686,032[d]	11,896,474[e]

a. Table compiled from: Catherine Elizabeth Reiser, *Pittsburgh's Commercial Development* (Harrisburg, 1951), p. 203; *Eighth Census of the United States: 1860. Manufacturing*, pp. 493–95.

b. These figures are for the county.

c. I calculated this figure by adding up the values of all iron products. This group included: agricultural implements; bolts and nuts; hardware; iron bar; sheet, castings, stoves, forgings, pipes, and railing; pig iron; machinery and steam engines; safes; and scales.

d. This figure is for the county.

e. This figure is for the city. The combined value for Pittsburgh and Allegheny was $14,672,888.

TABLE 2

COMPARATIVE POPULATION GROWTH OF CITIES*

City	1830	1840	1850	1860
Chicago		4,853	29,963	109,260
Cincinnati	24,831	46,338	115,436	161,044
Louisville	10,341	21,210	43,194	68,033
Philadelphia	161,410	220,423	340,045	565,529
Pittsburgh	12,568	21,115	46,601	49,217
St. Louis	5,852	16,469	77,860	160,773

* J. D. B. DeBow, *Statistical View of the United States* (Washington, 1854), p. 192; *Eighth Census of the United States: 1860. Mortality*, 1, xviii. Coupled with that of Allegheny City, Pittsburgh's population grew from 67,863 in 1850 to 77,919 in 1860.

TABLE 3

POPULATION INCREASE IN CITY AND COUNTY

Year	City[a]	Percent Growth	County[b]	Percent Growth
1810	4,768		25,317	
1820	7,248	52	34,921	40
1830	12,568	73	50,552	42
1840	21,115	68	81,235	60
1850	46,601	120.6	138,290	70
1860	49,217	5.6	178,831	30
1870	86,076	75	262,204	46.62

a. *Tenth Census of the United States: 1880. Social Statistics of Cities*, 1, 850.

b. Pennsylvania Bureau of Industrial Statistics, *First Annual Report of the Bureau of Statistics of Labor and Agriculture, for the Years 1872–73* (Harrisburg, 1874), p. 17.

TABLE 4

ETHNIC DISTRIBUTION IN PITTSBURGH IN 1850 [a]

Ward	Native	German	Irish	British	Negroes[b]
First	635	205	260	66	53
Second	638	119	239	131	107
Third	740	428	976	161	393
Fourth	583	107	329	80	85
Fifth	478	669	804	203	20
Sixth	531	139	712	121	741
Seventh	139	78	198	46	528
Eighth	238	324	421	243	29
Ninth	155	160	150	51	3

a. These figures represent the number of white males over twenty-one in each group, except for the Negroes. Native-born sons who lived with immigrant fathers were assigned to the nationality classification of their fathers. The figures on the white males came from a count in the manuscript census of 1850.

b. These figures represent the entire Negro population of the city—men, women, and children. They can be found in the *Census of 1850*, p. 158. The Hayti district along Wylie Avenue extended into the third, sixth, and seventh wards.

TABLE 5

DISTRIBUTION OF POPULATION IN PITTSBURGH ACCORDING
TO VALUE OF REAL PROPERTY OWNED IN 1850 *

Ward	None (percent)	$1–999 (percent)	$1000–4999 (percent)	$5000–9999 (percent)	$10,000–49,000 (percent)	Over $50,000 (percent)
First	81.4	1.8	7	4	4	1.4
Second	80.9	1.4	6	4	6.4	.9
Third	82.4	2.1	8.8	4	2.4	.35
Fourth	75.1	1.7	5.6	2.8	9.5	4.6
Fifth	96	.2	2	.6	.55	.15
Sixth	87.3	.2	8.7	1.6	1.95	.22
Seventh	72.1	3.4	19.5	2.3	1.5	.7
Eighth	92	.3	6.1	1.1	.9	.15
Ninth	90	0	7	2	1	0

* This table includes only white males over twenty-one and is based on the evaluation of real property listed in the manuscript census of 1850. Sons who lived at home with wealthy parents were included in the same category as their parents. If the wife of a man had separate property of her own, I combined the value of her property with that of her husband's and categorized him according to the total value of property owned in the family.

TABLE 6

COMPARISON OF PERSONS PER DWELLING IN PITTSBURGH
IN 1850 WITH VARIOUS INDICES OF WEALTH PER WARD

Ward	Persons[a] per Dwelling	Families per Dwelling	Average[b] Wealth, Real Estate	Average[c] Wealth, Furniture	Percent[d] Owning $10,000+
First	8.03	1.16	$336	$1.11	5.4
Second	8.08	1.08	268	.25	7.3
Third	6.88	1.25	164	.20	2.75
Fourth	8.20	1.14	308	8.29	14.1
Fifth	5.47	1.02	92	.76	.7
Sixth	5.75	1.13	59	.38	2.2
Seventh	5.57	1.03	58	.08	2.2
Eighth	7.46	1.16	38	.04	1.05
Ninth	5.13	1.01	21	.07	1.0

a. I calculated these figures by dividing the total population of each ward as listed in the published 1850 census by the number of dwellings in each ward as listed in the manuscript census of 1850. The populations of the wards may be found in the *Census of 1850*, pp. 158–59.

b. I calculated these figures by dividing the assessed value of the real estate in each ward in 1847 by the total number of people in that ward in 1850. The assessment figures may be found in the *Gazette*, Sept. 22, 1847. The figures for 1850 are not available.

c. I calculated these figures by dividing the assessed value of the furniture in each ward in 1847 by that ward's population in 1850. Because real estate figures include industrial property like factories, this index is probably the best to show the relative personal wealth in the wards. The furniture assessment may also be found in the *Gazette*, Sept. 22, 1847.

d. These percentages are based on the adult white males over twenty-one listed in the manuscript census of 1850.

TABLE 7

NUMBERS BELONGING TO CERTAIN OCCUPATIONAL TYPES IN PITTSBURGH IN 1850 [a]

Ward	Unskilled Laborers	Skilled Artisans	Profes- sional	Manu- facturers	Mer- chants	Bankers[b]
First	207	327	36	10	31	5
Second	185	228	69	36	54	13
Third	677	630	70	11	27	4
Fourth	219	240	67	29	75	10
Fifth	798	690	12	8	18	0
Sixth	528	381	36	6	22	3
Seventh	183	83	8	0	4	1
Eighth	620	252	10	5	9	0
Ninth	211	133	0	1	5	0

a. This table includes only white males over twenty-one.

b. I have included in this category men whose occupations are listed as "Gentlemen" in the census. These men were wealthy and retired or else wealthy enough not to have to work.

TABLE 8

WEALTH DISTRIBUTION AMONG WHIG AND DEMOCRATIC CANDIDATES, 1848–51 [a]

Group	Whigs[b]	Democrats[c]
$100,000 plus	4 (5%)	2 (3.5%)
$50,000–99,999	13 (18%)	5 (9%)
$10,000–49,999	19 (25%)	9 (16%)
$5,000–9,999	8 (10%)	8 (14%)
$1,000–4,999	11 (14%)	7 (12%)
$1–999	0	2 (3.5%)
None	21 (28%)	24 (42%)

a. The types of men included in this leadership table and in subsequent tables analyzing the backgrounds of party leaders and the sources from which that background information was gleaned are described in Appendix B. In each leadership table, percentages are based only on the number of leaders about whom I found information, not on the total number of men in each sample. This present table is drawn from a total sample of 97 candidates from each party.

b. N = 76.

c. N = 57.

TABLE 9

WEALTH DISTRIBUTION AMONG THE SECONDARY WHIG AND DEMOCRATIC LEADERS, 1847–51 *

Group	Whigs	Democrats
$100,000 plus	1 (1%)	0
$50,000–99,999	3 (4%)	1 (1.8%)
$10,000–49,999	16 (22%)	5 (10%)
$5,000–9,999	13 (18%)	6 (11%)
$1,000–4,999	14 (20%)	11 (20%)
$1–999	0	2 (3.6%)
None	25 (35%)	29 (53.5%)

* This table is drawn from a total sample of 119 Whigs and 107 Democrats.

TABLE 10

DISTRIBUTION OF WHIG AND DEMOCRATIC CANDIDATES, 1848–51,
AMONG OCCUPATIONAL CATEGORIES[a]

Occupation	Whigs[b]	Democrats[c]
Iron and glass manufacturers	13 (15.5%)	7 (9%)
Other manufacturers	12 (14%)	10 (12.5%)
Merchants	12 (14%)	8 (10%)
Shopkeepers and clerks	19 (23%)	11 (14%)
Bankers and brokers	3 (3.5%)	1 (1.3%)
Professional	11 (13%)	23 (29%)
Gentlemen	1	2
Artisans and skilled laborers	12 (15.5%)	16 (20%)
Unskilled laborers	1	2

a. This table is drawn from the same sample of 97 candidates from each
party as Table 8.
b. N = 84.
c. N = 80.

TABLE 11

DISTRIBUTION OF WHIG AND DEMOCRATIC SECONDARY LEADERS,
1847–51, AMONG OCCUPATIONAL CATEGORIES[a]

Occupation	Whigs[b]	Democrats[c]
Iron and glass manufacturers	8 (8%)	1
Other manufacturers	14 (15%)	12 (14%)
Merchants	11 (11.5%)	6 (7%)
Shopkeepers and clerks	28 (29%)	32 (37%)
Professional	11 (11.5%)	10 (11%)
Gentlemen	0	1
Artisans and skilled workers	21 (22%)	20 (23%)
Unskilled laborers	3 (3%)	5 (6%)

a. This table is drawn from the same sample of leaders as used in Table 9.
b. N = 96.
c. N = 87.

TABLE 12

DISTRIBUTION OF WHIG AND DEMOCRATIC CANDIDATES,
1848–51, AMONG NATIONALITY GROUPS*

Nationality	Whigs	Democrats
Native American	57 (73%)	45 (65%)
British	5 (6.4%)	3 (4%)
German	1	4 (6%)
Irish	15 (19%)	17 (25%)

* This table is drawn from the same sample of candidates as Tables 8 and 10. I found information on 78 Whigs and 69 Democrats.

TABLE 13

DISTRIBUTION OF WHIG AND DEMOCRATIC SECONDARY LEADERS,
1847–51, AMONG NATIONALITY GROUPS*

Nationality	Whigs	Democrats
Native American	52 (70%)	32 (48%)
British	4 (5%)	3 (4.4%)
German	3 (4%)	5 (7.6%)
Irish	16 (21%)	27 (40%)

* This table is drawn from the same sample of leaders as Tables 9 and 11. Percentages are based on the 75 Whigs and 67 Democrats about whom I found information.

TABLE 14

DISTRIBUTION OF WHIG AND DEMOCRATIC CANDIDATES, 1848–51,
AMONG RELIGIOUS DENOMINATIONS[a]

Religion	Whigs	Democrats
Presbyterian	23 (57%)	6 (17%)
Episcopalian	13 (33.3%)	11 (31%)
Methodist	1	0
Lutheran	1	0
Other Protestant[b]	2 (5%)	5 (14%)
Roman Catholic	0	13 (37%)

a. This table is drawn from the same sample of candidates as Table 8. Percentages are based only on the 40 Whigs and 35 Democrats about whom I found information regarding their denominational affiliation.

b. This category includes men who are identified specifically as non-Catholic and whom I assumed to be Protestant. The *Gazette* in 1858 printed a list of Democratic ward candidates and italicized those who were Catholic; the men whose names were not italicized and who were leaders in the period discussed in this chapter are the largest group of such non-Catholics included in this category. See the *Gazette*, Jan. 1, 1858.

TABLE 15

DISTRIBUTION OF WHIG AND DEMOCRATIC SECONDARY LEADERS,
1847–51, AMONG RELIGIOUS DENOMINATIONS*

Religion	Whigs	Democrats
Presbyterian	18 (50%)	2 (9%)
Episcopalian	12 (33%)	8 (35%)
Methodist	1 (3%)	0
Other Protestant	1	6 (26%)
Welsh Congregational	1	0
Roman Catholic	3 (8%)	7 (30%)

* This table is drawn from the same sample of leaders as Table 9. Percentages are based on 36 Whigs and 23 Democrats.

TABLE 16

PARTY VOTE AND PARTY PERCENTAGE OF VOTE IN PITTSBURGH, 1847–49 [a]

Election	Whig	Democratic	Native American	Free-Soil
1847 (County Commissioner)	1,824 (51%)	1,425 (40%)	278 (7.8%)	44 (1.2%) [b]
1847 (Governor)	1,897 (52%)	1,467 (40%)	247 (6.7%)	41 (1.3%)
1848 (Mayor)	1,642 (46.8%)	1,555 (44.3%)	312 (8.9%)	
1848 (Governor)	2,777 (59.8%)	1,863 (40.2%)		
1848 (President)	3,158 (58.8%)	1,977 (36.8%)		
1849 (Mayor) [c]	1,868 (48.3%)	1,515 (39.1%)	213 (5.5%)	230 (4.4%)
1849 (Sheriff)	1,763 (49.1%)	1,627 (45.4%)	193 (5.5%)	257 (6.4%)
1849 (Canal Commissioner)	1,819 (51.2%)	1,549 (43.6%)	183 (5.2%)	
1849 (Assembly) [d]	1,523 (43%)	1,808 (51.1%)	205 (5.9%)	

a. Election results may be found in the *Post*, Oct. 18, 1847; the *Gazette*, Jan. 15, Nov. 11, 1848, Oct. 15, 1849; and in the *Dispatch*, Jan. 13, 1849.

b. In 1847 the antislavery party was the Liberty party.

c. In the 1849 election for mayor there was also an independent candidate in the field, but he won only a very few votes.

d. These are the totals for Caleb Lee, Jonas R. McClintock, and C. B. M. Smith, the Native American candidate with the highest total vote.

TABLE 17

PRODUCT-MOMENT COEFFICIENTS OF CORRELATION BETWEEN WHIG VOTES AND VARIABLES, 1847–49 *

Variable	1847 (Governor)	1847 (County Commissioner)	1848 (Mayor)	1848 (Governor)	1848 (President)	1849 (Mayor)	1849 (Caleb Lee)	1849 (Sheriff)	1849 (Canal Commissioner)
Ethnic									
Native American	+.57	+.55	+.08	+.60	+.64	−.12	+.81	+.78	+.79
Irish	−.54	−.53	−.20	−.59	−.70	−.41	−.40	−.40	−.50
German	−.40	−.36		−.35	−.26	+.37	−.78	−.69	−.65
Property Holdings									
$25,000 plus	+.61	+.60	+.24	+.53	+.62	—	+.54	—	+.61
$10,000 plus	+.62	+.60	+.23	+.59	+.63	+.06	+.64	+.71	+.67
$5,000–9,999	+.40	+.38	.00	+.22	+.12	—	+.55	+.43	+.42
None	−.59	−.47	−.25	−.22	−.25	+.18	−.66	−.58	−.48
Occupation									
Manufacturers, merchants, and bankers	+.59	+.55	+.13	+.60	+.65	.00	+.66	+.72	+.70
Large manufacturers	+.45	+.47	—	—	+.64	—	+.57	+.62	+.64
Merchants	+.67	+.61	+.19	—	+.70	—	+.67	+.74	+.75
Clerks and shopkeepers	+.39	+.34	—	+.38	+.38	—	+.61	+.57	+.56
Professional	+.43	+.39	+.06	+.39	+.38	—	+.67	+.65	+.63
Skilled artisans	−.78	−.75	−.64	−.49	−.41	+.02	−.67	−.59	−.58
Unskilled laborers	−.31	−.25	+.23	−.33	−.42	+.25	−.56	−.54	−.55

* The coefficients of correlation in this table and in all subsequent tables of correlations are calculated with the Pearson Product-Moment formula which is explained in Appendix B.

TABLE 18

PRODUCT-MOMENT COEFFICIENTS OF CORRELATION BETWEEN DEMOCRATIC VOTES AND VARIABLES, 1847-49

Variable	1847 (Governor)	1847 (County Commissioner)	1848 (Mayor)	1848 (Governor)	1848 (President)	1849 (Mayor)	1849 (McClintock)	1849 (Sheriff)	1849 (Canal Commissioner)
Ethnic									
Total immigrant*	+.46	+.48	+.14	+.60	+.51	+.14	+.82	+.75	+.75
Irish	+.47	+.57	+.33	+.59	+.58	+.44	+.50	+.46	+.61
German	+.23	+.19	.00	+.35	+.18	−.24	+.63	+.58	+.47
Property Holdings									
$10,000 plus	−.47	−.50	−.23	−.59	−.45		−.62	−.65	−.61
None	+.44	+.39	+.18	+.22	+.14		+.65	+.54	+.38
Occupation									
Skilled artisans	+.55	+.54	+.47	+.49	+.29		+.52	+.51	+.44
Unskilled laborers	+.20	+.22	−.12	+.33	+.28	+.05	+.51	+.50	+.51

* This group includes all white males over twenty-one who were not native-born Americans.

329

TABLE 19

PARTY PERCENTAGES OF THE VOTE IN PITTSBURGH'S WARDS
IN THE VARIOUS ELECTIONS, 1847–49 [a]

	1847 Governor		1847 County Commissioner	
Ward	*Whig*	*Democrat*	*Whig*	*Democrat*
First	58%	32%	57%	31%
Second	57	40	57	38
Third	47	47	44	48
Fourth	64	29	65	28
Fifth	38	52	38	50
Sixth	50	40	51	41
Seventh	55	37	54	37
Eighth	56	38	57	37
Ninth	58	30	59	29

	1848 Governor		1848 President	
	Whig	*Democrat*	*Whig*	*Democrat*
First	63%	37%	64%	32%
Second	67	33	64	32
Third	52	48	50	46
Fourth	69	31	68	28
Fifth	52	48	56	41
Sixth	63	37	59	34
Seventh	57	43	58	38
Eighth	60	40	58	39
Ninth	69	31	65	25

Ward	1849 Mayor		1849 Assemblyman[b]	
	Whig	*Democrat*	*Whig*	*Democrat*
First	44%	34%	49%	41%
Second	46	40	54	44
Third	50	43	37	60
Fourth	55	33	52	42
Fifth	45	43	27	62
Sixth	45	39	49	48
Seventh	44	45	46	47
Eighth	50	43	37	59
Ninth	67	14	45	48

	1849 Sheriff		1849 Canal Commissioner	
	Whig	*Democrat*	*Whig*	*Democrat*
First	53%	38%	56%	36%
Second	60	38	62	35
Third	41	56	43	54
Fourth	64	32	63	33
Fifth	34	57	37	53
Sixth	56	40	57	40
Seventh	50	43	49	45
Eighth	41	53	46	49
Ninth	55	38	57	35

a. This table is based on the same election returns as Table 16.
b. These are the percentages for Caleb Lee and Jonas R. McClintock.

TABLE 20

PROPORTIONS OF ETHNIC GROUPS IN THE ADULT WHITE MALE
POPULATION IN PITTSBURGH'S WARDS IN 1850 *

Ward	Native	German	Irish	British	Other
First	53.2%	17.4%	22%	7%	.4%
Second	55.7	10	21	11	2.3
Third	31.1	18	42	7	1.9
Fourth	52.2	10	30	7	.8
Fifth	22	31	37	9	1
Sixth	35.2	9	47	8	.8
Seventh	29.5	17	42	10	1.5
Eighth	19.2	26.6	34	20	.2
Ninth	29.1	30	28	9	3.9

* This table is based on a tabulation of the white males over twenty-one
years of age in the manuscript census of 1850. I am deeply indebted to Paul J.
Kleppner of the University of Pittsburgh for sharing with me some of the
results of his research when I constructed this table.

TABLE 21

PROPORTIONS OF VARIOUS ECONOMIC GROUPS IN THE ADULT
WHITE MALE POPULATION OF PITTSBURGH'S WARDS IN 1850 *

Ward	None	$5,000– 9,999	$10,000– 24,999	$25,000– 49,999	$50,000 plus
First	81.4%	4 %	3 %	1 %	1.4 %
Second	80.9	4	4	2.4	.9
Third	82.4	4	2.2	.2	.35
Fourth	75.1	2.8	5.8	3.7	4.6
Fifth	96	.6	.4	.15	.15
Sixth	87.3	1.6	1.8	.15	.22
Seventh	72.1	2.3	1.5	0	.7
Eighth	92	1.1	.6	.3	.15
Ninth	90	2	1	0	0

* This table is based on the evaluation of real property owned by white
males over twenty-one as listed in the manuscript census of 1850. I also had
categories for those owning property worth $1–999 and $1,000–4,999, but since
there were no significant correlations between these groups and either the
Democratic or the Whig vote in these years, I did not include them in this
table.

TABLE 22

PROPORTIONS THAT MEN IN VARIOUS OCCUPATIONS CONSTITUTED OF THE ADULT WHITE MALE POPULATION OF THE WARDS OF PITTSBURGH IN 1850 *

Ward	Unskilled Laborers	Skilled Artisans	Small Manufacturers	Clerks, Shopkeepers	Professional	Large Manufacturers	Merchants	Bankers
First	19 %	30 %	13 %	30 %	3 %	1 %	3 %	.5 %
Second	17.6	21.7	9.1	35.1	6.5	3.4	5.1	1.2
Third	32.8	30.5	7.7	23.5	3.4	.5	1.3	.2
Fourth	21.1	23.1	7.8	30.4	6.4	2.8	7.3	1
Fifth	43.2	38	5.8	12	.6	.4	.9	0
Sixth	41.6	30	8.2	15	2.9	.3	1.7	.15
Seventh	49.4	22.4	10.8	13.8	2.1	0	1	.25
Eighth	58.2	23.7	8.3	7.5	.9	.5	.9	0
Ninth	48	30	9	10.7	0	.2	1.1	0

* This table is based on a tabulation and categorization of the white males over twenty-one years of age listed in the manuscript census of 1850. The types of men included in each group are identified in Appendix B. In the classification labeled "Bankers" I have included bankers, brokers, and those listed in the census merely as "Gentlemen."

TABLE 23

PARTY VOTE AND PARTY PERCENTAGE OF VOTE IN PITTSBURGH, 1849–53 [a]

	Whig	Democratic	Joe Barker	Native American	Free Democratic
1849 (Assembly)[b]	1,523 (43%)	1,808 (51.1%)		205 (5.9%)	
1850 (Mayor)	982 (22.3%)	1,575 (35.7%)	1,848 (42%)		
1850 (Congress)	1,536 (50%)	1,211 (39.5%)	142 (4.6%)[c]	175 (5.9%)	
1851 (Mayor)	1,147 (27.3%)	1,908 (45.5%)	1,140 (27.2%)		
1851 (Supreme Court Judge)[d]	2,372 (58.6%)	1,667 (41.4%)			
1851 (Governor)	2,554 (59.3%)	1,750 (40.7%)			
1852 (Mayor)	1,379 (38.2%)	1,429 (39.6%)	798 (22.2%)		
1852 (Congress)	2,088 (46.6%)	1,814 (40.7%)		204 (4.9%)	347 (7.8%)
1852 (Supreme Court Judge)[e]	2,239 (50.4%)	1,943 (44.1%)			224 (5.5%)
1852 (Sheriff)	1,788 (34.7%)	1,777 (34.5%)	1,330 (25.8%)		235 (4.6%)
1852 (President)	2,903 (54.5%)	2,046 (38.4%)		84 (1.6%)	295 (5.5%)
1853 (Mayor)	1,886 (48.2%)	1,568 (40%)		209 (5.1%)	251 (6.7%)
1853 (State Senate)	1,648 (44.3%)	1,681 (45.2%)		141 (3.7%)	252 (6.8%)

a. The returns for these elections may be found in the *Journal*, Jan. 9, 1850; *Post*, Jan. 15, 1851; *Gazette*, Oct. 15, 1849, Oct. 12, 1850, Oct. 18, 1851, Jan. 17, Oct. 16, 1852, Nov. 6, 1852, Jan. 12, Oct. 17, 1853.

b. These are the totals for Caleb Lee, Jonas R. McClintock, and C. B. M. Smith.

c. This is the vote for the candidate of the Protestant party.

d. These are the totals for James Campbell and the Whig candidate with the median vote out of the five Whig candidates.

e. This is the vote for George W. Woodward and his opponents.

TABLE 24

PRODUCT-MOMENT COEFFICIENTS OF CORRELATION BETWEEN WHIG VOTES AND VARIABLES, 1850–53

Variable	1850 Mayor	1850 Con-gress	1851 Mayor	1851 Gov-ernor	1852 Mayor	1852 Con-gress	1852 Sheriff	1852 Presi-dent	1853 Mayor	1853 State Senate
Ethnic										
Native American	+.60	+.83	+.28	+.81	+.37	+.78	+.86	+.83	+.66	+.65
Irish	−.06	−.39	−.32	−.51	−.09	−.60	−.49	−.51	−.45	−.57
German	−.71	−.81	−.27	−.51	−.52	−.59	−.76	−.67	−.59	−.43
British				−.38		−.13				
Property Holdings										
$25,000 plus	+.69	+.72		+.51		+.72		+.67	+.64	+.67
$10,000 plus	+.73	+.79	+.21	+.58	+.39	+.77	+.85	+.74	+.67	+.67
$5,000–9,999	+.37	+.53	+.16	+.43	+.29	+.57	+.61	+.52	+.33	+.42
None	−.76	−.50	−.03	−.20	−.05	−.49	−.58	−.35	−.31	−.49
Occupation										
Manufacturers, mer-chants, & bankers	+.64	+.80	+.34	+.64	+.44	+.82	+.88	+.81	+.68	+.67
Clerks and shopkeepers	+.47	+.72	+.16	+.57	+.32	+.68	+.79	+.69	+.47	+.49
Professional	+.66	+.81	+.28	+.53	+.51	+.73	+.86	+.74	+.59	+.53
Skilled artisans	−.57	−.55	−.49	−.22	−.33	−.62	−.60	−.42	−.57	−.63
Unskilled laborers	−.43	−.68	−.09	−.60	−.28	−.62	−.73	−.68	−.47	−.44

TABLE 25

PRODUCT-MOMENT COEFFICIENTS OF CORRELATION BETWEEN DEMOCRATIC VOTES AND VARIABLES, 1850–53

Variable	1850 Mayor	1850 Congress	1851 Mayor	1851 Governor	1852 Mayor	1852 Congress	1852 Sheriff	1852 President	1853 Mayor	1853 State Senate
Ethnic										
Total immigrant*	+.25	+.81	−.27	+.81	−.31	+.86	+.72	+.76	+.44	+.62
Irish	+.70	+.62	+.04	+.51	−.03	+.62	+.66	+.46	+.25	+.41
German	−.20	+.57	+.21	+.51	−.33	+.64	+.33	+.65	+.51	+.45
British		+.18		+.38		+.27		+.28		
Property Holdings										
$10,000 plus	−.37	−.75	+.43	−.58	+.35	−.79	−.61	−.67	−.43	−.51
None	+.17	+.32	−.31	+.20	−.42	+.36	+.14	+.31	+.10	+.24
Occupation										
Skilled artisans	+.38	+.44	+.23	+.22	−.10	+.44	+.16	+.43	+.52	+.29
Unskilled laborers	+.14	+.66	−.57	+.59	−.49	+.74	+.65	+.72	+.25	+.44

* The "Total immigrant" group includes all white males over twenty-one who were not native-born.

TABLE 26

PRODUCT-MOMENT COEFFICIENTS OF CORRELATION OF VOTES
FOR JOE BARKER AND VARIABLES, 1850–52

Variable	1850	1851	1852	Sheriff 1852
Ethnic				
Native American	−.27	−.71	−.64	−.32
Irish	−.38	+.35	+.01	−.22
German	+.79	+.61	+.79	+.74
Property Holdings				
$10,000 plus	−.43	−.80	−.69	−.41
None	+.59	+.43	+.43	+.70
Occupation				
Clerks and shopkeepers	−.33	−.79	−.77	−.39
Skilled artisans	+.29	+.31	+.36	+.73
Unskilled laborers	+.32	+.80	+.70	+.20

TABLE 27

PARTY VOTE AND PARTY PERCENTAGE OF VOTE IN PITTSBURGH, 1854–56 [a]

Election	Whig	Democratic	Know-Nothing	Republican	Others
1854 (Mayor)	2,166 (57.5%)	1,132 (30%)			465 (12.5%)
1854 (Governor)	2,786 (62.6%)	1,505 (33.6%)			155 (3.8%)
1854 (Congress)	2,795 (64.6%)	1,529 (35.4%)			
1854 (Supreme Court Judge)	1,457 (33.7%)	1,583 (36.6%)	1,281 (29.7%)[b]		
1854 (Clerk of Courts)	1,412 (34.9%)	1,241 (30.7%)	1,392 (34.4%)[b]		
1854 (County Register)[c]	*Fusion* 1,787 (46.3%)	1,668 (43.2%)			403 (10.5%)
1855 (Mayor)	2,406 (55.3%)		1,944 (44.7%)		
1855 (Canal Commissioner)		*Irwin* 2,111 (48.2%)	1,503 (34.3%)	653 (14.9%)	108 (2.6%)
1856 (Mayor)	*Volk* 1,030 (26.5%)	*Irwin* 1,115 (28.7%)	1,499 (38.6%)		234 (6.2%)

a. These election returns may be found in the *Gazette*, Oct. 16, 1854, Jan. 13, Oct. 17, 1855; and Jan. 9, 1856; the *Post*, Jan. 11, 1854.

b. In these elections the Native American candidates received the Know-Nothing vote.

c. In this election the Democratic candidate who had the Know-Nothing vote won a majority in the county as a whole although he failed to carry Pittsburgh.

TABLE 28

PRODUCT-MOMENT COEFFICIENTS OF CORRELATION BETWEEN
THE WHIG VOTES AND VARIABLES, 1854 *

Variable	Mayor 1854	Governor 1854	Supreme Court Judge 1854	Clerk of Courts 1854
Ethnic				
Native American	+.23	+.71	−.07	+.45
Irish	.00	−.32	+.13	+.16
German	−.54	−.74	−.21	−.71
Property Holdings				
$10,000 plus	+.20	+.50	+.13	+.52
$5,000–9,999	+.43	+.48	−.10	+.42
None	−.31	−.45	−.10	−.83
Occupation				
Manufacturers, mer-				
chants, & bankers	+.13	+.50	+.03	+.40
Clerks and				
shopkeepers	+.25	+.52	−.18	+.33
Professional	+.36	+.54	.00	+.54
Skilled artisans	−.50	−.51	−.54	−.62
Unskilled laborers	−.12	−.48	+.30	−.27

* The socioeconomic indices used in this table were the same as those used in Chapter 2.

TABLE 29

PRODUCT-MOMENT COEFFICIENTS OF CORRELATION BETWEEN THE DEMOCRATIC VOTES AND VARIABLES, 1854–55 [a]

Variables	Mayor 1854	Governor 1854	Supreme Court Judge 1854	Clerk of Courts 1854	Fusion[b] Mayor 1855	Canal Commissioner 1855
Ethnic						
Total immigrant[c]	+.26	+.57	+.34	+.67	+.67	+.49
Irish	+.41	+.42	+.34	+.13	+.65	+.43
German	+.04	+.41	+.15	+.61	+.22	+.22
Property Holdings						
$10,000 plus	−.08	−.32	−.16	−.36	−.40	−.31
None	−.12	+.29	.00	+.54	+.26	+.31
Occupation						
Skilled artisans	+.09	+.37	+.11	+.08	+.10	+.23
Unskilled laborers	+.11	+.29	+.10	+.54	+.52	+.27

a. These figures are calculated from the socioeconomic indices based on the manuscript census of 1850.

b. This column of figures represents the correlations between the variables and the Fusion vote for mayor in 1855.

c. These figures are exactly opposite what the correlation between the Democratic votes and the percentage of Native Americans would be since the group "Total immigrants" includes all white males over twenty-one who were not natives. Hence, the correlation between the Democratic vote for governor in 1854 and the Native Americans was −.57.

TABLE 30

PRODUCT-MOMENT COEFFICIENTS OF CORRELATION BETWEEN
THE KNOW-NOTHING VOTES AND VARIABLES, 1854–55 *

Variables	Supreme Court Judge 1854	Clerk of Courts 1854	Mayor 1855	Canal Commissioner 1855
Ethnic				
Native American	+.37	+.45	+.67	+.64
Irish	−.41	−.30	−.65	−.52
German	+.05	−.16	−.22	−.42
Property Holdings				
$10,000 plus	.00	−.02	+.40	+.37
$5,000–9,999	+.10	+.19	+.36	+.41
None	+.04	+.05	−.26	−.47
Occupation				
Manufacturers, merchants, & bankers	+.07	−.04	+.40	+.34
Professional	−.10	.00	+.21	+.26
Clerks and shopkeepers	+.18	+.30	+.43	+.38
Skilled artisans	+.37	+.45	−.10	−.45
Unskilled laborers	−.32	−.45	−.52	−.38

* These figures are calculated with the same tables and in the same way as those in Tables 28 and 29. For the mayoral election of 1855, they are exactly opposite in sign but equal in number to the correlations between these variables and the Fusion vote for mayor. Hence, the correlation between the professional group and the Fusion vote was −.21.

TABLE 31

CHANGES IN THE ABSOLUTE NUMBERS AND PROPORTIONS OF VARIOUS ETHNIC GROUPS IN PITTSBURGH'S WARDS BETWEEN 1850 AND 1860 [a]

Ward	Natives	Germans	Irish	British
First	−89 (−7.7%)	+31 (+2.3%)	+40 (+3.1%)	+3 (−1.3%)
Second	−152 (−1.6%)	−18 (+1.2%)	−24 (−2.9%)	−28 (−.4%)
Third	+39 (+1.8%)	+119 (+5.1%)	−22 (−1.6%)	−66 (−3%)
Fourth	−80 (−6.2%)	+43 (+3.7%)	−52 (−11.3%)	−37 (−3.1%)
Fifth	−29 (−.8%)	+314 (+15.5%)	−261 (−11.3%)	−90 (−3.7%)
Sixth	+108 (+6.1%)	+101 (+6.5%)	−150 (−10.7%)	−18 (−1.4%)
Seventh	+110 (+9.3%)	+85 (+8.6%)	−6 (−11.8%)	−23 (−6.6%)
Eighth	+66 (+8.4%)	+7 (+3.4%)	−126 (−7.8%)	−67 (−4%)
Ninth	+437 (+23.2%)	+43 (−12.1%)	+122 (+1%)	+30 (−1.9%)
Totals				
1850	4,137 (35.8%)[b]	2,229 (19.3%)	4,089 (35.4%)	1,102 (9.5%)
1860	4,547 (38.1%)	2,954 (24.8%)	3,610 (30.3%)	805 (6.8%)

a. This table is based on counts of the white males over twenty-one in the manuscript censuses of 1850 and 1860. The percentage difference listed for each group in each ward represents the change in the portion each group constituted of the total adult male population of each ward between 1850 and 1860 rather than the percentage change in each group represented by the increase or decrease in absolute numbers in that group. For example, in the first ward, the native Americans formed 53.2 percent of the population in 1850 and only 45.5 percent of the population in 1860. Hence, the decrease was −7.7 percent.

b. The percentages listed in the total sections are not changes, but are the proportions which the ethnic groups constituted of the total adult white male populations of the city in 1850 and 1860.

343

TABLE 32

PROPORTIONS OF ETHNIC GROUPS IN THE ADULT WHITE MALE
POPULATION IN PITTSBURGH'S WARDS IN 1860 *

Ward	Native	German	Irish	British	Other
First	45.5%	19.7%	25.1%	5.7%	4 %
Second	53.7	11.1	23.8	11.4	
Third	32.9	23.1	40.4	3.6	
Fourth	46	13.7	25.3	3.9	11.1
Fifth	21.2	46.5	25.7	5.3	1.3
Sixth	41.3	15.5	36.3	6.6	.3
Seventh	39.2	25.6	30.2	3.4	1.6
Eighth	27.6	30	26.8	15.6	
Ninth	51.7	17.9	23.7	6.7	

* This table is based on a tabulation of the white males over twenty-one years of age in the manuscript census of 1860. I am deeply indebted to Paul J. Kleppner of the University of Pittsburgh for sharing with me some of the results of his research when I constructed this table.

TABLE 33

PROPORTIONS OF VARIOUS ECONOMIC GROUPS IN THE ADULT WHITE
MALE POPULATION OF PITTSBURGH'S WARDS IN 1860 *

Ward	Less Than $100	$100– 999	$5,000– 9,999	$10,000– 24,999	$25,000– 49,999	$50,000 plus
First	63.8%	17.9%	3.6%	3.1%	.8%	.5 %
Second	52	18.5	5.9	6.5	2.2	1.1
Third	27.1	51.4	4.5	3.3	1	.13
Fourth	64.1	9.6	4.4	4.8	1.7	4.9
Fifth	43.1	37.8	3.5	2.1	.8	.23
Sixth	41	33.9	5.4	3	.8	.8
Seventh	45.8	28.6	2.5	1	1	.66
Eighth	46.1	33.3	1.9	1.8	.7	.59
Ninth	45.5	37	3.3	1	0	0

* This table is based on the evaluation of real and personal property owned
by white males over twenty-one listed in the manuscript census of 1860. When
sons lived at home, I included them in the same wealth category with their
fathers or mothers. I also had a category for those who owned property worth
$1,000–4,999, but since there were no significant correlations with this group,
I did not include it in the table.

TABLE 34

PROPORTIONS THAT MEN IN VARIOUS OCCUPATIONS CONSTITUTED OF THE ADULT WHITE

MALE POPULATION OF THE WARDS OF PITTSBURGH IN 1860 *

Ward	Unskilled Laborers	Skilled Artisans	Small Manufacturers	Clerks, Shopkeepers	Professional	Large Manufacturers	Merchants	Bankers
First	30.9%	31.6%	5.4%	22.8%	1.8%	1.6%	5 %	.8%
Second	22	26.1	5.5	28.2	6.3	3.4	5.3	3
Third	37.3	29.2	3.9	22.2	3.7	.3	2.7	.5
Fourth	23.6	20.9	4.4	28.8	7.4	4	9.4	1.4
Fifth	42.1	34.8	4.5	13.6	1.4	.9	1.9	.3
Sixth	32	30.4	7.8	20.5	2	1.6	4.9	.7
Seventh	36.4	36.7	5.9	14.4	2.9	1.2	1.5	1
Eighth	45.1	32.7	6.3	11	1.1	1.9	1.7	.1
Ninth	38	40.6	6.5	9.3	1.2	.9	2.9	.5

* This table is based on a tabulation and categorization of the white males over twenty-one years of age listed in the manuscript census of 1860. The types of men included in each group are the same as those included in the index based on the census of 1850, and they are identified in Appendix B. In the classification labeled "Bankers" I have included bankers, brokers, and those listed in the census merely as "Gentlemen."

TABLE 35

PROPORTIONS OF VARIOUS RELIGIONS IN THE
ADULT WHITE MALE POPULATION OF
PITTSBURGH'S WARDS IN 1860 *

Ward	Protestants	Catholics
First	80%	20%
Second	80	20
Third	60	40
Fourth	70	30
Fifth	55	45
Sixth	75	25
Seventh	85	15
Eighth	90	10
Ninth	85	15

* This table is taken from Paul J. Kleppner, "Lincoln and the Immigrant Vote: A Case of Religious Polarization," *Mid-America, 48* (1966), 176–95.

TABLE 36

PARTY PROPORTIONS OF THE VOTE IN PITTSBURGH'S WARDS IN
THE VARIOUS ELECTIONS, 1854 AND 1855 *

Ward	Mayor, 1854		Governor, 1854	
	Whig	Democratic	Whig	Democratic
First	59%	23%	73%	23%
Second	59	30	69	30
Third	65	31	58	40
Fourth	59	29	69	29
Fifth	39	40	46	48
Sixth	64	26	73	26
Seventh	54	38	60	35
Eighth	65	27	62	35
Ninth	54	19	62	24

TABLE 36 (cont.)

	Supreme Court Judge, 1854			Clerk of Courts, 1854		
	Whig	*Demo-cratic*	*Know-Nothing*	*Whig*	*Demo-cratic*	*Know-Nothing*
First	33%	28%	39%	33%	20%	47%
Second	30	38	32	36	26	38
Third	33	46	21	37	33	30
Fourth	40	33	27	43	25	32
Fifth	23	43	34	25	35	40
Sixth	40	29	31	39	20	41
Seventh	34	39	29	42	25	33
Eighth	46	37	17	29	47	24
Ninth	35	27	38	36	26	38

	Mayor, 1855		Canal Commissioner, 1855	
	Fusion	*Know-Nothing*	*Democratic*	*Know-Nothing*
First	36%	64%	38%	51%
Second	49	51	46	40
Third	68	32	60	24
Fourth	47	53	40	40
Fifth	62	38	59	20
Sixth	54	46	44	39
Seventh	57	43	45	39
Eighth	68	32	59	31
Ninth	40	60	30	43

* The election results may be found in the newspapers cited in Table 27. In the election for canal commissioner in 1855, the balance of the vote in most wards went to the Republican candidate.

TABLE 37

WEALTH DISTRIBUTION AMONG REPUBLICAN AND DEMOCRATIC CANDIDATES, 1855–57 *

Group	Republicans	Democrats
$100,000 plus	5 (15%)	3 (8%)
$50,000–99,999	4 (12%)	3 (8%)
$25,000–49,999	7 (20%)	5 (14%)
$10,000–24,999	6 (18%)	7 (20%)
$5,000–9,999	2 (6%)	6 (17%)
$1,000–4,999	7 (20%)	6 (17%)
$500–999	1 (3%)	1 (3%)
$100–499	1 (3%)	1 (3%)
None	1 (3%)	4 (11%)

* This table is drawn from total samples of 49 Republican candidates and 43 Democratic candidates. I found information on 34 Republicans and 36 Democratic candidates.

TABLE 38

WEALTH DISTRIBUTION AMONG SECONDARY REPUBLICAN AND DEMOCRATIC LEADERS, 1855–57 *

Group	Republicans	Democrats
$100,000 plus	7 (8%)	0
$50,000–99,999	6 (7%)	1 (2%)
$25,000–49,999	9 (10%)	3 (6%)
$10,000–24,999	16 (18%)	7 (13%)
$5,000–9,999	9 (10%)	9 (17%)
$1,000–4,999	24 (28%)	15 (28%)
$500–999	2 (2%)	2 (4%)
$100–499	8 (9%)	7 (13%)
$1–99	1 (1%)	0
None	6 (7%)	9 (17%)

* This table is drawn from a total sample of 137 Republicans and 88 Democrats.

TABLE 39

DISTRIBUTION OF REPUBLICAN AND DEMOCRATIC CANDIDATES,
1855–57, AMONG OCCUPATIONAL CATEGORIES[a]

Occupation	Republicans	Democrats
Iron and glass manufacturers	8 (19%)	1 (2%)
Other manufacturers and managerial [b]	4 (9%)	9 (21%)
Merchants	6 (14%)	3 (7%)
Shopkeepers and clerks	6 (14%)	10 (24%)
Bankers and brokers	3 (7%)	2 (4.5%)
Professional	10 (23%)	10 (24%)
Gentlemen	1 (2%)	2 (4.5%)
Artisans and skilled workers	4 (9%)	5 (12%)
Unskilled laborers	1 (2%)	0

a. This table is drawn from the same sample of candidates as Table 37. I found information on 43 Republican candidates and 42 Democratic candidates.

b. This group includes such men as a brickmaker worth $25,000, cabinetmakers, a mineral water manufacturer, a brewery master, a builder worth $25,000, and a master tin- and coppersmith.

TABLE 40

DISTRIBUTION OF REPUBLICAN AND DEMOCRATIC SECONDARY
LEADERS, 1855–57, AMONG OCCUPATIONAL CATEGORIES *

Occupation	Republicans	Democrats
Iron and glass manufacturers	7 (7%)	1 (2%)
Other manufacturers	8 (8%)	2 (3%)
Merchants	13 (12%)	8 (12%)
Managerial and Railroad officials	4 (4%)	3 (4%)
Bankers and brokers	2 (2%)	0
Shopkeepers and clerks	22 (22%)	23 (33%)
Professional	24 (23%)	17 (25%)
Gentlemen	2 (2%)	2 (3%)
Artisans and skilled workers	17 (17%)	11 (16%)
Unskilled laborers	3 (3%)	2 (3%)

* This table is drawn from the same sample of party leaders as Table 38, and the percentages are again based on the number of men found. I found information on 102 Republicans and 69 Democrats. I used the occupations listed in the manuscript census of 1860 and supplemented these with material taken from city directories.

TABLE 41

DISTRIBUTION OF REPUBLICAN AND DEMOCRATIC CANDIDATES,
1855–57, AMONG NATIONALITY GROUPS *

Nationality	Republicans	Democrats
Native American	26 (74%)	25 (68%)
British	0	2 (5%)
German	4 (11%)	3 (8%)
Irish	3 (9%)	7 (19%)
Other	2 (6%)	0

* This table is drawn from the same sample of candidates as Tables 37 and 39 and percentages are based on the number of men in each group on whom I found information. Information on ethnic background comes primarily from the manuscript census of 1850 and 1860. I found data on 35 Republicans and 37 Democrats.

TABLE 42

DISTRIBUTION OF REPUBLICAN AND DEMOCRATIC SECONDARY
LEADERS, 1855–57, AMONG NATIONALITY GROUPS *

Nationality	Republicans	Democrats
Native American	64 (71%)	37 (62%)
British	6 (7%)	1 (1.5%)
German	4 (4%)	5 (8%)
Irish	16 (18%)	16 (27%)
Other	0	1 (1.5%)

* This table is drawn from the same sample of leaders as Tables 38 and 40. Percentages are based on the 90 Republicans and 60 Democrats on whom I found information. The data on ethnic backgrounds come primarily from the manuscript censuses of 1850 and 1860.

353

TABLE 43

DISTRIBUTION OF REPUBLICAN AND DEMOCRATIC CANDIDATES,
1855–57, AMONG RELIGIOUS DENOMINATIONS[a]

Religion	Republicans	Democrats
Presbyterian	8 (50%)	2 (10%)
Episcopalian	3 (19%)	6 (32%)
Methodist	2 (12.5%)	0
Lutheran	1 (7%)	1 (5%)
Other Protestant[b]	2 (12.5%)	4 (21%)
Roman Catholic	0	6 (32%)

a. This table is drawn from the same sample of candidates as Table 37. Percentages are based only on the 16 Republicans and 19 Democrats on whom I found information regarding their denominational affiliation.

b. See Table 14, note b.

TABLE 44

DISTRIBUTION OF REPUBLICAN AND DEMOCRATIC SECONDARY
LEADERS, 1855–57, AMONG RELIGIOUS DENOMINATIONS *

Religion	Republicans	Democrats
Presbyterian	21 (63%)	1 (3%)
Episcopalian	8 (23%)	5 (16%)
Methodist	3 (9%)	0
Lutheran	1	0
Other Protestant	1	8 (26%)
Roman Catholic	0	17 (55%)

* This table is drawn from the same sample of leaders as Table 38. Percentages are based on the 34 Republicans and 31 Democrats about whom I found information regarding their denominational affiliations.

TABLE 45

PARTY VOTE AND PARTY PERCENTAGE OF VOTE
IN PITTSBURGH, 1848–56 *

Election	Whig	Democratic	Native American	Free-Soil
1848 (President)	3,158 (58.8%)	1,977 (36.8%)		230 (4.4%)
1852 (President)	2,903 (54.5%)	2,046 (38.4%)	84 (1.6%)	295 (5.5%)
1854 (Governor)	2,786 (62.6%)	1,505 (33.6%)	155 (3.8%)	
1854 (Clerk of Courts)	1,412 (34.9%)	1,241 (30.7%)	1,392 (34.4%)	

Election	Republican	Democratic	Know-Nothing
1855 (Canal Commissioner)	653 (14.9%)	2,111 (48.2%)	1,503 (34.3%)
1856 (Congress)	3,039 (52%)	2,588 (40.3%)	218 (3.7%)
1856 (President)	3,853 (54.5%)	2,881 (40.8%)	332 (4.7%)

* These results can be found in the *Gazette*, Nov. 11, 1848, Nov. 6, 1852, Oct. 16, 1854, Oct. 17, 1855, and Nov. 8, 1856; and in the *Post*, Oct. 20, 1856.

TABLE 46

PRODUCT-MOMENT COEFFICIENTS OF CORRELATION BETWEEN
WHIG, KNOW-NOTHING, AND REPUBLICAN VOTES
AND VARIABLES, 1854–56 [a]

Variable	Governor 1854	Canal Commissioner 1855	Congress 1856	President 1856
Ethnic				
Native American	+.71	+.82	+.65	+.59
Irish	−.32	−.40	−.37	−.45
German	−.74	−.71	−.58	−.54
Property Holdings				
$10,000 plus	+.50	+.14	.00	−.08
$5,000–9,999	+.48	+.11	−.24	−.35
$1,000–4,999		−.09	+.20	+.19
$100–999		−.66	−.54	−.48
Less than $100	−.45[b]	+.70	+.55	+.54
Occupation				
Manufacturers, merchants, and bankers	+.50	+.49	+.10	+.20
Professional	+.36	+.09	+.03	+.06
Clerks and shopkeepers	+.29	+.30	−.11	−.21
Skilled artisans	−.50	−.03	+.16	+.20
Unskilled laborers	−.16	−.55	−.24	−.13
Religion				
Protestant		+.66	+.82	+.88

a. The figures for the Whig vote for governor in 1854 are calculated from the indices based on the census of 1850 while those for the three other elections are based on scales constructed from the manuscript census of 1860. For correlations of the Know-Nothing vote for canal commissioner in 1855 and the indices based on the 1850 census, see Table 30.

b. In this election, this is the correlation between the Whig vote and the group owning "None."

TABLE 47

PRODUCT-MOMENT COEFFICIENTS OF CORRELATION BETWEEN
DEMOCRATIC VOTES, 1854–56, AND VARIABLES[a]

Variable	Governor 1854	Canal Commissioner 1855	Congress 1856	President 1856
Ethnic				
Total immigrant[b]	+.57	+.84	+.65	+.45
Irish	+.42	+.44	+.42	+.56
German	+.41	+.50	+.54	+.53
Property Holdings				
$10,000 plus	−.32	−.31	+.06	+.09
$100–999		+.51	+.46	+.56
Less than $100	+.29[c]	+.31[c]	−.51	−.63
Occupation				
Skilled artisans	+.37	−.13	−.19	−.20
Unskilled laborers	+.29	+.48	−.19	+.23
Religion				
Roman Catholic		+.46	+.81	+.93

a. The figures for the vote in 1854 are based on the scales constructed from the manuscript census of 1850, and the others are based on the scales constructed from the manuscript census of 1860. For correlations between the Democratic vote for canal commissioner in 1855 and the indices based on the 1850 census, see Table 29.

b. This group includes all white males over twenty-one who were not native-born.

c. These are the correlations between the group owning "None" according to the manuscript census of 1850 and the Democratic vote.

TABLE 48

PARTY VOTE AND PARTY PERCENTAGE OF VOTE IN PITTSBURGH, 1856–59 [a]

Election	Republican	Democratic	American
1856 (President)	3,853 (54.5%)	2,881 (40.8%)	332 (4.7%)
1857 (Mayor)	2,749 (51.7%)	2,323 (43.7%)	241 (4.6%)
1857 (Governor)	2,262 (50.5%)	2,035 (45.4%)	180 (4.1%)
1857 (County Commissioner)	2,131 (49.9%)	2,139 (50.1%)	
1858 (Mayor)	3,149 (62.1%)	1,915 (37.9%)	
1858 (Congressman)[b]	2,607 (54.4%)	2,181 (45.6%)	
1858 (County Commissioner)	2,590 (56.6%)	1,986 (43.4%)	
1859 (County Commissioner)	2,159 (57.3%)	1,628 (42.7%)	
1859 (State Senate)	2,311 (60%)	1,540 (40%)	
1859 (County Judge)	2,161 (57.9%)	1,571 (42.1%)	
1859 (Supreme Court Judge)	2,787 (56.6%)	1,932 (43.4%)	

a. These election returns may be found in the *Gazette*, Nov. 8, 1856, Oct. 17, 1857, Jan. 7, 1857, Jan. 7, 1857, Oct. 15, 1858, Oct. 15, 1859; and in the *Post*, Jan. 15, 1857, Oct. 16, 1858.

b. This is the vote in the Twenty-First Congressional District between James K. Moorhead and Andrew Burke.

TABLE 49

PRODUCT-MOMENT COEFFICIENTS OF CORRELATION BETWEEN REPUBLICAN VOTES AND VARIABLES, 1856-59

Variable	President 1856	Governor 1857	County Commissioner 1857	Congress* 1858	Supreme Court 1859	County Commissioner 1859
Ethnic						
Native American	+.59	+.49	+.42	+.42	+.59	+.47
Irish	−.45	−.33	−.36	−.60	−.48	−.48
German	−.54	−.37	−.30	−.41	−.48	−.29
Property Holdings						
$10,000 plus	−.08	.00	−.04	+.35	+.02	.00
$5,000–9,999	−.35	−.18	−.27	−.08	−.14	−.13
$100–999	−.48	−.40	−.43	−.73	−.55	−.46
Less than $100	+.54	+.39	+.44	+.66	+.62	+.55
Occupation						
Manufacturers, merchants, and bankers	+.20	+.25	+.22	+.47	+.32	+.30
Professional	+.08	.00	−.07	+.11	−.03	−.10
Clerks and shopkeepers	−.21	−.28	−.31	+.14	−.15	−.23
Skilled artisans	+.20	+.22	+.24	−.20	+.14	+.20
Unskilled laborers	−.13	−.12	−.12	−.32	−.20	−.13
Religion						
Protestant	+.88	+.62	+.72	+.75	+.83	+.56

* These figures are calculated with the returns for James K. Moorhead in Pittsburgh.

TABLE 50

PRODUCT-MOMENT COEFFICIENTS OF CORRELATION BETWEEN DEMOCRATIC VOTES AND VARIABLES, 1856–59

Variable	President 1856	Governor 1857	County Commissioner 1857	Congress[b] 1858	Supreme Court 1859	County Commissioner 1859
Ethnic						
Total immigrant[a]	+.45	+.54	+.42	+.42	+.59	+.47
Irish	+.56	+.40	+.36	+.60	+.48	+.48
German	+.53	+.36	+.30	+.41	+.48	+.29
Property Holdings						
$10,000 plus	+.09	+.10	+.04	−.35	−.02	.00
$100–999	+.56	+.49	+.43	+.73	+.55	+.46
Less than $100	−.63	−.56	−.44	−.66	−.62	−.55
Occupation						
Skilled artisans	−.20	−.30	−.24	+.20	−.14	−.20
Unskilled laborers	+.23	+.12	+.12	+.32	+.20	+.13
Religion						
Roman Catholic	+.93	+.75	+.72	+.75	+.83	+.56

a. This group includes all white males over twenty-one who were not native-born or who were native-born but living with immigrant parents.

b. These figures are based on the returns for Andrew Burke who ran against James K. Moorhead in Pittsburgh.

TABLE 51

WEALTH DISTRIBUTION AMONG REPUBLICAN AND DEMOCRATIC CANDIDATES, 1858–60 *

Group	Republicans	Democrats
$100,000 plus	3 (5%)	0
$50,000–99,999	6 (10%)	7 (14%)
$25,000–49,999	7 (11.5%)	3 (6%)
$10,000–24,999	14 (23%)	10 (20%)
$5,000–9,999	4 (6.5%)	8 (16%)
$1,000–4,999	13 (21%)	8 (16%)
$500–999	3 (5%)	1 (2%)
$100–499	6 (10%)	7 (14%)
$1–99	0	1 (2%)
None	5 (8%)	4 (8%)

* This table is based on the 61 Republicans and 49 Democrats on whom I found information out of my total lists of 91 Republican candidates and 83 Democratic candidates.

TABLE 52

WEALTH DISTRIBUTION AMONG SECONDARY REPUBLICAN
AND DEMOCRATIC LEADERS, 1858–60.*

Group	Republicans	Democrats
$100,000 plus	1 (2%)	1 (2%)
$50,000–99,999	1 (2%)	0
$25,000–49,999	4 (7%)	2 (4%)
$10,000–24,999	3 (5%)	6 (13%)
$5,000–9,999	12 (22%)	4 (9%)
$1,000–4,999	17 (30%)	13 (30%)
$500–999	1 (2%)	3 (6%)
$100–499	8 (15%)	8 (18%)
$1–99	1 (2%)	1 (2%)
None	8 (15%)	7 (16%)

* This table is drawn from a total sample of 80 Republicans and 82 Democrats although percentages are based only on the number of men about whom I found information. I found data on 56 Republicans and 45 Democrats.

TABLE 53

DISTRIBUTION OF REPUBLICAN AND DEMOCRATIC CANDIDATES,
1858–60, AMONG OCCUPATIONAL CATEGORIES [a]

Occupation	Republicans	Democrats
Iron and glass manufacturers	7 (9%)	4 (5%)
Other manufacturers and managerial [b]	11 (14%)	11 (15%)
Merchants	14 (18%)	8 (11%)
Shopkeepers and clerks	16 (20%)	23 (31%)
Bankers and brokers	3 (4%)	0
Professional	13 (16%)	11 (15%)
Gentlemen and farmers [c]	0	3 (4%)
Artisans and skilled workers	12 (15%)	13 (18%)
Unskilled laborers	3 (4%)	1 (1%)

a. This table is drawn from the same sample of candidates as Table 51. I found information on 79 Republicans and 73 Democrats. I used the occupations given in the manuscript census of 1860 whenever they could be found and supplemented these data with material from the city directories.

b. This group includes such men as wealthy brickmakers, cabinetmakers, a master tin- and coppersmith, and a railroad president.

c. Several of the Democrats, e.g. Edward Campbell, were listed merely as farmers.

TABLE 54

DISTRIBUTION OF REPUBLICAN AND DEMOCRATIC SECONDARY
LEADERS, 1858–60, AMONG OCCUPATIONAL CATEGORIES *

Occupation	Republicans	Democrats
Iron and glass manufacturers	5 (7%)	0
Other manufacturers and managerial	12 (16%)	5 (7%)
Merchants	6 (8%)	8 (11%)
Shopkeepers and clerks	24 (32%)	27 (38%)
Bankers and brokers	1 (1%)	0
Professional	5 (7%)	5 (7%)
Gentlemen and farmers	0	3 (4%)
Artisans and skilled workers	20 (27%)	19 (27%)
Unskilled laborers	2 (3%)	3 (4%)

* This table is drawn from the same sample of leaders as Table 52, and the percentages are again based on the number of men found. I found information on 75 Republicans and 70 Democrats. I used the occupations listed in the manuscript census of 1860 and supplemented these with data taken from the city directories.

TABLE 55

DISTRIBUTION OF REPUBLICAN AND DEMOCRATIC CANDIDATES,
1858–60, AMONG NATIONALITY GROUPS *

Nationality	Republicans	Democrats
Native American	51 (77%)	28 (56%)
British	2 (3%)	2 (4%)
German	3 (5%)	7 (14%)
Irish	8 (12%)	13 (26%)
Other	2 (3%)	0

* This table is drawn from the same sample of candidates as Table 51, and percentages are based on the number of men found. Information on ethnic background comes primarily from the manuscript censuses of 1850 and 1860. I found data on 66 Republicans and 50 Democrats.

TABLE 56

DISTRIBUTION OF REPUBLICAN AND DEMOCRATIC SECONDARY
LEADERS, 1858–60, AMONG NATIONALITY GROUPS *

Nationality	Republicans	Democrats
Native American	39 (65%)	28 (61%)
British	5 (9%)	2 (4%)
German	4 (7%)	4 (9%)
Irish	11 (19%)	11 (24%)
Other	0	1 (2%)

* This table is drawn from the same sample of leaders as Table 52. Percentages are based on the 59 Republicans and 46 Democrats on whom I found information.

TABLE 57

DISTRIBUTION OF REPUBLICAN AND DEMOCRATIC CANDIDATES,
1858–60, AMONG RELIGIOUS DENOMINATIONS [a]

Religion	Republicans	Democrats
Presbyterian	11 (48%)	4 (10%)
Episcopalian	8 (35%)	6 (15%)
Methodist	0	1 (2%)
Lutheran	2 (8.5%)	0
Other Protestant[b]	2 (8.5%)	14 (34%)
Roman Catholic	0	16 (39%)

a. This table is drawn from the same sample of candidates as Table 51. Percentages are based only on the 23 Republicans and 41 Democrats on whom I found information.

b. See Table 14, note b.

TABLE 58

DISTRIBUTION OF REPUBLICAN AND DEMOCRATIC SECONDARY
LEADERS, 1858–60, AMONG RELIGIOUS DENOMINATIONS *

Religion	Republicans	Democrats
Presbyterian	4 (30%)	1 (7%)
Episcopalian	7 (50%)	2 (13%)
Methodist	1 (7%)	0
Lutheran	1 (7%)	0
Other Protestant	1 (7%)	3 (20%)
Roman Catholic	0	9 (60%)

* This table is drawn from the same sample of leaders as Table 52, and percentages are based on the 14 Republicans and 15 Democrats whose religious affiliation I could identify.

TABLE 59

PARTY VOTE AND PARTY PERCENTAGE OF VOTE
IN PITTSBURGH, 1852–60 [a]

Election	Whig	Democratic	Other[b]
1852 (President)	2,903 (54.5%)	2,046 (38.4%)	379 (7.1%)

	Republican		
1856 (President)	3,853 (54.5%)	2,881 (40.8%)	332 (4.7%)
1860 (Governor)	4,228 (59.7%)	2,847 (40.3%)	
1860 (President)	4,396 (66.3%)	2,079 (31.3%)[c]	165 (2.4%)

a. These results can be found in the *Gazette*, Nov. 6, 1852, Nov. 8, 1856, Nov. 10, 1860.

b. In 1852 this was the vote of the Native American and Free Democratic parties; in 1856 it was the Know-Nothing vote for Millard Fillmore; and in 1860 it was the vote for John Bell.

c. This is the total Democratic vote for both the Douglas and the Fusion tickets.

TABLE 60

PRODUCT-MOMENT COEFFICIENTS OF CORRELATION BETWEEN
WHIG AND REPUBLICAN VOTES AND VARIABLES, 1852–60 *

Variable	Presi-dent 1852	Presi-dent 1856	Gov-ernor 1860	Presi-dent 1860
Ethnic				
Native American	+.83	+.59	+.48	+.41
Irish	−.51	−.45	−.64	−.56
German	−.67	−.54	−.34	−.33
Property Holdings				
$10,000 plus	+.74	−.08	+.09	+.13
$5,000–9,999	+.52	−.35	−.18	−.24
$100–999		−.48	−.69	−.66
Less than $100	−.35	+.54	+.74	+.65
Occupation				
Manufacturers, merchants, and bankers	+.81	+.20	+.35	+.35
Professional	+.74	+.08	−.07	+.03
Clerks and shopkeepers	+.69	−.21	−.05	−.10
Skilled artisans	−.42	+.20	+.07	−.24
Unskilled laborers	−.68	−.13	−.18	−.21
Religion				
Protestant		+.88	+.79	+.82
Former Party Votes				
Know-Nothings in 1855		+.81	+.75	+.63
Republican vote for President 1856			+.79	+.70
Whig vote for Scott 1852			+.41	+.31

* This table is based on the same returns as Table 59 and is calculated with the Pearson product-moment formula. The Whig returns were correlated with indices based on the 1850 census, and for the Whigs the correlation with the group owning less than $100 of property is with the group owning "None" in the 1850 census.

TABLE 61

PRODUCT-MOMENT COEFFICIENTS OF CORRELATION BETWEEN
DEMOCRATIC VOTES AND VARIABLES, 1852–60 [a]

Variable	President 1852	President 1856	Governor 1860	President[c] 1860
Ethnic				
Total immigrant[b]	+.76	+.45	+.48	+.60
Irish	+.46	+.56	+.64	+.50
German	+.65	+.53	+.34	+.52
Property Holdings				
$10,000 plus	−.67	+.09	−.09	−.17
$100–999		+.56	+.69	+.72
Less than $100	+.31	−.63	−.74	−.72
Occupation				
Skilled artisans	+.43	−.20	−.07	+.01
Unskilled laborers	+.72	+.23	+.18	+.36
Religion				
Roman Catholic		+.93	+.79	+.81
Former Party Votes				
Democratic vote for President 1852				+.56
Democratic vote for President 1856			+.81	+.88

a. The returns for 1852 were correlated with indices based on the census of 1850 while the returns for 1856 and 1860 were correlated with indices based on the census of 1860.

b. This group includes all white males over twenty-one who were not native-born or who were native-born but living with immigrant parents.

c. These figures were calculated with the total Democratic vote in the wards —that is, the vote for both the Douglas straight and the Douglas Fusion tickets.

Appendix B

Note on Methods and Sources

Throughout this study I have used certain quantitative techniques in order to construct a social profile of the city and in order to determine systematically how opposing political parties differed from each other. To facilitate this latter effort I have isolated and compared three elements of political parties—leadership, appeals to the electorate, and voting support. Some explanation of these methods and of the sources on which they were used will hopefully clarify the evidence on which this study is based and better enable the reader to evaluate that evidence.

CONTENT ANALYSIS

One way to distinguish exactly how one party differs from its opponent is to contrast the appeals—the programs and ideologies —the opposing parties presented to the voters to solicit support. Content analysis of such appeals reveals not only how the parties differed qualitatively in their treatment of the same issue but also how they differed quantitatively in their emphases, the amount of space given different issues and kinds of appeals such as economic, ethnic, slavery, or others. This technique also allowed me to measure how positions and emphases changed over time as the Whig party was replaced by the Republicans as the major foe of the Democrats. Content analysis is simply a close reading of the various appeals as well as a quantitative measure within fixed samples of platforms or editorials of the space devoted to specific issues or approaches to the voters. For an excellent introduction to this technique, one should see Bernard Berelson, *Content Analysis in Communication Research.*

Analysis of the appeals to the voters in Pittsburgh required examination of the programs written for national and statewide consumption as well as those launched specifically in Pittsburgh. Therefore, I examined the national platforms of the major parties in 1848, 1852, 1856, and 1860, the state platforms for the years 1847–60, and also the resolutions of city and county party conventions for those years. I also studied the editorial columns of the major local newspapers, the Democratic *Pittsburgh Morning Post* and the Whig-Republican *Pittsburgh Daily Gazette.* Such an investigation is necessary because local newspapers and resolutions, I believe, had much more impact in creating a party's image locally than did national and state platforms. Certainly the emphases of local appeals often differed from those of the state and national platforms. To measure quantitatively the emphases given different appeals, I counted the total words in a given national, state, or local platform devoted to issues and then calculated the percentage of that total which specific issues or approaches occupied. Quantitative investigation of the editorial appeals, on the other hand, involved measuring the column inches of space devoted to different issues. As I warned in the introduction, however, the fact that a party devoted more space to one issue than to another does not mean that voters thought about that issue the most or even responded to that particular appeal. Comparing such emphases is simply a way to demonstrate the differences between the parties so far as what they said.

The Manuscript Censuses

Both the analysis of the social structure of the city and the composition of its elite in 1850 and the investigation of the sources of leadership and voter support throughout the book rest heavily on data and indices culled from the manuscript schedules of population of the United States censuses of 1850 and 1860. Therefore, some description of these two censuses, the difficulties inherent in them, and their use in this study is necessary. The manuscript returns of 1850 and 1860 give the name, sex, age, race, place of birth, occupation, and value of property owned of every person in each ward of the city. Both of these manuscript censuses are available on microfilm at the National Archives and at the Carnegie Free Library of Pittsburgh.

To arrive at a portrait of the socioeconomic and ethnic makeup of the potential electorate of each ward and of the city's total population, I counted the number of white males over twenty-one years of age and then placed each man in his proper category of occupation, wealth as measured by the value of property owned, and ethnic group. For 1850, I also categorized the adult white males in Allegheny City. When sons over twenty-one lived at home, I attributed to them the ethnic and wealth characteristics of their fathers. For example, if a son born in Pennsylvania and owning no evaluated property lived with a father who was Irish and owned property worth $50,000, I included the son in the latter two classifications, assuming he was influenced by his environment and parents' values. Similarly, I added the value of any property owned by a wife or mother to that owned by a husband or son. With these categories I could determine the proportions that an occupational or ethnic group or economic class, as measured by the value of property owned, formed of the population of the city and of each ward.

Several qualifications about these data gleaned from the manuscript censuses must be made. First, it was impossible to distinguish between generations of immigrants and between naturalized and unnaturalized aliens. This latter consideration is important when these figures are used to identify voting support, for they show the numbers of white immigrant males, not the number of potential voters among the immigrants. More important, to make comparisons of the occupational backgrounds of leaders and voters manageable, it was necessary to combine numerous occupations into certain general categories or types. These are used in Chapter 1, in the occupational indices used to identify voting support, and usually in the tables on leadership in Appendix A, although these last are more detailed and precise. In assigning people to an occupational category, some mistakes are inevitable, and the process is not as systematic as it may seem. But I did try to be consistent, and the groups do allow some differentiation of the class status of certain occupations. The categories of "Banker," "Manufacturer," "Merchant," and "Gentlemen" are fairly self-explanatory. The last group included men who were described thus in the census. The group labeled "Professional" includes lawyers, doctors, newspaper editors, clergymen, aldermen, and civil engineers, but the first two occupations were by far the most numerous. Thus education, rather than professional standards, was the real criterion for inclusion in this group. In the category of "Clerks and Shopkeepers" I included tailors, butchers, and bakers who owned real property worth $300 or more because they probably owned their own shops. (Otherwise these men were included as skilled artisans.) There were also some men who listed no real property owned but who had three or four men of the same trade living with their families. I concluded that such men owned shops and that those nonfamily members living with them were helpers. I also included in this category clerks, toll collectors, street commissioners, grocers, druggists, tobacconists, confectioners, livery stable owners, and so forth. Some of these men were very wealthy, for unless a man was called a "wholesale grocer," I did not include him in the merchant category. In sum, the shopkeeper category is rather amorphous and includes men who, I assumed, belonged to the middle class because they owned property, had some managerial function, or did not work with their hands so much as artisans or laborers. But all gradations of the middle class were probably included. The category "Small Manufacturers" included such men as wagon makers, furniture makers, and brush makers who did not own much property. The "Skilled Artisans" were craftsmen such as blacksmiths, carpenters, bricklayers, and shoemakers and skilled operatives such as puddlers, boilers, and glassblowers. Some of these men were probably prosperous and independently employed, and the line between this category and that of "Small Manufacturer" is fairly arbitrary, although all "Small Manufacturers" were apparently self-employed. Those labeled "Unskilled Laborers" were the men listed in the census as "laborer," "riverman," "porter," or "drayman." These categories, then, are not flawlessly precise, but they do indicate the status differences within the working class, between manual and nonmanual occupations, and between employers and employees; moreover, within the upper-level occupations they specify function.

Several problems involved with utilizing the census material spring from the very significant difference between the property evaluations in the census of 1850 and those in the census of 1860. The first measured only the value of real property owned while the second measured the value of both real and personal property. Thus the second census is more complete and probably more accurate. There is especially a problem in using the 1850 census with those men whose property holdings were listed as "None." Since 84 percent of the adult male population belonged to this group, the complete accuracy of this census on property ownership is questionable. Some of the men in that group probably had personal property holdings or bank accounts of value. Moreover, several could have been reluctant to give accurate evaluations to the census taker if, for instance, they mistook him for a tax assessor. The evidence, then, is not unassailable. On the other hand, the vast majority of those listed as owning "None" were undoubtedly poor, and almost all of them were relatively poorer than those listed as owning some real property. Therefore, the measure is useful in showing the proportions of leaders or of the population less wealthy than those who owned some real property. That is, one can use the category "None" as a relative rather than an absolute indicator of the lack of wealth. For the sake of stylistic convenience, in this study I refer to those listed as owning "None" as poor or propertyless. The reader must remember that these terms are relative, not absolute, measures of wealth.

Another problem with the differences in the censuses is the difficulty of comparing figures based on data from the different censuses. As a whole, men listed in the 1860 census seemed wealthier because the value of personal property was also given. In the 1860 census, for example, many workers were listed as owning $100, $200, or $300 worth of real and personal property. Therefore, rather than using one group labeled "None" to indicate the poor, I constructed two more precise categories: a poor group which owned a total valued between $100 and $999, although most of the people listed in that group as counted in the 1860 census owned less than $500, and a very poor group which owned property less than $100, although most of these were listed as owning "None." These two groups, as will be shown later, followed sharply different voting patterns, and that fact makes any voting comparisons with the group owning "None" according to the 1850 census tenuous. Indices based on the 1850 census are used in the first four chapters, and those based on the 1860 census are used in Chapters 5, 6, and 7, and in the corresponding tables. Similarly, comparing the wealth of Whig and Democratic leaders in the late 1840s as measured in the 1850 census with the wealth of Republican and Democratic leaders in the late 1850s as measured in the 1860 census is very difficult. That the later leaders were wealthier as a group than the earlier sample is probably a function of the difference in the censuses. On the other hand, if an earlier sample were wealthier than a later sample, the differences between the groups was probably greater than the figures show because the first group was probably wealthier than the 1850 census revealed.

LEADERSHIP ANALYSIS

Another of the major methods used to analyze how opposing political parties differed was to compare the social backgrounds and origins of the most prominent men in the parties. To accomplish this task some indices of social status had to be established. Defining the exact nature and membership of social classes in the 1840s and 1850s was difficult, but I used as indices of social status property holdings, occupation, ethnic background, and especially religion and membership in elite churches. Residence in prestigious neighborhoods helped define the elite in Chapter 1, but since political leaders were normally drawn equally from all wards, residence could not be used as an index for political leaders. As mentioned above, I used the property evaluations listed in the manuscript censuses as measures of wealth; I used the 1850 census evaluations for the 1848–50 sample of leaders and the 1860 listings for the other two groups, except when I could find no information for the man in the 1860 census but had relevant data for him from the 1850 census. Because so few people in the city owned property valued over $10,000 (only 4 percent according to the manuscript census of 1850), I used that figure as a minimum index of the wealthy. For the ethnic background and occupations of the leaders I relied primarily on the manuscript censuses, but I supplemented these occupational data with information from the various city directories.

Religion was a major index of elite status. Both membership in the socially prestigious Episcopalian and Presbyterian churches and election to some lay office such as vestryman or elder denote, I believe, social prominence in the community. I also used as a source of religious affiliation delegates from various Protestant churches to the Pittsburgh Bible Society. Since these men were elected by their congregations to represent their respective churches, they enjoyed leadership status within that church if not in the community at large. Because my major sources for religious affiliation were the membership rolls of the prestigious churches and such lists of lay leaders, any change in the proportion of political leaders found on such lists indicates a change in the proportion of the elite who participated in party leadership. Thus, I argue

377

in Chapter 7 that, since fewer Republican leaders than Whig leaders could be identified as Presbyterians and Episcopalians, fewer Republicans than Whigs belonged to the social elite.[1]

A second problem involved in leadership analysis was to define precisely what a leader was and to choose comparable samples for different years. Three groups of leaders in different years form the basis of analysis in this study—Whigs and Democrats between 1848 and 1851, Republicans and Democrats in 1855–57, and Republicans and Democrats, 1858–60. For each group I selected two kinds of leaders—the men who ran for office and the men who ran the party. The first type consisted of the candidates who ran for Congress, the state legislature, county offices, the city councils, and mayor. I always confined my samples to men who lived in Pittsburgh itself except for some important candidates who lived elsewhere in Allegheny County. In order to obtain a wider sample of party leaders, I also compiled lists of men whom I label "secondary party leaders"—Pittsburgh delegates to city, county, state, and national party conventions which chose the parties' nominees, members of city and county party executive committees, and officers in various party clubs or committees. These men may have wielded more influence in the party and may also have been more

1. My sources for religious affiliation were the "Register for Trinity Episcopal Parish, 1808–1867" (MS, Trinity Episcopal Church, Pittsburgh); "Register of the First Presbyterian Church" (MS, First Presbyterian Church, Pittsburgh); "Church Records and General Register of the Third Presbyterian Church" (MS, Third Presbyterian Church, Pittsburgh). A list of elders of the First Presbyterian Church can be found in *Centennial Volume of the First Presbyterian Church of Pittsburgh, Pennsylvania* (Pittsburgh, 1884), p. 225. Another valuable source for members of the First Presbyterian Church is a published list of purchasers of pews in that church in 1855. *Gazette,* May 1, 5, 1855. The lists of vestrymen elected in the Episcopal churches and of the officers of Bible Societies can be found in the *Dispatch,* Apr. 26, 1859; *Post,* Jan. 11, Apr. 16, 1858; *Gazette,* Jan. 27, Apr. 7, 1858, Feb. 1, 1859, Jan. 17, 1860, Jan. 22, 1861. Lists of Catholic laymen can be found in the *Gazette,* June 16, 1851, Jan. 1, 1858; *Post,* Mar. 29, 1855, Sept. 22, 1857, Feb. 2, May 9, 1860.

representative of the types of men who belonged to the parties than were the candidates for office. For this group, like the candidates, I confined my lists to those who lived in Pittsburgh except for a few who lived outside the city but in the county. If a man was both a candidate for office and a delegate to a convention, I included him only in the candidate sample. Throughout this study I call the first type of leader "candidates" and the second group "party leaders" or "secondary leaders." Together these lists contained most of the active men in each party at each particular time. It must be noted that I could never find information about a total sample, and percentage figures in the text and footnotes refer only to proportions of those men whom I could find, not to proportions of the whole samples.

The leadership sample for 1848–50 in Chapter 2 included the candidates for the select and common councils in Pittsburgh in 1848, 1849, 1850, and 1851 as well as the nominees of both parties for mayor, state assembly, county offices, and Congress in 1848, 1849, and 1850. The list of Whig candidates also included Andrew Loomis, the Whig presidential elector in 1848, and Joseph Pennock, a prominent Whig who was not a candidate for the councils in those years but served on them from 1845–47. There were 97 Whig and 97 Democratic candidates in the sample. The list of secondary leaders in that chapter, which totaled 119 Whigs and 107 Democrats, included the ward delegates to the city and county conventions, the city's delegates to the state and national conventions, and the members of the parties' executive committees for the years 1847–51. The Whig list also included Thomas McKee, C. L. Magee, J. Von Bonnhorst, Charles B. Sculley, W. S. Haven, Samuel Roseburg, and G. L. B. Fetterman from the first and third ward Whig Vigilance Committee in 1847 and J. M. Crossan, N. Buckmaster, J. P. Rea, W. O. Leslie, and William Boyd from the executive committee of the Rough and Ready Club in 1848.[2]

2. The lists of these leaders can be found in the *Post*, Sept. 20, 1847, Jan. 4, June 22, 1848, Mar. 22, Dec. 19, 1849, Jan. 1, Mar. 21, Aug. 29,

The leaders included in the 1855–57 sample were similar types. The sample of candidates was drawn from the Republican, Union, and Democratic county and congressional tickets in 1855, 1856, and 1857 and the candidates of both Republicans and Democrats for city councils and other municipal offices in 1857. I specifically did not use members of the anti-Know Nothing council tickets of 1855 and 1856 as Democrats, for these were fusion tickets with Whigs. The sample of candidates for these years totaled 49 Republicans and 43 Democrats. My list of Republican secondary leaders included: delegates to the Republican county convention of 1855, the Republican county convention of June 1856, the Union county convention in August 1856, the city Republican convention in December 1856, and the two county conventions in 1857; the Republican vigilance committees for Pittsburgh in 1855, the city executive committee of 1857, the executive committee and vice-presidents for organization of the Frémont Club in 1856, and the committee of reception for the national Republican convention in Pittsburgh in February 1856; and the delegates from Pittsburgh to the state and national conventions of 1856. I specifically did not include delegates to the Anti-Administration convention in March 1856 as Republicans, for most of these men were then Know-Nothings. The sample of Democratic secondary leaders included: the delegates to the county convention in December 1855, the state convention in 1856, and the county and city conventions in 1856 and 1857; the vice-presidents, arrangement committee, and finance committee for the wards of the Allegheny County Buchanan and Breckinridge Club; and the officers of the last county convention in 1857. Altogether the sample of secondary leaders included 137 Republicans and 88 Democrats.[3]

Dec. 23, 1850, Feb. 27, Aug. 21, Sept. 8, Dec. 25, 1851; *Gazette*, Feb. 16, Oct. 15, 1847, Feb. 3, 17, June 15, 22, July 7, Aug. 24, Oct. 26, Dec. 28, 1848, Jan. 1, 1849, May 7, June 6, Sept. 18, 1850, Jan. 16, June 5, Dec. 15, 1851.

3. The lists from which the primary and secondary leaders were drawn

The Republican and Democratic leaders analyzed in Chapter 7 were leaders from 1858–60. The candidates were drawn from the Democratic and Republican city council tickets for 1858–60, the county and congressional tickets of the two parties for those years, and the Republican municipal candidates in 1858 and 1860. My sample also included Thomas M. Howe, the Republican presidential elector in 1860. I included only one man on the 1860 Democratic county and congressional ticket, George W. Cass of Allegheny City. Only one man from that ticket lived in Pittsburgh, and I could find no information about him. The total sample of candidates was 91 Republicans and 83 Democrats. My sample of secondary leaders included for the Republicans: delegates to the county conventions in May 1858, June 1859, and January and June 1860; delegates to the city convention of December 1859; members of the Republican county executive committee for 1860, and the officers of the Allegheny County Republican Club in 1860. It should be noted that all the delegates to the People's state convention in 1860 on whom I could find information were included in one of these other lists. Also included was John M. Kirkpatrick, chairman of the Republican county committee for 1859–60. For the Democrats my sample included: delegates to the county conventions in January, August, and December 1858, June 1859, and January and September 1860; delegates to the city convention in December 1859; and the Pittsburgh delegates to the state convention in 1860.[4]

Coefficients of Correlation and Voter Support

In order to identify the voter support of the parties in this study

can be found in the *Gazette*, Aug. 30, Sept. 26, 1855, Feb. 20, June 5, July 26, Aug. 21, 22, Oct. 14, Dec. 25, 1856, Jan. 1, 14, Mar. 19, June 25, 1857; *Post*, Dec. 20, 1855, Jan. 7, June 18, 24, Aug. 4, 28, Oct. 9, 1856, Jan. 1, 8, Aug. 27, 1857.

4. The lists of candidates and secondary leaders can be found in the *Gazette*, Jan. 5, 7, May 31, Aug. 24, Dec. 20, 1858, Jan. 10, 30, June 2, Dec. 12, 23, 1859, Jan. 4, 5, June 5, Sept. 6, 1860; *Post*, Jan. 7, Aug. 19, 28, Dec. 23, 1858, Jan. 5, June 28, 1859, Jan. 26, Sept. 30, 1860.

I have attempted to correlate election returns with socioeconomic indices of the voting population of the city. Because Pittsburgh was a small industrial city, its heterogeneous population of rich and poor, natives and immigrants, was packed closely together in the same wards. A few very wealthy men in a ward could raise its average wealth disproportionately. Instead of relying on averages or attempting to single out characteristic wards, therefore, I counted the number of white males over twenty-one and categorized them according to occupation, property holdings, and ethnic group as described above. Then I calculated the proportion that each ethnic group, occupational type, and economic class (as measured by the value of property holdings) constituted of the potential electorate of each ward and ranked the wards in a scale for each variable. In the later chapters I also used an index of the proportions of Catholics and Protestants in each ward found in Table 35. To identify the voting support, I then correlated the voting returns in each ward with these indices. For example, if I wanted to check the relationship between the native American population of the city and the Whig vote in an election, I would calculate the coefficient of correlation between the percentage of native Americans in the nine wards and the percentage of the Whig vote in that election in the nine wards. This is a ward-by-ward coefficient of correlation.

In this book the relationship between the socioeconomic variables and the voting returns is expressed as a coefficient of correlation. A coefficient of correlation of +1.00 indicates a perfect direct statistical relationship between two variables; a correlation of −1.00 indicates a perfect inverse relationship. Correlations of ±0.50 or greater indicate a significant relationship between variables. To calculate all coefficients of correlation in this study I used the fairly precise and complex Pearson Product-Moment formula (R is the coefficient of correlation; x is the deviation from the average in one variable; y is the deviation from the average in the other variable; N is the number of cases):

$$R = \frac{N(\text{sum of } xy) - (\text{sum of } x)(\text{sum of } y)}{\sqrt{N(\text{sum of } x^2) - (\text{sum of } x)^2} \sqrt{N(\text{sum of } y^2) - (\text{sum of } y)^2}}$$

Moreover, all coefficients of correlation are calculated on a ward-by-ward basis and on the basis of percentages in the wards rather than on the basis of raw numbers—i.e. the percentage of the Whig vote in each ward or the percentage that native-born Americans form of the electorate of each ward. Rather than repeating the cumbersome formula of ward-by-ward product-moment coefficients of correlation between the percentages of two variables, I generally refer in the footnotes merely to correlations between two groups or variables.

Some warnings about this technique and its use in this paper are imperative. Coefficients of correlation show a statistical relationship between numerical characteristics of the wards; they do not prove a causal relationship between those variables. For instance, if the example above produced a high positive correlation between the Whig vote and the native-born Americans, this figure only means that the Whigs were strongest where the native Americans were proportionately the strongest and weakest where native Americans were weakest. It does not prove that the native Americans in those wards voted Whig, although I have interpreted high correlations to indicate a tendency of a group to act in a certain way. Moreover, a high correlation certainly does not prove that native Americans voted Whig because they were native Americans, although after examining other evidence I often arrive at this conclusion. The statistical technique is useful in identifying who voted for whom, but it does not answer why. Another problem with the correlations is that there was no state census, so I had to use indices based on the 1850 and 1860 federal census returns to correlate with votes in the mid-1850s. Therefore, the results of such correlations may be suspect. This is a particularly difficult problem in Chapter 4 which covers the years 1854–56.

Other problems are also presented by the voting in Pittsburgh.

According to state law, only those who paid taxes could vote, yet a large portion of the electorate, especially as listed in the manuscript census of 1850, owned no property of value. Estimating how many of the poor were legally disfranchised by this law is impossible. In many cases the census of 1850 was probably inaccurate; it is certain that it did not measure personal property which was also taxed. In short, many of the group owning "None" probably did pay taxes and could vote. The same is probably true of the group owning "None" according to the census of 1860. The low correlations with that group and with unskilled laborers indicates that poorer people were probably apathetic about most issues and elections and did not vote when they could. When Joe Barker, the anti-Catholic demagogue, ran for mayor, however, newspapers complained that he drew out the votes of a rowdy, nonworking element which had never voted before. These men later probably voted Know-Nothing and then Republican. In any case, the lesson seems to be that these people could vote but had no interest in conventional issues.

Another problem raised in the voting study is the radically different voting patterns of the two poor groups in the index constructed from the 1860 census. The group owning less than $100 tended to vote very strongly Know-Nothing and Republican while the group owning between $100 and $999 voted strongly against the Republicans and for the Democrats. The evidence is even more confusing when compared with the voting behavior of the unskilled laborers, who should have been the poorest group in the community, for the correlations between that group and the Know-Nothings are strongly negative, and between that group and the Republicans they are slightly negative. The negative correlations with the Republicans are insignificant and probably mean that many unskilled laborers abstained from voting and that those who did vote divided their support among the parties. Even if one takes the negative sign to mean that more unskilled laborers voted against the Republicans than for them, and most evidently did vote against the Know-Nothings in 1855, this apparent inconsistency with the voting of the group owning less than $100 can still be explained. The answer to this paradox lies in the fact that the poorest group tended to be native-born American and probably Protestant while the group owning $100–999 tended to be immigrant. The correlations between the group owning less than $100 and the native Americans, Irish, Germans, and Protestants, were +.48, −.78, −.32, and +.33 respectively. The correlations between the group owning $100–999 worth of property and native Americans, Irish, Germans, and Catholics were −.54, +.65, +.46, and +.31 respectively. The disagreement with the voting patterns of unskilled laborers may also be explained by the extremely important findings in Stephan Thernstrom's, *Poverty and Progress: Social Mobility in a Nineteenth Century City,* pp. 155–56 and passim. Thernstrom found that native American and immigrant workers took different paths of social mobility. Native Americans tended to attain occupational mobility out of the unskilled laborer category more often than immigrants while immigrants achieved mobility by saving money and buying a house, not by rising into skilled occupations. The implications of this fact in Pittsburgh are that most unskilled laborers were immigrants who owned some property (that of many valued between $100 and $999) while the group owning less than $100 were native Americans who were skilled artisans or at least not unskilled laborers. That is, the group owning less than $100 and the unskilled laborers were not the same men, and their voting behavior would not necessarily be the same. The different voting patterns then would derive from ethnic and religious differences, not economic or occupational considerations. The correlations between the unskilled laborers and the groups owning less than $100 and $100–999 are −.54 and +.71 respectively. These figures give strong support to this interpretation and to Thernstrom's findings about the different behavior of immigrant workers and native American workers.

Finally, other techniques need to be explained. In several places in this study I use the terms "percentage increase (or decrease) of vote" and "arithmetic increment (or decrement) of percent." An example most simply defines these terms. If the Whig numerical vote in a ward was 100 in 1850 and 150 in 1851, the percentage increase of the vote was 50 percent. If the Whig proportion of the vote was 50 percent in 1850 and 60 percent in 1851, then the arithmetic increment of percent was 10. Throughout the study I also correlate the Democratic vote with the total immigrant group. These correlations are exactly the reverse of the correlations between the Democratic votes and the native-born portion of the population. For example, the correlation between the Democratic vote for governor in 1847 and the total immigrant group was +.46; therefore, the correlation between that vote and the native Americans was —.46.

Bibliography

PRIMARY SOURCES

Manuscript Materials

Information about politics in Pittsburgh in the late 1840s and 1850s in private correspondence is relatively scanty. Particularly the Whigs there apparently did not write many letters to major political figures. No single dominant state leader emerged in the Whig party who received letters from Pittsburgh. At the Library of Congress, the John McLean MSS contained some material on the 1848 campaign in Pittsburgh, but the Thaddeus Stevens MSS there were useless for this study. Much more information could be found on the Democratic party in Pittsburgh. The most helpful sources at the Library of Congress were the Jeremiah Sullivan Black MSS, the James Buchanan MSS, the Simon Cameron MSS, and the David Lynch MSS. The Edwin M. Stanton MSS contained nothing of use even though Stanton was married to the daughter of a prominent Pittsburgh merchant. Probably the most important sources for a study of Democratic politics in Pittsburgh and Pennsylvania were, however, the James Buchanan MSS and the William Bigler MSS at the Historical Society of Pennsylvania. Also consulted without profit at that depository were the Samuel Calvin MSS, the Lewis S. Coryell MSS, and the Wayne McVeagh MSS.

Material on the Know-Nothing and Republican parties is even less abundant. The best letters on the Know-Nothings in Pittsburgh are in the Simon Cameron MSS at the Library of Congress. The Edward McPherson MSS there also contain a few letters. These collections include letters on the Republican party in Pittsburgh. The Robert Todd Lincoln MSS at the Library of Congress, which are available on microfilm at the Yale University Library, contain important letters about the Republican campaign in Pennsylvania in 1860. The Salmon P. Chase MSS at the Library of Congress contain a few important letters for the years 1855 and 1856, but the John Covode MSS there were useless. At the Historical Society of Pennsylvania the S. P. Chase MSS had nothing of use, and the John Covode MSS at the Western Pennsylvania Historical Society in Pittsburgh included only two or three helpful letters.

The manuscript Robert McKnight Diary, at the Darlington Memorial Library of the University of Pittsburgh, was a great aid in recreating the social life of the wealthy classes in Pittsburgh in the late 1840s.

Censuses, Directories, and Church Records

Because the major problem of this study was the identification of men who led and supported the opposing parties, the sources used to trace their socioeconomic, ethnic, and religious background were very important. Most helpful were the federal manuscript census population schedules for 1850 and 1860, located at the National Archives but available on microfilm at the Carnegie Free Library in Pittsburgh. Unfortunately, there was no state or municipal census to supplement these federal returns, but city directories which listed the occupation as well as street address of heads of families and business directories proved a valuable aid. These directories were also helpful in tracing the rate of the city's economic growth. Of most use were: Samuel Jones, *Pittsburgh in the Year Eighteen Hundred and Twenty Six, Containing Sketches, Topographical, Historical, and Statistical; Together with a Directory of the City and a View of Its Various Manufactures, Population, Improvements, etc.* (Pittsburgh, 1826); Isaac Harris, *Harris' Pittsburgh Business Directory for the Year 1837; Includ-*

ing the Names of All the Merchants, Manufacturers, Mechanics, Professional & Men of Business of Pittsburgh and Vicinity (Pittsburgh, 1837) and *General Business Directory of the Cities of Pittsburgh and Allegheny, with the Environs* (Pittsburgh, 1847); Samuel Fahnestock, *Pittsburgh Directory for 1850, Containing the Names of the Inhabitants of Pittsburgh, Allegheny, & Vicinity* (Pittsburgh, 1850); Richard Edwards, *Pittsburgh Business Directory, 1854* (Pittsburgh, 1854); George H. Thurston, *Directory for 1856–'57 of Pittsburgh and Allegheny Cities, Birmingham, East Birmingham, South & West Pittsburgh, Temperanceville, Manchester, Duquesne, and Lawrenceville Boroughs* (Pittsburgh, 1856); *Pittsburgh As It Is: or Facts and Figures, Exhibiting the Past and Present of Pittsburgh, Its Advantages, Resources, Manufactures, and Commerce* (Pittsburgh, 1857); and *Directory of Pittsburgh and Allegheny Cities and the Adjoining Boroughs for 1860–61* (Pittsburgh, 1860).

Another important source of information was the membership records of prominent churches still in existence. Most helpful were: "Register and Role of Members of the First Presbyterian Church as complete as could be made in 1876 for 1876 from all Existing Records," MS, First Presbyterian Church (Pittsburgh); "Church Records and General Register of the Third Presbyterian Church," MS, Third Presbyterian Church (Pittsburgh); and "Register for Trinity Episcopal Parish, 1808–1867," MS, Trinity Episcopal Church (Pittsburgh).

Newspapers

I relied primarily on the major newspapers of each party in Pittsburgh and supplemented these with others when they were available. The *Pittsburgh Daily Gazette*, 1846–61, and the *Daily Commercial Journal* (Pittsburgh), 1848–55, were first Whig and then Republican papers. The *Gazette* was traditionally anti-Catholic and almost abolitionist in its antislavery sentiments. The *Pittsburgh Morning Post*, 1846–61, remained the major Democratic organ in the city, although its editors were prolabor and often in disagreement with the dominant clique of party leaders. Copies of the Bigler paper, the *Daily Union,* were not available. The *Pittsburgh Daily Dispatch,* available for 1847–50 and December 1854–60, claimed to be an independent sheet, but its editor followed a line from the Free-Soil party to the Know-Nothings into the Republican party. The most complete files of all of these papers are located at the Carnegie Free Library in Pittsburgh, except for the *Daily Commercial Journal,* which is available at the Western Pennsylvania Historical Society.

In the early stages of my research, I used several Philadelphia newspapers to locate state party platforms. They were the *North American and United States Gazette,* the *Pennsylvanian,* and the *Public Ledger.*

Public Documents

The printed returns of the United States census were of particular help for the first chapter to compare the population and economic growth of Pittsburgh to that of other cities. One should see: United States Bureau of the Census, *Seventh Census of the United States: 1850; Eighth Census of the United States: 1860. Population, Manufactures, and Mortality and Miscellaneous Statistics;* and *Tenth Census of the United States: 1880. Social Statistics of Cities, 1.*

One should see also certain state documents for voting requirements and more economic statistics: Pennsylvania, General Assembly, *Laws of the Commonwealth of Pennsylvania Passed at the Session of 1838–39* (Harrisburg, 1839); Pennsylvania, Bureau of Industrial Statistics, *First Annual Report of the Bureau of Statistics of Labor and Agriculture for the Years 1872–73* (Harrisburg, 1874).

Contemporary Writings

In the examination of the social and economic conditions of Pittsburgh I used: J. D. B. DeBow, ed., *The Commercial Review of the South and West* (New Orleans, 1847–55); Freeman Hunt, ed., *The Merchants' Magazine and Commercial Review* (New York, 1842–48); and J. D. B. DeBow, *Statistical View of the United States* (Washington, D.C., 1854).

SECONDARY SOURCES

The following list of secondary sources includes only those works that were most helpful in the preparation of this study or have been cited in the footnotes.

Books

Andrews, J. Cutler, *Pittsburgh's Post-Gazette: "The First Newspaper West of the Alleghenies,"* Boston, Chapman and Grimes, 1936.

Baldwin, Leland D., *Pittsburgh: The Story of a City*, Pittsburgh, University of Pittsburgh Press, 1937.

Baringer, William E., *A House Dividing: Lincoln as President Elect*, Springfield, Ill., Abraham Lincoln Association, 1945.

Barnes, Gilbert H., *The Antislavery Impulse, 1830–1844*, New York, Appleton-Century, 1933.

Benson, Lee, "Research Problems in American Political Historiography," in Mira Komarovsky, ed., *Common Frontiers of the Social Sciences*, Glencoe, Ill., Free Press, 1957.

———, *The Concept of Jacksonian Democracy: New York as a Test Case*, New York, Atheneum, 1964.

Berelson, Bernard, *Content Analysis in Communication Research*, Glencoe, Ill., Free Press, 1952.

Berwanger, Eugene, *The Frontier Against Slavery: Western Anti-Negro Prejudice and the Slavery Extension Controversy*, Urbana, Ill., University of Illinois Press, 1967.

Billington, Ray Allen, *The Protestant Crusade, 1800–1860: A Study in the Origins of American Nativism*, Chicago, Quadrangle Books, 1964.

Boucher, John Newton, ed., *A Century and a Half of Pittsburgh and Her People*, 4 vols. [Pittsburgh], Lewis Publishing Company, 1908.

Bradley, Erwin Stanley, *Simon Cameron, Lincoln's Secretary of War: A Political Biography*, Philadelphia, University of Pennsylvania Press, 1966.

Burgess, George H., and Miles C. Kennedy, *Centennial History of the Pennsylvania Railroad Company*, Philadelphia, Pennsylvania Railroad Company, 1949.

BIBLIOGRAPHY

Chandler, Alfred D., Jr., ed., *The Railroads: The Nation's First Big Business,* New York, Harcourt, Brace, and World, 1965.

Crandall, Andrew Wallace, *The Early History of the Republican Party, 1854–1856,* Boston, Gorham Press, 1930.

Crenshaw, Ollinger, "Urban and Rural Voting in the Election of 1860," in Eric F. Goldman, ed., *Historiography and Urbanization: Essays in American History in Honor of W. Stull Holt,* Baltimore, The Johns Hopkins University Press, 1941.

Davis, Stanton L., *Pennsylvania Politics, 1860–1863,* Cleveland, Bookstore of Western Reserve University, 1935.

Dusinberre, William, *Civil War Issues in Philadelphia, 1856–1865,* Philadelphia, University of Pennsylvania Press, 1965.

Eiselen, Malcolm Rogers, *The Rise of Pennsylvania Protectionism,* Philadelphia, University of Pennsylvania Press, 1932.

Fehrenbacher, Don E., *Prelude to Greatness: Lincoln in the 1850s,* New York, McGraw-Hill, 1964.

First Presbyterian Church, *Centennial Volume of the First Presbyterian Church of Pittsburgh, Pennsylvania,* Pittsburgh, William G. Johnston, 1884.

Fite, Emerson D., *The Presidential Campaign of 1860,* New York, Macmillan, 1911.

Fleming, George Thornton, et al., *History of Pittsburgh and Environs,* 4 vols. New York, American Historical Society, 1922.

Griffin, Clifford S., *Their Brothers' Keepers: Moral Stewardship in the United States, 1800–1865,* New Brunswick, N.J., Rutgers University Press, 1960.

Hamilton, Holman, *Prologue to Conflict: The Crisis and Compromise of 1850,* New York, W. W. Norton, 1964.

Hammond, Bray, *Banks and Politics in America from the Revolution to the Civil War,* Princeton, Princeton University Press, 1957.

Harper, Frank C., *Pittsburgh: Forge of the Universe,* New York, Comet Press, 1957.

Harrington, Fred H., *Fighting Politician: Major General N. P. Banks,* Philadelphia, University of Pennsylvania Press, 1948.

Hartz, Louis, *Economic Policy and Democratic Thought: Pennsylvania, 1776–1860,* Cambridge, Harvard University Press, 1948.

Hofstadter, Richard, *The American Political Tradition and the Men Who Made It,* New York, Knopf (Vintage Books), 1964.

394

Isely, Jeter A., *Horace Greeley and the Republican Party, 1853–1861: A Study of the New York Tribune*, Princeton, Princeton University Press, 1947.

Jaffa, Harry V., *Crisis of the House Divided: An Interpretation of the Issues in the Lincoln-Douglas Debates*, Garden City, N.Y., Doubleday, 1959.

Key, V. O., *Public Opinion and American Democracy*, New York, Knopf, 1961.

Klein, Philip Shriver, *President James Buchanan: A Biography*, University Park, Pennsylvania State University Press, 1962.

Kohlmeier, A. L., *The Old Northwest as the Keystone of the Arch of American Federal Union*, Bloomington, Ind., Principia Press, 1938.

Lorant, Stefan, et al., *Pittsburgh: The Story of an American City*, Garden City, N.Y., Doubleday, 1964.

Luthin, Reinhard H., *The First Lincoln Campaign*, Cambridge, Harvard University Press, 1944.

McCarthy, Charles, *The Antimasonic Party: A Study of Political Antimasonry in the United States, 1828–1840,* in Annual Report of the American Historical Association, *1,* New York, 1902.

McClure, Alexander K., *Old Time Notes of Pennsylvania*, 2 vols. Philadelphia, John C. Winston, 1905.

McCormick, Richard P., *The Second American Party System: Party Formation in the Jacksonian Era*, Chapel Hill, University of North Carolina Press, 1966.

McKinney, William Wilson, ed., *The Presbyterian Valley*, Pittsburgh, Davis and Warde, 1958.

Mandel, Bernard, *Labor: Free and Slave, Workingmen and the Anti-Slavery Movement in the United States*, New York, Associated Authors, 1955.

Mayer, George H., *The Republican Party, 1854–1966*, 2d ed. New York, Oxford University Press, 1967.

Morrison, Chaplain W., *Democratic Politics and Sectionalism: The Wilmot Proviso Controversy*, Chapel Hill, University of North Carolina Press, 1967.

Mueller, Henry R., *The Whig Party in Pennsylvania*, Columbia University Studies in History, Economics, and Public Law, 101, New York, Columbia University Press, 1922.

Nevin, Adelaide M., *The Social Mirror*, Pittsburgh, T. W. Nevin, 1888.

Nevins, Allan, *Ordeal of the Union*, 2 vols. New York, Charles Scribner's Sons, 1947.

——, *The Emergence of Lincoln*, 2 vols. New York, Charles Scribner's Sons, 1950.

Nichols, Roy Franklin, *The Democratic Machine, 1850–1854*, New York, Columbia University Press, 1923.

——, *The Disruption of American Democracy*, New York, Macmillan (Collier Books), 1962.

Porter, Kirk H., ed., *National Party Platforms*, New York, Macmillan, 1924.

Potter, David, *Lincoln and His Party in the Secession Crisis*, New Haven, Yale University Press, 1962.

Randall, James G., and David Donald, *The Civil War and Reconstruction*, 2d ed. rev. Boston, D. C. Heath, 1961.

Rayback, Robert J., *Millard Fillmore: Biography of a President*, Buffalo, Henry Stewart, 1959.

Reiser, Catherine Elizabeth, *Pittsburgh's Commercial Development, 1800–1850*, Harrisburg, Pennsylvania Historical and Museum Commission, 1951.

Rubin, Julius, "An Imitative Public Improvement: The Pennsylvania Mainline," in *Canals and American Economic Development*, ed. Carter Goodrich, New York, Columbia University Press, 1961.

Schlesinger, Arthur M., Jr., *The Age of Jackson*, Boston, Little, Brown, 1945.

Silbey, Joel H., *The Transformation of American Politics, 1840–1860*, Englewood Cliffs, N.J., Prentice-Hall, 1967.

Summers, Festus P., *The Baltimore and Ohio in the Civil War*, New York, G. P. Putnam's Sons, 1939.

Thernstrom, Stephan, *Poverty and Progress: Social Mobility in a Nineteenth Century City*, Cambridge, Harvard University Press, 1964.

Van Deusen, Glyndon G., *William Henry Seward*, New York, Oxford University Press, 1967.

Voegeli, V. Jacque, *Free but Not Equal: The Midwest and the Negro During the Civil War*, Chicago, University of Chicago Press, 1967.

Wade, Richard C., *The Urban Frontier: The Rise of Western Cities, 1790–1830*, Cambridge, Harvard University Press, 1959.

Ware, Norman, *The Industrial Worker, 1840–1860*, Boston and New York, Houghton Mifflin, 1924.

Zahler, Helene Sara, *Eastern Workingmen and National Land Policy, 1829–1862*, New York, Columbia University Press, 1941.

Articles

Arensberg, Charles C., "Evergreen Hamlet," *Western Pennsylvania Historical Magazine, 38* (1955), 117–33.

Aydelotte, William O., "Quantification in History," *American Historical Review, 71* (1966), 803–25.

Bernstein, Leonard H., "Convention in Pittsburgh," *Western Pennsylvania Historical Magazine, 49* (1966), 289–300.

Borit, Gabor S., "Old Wine into New Bottles: Abraham Lincoln and the Tariff Reconsidered," *The Historian, 28* (1966), 289–317.

Calvert, Monte A., "The Allegheny City Cotton Mill Riot of 1848," *Western Pennsylvania Historical Magazine, 46* (1963), 97–133.

Clark, Joseph S., Jr., "The Railroad Struggle for Pittsburgh," *Pennsylvania Magazine of History and Biography, 43* (1924), 1–37.

Gatell, Frank Otto, "Money and Party in Jacksonian America: A Quantitative Look at New York City's Men of Quality," *Political Science Quarterly, 82* (1967), 235–52.

Harrington, Fred H., "Frémont and the North Americans," *American Historical Review, 49* (1939), 842–48.

Hays, Samuel P., "The Social Analysis of American Political History, 1880–1920," *Political Science Quarterly, 80* (1965), 373–94.

Hunter, Louis C., "The Influence of the Market upon Technique in the Iron Industry in Western Pennsylvania up to 1860," *Journal of Economic and Business History, 1* (November 1928–August 1929), 240–81.

———, "Financial Problems of the Early Pittsburgh Iron Manufacturers," *Journal of Economic and Business History, 2* (November 1929–August 1930), 520–44.

Kleppner, Paul J., "Lincoln and the Immigrant Vote: A Case of Religious Polarization," *Mid-America, 48* (1966), 176–95.

Lofton, Williston H., "Abolitionism and Labor," *Journal of Negro History, 33* (1948), 249–83.

McCartney, Charles Edward, "The First National Republican Convention," *Western Pennsylvania Historical Magazine, 20* (1937), 83–100.

Man, Albon P., Jr., "Labor Competition and the New York Draft Riots," *Journal of Negro History, 36* (1951), 375–405.

Nichols, Roy Franklin, "Some Problems of the First Republican Presidential Campaign," *American Historical Review, 28* (1923), 492–96.

Purcell, Edward A., Jr., "Ideas and Interests: Businessmen and the Interstate Commerce Act," *Journal of American History, 54* (1967), 561–78.

Rayback, Joseph G., "The American Workingman and the Antislavery Crusade," *Journal of Economic History, 3* (1943), 152–63.

Shannon, Fred A., "The Homestead Act and Labor Surplus," *American Historical Review, 41* (1936), 637–51.

Silbey, Joel H., "The Civil War Synthesis in American Political History," *Civil War History, 10* (1964), 130–40.

Sponholtz, Lloyd L., "Pittsburgh and Temperance, 1830–1854," *Western Pennsylvania Historical Magazine, 46* (1963), 347–79.

Van Tassel, David D., "Gentlemen of Property and Standing: Compromise Sentiment in Boston in 1850," *New England Quarterly, 23* (1950), 306–19.

Wolstoncroft, Joseph P., "Western Pennsylvania and the Election of 1860," *Western Historical Magazine, 6* (1923), 25–38.

Unpublished Theses and Papers

English, Helen Dorothy, "The Political Background and Republicanization of Allegheny County, 1844–1856," unpublished M.A. thesis, University of Pittsburgh, 1936.

Kleppner, Paul J., "Immigrant Voting Behavior: Pittsburgh, 1860," unpublished seminar paper, University of Pittsburgh, 1963.

Myers, C. Maxwell, "The Rise of the Republican Party in Pennsylvania, 1854–1860," unpublished Ph.D. dissertation, University of Pittsburgh, 1940.

Thompson, James Howard, "A Financial History of the City of Pittsburgh, 1816–1910," unpublished Ph.D. dissertation, University of Pittsburgh, 1948.

Index

View of Pittsburgh in 1853. Courtesy of Carnegie Library of Pittsburgh.